THE
NEW NATURAL
FOOD GARDEN

THE
NEW NATURAL
FOOD GARDEN

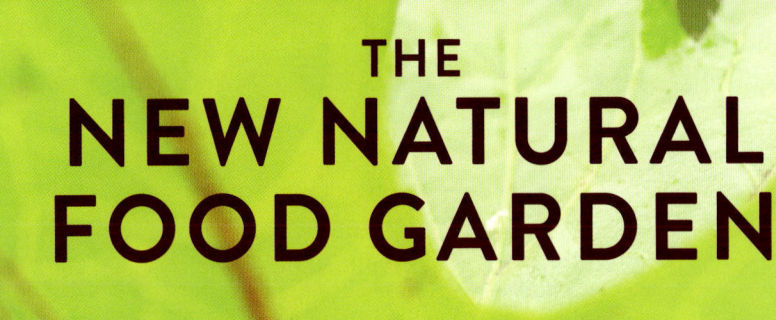

A COMPREHENSIVE GUIDE
to Growing a Bountiful
Harvest with Less Work,
in Partnership with Nature

NATALIE BOGWALKER

CHLOE LIEBERMAN

Photography by Sarah Tew

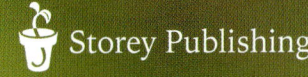
Storey Publishing

DEDICATION

For Hazel and Felix, and all children,
May your bodies and souls be nourished by the Earth.

For the mystery that brings rain, quickens seeds, and alights our hearts,
May we humans re-member our part in the sacred dance.

*The mission of Storey Publishing is to serve our customers by
publishing practical information that encourages
personal independence in harmony with the environment.*

EDITED BY Carleen Madigan and Sarah Slattery
BOOK DESIGN BY Carolyn Eckert and Bredna Lago
COVER DESIGN BY Bredna Lago
TEXT PRODUCTION BY Jennifer Jepson Smith

COVER AND INTERIOR PHOTOGRAPHY BY Sarah Tew Photography
ADDITIONAL INTERIOR PHOTOGRAPHY BY © Andrii Yalanskyi
/iStock.com, 206; Frank Salzano, 85 l.; © Frazao Studio Latino
/iStock.com, 246 2nd fr. t.; © H. Mark Weidman Photography
/Alamy Stock Photo, 31; © HHelene/Shutterstock.com, 217 b.l.;
© Irina Starikova1811/Shutterstock.com, 245; © J.J. Gouin
/Shutterstock.com, 109; Jeff Wales Photography, 57 t., 101, 261 c.r.,
270, 302; Jenny Tenney Friedrichs, 217 2nd fr. b.l.c.; kallerna/CC
BY-SA 4.0/Wikimedia Commons, 127; Maja Dumat/CC BY 2.0
/flickr, 32; Mallory Lance, 268, 284, 304, 325; © malshkoff
/Shutterstock.com, 94; Mars Vilaubi © Storey Publishing, 217 b.l.c.;
Mason McDonald, 286, 320; Merideth Garrigan, 90 c., 328; © Mr.
Meijer/Shutterstock.com, 217 b.c.r.; NASA/ESA/R. Kirshner
(Harvard-Smithsonian Center for Astrophysics and Gordon and
Betty Moore Foundation)/M. Mutchler and R. Avila (STScI), 100;
© Nataliia Kuznetcova/Shutterstock.com, 246 b.; Natalie Bogwalker,
22, 26, 86 b.l., 217 t.r.c., 220, 234, 246 5th fr. t., 275 c.l., 280, 289,
316, 327; Courtesy of Native Seeds/SEARCH, nativeseeds.org,
30; © Orest lyzhechka/Shutterstock.com, 217 t.c.l.; © Pilar Picas
/Shutterstock.com, 217 2nd fr. b.r.; Rob Bertholf/CC BY 2.0/flickr,
125; © Sarah Macor/Shutterstock.com, 123 r.; © ShamAn77
/Shutterstock.com, 217 2nd fr. t.r.; © sophiecat/Shutterstock.com,
279; Wayne S. Teel, 123 c.l., 129; Courtesy of Wild Abundance, 267 t.

TEXT © 2026 by Chloe Lieberman and Natalie Bogwalker

Foreword by DeLesslin "Roo" George-Warren
"How Long Do Seeds Last?" on page 163 courtesy of Johnny's
Selected Seeds Grower's Library

Storey books may be purchased in bulk for business, educational, or
promotional use. Special editions or book excerpts can also be created
to specification. For details, please contact your local bookseller or the
Hachette Book Group Special Markets Department at special.markets
@hbgusa.com.

Storey Publishing
210 MASS MoCA Way
North Adams, MA 01247
storey.com

Storey Publishing is an imprint of Workman Publishing, a division of
Hachette Book Group, Inc., 1290 Avenue of the Americas, New York,
NY 10104. The Storey Publishing name and logo are registered trade-
marks of Hachette Book Group, Inc.

ISBNs: 978-1-63586-940-8 (paperback); 978-1-63586-941-5 (ebook)

Printed in China by Toppan Leefung Printing Ltd. on paper from
responsible sources
10 9 8 7 6 5 4 3 2 1

TLF

Library of Congress Cataloging-in-Publication Data on file

Contents

FOREWORD
Remembering How to Be with the Land,
by DeLesslin "Roo" George-Warren,
Citizen of Catawba Nation viii

PREFACE
The Farce of the "One Right Way" 1

INTRODUCTION
Learning to Think Holistically 2

**1 Designing & Planning
Your Garden** 13
Why Do You *Really* Want to Garden? 14
Your Garden Design 18
What a Garden Needs 19
Garden Location and Layout 22
Rows vs. Beds 26
Styles of Garden Beds 28
Terraces and Terracing 31
Container Gardening 32
What Crops Do I Plant? 35
Considerations for Crop Placement 37
How Much Do I Plant? 38
Making Your Garden Plan 39

2 Tools & How to Use Them 45

Tool Quality and Care 46

Bare-Bones Tools 48

Tools to Tend the Gardener 50

Small Hand Tools 52

Tools for Moving Things Around 54

The Magical World of Hoes 56

Big Digging Tools 58

3 Starting a Garden from Grass 61

Ways to Transform Grass into a Growing Space 62

Setting Up Raised Beds 65

Double-Digging 69

Tilling with a Machine 72

Sheet Mulching and Lasagna Gardening 75

Basic Solarization and Occultation 78

Bogwalker's Badass Topsoil Technique 84

Crimping Cover Crops 88

Getting Soil Ready for Seeds and Plants 90

4 Soil & Fertility 93

Soil 101 94

What Makes Soil Good for Growing Vegetables? 96

How to Do a Soil Test and Why 105

Fertility 101 107

Vegetable Fertility Needs 112

Managing Fertility 113

Growing Mediums for Containers 117

5 Feeding What Feeds You: Fertilizers & Amendments 123

Compost and Worm Castings 124

Manure 125

Biochar 129

Wood Ash 131

Urine 131

Store-Bought Fertilizers and Amendments 134

Cover Crops 140

Making Compost 140

6 How to Plant a Seed & Get It to Grow 157

The Magic of Seeds 158

Germination and Seed Viability 160

Ordering Seeds 162

Overview of Planting Methods 170

Setting Up a Seed-Starting System 174

Growing Your Own Transplants 180

Transplanting Baby Plants 184

How to Buy Strong Transplants 190

Direct Sowing 191

When to Plant What 194

7 Caring for Plants When They Are Growing 199

Water and Irrigation 200

Feeding Growing Plants 207

Thinning 210

Weed Management 213

Mulch 221

Trellises and Trellising 229

8 Dealing with Pests & Diseases 239

Holistic Overview of Pests and Diseases 240

Pest ID and Life Cycles 244

Plant Disease ID and Management 245

No-Spray Ways to Combat Pests and Diseases 250

Organic Pesticides and How to Use Them 254

9 Harvesting & the End of the Growing Season 261

Consider Harvesting When Planning 262

Harvesting Methods 263

Post-harvest Processing 269

The Lifespans of Annual Vegetables 272

Sharing the Harvest 273

Vegetable Profiles & Growing Guides 275

Guide to the Vegetable Profiles 276

Arugula 278

Basil 280

Beans 282

Beets and Chard 284

Broccoli and Cauliflower 286

Cabbage 288

Carrots 290

Cilantro 292

Corn 294

Cucumbers 296

Dill 298

Eggplant 300

Garlic 302

Kale and Collards 304

Lettuce 306

Muskmelons 308

Okra 310

Onions 312

Parsnips 314

Peas 316

Peppers and Chiles 318

Potatoes 320

Radishes 322

Spinach 324

Sweet Potatoes 326

Tomatoes 328

Turnips and Rutabagas 330

Watermelons 332

Winter Squash and Pumpkins 334

Zucchini and Summer Squash 337

Timing Tables 339

APPENDIX

When to Sow, Plant, and Harvest Based on Temperature and Season 356

Seed Spacing, Depth, and Amounts of Seeds Needed 358

Plant Spacing for Garden Beds 360

Determining the Right Plant Spacing 361

Possible Yields of Common Vegetables 362

Acknowledgments 363

Resources to Download from the Growing Wise Gardening School 364

Index 365

Remembering How to Be with the Land

By DeLesslin "Roo" George-Warren, Citizen of Catawba Nation

I grew up going with my grandfather to what we called the Church Farm, a beautiful piece of land surrounded by a dense forest with a few large fields for farming. The land had been sold to a local church for no more than $5 with a promise to hold it in trust for our people, during a time when the federal government sought to end our existence as a tribal nation by way of legislative action.

I vividly remember my grandfather sitting on the back of his truck in the oppressive South Carolina heat, cutting seed potatoes into pieces, each with a few eyes. He would direct my brother and me to place the pieces in long rows in the parched, freshly tilled red clay soil. At the end of the season, my grandfather would be there again, on the tailgate, while, heat still blazing, we dug the now-mature bundles of potatoes from the well-baked ground. The heat didn't help my grandfather in his efforts to persuade me—I knew that day that I would never become a farmer.

Many years after those childhood summers, after I graduated from college, and after the passing of my grandfather who had served almost three decades as an elected official for my tribe, I returned to my community. Initially my hope was to continue the work of revitalizing our language. The last fluent speaker of Catawba passed away in 1959, the same year that the US Congress passed a law to "terminate" Catawba Nation. Because of those decades without fluent speakers, our language lacked terms to describe modern life, such as *cell phone, television,* and *computer.* But what our language has always had is a rich lexicon of words for the land, the river, the plants, and the other-than-human animals with whom we share our home. It was apparent to me that we couldn't revive the language without reconnecting with the land.

But relearning how to have a relationship with the land wouldn't be easy. Catawbas, other Indigenous communities, and non-Indigenous communities alike in the United States are all standing on landscapes irrevocably changed by five hundred years of colonialism. This is apparent when we look out on a concrete jungle, or on the acres of chemically augmented farm fields that feed most of us. But it is also apparent in the dense, scraggly forests that have become synonymous with "wilderness," a far cry from the purposefully cultivated landscapes that Catawbas and many other communities once knew and tended.

Some people laugh when I say that Indigenous people are not forest elves with instinctive knowledge of the land. In fact, Indigenous people are just like the rest of humanity—curious, observant experimenters. The land-based knowledge held by Native communities is not innate but the product of hundreds of generations in relationship with the same landscape. It is inscribed in dances, songs, stories, and shared labor, then revised and contributed to by each generation due to new understandings and changing contexts. This hard-earned knowledge has been crucial to the ways our ancestors fed their families with a diversity of nourishing plants and animals.

Colonists understood that this knowledge was a powerful force, and they created boarding schools and other mechanisms to block it from being transferred across generations. Today we are left with the few fragments our ancestors were able to protect. It's a heartbreaking place to be: knowing of loss but unable to identify exactly what was lost. And yet there is hope, because we are also left knowing that if our ancestors learned everything they knew about their home, the land, through observation and experimentation, then we can do that, too. Starting from scratch wasn't an option, so I knew I'd need some help getting there.

LEARNING TO REMEMBER

In 2018 I participated in a permaculture design course led by Natalie Bogwalker. I saw that her rich, thriving plot of land was living proof of both her hard work and the knowledge she'd gleaned through observation, intervention, curiosity, and experimentation. I suspected that, unlike those long, red clay rows of potatoes back on the Church Farm, here was the glorious result of a sustainable approach to vegetable gardening.

The knowledge of when to plant a seed, how to organize a garden, and how to rest the land isn't innate to anyone, but it can be learned over long periods of time through observation, experimentation, and experience. But many people, like myself, realize that we don't have generations to start growing the resiliency we so desperately need. Thankfully this book and the knowledge shared by Natalie and Chloe in their courses offer a jump start to that learning.

It is remarkable to consider how Indigenous land-based knowledge was gleaned by academics and codified as permaculture, only to travel through a network of students and teachers all over the world and back to my own tribal community. After getting here, it has shed light on our past, to a time before the rows of heavily tilled monocrops that I grew up with. It is charting a new way of interacting with the land that puts aside the clear-cutting, industrialization, and chemical warfare that have become synonymous with modern agriculture. Indeed, perhaps the most exciting development of the permaculture

movement has been the rise of purposeful and thoughtful collaborations with Indigenous communities, which are where the central principles of permaculture arose from in the first place.

My studies with Natalie so many years ago kick-started a renewed commitment to doing land-based work in my community. That has blossomed into numerous exciting projects and a whole team of passionate Catawbas who are leading the way. Since 2018 my community has been able to reconnect with and cultivate our delicious, beautiful heritage corn variety. Eschewing tilling and chemical fertilization, we're committed to a more biodynamic approach to soil management. We've even reignited the traditional practice of using controlled burns to shape and enrich the land. By working with the fields, the forest, the river, and now with fire, we're developing and growing a landscape more reminiscent of that which our ancestors knew and that can sustain our people today. It's amazing to see what one small seed can grow into.

Whether this is your introduction to vegetable gardening or simply a refresher, whether you are cultivating a multiacre vegetable garden or a few rows in your backyard, I predict this book will be your seed of inspiration for developing a deeper relationship with the land and the plants that sustain you. And remember, regardless of where you are growing, you are stepping into a dance between humans and the land that has been unfolding for millennia and, with your help, will continue to unfold for many generations to come. Now let's get to work.

Hawu Kuri,
Roo

The Farce of the
"One Right Way"

Three gardeners walk into a bar. The first one cheerfully places a lime green cucumber on the table and declares she does square-foot gardening.

Not to be outdone, the second gardener proudly presents a pile of tender, young green beans next to the glowing cucumber, explaining that thoughtfully managed biointensive growing yielded these emerald beauties.

Finally, a third gardener unwraps a worn bandana to reveal two lush tomatoes. She explains that they grew unexpectedly in a 5-gallon bucket filled with composting food scraps her neighbor had thrown away.

Who did it right?

The bartender, of course! She was wise enough to invite a variety of gardeners to share their diverse knowledge and bounty, celebrating different perspectives instead of seeking only one right way. The bar was a juice bar, in case you were wondering.

There is obviously no "one right way" to grow vegetables, and there is no such thing as a perfect gardener. What works best in any given situation depends on the gardener's goals, land, tools, and intentions. After decades of teaching thousands of gardeners (and forever learning ourselves), we now have the joy of sharing our breadth and depth of knowledge with you in this book.

In the following pages, you'll discover detailed step-by-step guidance on many of the techniques we've found to be most effective. You'll also benefit from our combined 45 years of gardening successes and failures, which will save you some time! You'll get to hear what we think about various approaches, including when we think each is appropriate, and how to navigate through your own choices. This book will show you how to garden, but, perhaps more importantly, it guides you to become the leading expert on *your* garden. Our hands-on, heart-listening experience becomes yours. With tools and approaches rooted in the Indigenous science of permaculture, you'll learn how to observe, interact, take notes, and harvest from your own "mistakes," all while building a deeply rewarding relationship with your garden and coming up with a gardening style that's your own.

Learning to Think Holistically

Growing a garden can hold deep meaning for many different reasons. One reason that's often overlooked is the power of experiencing your garden as a direct point of contact between you, as a human animal, and the rest of the living world.

At this moment in history, many of our daily lives are permeated with human-created and human-oriented technologies: computers, smart phones, cars, social media, robo-vacuums . . . the list goes on. They mediate our relationships with one another and with the rest of life. And don't get us wrong, some of these can be super helpful and arguably very life enhancing—like listening to a compassionate communication podcast on the way home from dropping kids off at school or looking at the long-term forecast to know if it's safe to plant tomatoes in the early springtime. And yet, we think of the "good old days" before we had all these devices and intermediaries with fondness and longing. We wish to feel deeply connected with life—part of it, rather than apart from it.

"The garden" appears in mythologies from many cultures around the globe—particularly the idea of leaving the garden, or some other beautifully balanced place, in order to trudge toward human "progress," and with it the civilizing forces that have led to modernity. Returning to this metaphorical garden is a yearning that lives in many human hearts, and it's a journey that can begin in the vegetable garden.

Indigenous wisdom has always known what more and more scientific studies now also reveal: In no uncertain terms, humankind is simply one actor in a much grander drama of unfolding life. Plants share with each other, they warn each other about dangers, and they make sacrifices for their offspring. The soil is a vibrant community teeming with billions of organisms, many of whom we haven't studied long enough to even name, and some of whom also live inside our digestive tracts, making it possible for our bodies to function. Winds know no borders and carry stories of wildfires from the West Coast to the East and beyond, painting sunsets red while the entire planet feels the heat of burning forests. We are all in this together.

Since many of us were not taught that we are members of this "family of things," as poet Mary Oliver put it, trusting interconnectedness deep in our beings can be tricky. But when we lean toward the earth and touch that dark and fertile place of possibility, when we offer ourselves in service to that which feeds us, the family of things becomes tangible and real. It is obvious and inviting. No longer conceptual, romantic, or philosophical, the reality of reciprocity and mutual aliveness is just how a garden grows, and how we grow with it.

> *There are a host of reasons to grow a garden. . . . One that's often overlooked is the profound effect of experiencing your garden as a direct point of contact between you, as a human animal, and the rest of the living world.*

Our Holistic Lens

Many factors have influenced our holistic approach to gardening, the garden itself being one of them. Additionally, during our childhoods we were both lucky enough to have adults around who honored and encouraged our curiosity and connections with wild places. Later we both ended up studying agroecology in college and spent several years afterward traveling and living in various climates and regions, always with the anchor of growing food and community and learning from the people and plants who called those places home. Our teachers have been many: from older men displaced by the Spanish Civil War, yet firmly committed to gardening techniques from their home villages, to nerdy professors with PhDs pioneering new approaches to agricultural science.

On our parallel paths, we both discovered and studied permaculture, a modern design system for using and applying holistic thinking. It resonated instantly with both of us because it's based on the living systems that we've been learning from since we were kids picking wild blackberries. Contrary to what many believe, permaculture isn't a gardening technique but rather a collection of principles and approaches for engaging with whole systems—the interconnected webs of life that all people and gardens are a part of. It gives a contemporary framework for an approach to making connections with life, gardening, and land similar to what Indigenous peoples all over the world (including your own ancestors, if you trace your lineage back far enough) have been doing for millennia. Of course, Indigenous worldviews and practices are diverse, nuanced, and much more complex than the modern practice of permaculture. Permaculture offers tools to cooperate with the rest of the living world rather than trying to dominate it—an approach to relating to systems holistically, just like we're doing with this book!

Our friendship and gardening collaborations didn't start until we were in our thirties, after we had both gardened for many years and had a lot to share. The fire and passion that burns in each of us around connecting with the earth and our human lineage through gardening has led us to cocreate resources that have guided thousands of people into the magical world of growing food. You can learn more about our individual journeys, our work, our online gardening classes (including free ones), and our company, Growing Wise (see page 364).

A vegetable garden is a diverse ecosystem, filled with all kinds of life; approaching it with curiosity can be deeply rewarding.

Permaculture and Vegetable Gardening

Many of the agricultural practices popular in permaculture are based on perennial crops, like fruit and nut trees. Annual vegetables, in contrast, are the black sheep of permaculture. Industrial, extractive, profit-driven vegetable and grain production, with their harmful impacts and unsustainable demands, were what many of the "fathers" of permaculture sought alternatives to. But, of course, annual plants play vital roles in balancing ecosystems, and annual vegetables (and grains, and the animals that eat them) are what feed most humans most of the time!

When we apply the principles and underlying philosophies of permaculture to vegetable gardening, the whole experience is improved. These approaches lead to more resilient systems in our gardens, which result in gardens that come to thrive over time. They more easily respond and adapt to pressures, such as pests, droughts, and withdrawal of care (like if the gardener breaks her ankle, for example).

Permaculture is based on holistic thinking, and holistic thinking, by definition, requires that we engage with whole systems in a subject-subject relationship (rather than subject-object); every part of every system influences and works with every other part—including you, including us.

Perennial crops, like this pawpaw, are popular in permaculture. Annuals (most vegetables) are often overlooked but are essential food sources, especially outside of the tropics.

The term *permaculture* is a marriage of the words *permanent* and *agriculture* and was coined in 1978 by Bill Mollison and David Holmgren. Mollison was then a senior lecturer in environmental psychology at the University of Tasmania, and Holmgren was a graduate student at the Tasmanian College of Advanced Education. They both observed how industrial agriculture was degrading land and water and would ultimately be unsustainable over the long term.

Mollison and Holmgren were expanding upon the work of American agricultural scientist Franklin Hiram King, who wrote *Farmers of Forty Centuries; Or, Permanent Agriculture in China, Korea, and Japan* (published 1911); American geographer Joseph Russell Smith, who wrote *Tree Crops: A Permanent Agriculture* (1929); and Australian agronomist and engineer P. A. Yeomans, who wrote *Water for Every Farm* (1964), in which he describes a "permanent agriculture" that could be sustained indefinitely.

All of these white guys occupied social positions that allowed their work and ideas to be taken seriously by society at large, and they all did some very valuable study and practice, but none of them came up with their ideas out of nowhere. The philosophies and even specific techniques of permaculture stem from generations-old relationships between humans and the other-than-human world. In a 2019 online PBS article, writer Rohini Walker notes that permaculture is an "indigenous science of working in partnership and reciprocity with the land and cycles of nature." Bill Mollison and David Holmgren give credit for many of the foundational ideas of permaculture to the aboriginal Tasmanian land stewards with whom they studied.

Our Gardening Principles Inspired by Permaculture

At the core of permaculture is a set of 12 principles laid out by founders Bill Mollison and David Holmgren that came from observing ecosystems that hadn't been altered by industrial humans. The principles communicate patterns to design into our human-centered spaces in order to make them function more like wild nature and landscapes

Incorporating permaculture into your garden can yield armloads of beets, but it's also a way to incorporate nontangible goals, like gardening with kids.

that have been tended by people for generations. One of Natalie's mentors and a locally renowned permaculture teacher, the late Patricia Allison, adapted and expanded upon these original 12. We've grown our own tendrils of knowledge, so to speak, from the roots put in place by these colleagues and guides and have further adapted and expanded upon what Patricia Allison came up with.

Following are our 20 gardening principles, inspired by permaculture, with examples of how they might be applied in real-life situations. Principles are not rules, exactly, but rather guiding ideas that have numerous applications across a wide field. They often come into our planning and decision-making processes in the form of questions: *How could this system produce less waste? How could the waste that's produced here be used?* We invite you to relate with these principles with a sense of curiosity and play as you apply them to your garden, and to life in general.

1. **Observe and interact.** Put in the time and attention to understand what's already happening before you take action, then experiment with small actions, pausing in between to see how the system responds.

   Example: Take note of which parts of the garden are shady or sunny during different times of day and seasons throughout the year, then adjust what is planted where so that everyone gets the sun they need. Alternatively, you could trim or thin trees as needed to increase sun for the garden and watch again what the impact is.

2. **Obtain a yield.** Each part of a system should produce something of value to someone or someones (e.g., you, your human neighbors, soil organisms, pollinator insects, songbirds). If your vegetable garden is not yielding food for you or for the soil or wildlife, it's time to make adjustments.

   Example: You plant Jerusalem artichokes because they are a cool perennial vegetable, then you discover that your body doesn't digest them well. If you have livestock, you learn that they like to eat the artichokes, so you keep them to feed your critters. If you don't have animals to feed them to, you dig them up, give them away, and plant something else instead.

3. **Build in redundancy.** Be sure to have multiple ways to meet important needs; have a backup plan (or three).

   Examples: Set up rain barrels to catch water from your roof, use a well and tap a spring, or make sure you have access to town or city water; should any single water source fail or be temporarily out of commission, you'll still be able to water your garden. Plant stinging nettles (a delicious perennial vegetable), berry bushes, nut trees, and other perennial crops, and tend annual vegetables so that you have multiple sources of food requiring different conditions and inputs.

4. **Catch and store energy.** Design a system to accumulate energy, materials, and information in the most useful forms and locations.

   Examples: Collect water in a rain barrel or tank that's above your garden rather than at the same elevation or below so that gravity can bring it to your crops as needed. The practice of growing vegetables stores the energy of the sun and rain in the form of food.

5. **Ensure multiple functions.** Every element in a system should serve multiple functions.

   Examples: You build a trellis to service peas and, after the peas are finished, cucumbers. You allow chickweed to come in as a ground cover in winter, harvest it for salad, and take advantage of it as a soil conditioner and for fertilizer when it's returned to the ground.

6. **Produce no waste.** Design so that "waste" streams/by-products from one system become input for another; rethink, reduce, repair, reuse, recycle. Think of waste as an action, not just a thing.

    Examples: Share any extra vegetables with neighbors, as feed to animals, or as compost that is returned to the soil. Clean out plastic potting soil sacks and reuse them as storage for row cover and other materials. Splurge on durable seedling trays instead of using cheap disposable ones.

7. **Observe and replicate natural patterns and cycles.** Great design exists everywhere on Earth; notice and learn from the ways systems organize themselves without human interference. Notice already-existing patterns and relationships, and mimic those that are beneficial.

    Example: Observe how forest soil is never exposed but is naturally mulched with fallen leaves; follow suit and gather leaves or use straw or hay to mulch the garden to protect the soil from the sun and compaction, and to reduce weed load.

8. **Use and value renewable resources.** Whenever you can, choose a renewable option rather than a finite resource.

    Examples: Create a trellis with bio-degradable material, such as bamboo and jute string—or something reusable, like a metal fencing panel—rather than single-use plastic netting. Choose seedling potting mixes that contain coconut coir instead of sphagnum peat moss, because coconuts are a more renewable resource than peat bogs. Use leaves, straw, hay, or UV-resistant plastic that lasts for years instead of thin, disposable film plastics. And take good care of whatever materials you select so you get maximum use of them before they head to the landfill.

9. **Design from patterns to details.** Always look at the big picture first; be sure you're not missing the forest for the trees. Make the most important and permanent decisions first and wisely, and let smaller choices gather around those patterns.

    Examples: When establishing your garden, design for general areas or beds (pattern) through which crops will rotate rather than getting caught up in the exact garden plan for the whole first year (details). Create beds or rows that can host various kinds of crops over time. If you're setting up an irrigation system, choose strategic locations for spigots (pattern), then try out different kinds of irrigation (details) to find the one that will work best.

10. **Site elements based on zones and sectors.** Place elements that you need frequent access to in convenient locations (close or on contour; in other words, not uphill or downhill but level with), and place elements that need less regular tending farther away.

The fence panel on the left supports tomato plants. The bamboo quadripods on the right do the same job. Metal is reusable and bamboo is renewable; they both work great.

Every bit of this garden is bursting with color and texture. This is what it can look like to value diversity and use edges.

Examples: Rotate crops that need more attention and more frequent harvesting, such as tomatoes, greens, and cilantro, closest to your kitchen entrance (as long as the spot is good for growing and gets enough sun), and rotate storage crops, like onions, potatoes, sweet potatoes, and squash, in the farthest growing space. Store your tools and bulk materials like mulch as close to the garden as possible (but see example 11).

11. Be mindful of relative location.
Put things that need each other and feed each other close to each other.

Examples: Place the compost bin or pile in a spot convenient to both the kitchen and the garden. Store garden tools close enough to use them, but not so close that the shed will shade the crops that need sun. If possible, put the water barrel below the low end of your roof and above your garden (different principles often guide us to similar actions).

12. Use edges and value the marginal.
Pay attention to the physical edges of a place and utilize them, too. Recognize and utilize what's "off the beaten track."

Examples: Create a little shelf or box on the fence line with your neighbor to share your extra veggies with them.

Put a bench or hammock at the edge of the garden for resting and reflecting. Reintroduce hedgerows: In many parts of the world, gardeners and farmers plant hedgerows so that the wild gets to be wild between growing spaces; these wild spaces host many creatures who eat garden pests.

13. Explore and value diversity. Life gets pretty boring when everything is the same; monoculture (for plants as well as people) can be a dangerous thing that leads to disease and closed-mindedness. Make sure to cultivate diversity in elements as well as relationships between elements.

Examples: Plant a variety of vegetables to ensure that enough of them thrive and yield well when others fail. Plant open-pollinated varieties of vegetables that are more genetically diverse and, therefore, more adaptive to stressors like pests and climate changes. Plant a diversity of flowers for beauty, to feed pollinators, and to attract predatory insects for pest control.

14. Apply feedback. You will make mistakes, so learn from them, share them, revel in them. The same goes for your successes.

Examples: If your sweet potatoes yield lots of tiny potatoes and few of

with a different variety, or just being satisfied with a shorter tomato season.

16. Stack and pack. Use vertical as well as horizontal space to place elements, the way that a forest does. Think about stacking in space as well as time.

    Example: This can be tricky in a veggie garden. If you pack plants in too thickly, you risk decreasing airflow and encouraging fungal and pest problems (especially within the same species of plant). However, there are some great ways of "intercropping" to utilize vertical space both above and below the ground. One pairing that works well: beets and onions. Onions are tall and skinny above the ground, beets broad and wide. Belowground, beets reach deep, while onions stay shallow.

17. Use appropriate technology. Choose and use tools that are as effective as possible for a given task, while being as comfortable and enjoyable as possible and causing a minimum amount of harm to the planet.

    Examples: A stirrup hoe kills weeds while saving your back and the soil. While we promote no-till systems over the long term, plowing and discing or another kind of tilling might make sense for your first year. If you have a hard time kneeling and bending to tend a garden, buying or building tall raised beds could be a great choice.

18. Creatively use and respond to change. Approach design, the world, and life in general as a fluid process in which each change contains opportunities. Pay attention; the journey really is the destination. Change is upon us, especially with an unstable climate; understand it, roll with it, creatively respond to it.

Here, beets and onions grow in the same bed. Onions have shallow roots, but beets' roots are deep. This is "stacking and packing" above- and belowground.

them are big enough to eat, maybe the following year they should be planted farther apart or planted earlier in the season. If you have a bumper crop of green beans, explore the possible reasons why: Planting time? Fertility? Variety? Location? The weather that year?

15. Find small and slow solutions. Go slowly and thoughtfully so that you can observe impacts of changes, respond to that feedback, and use the least amount of energy to reach a desired outcome.

    Example: Just because your tomatoes died from late blight in August does not necessarily mean you should build a resource-intensive greenhouse to always grow them in. Consider simpler solutions, like pruning for airflow, building more vertical trellising, experimenting

Examples: Plant crops and varieties of crops that are tolerant of variable temperatures, drought, and flood (this is much easier to do with annual crops than perennials, as you can respond and experiment each season). If you plan to have a baby, go to graduate school, or take on a new and big responsibility during the growing season, plant lots of cover crops and rest the soil rather than grow a huge garden that will need your time, attention, and energy.

19. Value and feed neighborly relations. Just like trees gift one-fifth of their sugars to the mycelia and bacteria in the soil, give to your neighbors and see how they may enrich your life in ways that you can't even imagine.

Examples: When you share veggies with your neighbors, they will likely share with you—they might share vegetables, their knowledge of fixing lawnmowers, or less-tangible things that are just as inspiring. If you learn something about gardening in your area or discover a great variety for your microclimate, share that information, too.

Leaving a basket of veggies on your neighbor's doorstep reduces waste and feeds positive relationships.

20. Use the right material in the right place. Birds know just the right materials with which to build and line their nests; we humans can learn from this discerning expertise.

Examples: Unless you are at a rental house where the future of the land is uncertain, use material that won't rot right away to build your raised garden beds. Even though wood chips can be great mulch for perennials, they don't work so well in annual veggie beds (with some exceptions . . . like always; see page 221 for more on mulching).

Our Wish for You

We plant gardens because we love to eat fresh vegetables, and because we want to nourish ourselves and our families without toxic chemicals. We sow and harvest, paying for our food with work and care instead of our dollars. Our lawns and yards transform into unruly bursts of color and texture and leaf and life so that we can walk outside and enjoy that wild beauty every time we make a salad. And through this simple act of tending a few vegetables, we feel more human, more animal, more fully present with the wondrous world.

This is our hope for you, dear reader: that you walk through the garden gate into a world of awe and beauty, that it gifts you with an abundance of delicious food to enjoy and share. Of course, not everything you plant will grow and thrive, not every year will yield a bumper crop, and your life might pull you away from tending the garden at a crucial moment. Not to worry! The focus shouldn't be only on measurable outcomes (like pounds of vegetables) but also on the minor miracles happening in your garden every day. Stay open and curious. Let your garden coax you into connecting with the bigness and benevolence of this glorious life, an awareness that will be your most important yield and your most abundant harvest.

1
Designing & Planning
Your Garden

Why Do You *Really* Want to Garden? 14

Your Garden Design 18

What a Garden Needs 19

Garden Location and Layout 22

Rows vs. Beds 26

Styles of Garden Beds 28

Terraces and Terracing 31

Container Gardening 32

What Crops Do I Plant? 35

Considerations for Crop Placement 37

How Much Do I Plant? 38

Making Your Garden Plan 39

Why Do You *Really* Want to Garden?

Even if you have an established garden plot or have been gardening for a while, we strongly encourage that you give this exercise a try. It's simple and easy, and it will help you get in touch with your needs, desires, and hopes (as well as your limitations!) pertaining to your garden. It allows you to practice thinking holistically and can also lead to a much more intentional and joyful gardening experience.

Holistic thinking in this instance means that we consider all the various reasons we want a garden in the first place and all the various *kinds of reasons*. Then we can assess how they intersect and interact with one another.

You can download a digital version of this exercise as a worksheet on our website (see page 364).

REASONS FOR GARDENING

Circle any reasons that feel true for you from each category and add any others that come to mind.

PRACTICAL
- Have lots of food to eat.
- Practice self-sufficiency (e.g., food, seeds, knowledge of growing).
- Grow enough vegetables to share.
- Utilize the space that's available to me.
- Other:

ECOLOGICAL/ENVIRONMENTAL
- Lower my carbon footprint.
- Grow organically and avoid supporting agrochemical industry.
- Attract and feed beneficial insects like honeybees.
- Conserve water by utilizing mulch and other water-saving practices.
- Encourage a healthy soil ecosystem.
- Transform a barren landscape into a bountiful one.
- Other:

PERSONAL AND SPIRITUAL
- Build a tangible relationship with the more-than-human world.
- Celebrate the glory of creation.
- De-stress and unwind with my hands in the dirt.
- Cultivate beauty to enjoy and to share.
- Connect with the foods/medicines of my ancestors and/or my local land.
- Other:

FAMILY AND COMMUNITY
- Grow enough to share with a food bank, neighbors, and so forth.
- Share knowledge about gardening in my area.
- Garden with kids, elders, and/or other community members.
- Have homegrown seeds and/or plant starts to share.
- Create a beautiful place to invite friends.
- Be a living example of connecting more directly with my source of sustenance.
- Other:

HEALTH
- Increase my access to fresh foods.
- Grow and eat vegetables without agrochemicals.
- Gain hands-on education about healthy food.
- Build connection and meaning.
- Other:

Natalie and her daughter, Hazel, prepare for a garlic braiding party. This garden chore can yield beauty, connection, and good storage garlic.

QUESTIONS FOR REFLECTION

Review what you've circled and explore the questions below. Refer to the reflections we've provided for ideas.

Q: Which reasons are overlapping or synergistic and can coexist and support one another?
A (sample): Choosing to garden without agrochemicals is supportive of the environment, the community, and your health; it may also be in line with your personal and/or spiritual beliefs. Incorporating organic practices in your gardening plan, then, will be synergistically supportive of several aspects of your values.

Q: Which reasons are potentially antagonistic, at odds, and/or cancel each other out? Brainstorm ideas for how you might strike a balance.
When you make balance a priority before you even get started, this sets you up for satisfaction with and success in your garden. You'll be less likely to get overwhelmed or feel disappointed and more likely to move confidently toward your goals and vision.
A (sample): The goal to grow as much food as possible and the desire to tend a garden with children might be at odds with one another. In our experience, gardening with little kids is incredibly rewarding but also slower and less "productive" than gardening with most adults, or alone. As a solution, and in the spirit of balance, you might dedicate one garden bed, or one block of time each week, for engaging with children in the garden. The rest of your physical or temporal space can be reserved for more "efficient" adult food growing. It's a win-win!

THE DISTINCTION BETWEEN
GARDEN DESIGN AND GARDEN PLANNING

From the big picture to the smallest details, designing and planning your garden will not only help you envision just how your garden will grow, what you will plant, and more, but it will take another vital factor into consideration: you, the gardener, and your relationship to the land, the plants, and your resources. This zooming out and zooming in brings the realities of your daily life into the fold.

Discard the idea that planning is meant to be a one-time activity leading to a fixed and measurable goal. Your garden, and your life, are too wild and beautiful and full of vitality to be controlled in this way. Instead, we approach both design and planning as ways to actively participate in the relationship between you and

your garden. This process can absolutely lead to success in the form of a beautiful garden, an abundance of delicious vegetables, and an enriching experience along the way, but the way it leads you there will change over time. Since you and your garden will continually evolve and bring forth surprises, your design and plan will benefit from doing the same.

GARDEN DESIGN. Any traditional permaculture design map includes only permanent and semipermanent elements: trees and other perennial plantings, buildings, ponds, locations and layouts of annual vegetable growing areas. Specific types of vegetables, and where they will go within an annual vegetable garden, are not part of an overall design. That's

A permaculture design map includes more permanent infrastructure (buildings, ponds, perennial plantings) and gardens. Specific vegetables don't belong here but on a garden plan (see drawings on facing page).

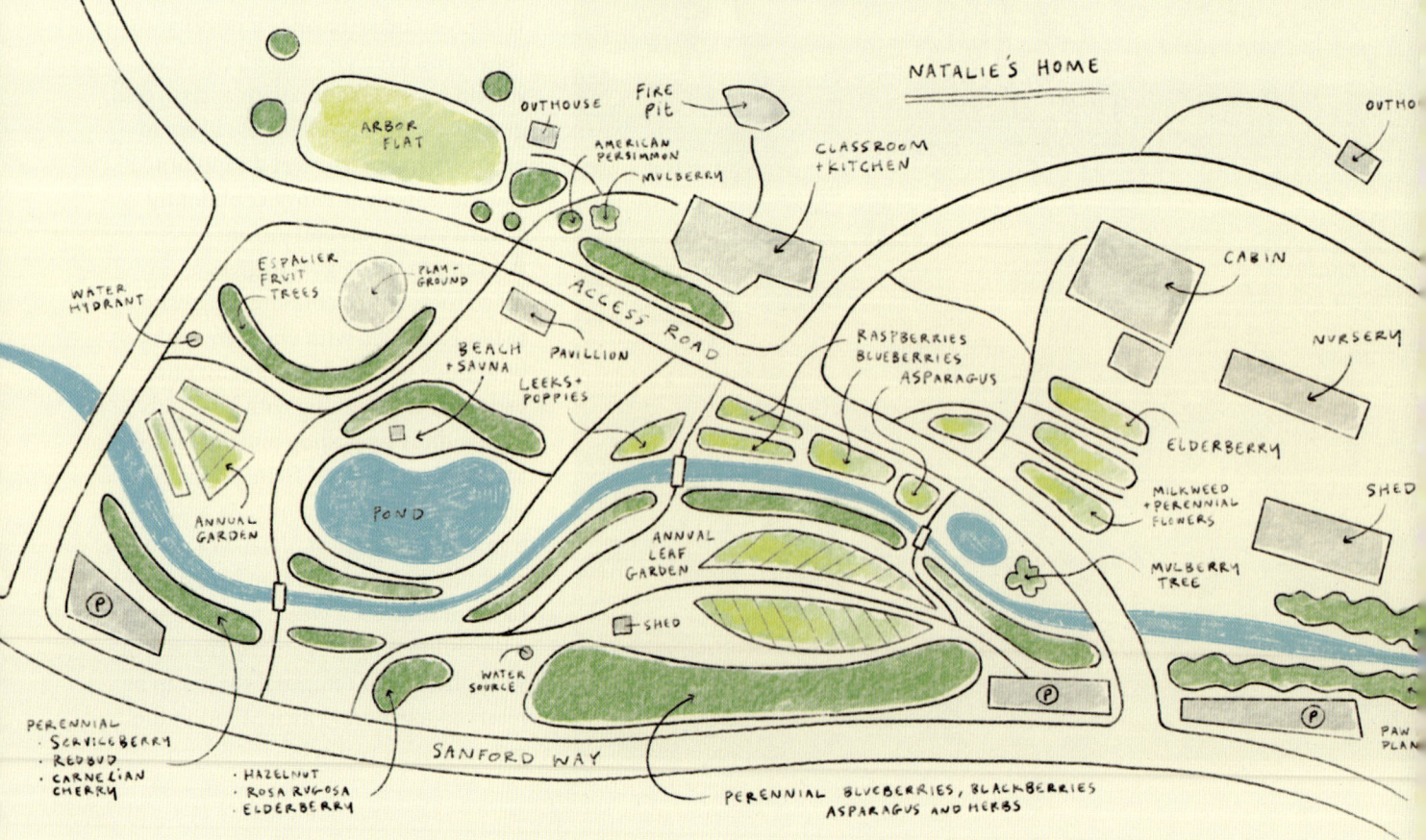

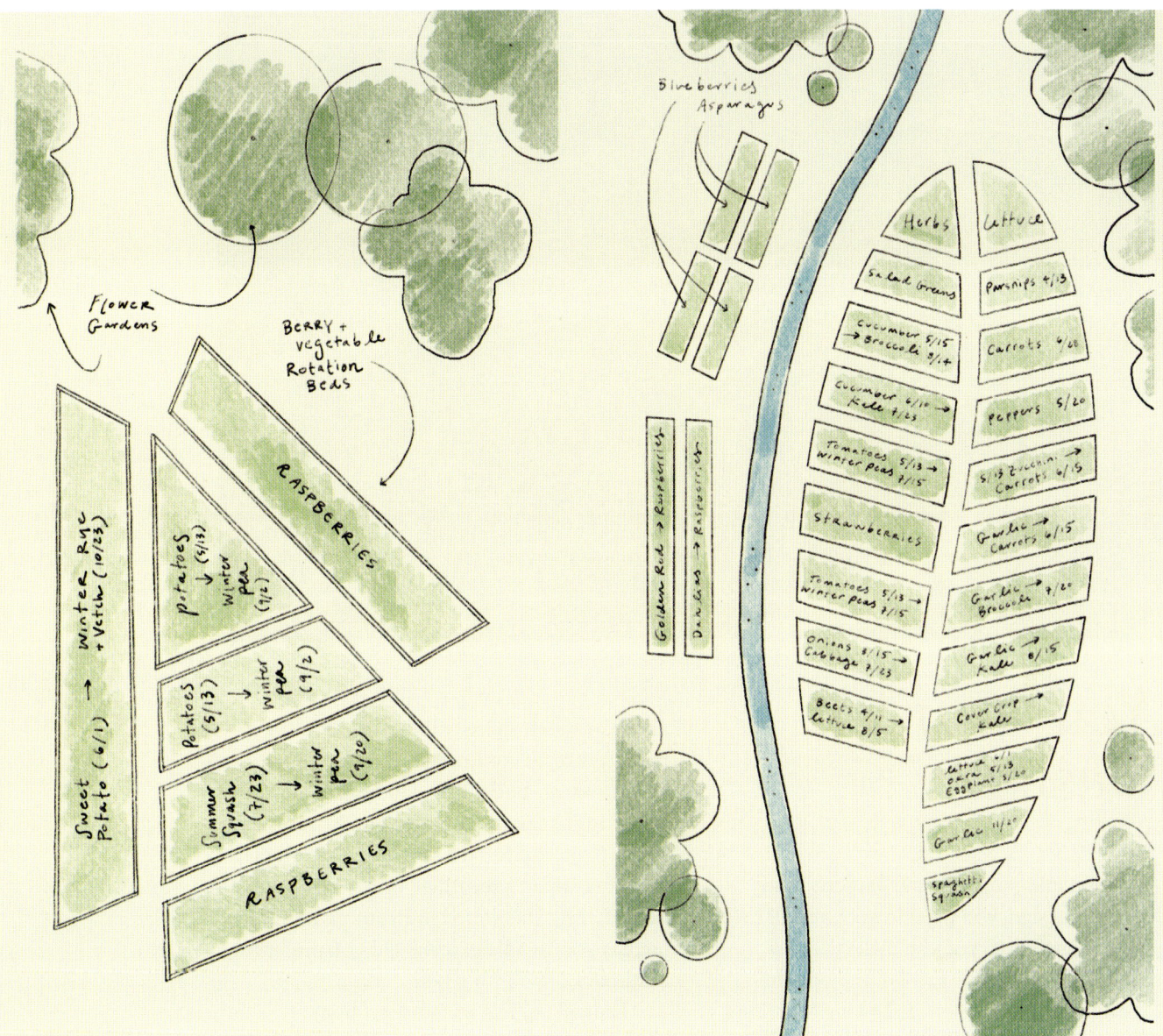

A garden plan shows specific vegetables. A new version of this kind of garden plan is made each year and adjusted as plans change and plantings are made; bed shapes and layout (garden design) won't change.

because planting the same annual vegetables in the same places year after year is a recipe for increased pests and diseases, along with soil depletion. However, using the same garden beds and general layout year after year can work well.

Whether or not you intend to create a full-on permaculture design map for your landscape, it's a good idea to make a permaculture-inspired garden design before you get into the details of your planting plan. This will include things like where the garden is in relation to other factors, such as water, sun, wind, the kitchen, and so on. Additionally, it will consider infrastructure, such as raised beds vs. rows, a

garden shed for storing tools, fences, and whatever else you're working with. The design map might include markers for "kitchen garden" and "storage crop garden" as well as for paths or roads for garden access. Garden design is foundational but only semipermanent (in most cases), so you'll be able to refine and adjust over time.

GARDEN PLAN. Once you have this overarching garden design, you can move on to the creation of a planting plan for the coming season. This plan will include which specific vegetables you'd like to plant and where. You'll create a plan annually, or even seasonally. (More on this process toward the end of this chapter.)

Raised beds should be considered part of the overall garden design. That's because the beds themselves will be there a long time, though veggies growing in them will change.

Your Garden Design

To begin mapping out your garden's foundational design, you need to ask yourself the right questions so you can make the best choices for you, your garden, and your life. Thoughtfully answer the following questions, then turn to the appropriate section in this chapter for further details.

Needed elements. Do you have an area with enough sun for growing vegetables? What is the quality of the existing soil? Is water easily available? Do you have the time to start plants from seed or the funds to purchase starter plants? Can you give a garden the attention and love it needs to thrive?

Location and layout. Where will your garden grow? How close is this spot to your kitchen, a water source, a wildlife habitat, your tool shed? Do you want a square or rectangular garden, or would you prefer a more whimsical shape? How much sun will your garden get in this spot? How will you access it? Do you want to be able to bring a wheelbarrow or cart into the garden? Who will be gardening, and how much space will they need in the pathways to be comfortable?

Rows vs. beds. Will you be growing storage crops like corn, potatoes, squash, and dry beans that require a lot of space? Do you plan to use a tractor, a rototiller, or a two-wheel walk-behind tractor to tend your garden? How large is your whole garden? Do you prefer the aesthetics of beds or rows?

Raised vs. flat vs. sunken beds. If you're opting for beds, do you want or need to raise them up because of compacted, polluted, or soggy soil; so they require less stooping; or for simple aesthetic reasons? Do you have access to tools and materials to construct raised beds? If you live in a desert, will sunken beds help maintain moisture in the soil?

Terraces. If you're gardening on a slope, is it steep enough to require terraces? Do you have the resources to build terraces? Will terraces help you access the garden comfortably?

Container gardening. Might you move from your current place in the not-too-distant future? Is a porch or patio your only available gardening space? Does the soil in your yard contain toxins? (See page 105 for how to test your soil.)

What a Garden Needs

When determining where to locate your garden, consider these basic elements that gardens need to thrive.

Sun. To grow most vegetables, you'll need a minimum of six hours of sun per day. Vegetables generally need more sun than some flowers and other landscape plants. They bravely and generously grow huge parts of their bodies—leaves, fruits, roots, or seeds—for us to eat. We humans have coaxed them into this arrangement over many generations, and part of our end of the bargain is to plant them where they get plenty of sun. Growing enough of themselves to feed us takes a lot of energy, and the primary place where plants get energy is sunlight. If you don't have a garden space that gets lots of sun, you may still be able to grow greens, but you won't have great success with fruiting crops like tomatoes, peppers, and melons.

Good soil and fertility. Starting with earth that has a loose, fluffy texture, lots of organic matter, and a high nutrient and mineral content will jump-start your garden. If possible, choose a garden location where the soil is already inviting to vegetables and continue caring for it to improve these qualities. While sand, compacted clay, and gravel beds are all possibilities for fertile growing spaces,

Sunflowers aren't the only sun-worshippers in the garden; all crops need sunlight, and those that yield flowers or fruits need the most.

each of these will require much more serious time and inputs than an area that already has moderately fertile soil. If you'll be container gardening, it's worth investing time and money into getting a high-quality soil mix or growing medium, as happy soil is vital for growing happy plants. (To learn more about soil fertility, see page 107.)

Water. No matter your climate, you'll want a way to irrigate your garden. Seeds need water to sprout, and roots need it to transport nutrients. Because the sun pulls moisture out of leaves every day, growing plants require significant amounts of water every moment of their lives. If you live in a rainy place, watering may be a once-in-a-while activity, whereas you desert dwellers might have a daily relationship with it. There are elegant ways to reduce watering needs in your garden, including crop choices, planting methods, and mulching (more on these in later chapters), but there's no way around your garden's need for water. Be sure that wherever you put your garden, you have easy access to this magical resource!

Plants. A garden with sun, soil, and water isn't a garden at all without plants! Whether you sow seeds directly into the earth, grow

All plants need water to grow; making sure they get it is part of how we hold up our end of the bargain.

PUTTING DOWN ROOTS

Behold the awesomeness that is the rhizosphere (the area of soil right around the roots), from which plants take up water and nutrients, breathe air, and chemically converse with billions of microorganisms. If sunlight is like sugar to a plant—and plants do turn sunlight into sugars!—then fertility from the ground is like protein, fat, and vitamins, which the plant is able to make and share with us, thanks to soil nutrients and organisms.

Plants, like humans, need a variety of nutrients to grow well. Indeed, the complex, beautiful, mysterious, and mostly unseen work of the roots is what allows the aboveground parts of a plant to thrive. And contrary to popular belief, the flow of life from soil to roots is not a one-way street. Plants release juicy root exudates into the soil that nourish the organisms who, in turn, help those same plants receive soil nutrients in chemical forms that they can actually use. Here is just one of many examples of the cooperative nature of living things that you'll find in this book, and in your garden.

transplants in pots, or buy baby plants, the health and vitality of your plants will determine the success of your garden. (For more on garden plants, see page 35.)

Attention and love. Enter the gardener. *You* are as crucial an element in your garden as the other-than-human parts like sun, soil, and water. Itself a human-created landscape, your garden requires human attention and love to flourish. If your garden can't be situated where you live and you need to travel to tend it (such as a leased field, a plot in a community garden, a friend's backyard), you can still give your growing patch the attention and love it needs by weaving gardening into your daily routine. Make a regular date with a friend, for instance, who lives closer to the garden, or stop by your plot after picking your kids up from school. Wherever your garden grows, by observing and attending to it regularly, you will catch issues early, before they become problems that require more physical effort to solve down the line.

Pruning and trellising tomato plants helps prevent fungal diseases. It's also a lovely way to have a hands-on relationship with the plants as they grow.

Garden Location and Layout

Once you've chosen the general location that will give plants the elements they need, it's time to home in on the layout. There are a lot of different approaches to laying out a garden. Your decision will depend on what works best for you and your environment.

FACTORS TO CONSIDER

As you set up a new garden location, or expand or improve an existing one, here are some more factors to explore and consider.

Water flows downhill. If your garden is sited on a slope or hill, lay out your beds to run level along the contour of the slope—that is, place the beds side to side, not up and down the hill. The idea is to help trap water, prevent soil from washing away during storms, and make your garden easier to traverse and care for. A much more intensive way to do this is by creating berms (mounds) and swales (ditches) next to each other, along level contour lines on the landscape. This much-beloved permaculture practice dramatically alters the landscape and is especially suited to drier areas, where gardeners want to capture every drop of water possible.

Sun shines from the south. (Or from the north, if you're in the Southern Hemisphere). Observe the path of the sun over time to make the most informed location and layout decisions. If it's an option, locate your garden in a spot that doesn't have anything tall to the sunny side. Know that outside of the tropics, the sun travels on a higher path during summer and a lower path during winter—a section of your yard that is sunny in summer may be in shade in wintertime, or vice versa. Sometimes a shadier corner of the garden in summer is actually a boon, as it creates a cooler, more favorable microclimate for heat-sensitive crops like lettuce and cilantro.

Beauty matters. Your garden will be a visual and energetic part of your life. The more beautiful you think it is, the easier it will be to love and care for. Choose a location and layout that is aesthetically pleasing to you, without making it too complex and difficult to tend. Some simple ways to increase beauty in the garden are to build arbors or trellises,

BERMS AND SWALES

To create a berm and swale, dig out a long trench on the contour of a slope and build up a long mound of soil parallel to it; this is where you'll plant. Water is slowed by this sculpted topography and captured in the swale so that it percolates down into the soil rather than running off. On gentle slopes, simply orienting your garden beds or rows on a contour accomplishes a similar effect, though on a smaller scale. If you're dealing with a serious slope, berms and swales or terraces may be necessary to retain soil and water and allow easy access to your garden.

You'll be more inspired to care for a garden that you think is beautiful; incorporating flowers is an easy way to increase beauty.

plant flowers, include perennials around borders or at the end of beds (bed-ends), and vary the layout.

Maintaining a garden takes more work than planting one. Preparing the soil, sowing, and transplanting are the first fundamental steps in caring for garden plants. You'll also be thinning, weeding, mulching, watering, fertilizing, and harvesting, which can each be a lot of work, too (see Chapters 6–8). Keep all of this in mind when you choose what size to make your garden.

We've witnessed many people (including ourselves!) design gardens that were way too big and ambitious. One way to avoid overdoing it is to go large, but plan to work on building the soil in *half* the area rather than growing vegetables in the whole space at the onset. If and when you want to expand, you'll have a lovely and fertile place in which to spread out. If the smaller area turns out to be enough, you'll have prepared a fertile spot to move into for longer-term rotations. There's great humility in accepting our human limitations, and also a great freedom that can sprout from that humility.

Access is essential. Whether you're planting, weeding, watering, fertilizing, building a trellis, harvesting, or sitting and smelling the flowers, you need to access your garden with ease. If you're growing a larger garden, it's really nice to have pathways wide enough for a cart or wheelbarrow. If you'll be watering by hand, having a spigot or hose close by is a huge plus. Also, think about what you'll bring into and take from your garden (tools, water, transplants, a picnic table, large rocks, raised-bed materials, heavy baskets of vegetables, your toddler), and design accordingly. Remember that some plants might overflow their beds (looking at you, squash); you might curse very narrow paths down the line if they are overtaken by vegetation.

Your body dimensions are your ruler. A rule of thumb is to create garden beds that are no wider than twice your arm length (otherwise you won't be able to reach the middle of the bed). Some folks like narrower beds, some like wider, depending on their size and ease or limitation of movement. If you use mobility support like a cane or wheelchair, you may benefit from wider pathways, or even super-tall raised beds, so you can move about comfortably. Make sure your garden works for *your* body.

Steer clear of allelopathic plants. Some plants release chemical compounds that inhibit the growth of other plants. This is

CREATIVE INSPIRATION FROM DIFFERENT TIMES AND PLACES

Researching different gardening approaches from around the world and throughout time reveals a beautiful diversity of human creativity when it comes to interacting with the land and landscape. May the following examples inspire you!

FARMERS IN THE PERUVIAN ANDES, and in many other mountainous regions of the world, have been building and using andenes (stairstep-like terraces) for thousands of years. Some of these beautifully constructed andenes were built more than four thousand years ago and are still in use today!

IN MESOAMERICA, complex and incredibly generative milpa farming has been practiced for more than seven thousand years. These systems can include regular fallow periods, fertilization practices, specific planting times, rotations that can be longer than a single human lifespan, and unique, locally adapted varieties of up to a dozen or more plants, most often including the beloved "three sisters": corn, beans, and squash.

RICE FARMERS THROUGHOUT ASIA utilize the paddy system to grow their crops in flooded and semiflooded marshy areas near rivers and in terraces. This practice originated in the Yangtze River basin in southern China more than six thousand years ago.

ANCIENT MESOPOTAMIANS created massive stone ziggurats (pyramid-shaped structures) that featured terraces where trees, flowers, and other plants grew—the original rooftop gardens! In that way, people were able to maintain cool and inviting gardens in the midst of hot and dry cities.

IN THE YUCATÁN PENINSULA, people have been building and using raised beds for growing vegetables for thousands of years. In this region with very thin topsoil and heavy pressure from critters that will eat crops, gardeners use sticks and leaves to build table-height canchés (raised beds) for growing vegetables. Lower raised beds made of rocks and sticks are also common in this region.

called allelopathy. If you lay out your garden near such plants, you may be very disappointed with your yields. Shown on the next page is a list of common allelopathic plants and the crops that are most sensitive to them (avoid planting these close to one another).

Right angles are usually easier to build and maintain. If you are using wooden material for raised-bed frames, it's easier to create rectangular or square beds than round or oddly shaped beds; similarly, plowing or tilling a squarish area is also a lot more practical than another shape. Building trellises and hoeing in straight lines is much simpler than accomplishing those tasks in curved or wiggly lines. We have definitely seen gardens shaped like mandalas, spirals, and suns, and Natalie's garden is leaf-shaped, with angled, wooden

raised beds. These shapes are arguably worth the extra work if they make you happy or serve other functions. Natalie's leaf-shaped garden performed way better in Hurricane Helene than a grid pattern of beds would have. Follow your bliss, but don't make your life harder than it has to be!

Planting in straight rows saves a lot of energy. We've tried planting in a honeycomb pattern to maximize plants in a given area and have found that the small amount of space this saves, particularly in medium to large gardens, isn't worth the hassle. Honeycombs are much more difficult to weed with a hoe and to mulch. In the cases of container gardening and small-scale gardens, honeycomb planting may be worth the extra maintenance for the amount of space it saves. Otherwise we go

Running a stirrup hoe alongside these young turnip plants to remove weeds is a cinch because they're planted in straight rows.

for straight lines so we can weed and mulch efficiently.

Keep your holistic goals in mind. As you create your garden layout, don't lose sight of your holistic goals (see the holistic inquiry exercise at the beginning of this chapter). You may want to sacrifice some bed space for a picnic area, or you may choose to make wider pathways so children can easily tell the difference between paths and beds and avoid trampling vegetables. One of the beauties of your garden is that it's *yours*; you get to have a conversation with the landscape and other-than-human inhabitants in order to find a shape that honors everyone's place.

Allelopathic Plants

ALLELOPATHIC PLANT	ESPECIALLY DETRIMENTAL TO THESE CROPS
Black walnut	Members of Solanaceae family (a.k.a. nightshade)
Eucalyptus	Wheat
Goldenrod	Lettuce, possibly others
Pine	Wheat, corn, other grasses, possibly other vegetables
Redwood	Most vegetables
Rhododendron	Decomposing leaves may inhibit germination of seeds in nearby soil

Rows vs. Beds

Some gardens are grown like fields, with space to walk between each row of plants—a method known as row cropping. Others utilize beds (raised or in-ground), which usually have rows or clusters of vegetables within them. Still other gardens grow in containers (see page 32 for more about container gardening). It's helpful to familiarize yourself with each of these approaches, including their advantages and disadvantages, so that you can create a workable design for your garden.

Keep in mind that you don't have to choose one or the other! You can have a field where you grow row crops, raised beds for other vegetables, and even a set of containers on your porch for plants that need extra care or a specific soil type, or that you just love having nearby. Natalie's garden, for instance, includes raised beds with wooden sides, flat beds, row cropping, and even some containers. Chloe also uses a combination of flat beds and row cropping. You are free to mix and match based on your needs and resources.

ROWS

When row cropping, a sizable block is prepared for planting, and then crops are sown or transplanted in rows throughout the block. Generally speaking, row cropping is best suited for large areas. This is especially true if you'll be using a rototiller or tractor, or if you

Natalie's garden is a gorgeous leaf shape. This goes against our advice to use straight lines, but the diagonal beds help shed floodwater.

We've witnessed many people (including ourselves!) design gardens that were way too big and ambitious. One way to avoid overdoing it is to go large, but plan to work on building the soil in half the area, rather than growing vegetables in the whole space at the onset. If and when you want to expand, you'll have a lovely and fertile place in which to spread out.

plan to kill grass and/or weeds in an area by excluding light with a large specialized tarp (a process known as solarizing/occulting; see page 78 for details). Indeed, weeds will grow in any exposed soil between rows, so regular maintenance, such as mulching, hoeing, or mowing, will be required.

A notable advantage to row cropping is that you're not limited by the width of a bed. Corn, dry beans, potatoes, sweet potatoes, and winter squash are all typically grown in fairly large quantities, so planting them in blocks of rows makes more sense than using several beds. Some of these crops also need room to sprawl and vine (squash and sweet potatoes). Corn, which is wind pollinated, won't yield well unless it's planted in at least a 4- by 4-foot block, and dry beans don't yield enough to be worth the effort unless you grow a lot of them.

BEDS

Beds can be easier to manage than rows, especially over time. They're less likely to be stepped on and compacted, so you can continue building and conditioning the soil season after season without much disturbance. Also, the psychology of managing several distinct beds is very different from managing a large field. Even if they take up the same space as rows, beds can somehow feel more manageable to our minds, maybe because it's easier to focus on each one individually at any given time.

Keep in mind that the pathways between beds will need to be managed in some way, especially if you live in a rainy area where weeds grow even where you don't irrigate. One option is to leave paths bare, hoeing them periodically as weeds begin to grow. Because this can be labor intensive, and bare paths get muddy in wet climates, our favorite approaches are to either sow a mix of grass and white clover to be mowed regularly or to mulch *heavily* with something pleasant to walk on, like bark mulch or partially decomposed wood chips.

Potatoes need weeding and hilling during their growth; planting them in long rows makes both of these tasks simpler.

PLANTS THAT MAKE GOOD NEIGHBORS

In wild nature, in many traditional agricultural systems, in some large-scale modern fields, and in lots of hopeful organic gardens, different crops are planted in the same beds or rows together. This practice is broadly called *intercropping* or *polyculture*, with a subterm, *companion planting*, that refers to planting things together because of a purported benefit to the growth of one or both.

Companion planting was popularized in the 1970s. Since then, many of those ideas have been revealed as fanciful folklores that don't play out in real-life gardens. There are definitely healthy and productive polycultures all over the world, but they are usually quite nuanced and complex. At the scale we're working, we've found that our gardens are quite diverse and have many of the benefits of intercropping even as we plant each crop in a little "neighborhood" block.

Additionally, managing two or more crops in the same space can be difficult, and if it's done poorly (especially the timing of planting and of weeding), it can result in poorer yields of both. We do, however, sometimes plant annual herbs, lettuce, or arugula between or next to taller plants to maximize space, or to benefit from a cooler microclimate in the shade of the taller plants in summertime. Natalie usually interplants beets and onions, also for space saving. And we love to plant marigolds here and there throughout the garden, mostly because they're beautiful. People claim marigolds deter pests, but there are no scientific studies that back this up, except some promising evidence that they reduce populations of harmful soil nematodes.

Styles of Garden Beds

Garden beds can be flush with the ground, raised and supported with sidewalls, or sunken into the ground, depending on your climate and needs. As you may suspect, the first two styles are more common. In fact, sunken beds are really only appropriate for dry, desert conditions; Natalie learned about them when she was gardening in Arizona.

Some factors to consider when choosing between flat and raised beds include the permanence of your garden, what resources you have to invest, the quality of your in-ground soil, and your aesthetic preferences.

FLAT BEDS

The simplest option for creating a garden bed is to keep it at the same level as the soil around it. This method makes sense only if the soil that you are starting with is reasonably suited for gardening—meaning it's not waterlogged, loaded with toxins, or extremely dense and hard. Over time, with good management, flat beds "puff up" and appear slightly raised. When you add loft (air) and organic matter through mulching, mixing in compost, growing cover crops, and avoiding compaction of the soil, soil tilth (or fluffiness) will improve, and the soil level actually rises as organic matter and air build up.

Pros of Flat Beds

- Simple and fairly quick.
- Flexible—you can change your mind about where a flat bed is, or turn it back into lawn or a path with ease.
- Easy to weed with a stirrup hoe.
- No sidewalls to maintain.
- Do not require construction or purchased materials (although you may buy compost, mulch, amendments, and more).

Raised beds like these have a very clear distinction between bed space and path space. The paths here are covered in low-maintenance decomposed granite.

- No need to dig deep into the soil to excavate and then rebuild soil, as you'd need to do in a sunken bed.

Cons of Flat Beds

- Not appropriate in soggy, poisoned, or overly heavy soils.
- Soil that builds up more than 6 or so inches above the path will eventually tumble into the pathways.
- Weeds easily crawl from paths into beds, making flat beds much harder to keep free of weeds than raised beds with sidewalls.
- More challenging to keep children and pets from trampling soil and crops without the delineation of sidewalls.

RAISED BEDS

If you wish to manage at least one section of your garden on a small to medium scale, raised beds can be a wonderful option because they make it easier to maintain and build soil tilth and health. They keep the garden soil separate from the well-traveled paths and make it much easier to tend the soil in a methodical manner.

Raised beds can be constructed by hand or purchased as kits. You can fill them with the natural soil you've got, adding compost and cover cropping, as well as doing other

soil-tending techniques to get going. You can alternatively and/or additionally purchase soil or amendments to fill them. We say "and/or" because even if you work with the soil you've got, you may want to acquire manure, compost, cover crop seeds, mineral amendments, or powdered fertilizers. If the soil below your raised beds is not suitable for growing, you'll need to bring in more imports, probably including imported soil itself. For details on setting up raised beds, including possible materials for building, see page 65.

Pros of Raised Beds

- Eliminate compaction of soil in beds from foot traffic.
- Can be built on top of questionable soil by using imported material or with mostly native soil.
- Minimize weeds jumping from paths into beds.
- Protect crops when minor flooding occurs.
- Possible to direct sow crops earlier than in flat beds or rows because elevated soil typically heats up and dries out faster than the surrounding soil.
- Can be elevated high enough to make gardening more accessible to gardeners with less flexibility or mobility.
- Prefabricated metal raised beds are easy to install.

Sunken beds make sense in hot desert areas. They keep soil moist and cool.

Cons of Raised Beds

- Not practical for very large gardens.

- Harder to weed with a stirrup hoe.

- Semipermanent—not appropriate if you think you'll need to move the bed or garden.

- Often require a good bit of off-site materials, which usually cost money.

- Cheapest and easiest materials do not stand the test of time: Pine slabs (waste products of the milling process available at local sawmills for free or cheap), coniferous rough-sawn boards, repurposed pallets, and untreated "white wood" boards will rot in one to five years, depending on your climate.

- Finding nontoxic and rot-resistant materials to build them can be challenging, pricey, and/or a lot of work.

- Many materials commonly used have questionable levels of toxicity, such as treated wood and railroad ties.

- Prefabricated metal raised beds are getting more affordable but are still not cheap.

SUNKEN BEDS

These beds make sense in places where the climate is dry and windy and the air temperature is too hot for many vegetables to grow without assistance. Sunken-bed plants grow in soil moderated by the constant, cooler temperature of the deeper earth, and the bed depth retains moisture and protects plants from strong winds. Creating sunken beds is a lot of work: A 3- by 8- foot or longer area of soil is excavated to a depth of about a foot, and a 2- to 3-inch-thick layer of compost or rich topsoil is put in this wide trench; plants are then installed directly in this soil. But these beds allow you to cultivate crops that would otherwise suffer from heat, which makes this approach ideal for growing in the desert.

Pros of Sunken Beds

- Do not need the infrastructure of raised beds.

- Keep plants cool in super-hot areas.

- Retain moisture better than raised beds, flat beds, or rows.

Cons of Sunken Beds

- Only appropriate where temperatures are extremely hot.

- The sunken bed slowly becomes less deep as you build soil.

- It's a lot of work to dig such big holes!

- Lowers soil temperature, so can delay germination for spring plantings.

- Any thick topsoil must be removed and transported elsewhere.

Terraces and Terracing

There are many ways to create terraces for gardening. These have beautiful stone retaining walls, allowing for steeper sides.

Terracing is an ancient practice that has allowed people to grow food on hills and mountainsides for millennia (see Creative Inspiration from Different Times and Places, page 24). Put simply, it involves molding the earth on a slope into a more stairstep shape, which creates flat areas for growing. In many cases, retaining walls hold the soil in place. Terraces can be any size, from a single, small garden bed to a series of strips hundreds of feet long. The width of a terrace is governed by the steepness of the slope: Gentler slopes can afford fewer, wider terraces, while steep slopes require thinner, more numerous terraces. Generally it doesn't make sense to build terraces that are less than 3 feet wide.

WHAT SITUATIONS CALL FOR A TERRACE?

Terracing is a lot of work and heavily disturbs the soil. Additionally, building an appropriate retaining wall, whether out of wood, metal, or, like the ancients did, stone, requires skill and the right materials. However, if you're working with a steep situation, terracing might be the key to having a garden. If your potential garden is on a gentler slope, to terrace or not is a judgment call you'll have to make. If you're not sure, we suggest trying to garden without terracing; if it works, no need to terrace.

Whatever the terrace size, be sure to leave space uphill of your growing area to walk and navigate with tools. If your slope allows enough space for a wheelbarrow, that's excellent. You'll need to access a terrace garden and tend to it in the same ways as any other garden.

WANT A LARGE TERRACE GARDEN?

If creating a large-scale terrace ends up being the right choice, the job will be made much easier with heavy machinery. This can mean hiring someone to create the terraces, or renting a mini excavator and/or skid steer and operating them yourself. Of course, terraces can also be made by people power and hand tools. This kind of project is a great candidate for a community work party, as it's pretty backbreaking labor and will take a long time with just one or two people.

Container Gardening

The idea of growing food in containers may seem like a modern adaptation to high population density and city living, but it's actually quite old. In fact, traditional Mayan gardeners in the Yucatán Peninsula have been building raised wood-and-banana-leaf canchés for centuries (see Creative Inspiration from Different Times and Places, page 24). In parts of India, the first seeds of the planting season are sown in baskets of soil, and the new plants are floated down the river as an offering.

Container gardening provides versatility and enables you to grow food even if you don't have access to a patch of earth, or if you want to expand your garden upward or edge-ward. There are entire books and courses dedicated to the how-tos of container gardening, but in our permaculture approach, we like to integrate container gardening into gardening in general; the pattern is gardening, the detail is the container. This said, you may want to access additional resources that take deep dives into container-gardening culture; follow the link to our website found on page 364 for some suggestions.

Container gardening isn't an all-or-nothing choice. Many people grow some plants in the ground and others in containers.

What if every patio were a garden? With creative container gardening, that could become a reality. Container gardening is also a great choice if you rent your home.

Here are a few scenarios for which container gardening can be a great fit.

- You don't have ground to plant in.
- You know that the soil around you is high in toxins, like heavy metals or pesticide residues.
- You want to plant things where the soil is poor, rocky, or otherwise unsuitable.
- You aren't sure how long this garden space will be available to you.
- You are dealing with a shady spot and want to move plants around to get maximum sunlight.
- You have physical constraints that make gardening in the ground difficult or impossible (in this case, containers would best be raised up on a table or platform).
- You are unsure where you want to put in a forever garden and want to play around with your garden location.
- You don't have time or energy to prepare the ground and want to put seeds in *now*.
- You want to grow plants that won't survive winter where you live (for example, lemon trees and some Mediterranean herbs where we are in southern Appalachia); in this case, you would need a sunny spot indoors or a greenhouse to keep the plants over winter.
- You are available to water and fertilize your container garden very regularly, as they need more of both than in-ground gardens do. (See Chapter 4 for more on soil mixes and fertility.)

While containers come in all shapes and sizes, and gardeners have been known to adapt all manner of objects as planters, there are reliable common containers that you can choose from.

Plastic pots are cheap, lightweight, and easy to get your hands on. Plus they're durable, simple to store, and, in most cases, made of UV-resistant plastic. Pots like this are usually black and absorb a lot of heat from the sun, which can dry out the container

soil, although the plastic material doesn't let moisture evaporate through the pot itself. All plastic is eventually destined for the landfills and oceans of the world, where it harms living creatures and systems. Please note, 5-gallon buckets are popular and fun to garden in, but the plastic they're made of is *not* UV resistant like nursery pots. After a season or two in full-time full sun, 5-gallon pots will become brittle and start to break apart.

Unglazed ceramic pots (terra-cotta) are moderately expensive and quite heavy and breakable, but they are also pretty, nontoxic, and fairly easy to get hold of. Because they are not glazed, moisture can evaporate through the pot itself. If you live in a humid climate, this natural water loss can be a boon; plants are less likely to get waterlogged. But if you live in a drier place, using a terra-cotta pot can mean you'll need to water at least daily, even twice a day at the height of summer.

Glazed ceramic pots can be quite beautiful, as well as expensive and heavy. They retain moisture better than unglazed pots, and, if they're a lighter color, deflect some of the sun's searing rays. Some glazes, however,

CONSIDERING CONTAINERS

You can grow plants in just about any container that will hold soil and let water drain. What else should you consider when searching for the best containers to fit your situation?

- Accessibility and price
- Size and weight
- Aeration
- Potential for leaching toxins
- UV stability
- Aesthetics

contain lead, especially those on older pots, so be careful there. Also, like terra-cotta, they're breakable, so they're not the best choice if you'll be moving them frequently.

Fabric pots are extremely lightweight, durable, and relatively affordable. If you can't find them locally, you can purchase them online. Fabric pots are made of woven/felted poly (plastic) fibers and are porous, meaning moisture will evaporate through them. Most fabric pots are black, so they get hot and dry out quickly. An advantage of the material's breathability is that fabric pots air-prune roots (the roots stop growing at the edge of the pot, where they sense air, rather than spiraling and becoming pot-bound). Also, fabric pots come in a wide range of sizes and shapes, and even larger ones are relatively inexpensive.

Metal containers made of galvanized metal created specifically for growing plants are wonderful, whereas ungalvanized containers will likely rust after some time. Galvanized metal is coated with zinc to prevent rusting, and zinc is an essential nutrient for both plants and humans; it also won't leach unless it's in an acidic environment (so toxicity isn't a real concern). Metal containers meant for plants are becoming more readily available in a variety of shapes and sizes. They are usually sold ready to assemble with minimal tools.

Wooden containers, like old drawers or decrepit chests, can be fun and whimsical, though they will eventually rot (some sooner rather than later). Before using them to grow vegetables, make sure any original finishes or paints left behind are nontoxic. Prefab wooden growing containers like planter boxes, or repurposed half whiskey barrels are lovely, though they can be pricey.

Bathtubs, toilets, and other miscellany are cute and clever ways to add flair to a garden. You may be able to find random household items like this for free, which is best since buying these items new can get expensive. Just be sure to test any enamel coating or paint on used items for lead to ensure they're safe before you create a funky container garden with them. (Simple home lead-testing strips are available at most home improvement stores.) Keep in mind, too, that once these objects have soil and plants in them, they're not easy to move.

LEFT: Flowering Thai basil is a great candidate for growing in a fabric pot.

RIGHT: Beautiful and happy chard thrives in a large metal container at a café, where it's destined for the kitchen.

What Crops Do I Plant?

If you love beets, plant lots of them in the springtime, make pickles in the summer, and store some for winter.

A dazzling array of vegetables, fruits, and herbs can grow in your garden. So how do you decide? The following list of questions will help you explore your options and select what to plant next—whether you are at the beginning of your gardening journey or you already have seasons of experience on the same plot. Use it to home in on and ultimately determine what you love to grow, harvest, and eat, in addition to what works well in your garden.

You can download a handy printable chart, along with a video of Chloe diving deeper into the process of choosing what to grow, on our website (see link on page 364).

Note: Not every question will apply to every crop you're considering.

Questions to Ask Yourself

- Do I love to eat it?
- Does it grow well in my area?
- Does it grow well in my conditions?
- Is it pricey to buy?
- Is it way better when freshly picked?
- Is it easy to grow (low input)?
- Do I have a personal and/or cultural connection with it?
- Can I easily get seeds or transplants?
- Can it grow without special infrastructure like a trellis?
- Is it the right season to plant it here?
- Can I grow a meaningful amount in the space I've got?
- Is it hard to find in the grocery store or market?

Refer to the vegetable profiles beginning on page 275 for more information on particular

crops. You can also ask neighbors or use the internet to find answers to questions that go beyond personal preference.

The vegetables with the most "yes's" to these questions have a lot going for them and are worth strongly considering. More weight should be put on the first three: Do I love to eat it? and Does it grow well in my area and conditions? If something doesn't get a lot of "yes's" but you still really want to grow it, go for it! Just know that this plant may present certain challenges or might not be an efficient or economical choice if you're trying to optimize yields.

These beds of cucumber look like they're "passing the torch"—the left being the second succession ready to begin producing while the right winds down.

GARDENING IN TIME: SUCCESSION PLANTING

Your garden doesn't just live in space; it also lives in time. This means it changes over time and that different crops will be at different parts of their life cycles during different times of year. When one plant is done growing, another can take its place. Considering this is part of garden planning and will become more intuitive as you get to know the rhythm of each crop's life. Two ways that we include time in our longer-term planning are with succession planting and crop rotation.

SUCCESSION PLANTING: Planting the same crop more than once in different places, with an appropriate amount of time in between, to extend the harvest window (when one planting is done producing, you start harvesting from the next). See crop-specific succession planting info in the vegetable profiles beginning on page 275.

CROP ROTATION: Planting something different in the same place, after the first crop has finished, to vary the impacts on soil and to break up pest and disease life cycles. You can download a video lecture about crop rotation that includes some sample rotations. See page 364 for the link to our website.

Considerations for Crop Placement

Sprouting broccoli, like this 'Piracicaba', yields multiple harvests and deserves an accessible location. Heading-type broccoli is only harvested once and can be located farther away.

When you are placing your crops in your garden map (if you made one; see page 39), or when you're ready to plant, consider the following.

Access. Crops that require frequent harvesting or tending—such as cilantro, green beans, sprouting broccoli, kale, lettuce, peppers, tomatoes, and zucchini—should go in the most accessible parts of the garden. Crops that need less frequent tending—such as dry beans, field corn, potatoes, sweet potatoes, and winter squash—should go in the less accessible areas.

Beauty. What looks beautiful to your eye? Consider shapes, colors, and textures.

Sun exposure. Identify a spot with prime sunny conditions.

Plant height. Put sprawling plants near taller plants and/or edges. Place taller crops like corn to the north (or south, if you're in the Southern Hemisphere) of shorter crops so the little ones won't be shaded out (unless you want to create shade, in which case, plant them on the shady side). This applies equally to crops that will climb a tall trellis, thus becoming tall.

Crop groupings. Place related crops near each other in blocks (not intercropped in the same bed) so that future crop rotations will be simplified.

Crop rotations. Avoid planting the same type of crop in the same place year after year.

How Much Do I Plant?

Just like choosing which crops to grow, deciding how much to plant and where (within your garden) will require an ongoing process of refinement over several seasons of growing. We know of no gardener who has ever grown the exact "right" amount of everything in any given year, so don't let this process get too stressful!

If you plant the exact same amount of carrots from one year to the next, your yields will not be identical: Germination rates vary based on temperature fluctuations, and this variability will increase as the climate continues to change; a very courageous bunny might come onto the scene who wasn't around last year; and/or the compost you add this year might have just the right balance of nutrients to grow super carrots. The variables are almost endless and don't just include how many seeds or plants you put into the ground. Gardening is always an adventure!

All that being said, you can tap into brainpower and the type of interactive holistic planning we use and teach to create a solid plan from which to begin.

Following is a system Natalie has developed and refined over decades of gardening to plan out her garden at various locations. For planning out her current 28-bed garden, she goes through all of these steps in 20 to 45 minutes each February. Pretty efficient, given the amount of space. The first time you do it, it will likely take you longer, but year after year, it will become easier and easier. Chloe doesn't map things out like this but rather is guided by an intuitive sense of how much of each crop she'll use, as well as careful records over time. This less exact approach has worked well for her because she's had nearly one-third of an acre to grow on, meaning there's usually plenty of space for everything.

We suggest you go through Natalie's process below, especially if you're new to gardening, and then adjust and tweak it over time to work best for you. If measuring and mapping make you crazy, just skip it and get some plants in the ground or come up with your own approach.

The step-by-step process on the following pages will help you to start from square one with planning your garden if you haven't grown in a space before. We present this as a plan for planting in garden beds because that has been the most common growing method for our students. You can, however, apply this technique to growing in rows or planting individual plants in planter boxes.

Some parts of this process, specifically steps 5 and 6, can be rather cumbersome, as they involve a lot of calculations. Once you get to know how much garden space it takes to grow the quantity you want to harvest, you can drastically simplify these steps.

If you are growing in rows or planter boxes, you are in luck. In step 2 you can count up the total space you have in whatever format you have, and in step 5 you can still refer to the chart in the appendix, but just look at the column that applies to how you are growing.

It's easy to grow too many cucumbers all at once. Thankfully they make great pickles.

MAKING YOUR GARDEN PLAN

1. DRAW A SIMPLE MAP OF YOUR GARDEN.
It doesn't need to be exactly to scale, but it's easier to visualize if the map proportions strongly resemble the real thing.

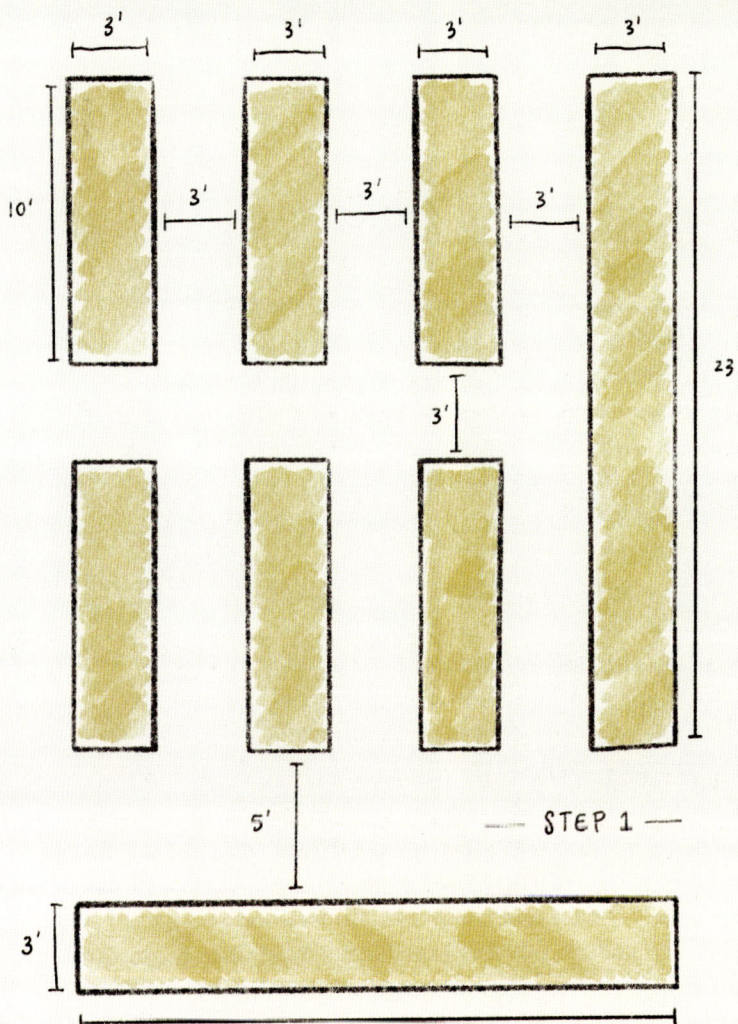

— STEP 1 —

2. DETERMINE AVAILABLE BED SPACE.
Measure the length of your beds and add all those numbers together. We like to use linear feet of bed length more than square feet of bed space because it keeps things simpler.

If you have an oddly shaped area or several different areas, simply measure the length of each and add them together. Don't worry if beds have slightly varying widths. You don't need to be obsessively precise, unless that is your joy.

For example:
6 beds × 10 feet long = 60 linear feet
1 bed × 24 feet long = 24 linear feet
1 bed × 21 feet long = 21 linear feet
Total = 105 linear feet of 3-foot-wide beds

3. DREAM UP WHAT YOU WANT TO GROW. List the plants that you decided to grow based on the questions you asked yourself on page 35. You can go with your dreams and desires in this step; don't get caught up in what will actually fit in your garden or what you already know how to grow; in the next step you'll be able to rectify your dreams with reality.

Crops by Planting Season

Note that these time frames are for temperate areas. For more specific timing for your area, go to the Timing Tables that start on page 339.

EARLY SPRING PLANTED CROPS	MID-SPRING PLANTED CROPS	MIDSUMMER AND FALL PLANTED CROPS (FOR FALL AND WINTER HARVESTS)
Arugula	Basil	Arugula
Beets and chard	Cilantro	Beets and chard
Broccoli and cauliflower	Corn	Broccoli and cauliflower
Cabbage	Cucumbers	Cabbage
Carrots	Dill	Carrots
Cilantro	Eggplant	Cilantro
Lettuce	Lettuce	Garlic
Onions	Muskmelon	Kale and collards
Parsnips	Okra	Lettuce
Peas	Peppers and chiles	Peas
Potatoes	Pole beans	Radishes and daikons (short and long season)
Radishes (short season)	Potatoes	Spinach
Spinach	Radishes (short season)	Turnips and rutabegas
Turnips	Sweet Potatoes	
	Tomatoes	
	Watermelons	
	Winter squash and pumpkins	
	Zucchini and summer squash	

4. SEPARATE CROPS BY SEASON. It is helpful to sort the list of veggies you'd like to grow according to the season they will be planted. Note that some crops can be planted in multiple seasons. You can plant these in just one season or multiple times for multiple harvests. Keep in mind that some crops will need to be sown indoors long before their planting time out in the garden. The table above refers to when plants are direct sown or transplanted into the garden, not when they are sown indoors. Refer to the vegetable profiles starting on page 275 for info on which crops are transplanted vs. direct sown.

5. DETERMINE GARDEN SPACE FOR EACH VEGETABLE. How much will you, your family, and your community eat fresh, and how much might you preserve? Keep in mind that food preservation takes time and energy! Be realistic with how much canning, freezing, drying, and pickling you're able to do. Refer to Possible Yields of Common Vegetables on page 362 in the appendix to help guide how many bed feet of each crop you want to grow. Put this number next to the crops you've listed in previous steps.

See the following chart for an example.

Desired Bed Space for This Year's Crops (in Feet)

EARLY SPRING PLANTED CROPS	MID-SPRING PLANTED CROPS	MIDSUMMER AND FALL PLANTED CROPS (FOR FALL AND WINTER HARVESTS)
Beets 10 (shared)*	Pole beans 10	Cabbage 10
Onions 10 (shared)*	Cucumbers 10	Kale 15
Chard 5	Peppers 5	Broccoli 5
Parsnips 5	Canning tomatoes 20	Arugula 5
Lettuce 5	Slicer and cherry tomatoes 10	Carrots 10
Peas 10	Bush beans 10	Cilantro 5
Potatoes 10	Eggplant 10	Garlic (late fall) 20
	Lettuce 10	Daikon 5
	Dill—smattering	Lettuce 5
	Cilantro 4	
	Winter squash 10	
	Zucchini 10	
	Basil—planted w/tomatoes	
Total: 45	**Total: 109**	**Total: 80**

*Note that beets and onions can be planted at different times in the same bed space, so the total number just includes 10 linear feet of bed space total for them rather than 10 linear feet of bed each.

Once you've added desired space next to crop names, total the linear feet needed per season using the following formulas. *Note that most fall gardens, which are planted in midsummer, take up less space than spring gardens, so less specific planning has to happen to make everything fit. This is why we go through the more detailed planning process just for spring planting.*

Total feet for spring = early spring planted crops + mid-spring planted crops

Total feet for summer into fall = all midsummer and early fall planted crops

To calculate **total feet for spring** using the crops in our example:

> 45 (total linear bed feet for early spring long-season crops)
>
> + 109 (total desired mid-spring crops)
>
> = 154 feet (total desired space for early spring and mid-spring planting)

The **total feet for planting in the summer for fall and winter harvests** for the crops in our example is 80 feet.

TIP: *If your beds are a fairly consistent size, you can simply calculate the number of beds (or fraction thereof) per crop, instead of the specific feet; this is what Natalie does. If you have grown a garden before and have data from past seasons (e.g., how much bed space you dedicated to each vegetable, whether it was too much, too little, or just right), this will be extremely helpful for determining how much to grow this year.*

Real Bed Space for This Year's Crops (in Feet)

EARLY SPRING PLANTED CROPS	MID-SPRING PLANTED CROPS	MIDSUMMER AND FALL PLANTED CROPS (FOR FALL AND WINTER HARVESTS)
Beets 10 (shared)*	Pole beans ~~10~~ 5	Cabbage 10
Onions 10 (shared)*	Cucumbers ~~10~~ 5	Kale ~~15~~ 10
~~Chard 5~~ (I don't actually like the way it tastes)	Peppers ~~5~~ 3	Broccoli ~~5~~ 10
Parsnips ~~5~~ 4	Canning tomatoes 20	Arugula 5
Lettuce ~~5~~ 3	Slicer and cherry tomatoes ~~10~~ 5	Carrots 10
Peas ~~10~~ 5	Bush beans ~~10~~ 5	Cilantro 5
Potatoes 10	Eggplant ~~10~~ 5	Garlic (late fall) ~~20~~ 15
	Lettuce ~~10~~ 3	Daikon 5
	Dill—smattering	Lettuce ~~5~~ 10
	Cilantro 4	
	Winter squash 10	
	Zucchini ~~10~~ 6	
	Basil—planted w/tomatoes	
Total: 32	**Total: 71**	**Total: 80**

6. RECONCILE DESIRE AND REALITY.

Unfortunately, and fortunately, we are bound by physical reality. What we want to plant and harvest may be much more than we have space for. To see if this is the case, compare the total feet (or beds) of what you came up with above with the actual space you have in your garden.

If the total feet you came up with in step 5 is less than the size of your garden, you can easily fill the rest with low-maintenance cover crops, flowers, or extra veggies. If the total feet you came up with in step 5 is greater than your actual bed space, you will need to ask yourself some hard questions, such as: Which crops might you not end up eating? Which are easy and inexpensive to buy at the store? Go back to your answers in the What Crops Do I Plant? section (page 35) and see what it makes sense to reduce or nix this year.

In our example, we would need 154 feet of bed space to grow all the crops that we desire in the spring. We only have 105 linear feet of bed space available, so in order to rectify our desires with reality, we either need to add 49 feet of bed space or tamp down our desires.

Check out the table above to see how we adjusted our planting plan to match the bed space we have available.

TIPS: *If you are a first-year gardener, we recommend paring your list down to just five or so crops. You also must consider your time and energy. Even if you have an abundance of available space, you don't need to make all of it into a garden. It can be great for the soil, and for your peace of mind, to grow cover crops on a portion of the land, especially for the first few years. You can learn all about cover crops on page 140.*

7. PLACE YOUR CROPS ON THE MAP. We like to put each crop in a single block rather than spread out throughout the garden, so that they can be rotated more effectively. Sometimes we fill a whole bed with one crop, and sometimes we plant two crops in one bed, choosing vegetables that have a similar length of season or are in the same plant family. This, again, is to ease future crop rotations.

We generally map out the early spring and warm season plantings—not fall crops. We tend to place fall crops where they fit as other crops make space for them, being sure to rotate plant families (see sidebar on crop rotation, page 36). Also note that some crops, like peas and lettuce, may finish up before mid-spring planting, so there may be some extra space for mid-spring crops to be planted; the planning process is dynamic and not set in stone.

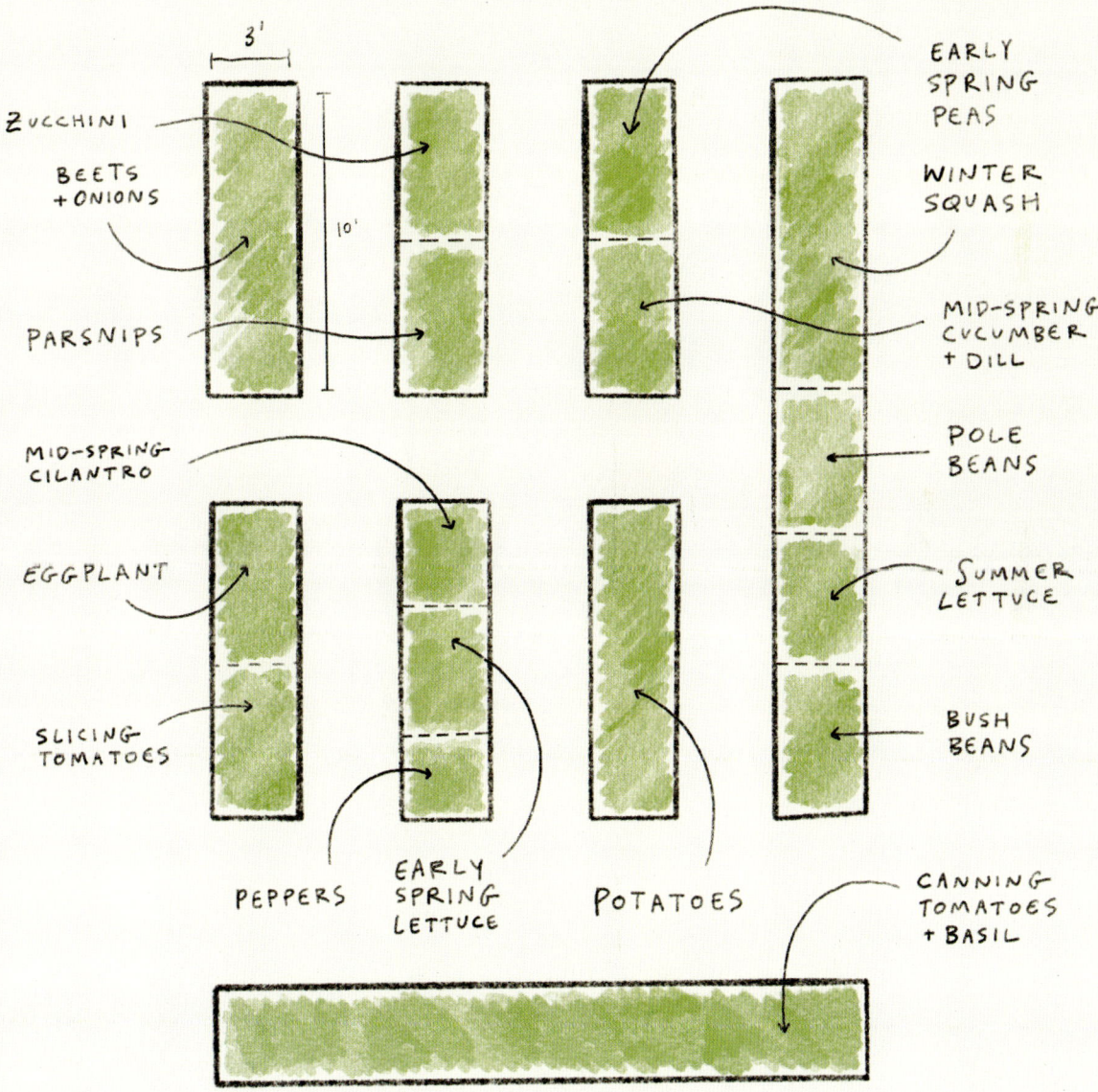

2
Tools
& *How to Use Them*

Tool Quality and Care 46

Bare-Bones Tools 48

Tools to Tend the Gardener 50

Small Hand Tools 52

Tools for Moving Things Around 54

The Magical World of Hoes 56

Big Digging Tools 58

Hoes come in many shapes, sizes, and qualities. The sturdy one (left) is part furrowing hoe, part chopper-digger. The flimsy one (right) is less useful.

Tool Quality and Care

Having the right tool for the job can mean the difference between satisfaction and struggle. Our favorite and most-used garden tools are our companions in the garden, and we recommend that you acquire at least the basics while also finding your own reliable favorites. Try out tools and choose ones that you love rather than collecting all the latest garden gadgets. If you keep them in good shape, most tools will last a lifetime.

QUALITY

You get what you pay for when it comes to garden tools. Many low-quality shovels, forks, and rakes will break under regular use by serious gardeners. That said, you don't necessarily have to start out with the most expensive, professional-grade tools; this is a good time to walk the middle path.

Keep these elements in mind whether you are shopping for new or used tools.

- Hand-forged steel is stronger and more durable.

- Sturdy handles and handle attachments last longer.

- With used tools, look for the absence of rust, or superficial rust only (a little rust is inevitable, but check to see if it's compromising the integrity of the tool).

- Avoid hoes and shovels with chips and nicks.

- Look for the right size for your body, something that feels good in your hands.

- Wooden handles should be smooth and not splintery.

- As much as possible, select tools with little or no plastic.

Wall-mounted brackets, also called "garage hooks," are handy for storing tools. These are on the north side of a shed, which protects them from direct sunlight.

MAINTENANCE AND CARE

Your great garden tools are more likely to stay great if you take care of them. Treat your tools like the honored helpers they are.

Keep your tools clean. Don't leave them out in the garden under the sun and rain, and don't leave them covered with dirt. Ultraviolet light from the sun degrades both wooden and plastic/fiberglass handles, while rain can lead to rust and rot. Leaving dirt on tools will also increase the chance of rust. If you don't have a garden shed, lean your tools up under the eaves, on a porch, or in any covered space; this will significantly prolong their lives.

Oil wooden handles. We recommend sanding or scraping handles smooth and applying a layer of oil at least once a year. Boiled linseed oil that doesn't have any chemical drying agents is a great choice. Simply moisten a rag with the oil and rub it along the length of the handle, then let the oil dry overnight.

WHERE TO STOCK UP ON TOOLS

Big-box home improvement centers may have decent tools, though they usually don't have great hoes. Flea markets, thrift stores, and yard sales can sometimes be gold mines for gently used tools, if you know what to look for. And believe it or not, handcrafted garden tools are still being made by skilled blacksmiths in the US and other countries; these are some of the best you can find.

Remove rust from metal parts. Those parts deserve care, too. Their main enemy is rust, with the dulling power of dirt and rocks coming in second. A few times a year, and especially before storing tools for the off-season, clean off any rust with a wire brush (soak the metal parts in vinegar for a few hours or overnight before brushing if the rust is bad). Then dry the tool completely, sharpen as needed, and rub down with boiled linseed oil to offer a protective coating.

Keep tools sharp. Sharpening your tools isn't too tricky to do moderately well. For dirt-chopping tools like hoes and shovels, running a simple flat file (also known as a mill file) down the cutting edge in *overlapping strokes* will quickly restore sharpness to dulled metal. Files cut in only one direction, usually away from you, and it's important to keep a consistent angle between 30 and 40 degrees to create a uniform cutting edge. For smaller tools, like pruners, a whetstone or diamond stone is better suited. You can learn how to use a stone (which takes some skill), or bring your pruners to a sharpening service at least once a year.

Bare-Bones Tools

There are more tools available than any gardener, expert or not, would know what to do with. While it can be fun to experiment with new and specialized tools, we always return to the standby basics.

Hands. Your hands are your number one gardening tool. They are involved in direct sowing on a home gardening scale and are used for pulling weeds within rows, hand pruning, transplanting, applying amendments and holistic sprays, loving your plants and soil, manipulating all other tools, and harvesting. Make sure when you are using your hands (and arms) that you rotate which side you're using, even if that feels awkward. Switching sides is good for the brain and has a big impact on the long-term health of your body, especially your back.

Shovel (any kind). Shovels are useful for digging holes, uprooting weeds, moving materials around, scraping the soil surface, and harvesting root crops. Depending on the task, it might be easier to use a specialized shovel

LEFT: A sharp knife with sheath and/or bypass pruners are some of the most frequently used and versatile tools.

RIGHT (from top to bottom): Gloves protect hands; the stirrup hoe leads to weeding with ease; harvesting zucchini is made easy with a sharp knife.

Even Chloe's young son Felix knows the value of good tools. Here are the basics: hard rake, shovel, hori hori, and pruners.

(more on some of these below), but in a pinch, almost any shovel can work.

Hard rake. A hard rake is helpful for working with mulch, compost, and other materials and is essential for smoothing out beds. The tined side is used for moving around coarse materials, and the flat (back) side is used to smooth beds perfectly flat in preparation for direct sowing. To maximize usability and enjoyment of this tool, make sure your hard rake has both a sturdy handle attachment and a long handle. A leaf rake is a different tool and is pretty much only useful for, you guessed it, raking up leaves.

Knife or pruners. A cutting tool like a knife or a pair of pruners will come in handy during many garden tasks like pruning, cutting string when trellising, and harvesting. Certain tasks are better suited for one or the other tool, but they can do each other's jobs fairly well.

Knife. We like a sturdy Morakniv brand knife, especially one with a handy sheath so it can rest safely at the ready; this brand is well made and fairly affordable. A high-carbon steel blade is easier to sharpen but will rust. A stainless steel blade won't rust at all, though it's a challenge to sharpen by hand.

Pruners. The world of pruners is vast, but unless you're tending lots of perennials, you don't need to dive in too deeply. The most useful, versatile, and durable type is a simple bypass pruner. Felco is the best brand, in our opinion, though it's also fairly pricey; Corona is decent and more affordable. If you can, purchase pruners in person, at a brick-and-mortar shop, so you can find a pair that feels good in your hands. As with a knife, having a sheath for your pruners means you can wear them on your hip and have them available as needed.

Trowel or hori hori. A trowel is a small handheld digging tool that looks like a little shovel; a hori hori is a Japanese garden tool that is also used for digging but looks more like a knife (some folks call these garden knives, though they aren't actually knives). Either of these tools is useful for digging up taprooted weeds growing close to crops, harvesting root crops, making furrows for planting, dividing plants, and transplanting. The hori hori is flat and can ride comfortably in a sheath attached to your belt. It also has a serrated edge that can be used for coarse cutting. Garden trowels tend to have angled handles, making them more awkward to stow in a sheath or pocket, but their shape offers the advantage of a fulcrum for dislodging particularly persistent roots.

TAKING CARE OF YOUR HANDS

If you prefer bare hands to gloves, your skin will tend to dry out or crack from soil contact, so take the time to clean and moisturize them. After repetitive tasks with your hands, wiggle and stretch your fingers. The movement feels good and will help you continue gardening comfortably for a long time. In our online gardening classes, we have a whole lesson on stretching and staying limber.

Tools to Tend the Gardener

We are human animals, and gardening can feel difficult because of the heat, bugs, sun, and general skin irritations from being around soil and plants. There's no need to give up or get discouraged by these realities; just get prepared. Also, there's no need for heroism here—it's worth the time and effort and potentially dorky appearance to take care of your body so that gardening feels comfortable and sustainable.

Water bottle. A metal water bottle that won't break if tossed on the ground or accidentally hit with a tool is ideal. Insulation can help keep water cool even if it's left out on the sunny ground.

Hat. We rarely enter the garden without a sun hat, even in winter. Baseball caps are quick and easy and can be stored without getting smooshed, but they don't shade your shoulders or neck. Wide-brimmed straw hats provide maximum shade but can be cumbersome in windy conditions and need to be stored hanging up to stay in good shape. Wraparound-style, doughnut-shaped hats or visors are great for folks who like to wear their hair in a bun or ponytail on top of their head, and they also provide more airflow through the hole. In the cooler months, we usually layer a knitted cap over a baseball hat to achieve both warmth and sun protection.

Long-sleeved shirt. If you look out at agricultural fields the world over, folks are wearing lots of clothes, no matter the temperature. Covering our skin with lightweight cotton fabric protects us from sunburn and abrasion by plants and can also keep us cooler. We love getting inexpensive flowy and sometimes flowery button-up cotton shirts from thrift stores so we don't feel bad when they get dirty and ripped. On really hot days, you can dunk your long-sleeved shirt in water, wring it out, and then put it back on for an air-conditioner effect.

Sunscreen. If you opt for exposed skin while gardening and you're out for long

Some people swear by gloves, while others never use them. If you go for gloves, make sure you get a pair that fits well.

periods in the middle of the day, it's worthwhile using sunscreen. Several of our gardener friends have had to deal with skin cancers; the danger of sun exposure is no joke.

Bug spray. Covering up with loose clothing is our favorite way to deter biting insects, but sometimes bug spray is helpful, too, especially on ankles and wrists.

Snacks. During some seasons, the garden will provide built-in snacks. Even so, it's a good idea to bring fat- and protein-rich accompaniments with you. Gardening can be physically demanding, so giving your body the fuel that it needs to work hard is important. Snacks are especially helpful if you're trying to get children to join you in the garden! Some of our favorites are jerky, nuts and seeds, and hummus, goat cheese, or pesto for dipping fresh veggies.

Gloves. Garden gloves help protect our hands from thorns, abrasion, moisture, cold, and the drying impacts of soil. Some folks rarely use gloves, while others don them every time they garden. Chloe has taken to wearing them more often over the years, especially while hand weeding; Natalie tends to put them on only as needed for thorny plants or repetitive tool use. There are lots of types of gloves, and the best way to choose a pair is to go to a store where you can try on several. Our favorites for weeding and soil contact are Atlas brand latex-coated gloves that are made of flexible fabric with a latex coating on the underside, so they're mostly moisture-proof. An insulated version of these is quite nice for fall and winter gardening. Plain leather gloves are more comfortable for tool use and also more resistant to thorns. We like to have a pair of each on hand.

Music, audiobook, or gardening video. Particularly when you've got repetitive tasks like weeding to do, it can be nice to accompany gardening with music or an audiobook. If you're still learning and want company that also offers guidance on how to do gardening tasks, we recommend joining our online gardening classes and bringing a device into the garden so you can watch and learn as you go. Gardening with friends is, of course, a great option, too.

RESTING WHILE GARDENING

In her book *The Resilient Gardener: Food Production and Self-Reliance in Uncertain Times*, Carol Deppe shares her practice of bringing a folding cot out to the field when she's harvesting potatoes. We love this idea! If any one of us hopes to be gardening into our 60s and beyond, like Deppe, we need to pace ourselves and make sure to rest and to eat. Designing a shady bench or swing into the garden layout is one great way to incorporate a rest space. Or just lying down in a garden path for a moment and watching the clouds go by is always an option.

Small Hand Tools

These little tools will help with a variety of tasks—from weeding to pruning to harvesting and more.

Hori hori. When we are in the garden, we almost always have one of these knifelike digging tools strapped to our hip, and if we don't, we frequently wish that we did. That's why we consider it one of our bare-bones tools (see page 49).

Pruners. Chloe has had her pair of pruners for more than 15 years! An important garden companion indeed. See more on pruners on page 49.

Knife. It can be nice to have a garden knife that's a little rougher and tougher than your everyday pocket knife. See page 49 for our recommendations when it comes to knives in the garden.

Wire weeder. This funny little tool looks more like a toy and is hard to imagine being very useful, but it is! It's a handheld weeder that can be pressed gently against the soil surface and scraped back and forth to uproot small, emerging weeds. Its action is similar to the beloved stirrup hoe, but on a smaller scale. The wire weeder is especially useful for weeding very close to transplanted or emergent crops in spaces that are too tight for a stirrup hoe.

Hand hoe (and cultivator). There are several types of little hoes. Natalie knows someone who designed a model that straps to and is cupped by the hand—it works fabulously for small weeding projects. Commercially made hand hoes either have a single very sharp side for slicing roots just below the surface or a less-sharp "hoe" blade on one side with a three-tined cultivator on the other. Chloe likes to use a hand hoe to open holes for transplanting as well as for weeding and cultivating. This tool is not

LEFT: Knife and sheath, hand hoe, hori hori, trowel, kama, and pruners

RIGHT: This funny little tool is called a wire weeder, and it makes removing tiny weeds from amid slightly less tiny crops quite easy.

essential for basic gardening, but it can come in handy in many circumstances and is a smaller investment than some larger tools.

Trowel. Neither of us tends to use trowels all that much, though they can be helpful during transplanting. They come in many shapes and sizes and are readily available at almost any home or garden store. See more on trowels on page 49.

Kama. This wonderfully versatile and sharp Japanese hand sickle can cut all sorts of things, such as weeds, some grains, and the stalks of old crops. The kama can mow down cover crops and thus is very useful in no-till systems. It can also be used to harvest crops. It requires frequent sharpening to stay in good shape. To do this, we select a curved whetstone meant for sharpening scythes.

The kama has a curved blade that's great at slicing weeds and cover crops . . . or your own arm or leg if you're not careful!

USE A KAMA WITH CAUTION

You use a kama by holding up the plants you're cutting with your nondominant hand and cutting them with the kama in your dominant hand, or by slicing upright plants in a smooth arc. In either case, hold the kama's blade close to the earth unless you need to cut higher on the plant. The blade is more effective if you use a slicing action rather than simply pulling the blade toward you. When it's in good condition, the kama's large blade is incredibly sharp. Make sure that your nondominant hand and any other body parts are well out of the way of the slicing action. Natalie has had several apprentices cut their hands with this tool, so be careful!

Tools for Moving Things Around

The right tools for transporting amendments, crops, and miscellany can help save your back and your time. The following are suited to various needs and sizes of gardens.

Wheelbarrow. This simple and familiar tool is a really big deal if you have a medium to larger garden. It is incredibly helpful for moving around soil, compost, leaves, weeds, and, if you have a bumper harvest, crops. We prefer the traditional three-wheeled barrows over modern four-wheel versions because three wheels are more maneuverable than four. Be sure to get a wheelbarrow with a "flat-free" tire or add one onto the wheelbarrow you have. These solid rubber tires will never go flat, even as you traverse thorny, rocky, or otherwise hazard-ridden ground.

Garden cart. If your garden is on the big side, a garden cart can be very useful. It differs from a wheelbarrow in a few crucial ways. First, the cart itself is a flat-bottomed box rather than a slant-bottomed trough, which means it can carry bigger loads than a wheelbarrow. Trays and boxes can be stacked neatly in a garden cart without risk of damage. Second, the cart has two large wheels, like bicycle wheels, with front legs made of sturdy metal, so it's very stable when parked. On the downside, it's more cumbersome than a wheelbarrow. Chloe uses it to haul around tools, mulch, seedlings, children, produce, and more. If your garden is on the smaller side, a wheelbarrow will serve you very well and you probably don't need to invest in a garden cart, which is rather pricey.

Buckets. These help with any number of tasks. You can transport amendments or cover crop seeds; mix up and dilute liquid fertilizers; and harvest your crops—just be sure to use different buckets for harvesting produce and mixing fertilizers. They are also great for hauling weeds to compost piles. If you don't have a wheelbarrow, or if your wheelbarrow can't get into a tight space, you can use buckets to haul soil and other materials. We use 2- or 5-gallon buckets, which can be purchased or sometimes acquired for free from grocery store bakeries (which use them for cake frosting!). Some folks really like flexible buckets

A lot of the work in the garden is simply moving things around: amendments, compost, mulch, and harvested vegetables. These tools help make it happen.

(also called flex tubs)—basically buckets made of a soft material that you can grab with one hand like a basket; they're sold at garden centers. *Tip:* If you are carrying buckets with heavy contents, carry two at a time (one in each hand) to balance the act and save your back.

Baskets. Very versatile, baskets can hold the harvest or carry things like seeds, snacks, water bottles, and your garden journal. Having a variety of sizes and styles can make for an efficient day in the garden—no extra trips,

everything you need at the ready. All woven baskets are still made by human hands and have a very different feel than industrial plastic vessels like buckets and crates.

Pitchfork or hayfork. These big forks are used to move light materials like leaves, hay, straw, and wood chips. An appropriate pitchfork or hayfork is way more effective at these tasks than a digging fork or a shovel, so it's worth getting one of these more specialized tools if you'll be moving a lot of loose materials.

WHICH FORK DO I USE?

Distinguishing a digging fork from a pitchfork or hayfork is easy. The digging fork has stout, flat, square-edged, straight, or nearly straight tines that are shorter and thicker than any pitchfork or hayfork; their handles are usually shorter, too. The differences between pitchforks and hayforks are subtle. They both have long, rounded, slender tines that curve upward. Hayforks tend to have fewer and longer tines than pitchforks, as they're made for moving hay, which clumps and clings. Materials like leaves or wood chips will fall through the tines of a hayfork and require a pitchfork with its tighter tines. *Caution:* If you try to use a pitchfork or hayfork to dig, you may break or seriously damage the tool!

DIGGING FORK

PITCHFORK

The Magical World of Hoes

Hoes include all kinds of chopping, weeding, digging, and cultivating tools and are some of the most useful tools to have on hand. There are many, many types of hoes, each with its own specific purpose. Here we cover the ones we think are most useful in the garden.

Basic hoe (a.k.a. field hoe, eye hoe). This sturdy hoe is made for gardening and is much more effective than the generic type of hoe you might find at the hardware store. Its heavy, solid-metal head has a slightly curved blade that flares out. It has a strong handle attachment and, usually, a fairly long handle. The shape of this hoe makes it more effective and ergonomic to swing, as the weight of the tool helps plant it into the ground for productive weeding, soil turning, or even shallow digging.

Tips

- Find a hoe heavy enough to do the job, but not too heavy for you.

- Move the hoe using your arms, legs, and core rather than your back.

- Create a solid fulcrum as you swing by bracing your abdominal muscles, and find a rhythm to your swings using your hips. (Experiment to come up with the best technique for your body.)

- Adjust the following as needed: the angle of the hoe (let a corner of the hoe hit the ground first, then the full blade), the force of the tool's impact with the ground, and the firmness of your grip on the handle.

Stirrup hoe (a.k.a. hula hoe, scuffle hoe). This is one of the most frequently used tools in our gardens. Its various names describe both its shape (either a stirrup or a Hula-Hoop), and its action ("scuffling" the ground to disturb weed seedlings by gently cultivating). It's quick and easy to weed with this tool

THREE-TINE HOE   FURROWING HOE   GRAPE HOE   FIELD HOE   STIRRUP HOE
(A.K.A. HAZEL HOE)

in areas without mulch and where weeds are still seedlings. It only disturbs the soil about ¼ inch down, leaving deeper soil alone. It's less likely to stir up weed seeds or disrupt important micro- and macroorganisms living below the surface.

Tricks and Techniques for Using a Stirrup Hoe

- Hold it firmly: Try a grip with your thumbs downward toward the metal tool, then up toward your body; see what feels more secure.
- With the tool resting on the soil surface, drag it back and forth so that it slices down about ¼ inch.
- To save your back, tighten your core muscles and hold your upper body straight, rocking back and forth at your hips to create the scuffling action.

Three-tine hoe. Once Chloe discovered this tool, she pretty much stopped using a digging fork to loosen soil. The head of the three-tine hoe is similar to a digging fork in that it has stout, square-edged tines between 6 and 8 inches long. The difference is that this "fork" is mounted to the handle at an angle, like a hoe.

Tricks and Techniques for Using a Three-Tine Hoe

- When you swing this hoe, let it dig into the soil with its own weight.
- Push on the handle to use the angle of attachment as a fulcrum. This will easily loosen the soil without requiring you to bend over.

Grape hoe (or hazel hoe). This beast of a hoe has a wide, heavy head that's very effective at scraping the ground for weeding or moving soil. It usually has a short handle and is especially good for use on slopes and terraces.

  Furrowing hoe. If you'll be planting rows or beds that are more than a few feet in length, a furrowing hoe might be worth the investment. It's small and lightweight with a

TOP: Using a hoe properly is so ergonomic that you can do it with a baby on your shoulders!

BOTTOM: Natalie easily makes a furrow for planting seeds with the triangular furrowing hoe.

57

triangular or diamond-shaped head. It's great for preparing the furrows to direct sow into, and for marking out straight rows to transplant into.

Tricks and Techniques for Using a Furrowing Hoe

- Simply drag this hoe along the soil, allowing its weight to press in and make a nice furrow for planting.
- Press down more firmly for deeper furrows, to receive larger seeds.
- The shape of the hoe naturally pushes soil aside.

Lots more! If you notice yourself doing a garden task and wishing there were a tool to help you, it's likely that one exists. Specialized hoes are abundant. Rogue Hoe and Homestead Iron are wonderful companies to explore in your search of the perfect hoe for the job.

Big Digging Tools

When you need to do some digging in the garden—whether to harvest crops, dig a trench, or transplant a big plant—the following tools are helpful.

Digging fork. This tool is used primarily for harvesting root crops and for loosening soil. It's got shorter, squared, stout tines compared to a pitchfork, and it usually has a shorter handle, too. The digging fork is great for exactly what its name promises, although Chloe prefers the three-tine hoe for soil loosening (see page 57). It's important to note that a pitchfork is different from a digging fork, is not made for digging, and will suffer greatly if used in this way (see the facing page for more on forks).

BROAD FORK

DIGGING FORK

DIGGING SHOVEL

FLAT SHOVEL

SPEARHEAD SPADE

LEFT: The force of a digging shovel is easily increased by using your body weight to push it down.

RIGHT: A digging fork is the best tool for harvesting potatoes and other root crops. It can also be used to aerate without disturbing soil layers.

Flat shovel. Perfect for scooping and scraping, this shovel is ideal for moving around loose, nonfibrous material like soil or compost. If it's super sharp, you can surface weed with it by skimming about ¼ inch deep into the topsoil. (The stirrup hoe does this same job, however, and is much more ergonomic; see page 56.) The flat shovel can also be used for leveling out paths and taking high points out of beds. Flat shovels are not great at digging, though they will work in a pinch.

Digging spade and spearhead spade. These sturdy shovels with shorter *T*- or *D*-shaped handles are made for digging, not for scooping (flat shovels are better for that). The digging spade has a square head, while the spearhead spade has a pointier shape (see facing page). Although these tools are more expensive and garden-specific than a run-of-the-mill digging shovel, they're worth it if you plan to do a lot of double-digging or lots of tree and shrub planting.

Digging shovel or round shovel. This familiar tool usually has a pointed blade (in the case of the digging shovel) or a rounded blade. It's generally used to dig up weeds with taproots (roots growing vertically and deep, rather than laterally and closer to the surface), and for harvesting root crops (if you don't

have a digging fork). A digging shovel can also be used to remove soil where you don't want it, or to build a sunken or double-dug bed. Digging shovels are helpful for moving materials like compost or mulch around, though they hold less material per scoop than flat shovels or forks. The only time you might select a digging shovel over a fork or flat shovel for moving stuff around is if your other tools have a hard time penetrating into the material; in this case, the point of the digging shovel would make things easier.

Broad fork. This specialized tool is used for loosening soil deeply in an efficient way. It is basically a giant digging fork that you stand atop, using a combination of your body weight and a wiggling motion to drive deeply into the ground. Some folks love these because they aerate soil without disrupting soil strata (the qualities and organisms that characterize different layers of the soil). A broad fork is particularly useful for the second step in double-digging and for loosening hardpan (compacted claylike soil below the topsoil) that may be present if you're gardening in a place that has been continuously plowed. Broad forks are pricey as well as physically big and heavy. They're not a go-to for us, but some folks swear by them.

3
Starting a Garden
from Grass

Ways to Transform Grass into a Growing Space 62

Setting Up Raised Beds 65

Double-Digging 69

Tilling with a Machine 72

Sheet Mulching and Lasagna Gardening 75

Basic Solarization and Occultation 78

Bogwalker's Badass Topsoil Technique 84

Crimping Cover Crops 88

Getting Soil Ready for Seeds and Plants 90

Ways to Transform Grass into a Growing Space

So, you have grass—and you want a garden. There are several ways to make this glorious transformation happen, but figuring out which method to use can feel overwhelming. You may have heard folks either espousing or criticizing any of the methods we cover in this chapter. The truth is that each approach has benefits and downfalls. There is no right or wrong choice; it's just a matter of what works for you and how you want to manage your garden in the long term. You can download and watch a video of us discussing *when* you can start a garden on our website (see link on page 364).

BE OPEN TO TRYING DIFFERENT METHODS

As you've probably noticed, we try to stay open-minded and curious and believe that most tools and techniques have their appropriate place. A testament to this is that we've tried all of the techniques for transforming grass (or a weedy field) into a garden that we describe here. We've learned that, generally speaking, you can create a growing space more quickly if you invest more physical inputs (e.g., time, labor, amendments). But if what you mainly have to invest is *time,* you can create a fertile garden with many fewer physical inputs.

BE PATIENT THE FIRST YEAR

No matter which technique you use, the first year in your newly established garden will be a period of adjustment. The land will need time to settle after disturbance and adapt to its new role as the home of annual vegetable crops. When we dramatically change what kinds of plants are growing in a particular area—perhaps adding mineral and biologic amendments, irrigating with groundwater, exposing soil to direct sunlight, possibly mixing up soil strata and structure, and otherwise meddling with the ecosystem that was there—it takes time for things to adjust.

This doesn't mean you can't have a fabulous vegetable garden immediately after eliminating the grass—you can. This is just an invitation to be aware of what's happening. Don't get discouraged if everything doesn't look amazing that very first season. Fortunately and miraculously, the earth is alive with a bustling community of organisms and varied structures that respond to disturbance with resilience.

> *You can create a growing space more quickly if you invest more physical inputs (e.g., time, labor, amendments). But if what you mainly have to invest is* time, *you can create a fertile garden with fewer physical inputs.*

Six Ways to
START A GARDEN FROM GRASS

RAISED BEDS
(PAGE 65)

DOUBLE-
DIGGING
(PAGE 69)

TILLING WITH
A MACHINE
(PAGE 72)

SHEET MULCHING/
LASAGNA GARDENING
(PAGE 75)

SOLARIZATION/
OCCULTATION
(PAGE 78)

BOGWALKER'S BADASS
TOPSOIL TECHNIQUE
(PAGE 84)

Comparison of Techniques for Turning Grass into Garden Beds

When selecting a method for transforming grass into a growing space, consider the amount of labor, waiting time, material inputs, and money, as well as the method's effect on the soil, to determine which is right for you.

METHOD	WAIT TIME TO PLANT	ENERGY INPUT (LABOR)	MONEY INPUT	EQUIPMENT AND MATERIALS REQUIRED	CAN IMPROVE SOIL QUALITIES?
Raised bed with imported materials, including soil	Short	Medium to high	High	Raised-bed walls and tools to install them, soil, amendments	Yes
Raised bed with native soil	Short	Medium to high	Medium	Raised-bed walls and tools to install them, optional amendments	Depends on amendments
Double-digging	Short	High	Low	Digging fork and shovel or spade, finished compost and other optional amendments	Yes
Single-digging	Short	High (though lower than double-digging)	Low	Digging fork and shovel or spade, finished compost and other optional amendments	Yes, though less potential than with double-digging
Tilling with a machine	Short to medium	Low to medium	Low to high (depends on machine access)	Rototiller or tractor with appropriate implements, optional amendments	Majorly disturbs soil structure, but using this technique to incorporate amendments can improve fertility
Sheet mulching/ lasagna gardening	Medium	Low	Low	Scavenged materials, like cardboard, paper, leaves, vegetable scraps, yard waste, and other organic debris; can include compost and purchased amendments	Yes
Solarization/ occultation	Long	Low	Low to medium	Large specialized tarp to cover garden area, optional compost and amendments (see page 79 for info on tarp qualities)	Yes, with amendments
Bogwalker's Badass Topsoil Technique	Long	Medium	Low to medium	Large tarp to cover garden area, compost, amendments, wood chips, cover-crop seed (see page 79 for info on tarp qualities)	Yes

Setting Up Raised Beds

Lumber scraps can be turned into raised beds. While this is cheap and easy, such a bed may fall apart within a year or two. (See the table on page 67 for a comparison of building materials.)

In this method you create a planting space by containing soil within a structure with sidewalls. Your raised bed may or may not have a barrier on the bottom, depending on what lies beneath. If you're dealing with persistent toxins in your native soil, like lead, or persistent weeds, like Bermuda grass, you'll definitely want to create a barrier out of landscape fabric or thick layers of cardboard so that these unwanted elements don't creep into the bed itself. If your soil is free of toxins or persistent weeds, it's cheaper and easier to simply build walls and forgo a significant bottom barrier.

Raised beds can be as low as a few inches off the ground or as tall as you want them to be for ease of tending, as long as you have materials to build and fill them. A common height is 8 to 15 inches, and prefabricated raised beds are available anywhere from 10 to 32 inches high. If back problems preclude you from gardening at ground level, or if you or a fellow gardener uses a wheelchair, going with extra-tall garden beds could transform the gardening experience.

How to Set Up a RAISED BED

1. **CLEAR VEGETATION.** Mow the existing grass or vegetation as short as possible in and around the raised bed's location.

2. **LAY IT OUT.** Mark out the bed's footprint directly on the ground where the bed will be located. You can use stakes and string to make straight lines and sprinkle a light-colored powder like garden lime or even flour to mark the bed edges so you keep track of them as you build.

3. **LAY DOWN BARRIER MATERIAL,** if using. Apply a layer of cardboard, several layers of newspaper, or a piece of tight burlap within the bed's footprint. If the site has aggressive weeds, you might use a sturdier weed barrier fabric or several layers of cardboard. If a soil test reveals the presence of persistent toxins, consider putting down a layer of naturally rot-resistant wood (not pressure treated), which plant roots will take longer to penetrate.

4. **BUILD THE STRUCTURE.** Assemble a purchased raised-bed kit or create your own raised bed using rot-resistant wood, salvaged roofing metal, or other salvaged or innovative material. Be wary of railroad ties, chemically treated or pressure-treated wood, as well as untreated non-rot-resistant wood. See the table Comparing Materials for Building Raised Bed Walls on the facing page to evaluate the pros

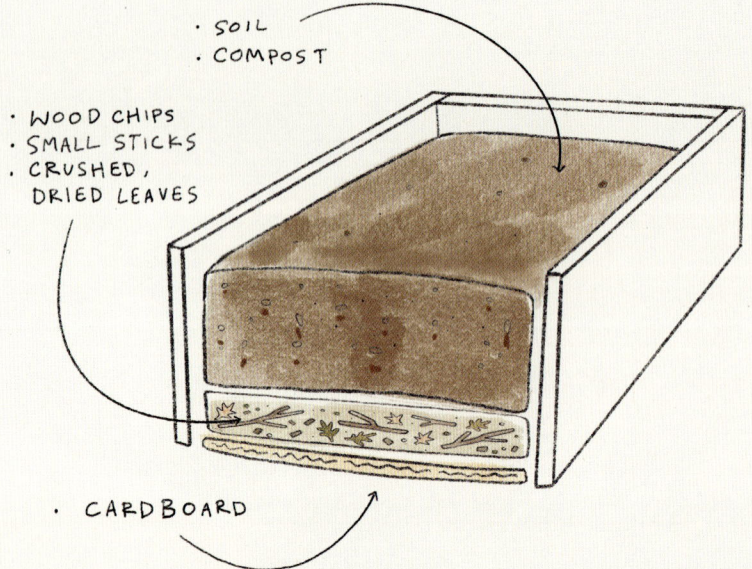

· SOIL
· COMPOST

· WOOD CHIPS
· SMALL STICKS
· CRUSHED, DRIED LEAVES

· CARDBOARD

and cons of different materials. For more detailed instruction on how to build a raised bed out of wood, check out *Building Raised Beds* by Fern Marshall Bradley or *Homestead and Chill* on YouTube.

5. **FILL THE STRUCTURE.** If the bed is over 12 inches tall, begin by adding wood chips, tightly packed twigs and small sticks, shredded leaves, bark, or other bulky organic material. Then cover with 8 to 12 inches of soil and optional compost and amendments. If the bed is shorter than 12 inches, simply fill it with soil and optional compost and amendments.

INSPIRED BY HÜGELKULTUR

Filling the bottom of a bed with bulky organic material is a permaculture practice inspired by hügelkultur, or mound culture, a traditional German and Eastern European technique that utilizes an underlayer of woody debris to lend long-term fertility, aeration, and water-holding capacity to garden beds. In this case it also reduces costs associated with buying soil, compost, or manure to fill your raised bed.

Comparing Materials for Building Raised Bed Walls

Here is a comparison of different kinds of materials you might use to build a raised bed. Note that thicker pieces of wood will take longer to rot, whatever kind of wood they are.

MATERIAL	DURABILITY	COST	TOXICITY	READILY AVAILABLE?	ECOLOGICAL FOOTPRINT
Concrete blocks (new)	High, 15+ years	High	Low	Yes	High; making concrete is a significant carbon emitter
Galvanized metal	High, 15+ years	Medium	Low	Yes	Medium
Manufactured plastic lumber	High, 15+ years	High	Low	Yes	Complex; a form of recycling, but they're still made of plastic
Railroad ties	High, 15+ years	Medium high	High	Maybe	Complex; initial footprint is high, but this use is a form of recycling
Stone	High, 15+ years	Low (high if purchased)	Low	Maybe	Low, especially if locally sourced
Urbanite (recycled concrete)	High, 15+ years	Low	Low	Maybe	Complex; the initial manufacturing is high, but this use is a form of recycling
Wood (chemically treated)	Medium, 5–15 years	Medium	Medium	Yes	Medium
Wood (flame treated)—pine, spruce, fir, and most hardwoods that have been superficially burned	Medium, 5–15 years	Medium low, high labor	Low	DIY (do it yourself)	Low, especially if locally sourced
Wood (rot resistant)—cedar, cypress, redwood, or locust	Medium, 5–15 years	High	Low	Maybe	Low, especially if locally sourced
Wood (untreated)—pine, spruce, fir, and most hardwoods	Low, 2–5 years	Medium low	Low	Yes	Low, especially if locally sourced

RAISED-BED MATERIALS

Currently there are many raised-bed wall options. You can purchase kits for metal beds in pretty much any shape or size you desire. An advantage of these is that they'll last a long time, and they're easy to assemble. Their growing popularity means the price of these kits is going down, but they're still not exactly cheap.

Alternatively, you can build raised beds out of wood, manufactured plastic lumber made from recycled soda bottles, salvaged concrete blocks, or even stones. Keep in mind that if you plan to garden in a given place for a while, it's nice to use a material that won't rot quickly, that has low to no toxicity, and that, ideally, has a low carbon footprint.

FILLING RAISED BEDS

Your choice of raised-bed soil mix will have a huge impact on your garden's success. Soil is the foundation for healthy plant growth, so using the best mix you can afford or locate will provide lasting benefits. For a detailed discussion of soil, fertility, and amendments that will boost the health of your soil, check out Chapters 4 and 5.

Native topsoil. If you have a place to dig native soil, such as an area where you're doing earthmoving anyway, use that *topsoil* in your raised beds—along with compost and any other necessary amendments. (Don't use layers excavated from farther down in the earth, like those resulting from digging a foundation or septic field; deeper subsoil lacks organic matter that makes soil good for growing). Using native topsoil will not only be cheaper than purchasing everything you need to fill the beds, it will also impart structural, chemical, and biological elements of that place into those beds. In our experience plants seem to grow better when they have contact with at least some native soil.

Purchased topsoil. If you don't have access to topsoil to dig and add to your beds, you may be able to purchase it in bulk by the yard or by the truckload. Ask around—local landscapers generally have a wealth of knowledge—to find good sources of both topsoil and compost to purchase in bulk. Buying these things in small bags can get pretty pricey, and sometimes material labeled as topsoil in garden stores is actually just a mixture of soil conditioner (ground bark from the timber industry), fertilizer, subsoil, and perhaps sand and small gravel. Be sure you know what's in anything you buy before adding it your raised beds.

Compost and amendments. A basic soil recipe for raised beds is three-quarters soil and one-quarter finished compost, applied on top of the bulky base material, if the beds are deep enough (see page 66). Other amendments (such as organic fertilizers, decomposed manure, worm castings, or mineral powders) can improve soil quality; add them, if you have the ability. Note that it's best to add mineral powders in very small amounts or after testing the soil that you are starting with. If you add too much of these powerful amendments, the resulting soil could actually become impossible to grow in. If your native soil has a high clay content, it might behoove you to add a little sand or sandy soil into the mix to improve drainage. For details on the various things you can add to raised beds, see Chapter 5.

This homemade metal raised bed, with woodchips below and soil and compost on top, is in the greenhouse and ready to significantly extend the gardening season.

Double-Digging

Double-digging is a fabulous method for preparing lusciously fluffy garden beds quickly—if you've got a strong back and plenty of energy! This technique was developed by Alan Chadwick in the 1960s as part of his Biodynamic French Intensive Method for gardening. He was specifically looking to bring "marginal" or less-fertile land into food production quickly and effectively.

Double-digging is thoroughly described and promoted by Chadwick's friend and mentee John Jeavons in his classic book *How to Grow More Vegetables* (and Fruits, Nuts, Berries, Grains, and Other Crops) *Than You Ever Thought Possible on Less Land Than You Can Imagine*. This awesome book was popular when we were in our 20s; it inspired us just as we were really getting into gardening. We both spent many sweaty hours double-digging yards around community houses we lived in during our college years and growing great, quick veggie gardens as a result.

WHAT IS DOUBLE-DIGGING?

The basic idea of double-digging is to turn and mix compost into the top 6 to 8 inches of soil while deeply aerating the subsoil to make it more welcoming to plant roots. It involves some deep digging, but to maintain the natural soil strata, the upper layers of soil don't get mixed with the lower layers.

One benefit of this method is that it's pretty low cost. All you need is a digging fork, a shovel, and some compost . . . and did we mention a strong back and lots of energy? It's also a great way of getting a garden going quickly, even in rather poor soil, without the expense and potentially negative impacts of machine tilling (see page 72).

WHY (AND WHY NOT) USE DOUBLE-DIGGING?

We've pretty much abandoned this method in our middle age, but that doesn't mean it's not the right choice for you! Since our gardens are established in places where we plan to be for the foreseeable future, we don't need to break new ground in a hurry, so we've been able to take the time and invest in the materials needed for slower, lower-labor ways to prepare beds, such as solarization/occultation (see page 78).

Chloe recently helped double-dig some beds in a friend's pitiful-looking lawn as part of a demo for our online gardening classes, and the resulting vegetables that very first year were pretty impressive. This method works incredibly well, if you're up for doing the work.

An important note: Many folks who espouse double-digging do it *annually*. This, in our opinion, is unnecessary and potentially harmful to the soil, as it creates quite a bit of disturbance. If you decide to use the double-digging technique, employ it as a strategy for establishing garden beds, then explore other methods for preparing those beds for planting year after year.

A key step in double-digging is laying compost atop the area before digging; this adds fertility and improves soil texture right away as it's mixed in.

How to Create a Bed Using
DOUBLE-DIGGING

You can access a video of Chloe demonstrating double-digging on our website (see link on page 364).

1. **MOW THE EXISTING GRASS OR VEGETATION.** You can leave this grass or use a flat shovel or hoe to scrape back any sod (add it to the compost pile), leaving exposed soil, depending on how concerned you are about the grass coming back.

2. **MARK OUT THE EDGES OF THE BED.** Stakes and string, sprinkled lime or flour, flags—use whatever works!

3. **ADD A 2- TO 3-INCH LAYER OF COMPOST.** Include any other soil amendments. As you create the layer, stay within the bed's boundaries.

4. **DIG A TRENCH.** Beginning at one end, dig a trench one shovelful deep across the width of the bed. Set this soil aside on a tarp or piece of cardboard, or place it in buckets or a wheelbarrow.

5. **AERATE THE SOIL.** Insert a digging fork or broad fork (not a pitchfork) along the bottom of the trench to the full depth of the digging fork. This might take some wiggling. Once inserted, move the handle forward and backward in order to aerate the soil without disturbing its layers. Move the fork forward 4 inches or so, insert, and move the handle forward and backward. Repeat until the bottom of the little trench is fully aerated.

6. **DIG A SECOND TRENCH.** Use the shovel to make a new trench right next to the trench you just forked, putting the soil you remove directly into the first trench, rather than on the cardboard or in buckets. As you move the soil, break it up so that it's loose and fluffy.

7. **REPEAT STEP 5**. Deeply aerate the subsoil beneath your second trench with the digging fork or broad fork.

8. **REPEAT STEPS 6 AND 7.** Work in this manner until you have made your way all the way down the bed.

9. **FILL IN THE LAST TRENCH** with reserved soil from the first trench.

10. **RAKE THE ENTIRE BED FLAT.** Use first the tine side of the rake, and then the back side of the rake to make an even and inviting seed bed.

SINGLE-DIGGING OPTION

If double-digging feels like too much work but you'd like to create in-ground garden beds quickly with few material inputs, single-digging is an option. The beds prepared with this admittedly shortcut approach are not quite as fluffy and rich, but it's nonetheless a fine way to get a garden started in a hurry, especially if the subsoil where you're gardening is permeable instead of impenetrable clay or hardpan.

Start with the first three steps for double-digging, then, instead of digging the trench and moving soil aside as you deeply aerate, simply use a digging fork to turn and aerate the top 6 to 8 inches of soil as you mix in the compost. (You can access a video of Chloe demonstrating single-digging on our website—see page 364.)

Tilling with a Machine

Tilling with a machine is the fastest way to break ground in a large area, with the least amount of physical work; this is why it's common on big farms. Many large-scale farmers till every spring, and again after each crop matures. Although this practice can be very hard on the soil, ultimately leading to lower productivity, it's quick and relatively cheap, so it fits right in with money-driven industrial agriculture.

Is it appropriate for a home garden? Well, machine tilling can be the right move to get a new garden bed established quickly, or to integrate minerals or other amendments through soil layers. It's just not something we recommend relying on year after year in an intensive manner.

Positive Results of Tilling

- Removes weeds or grasses quickly and effectively (when done properly).
- Aerates dense soil.
- Releases a flush of fertility from organisms that are killed in the process.
- Incorporates soil amendments effectively.
- Aids in getting a large space ready (very quickly!) for planting.

Consequences of Tilling over Time

- Can increase erosion (water and wind carry soil away).
- Leads to loss of topsoil and organic matter.
- Compacts the soil beneath where the tiller reaches, creating hardpan.
- Brings weed seeds to the surface, where they can sprout.
- Dramatically disturbs the complex and sensitive physical and biological communities in soil that help support plant growth.

TIPS FOR REDUCING SOIL DAMAGE FROM TILLING

Don't till if the soil is either soggy or bone-dry. Wait until it's loosely moist and doesn't form a tight ball or turn to dust when squeezed. Add organic matter as you till, such as compost, manure, or cover-crop residue. If possible, till on an overcast day (sunlight "cooks" nitrogen and other nutrients out of the soil).

Sow seeds and/or cover the soil with mulch soon after tilling; don't let soil stay exposed for a long time.

Working wet soil can be very detrimental, leading to large clumps and soil compaction.

The sections in this chapter on lasagna gardening (see page 75) and solarization/occultation (see page 78) provide good guidance on how you can prepare planting space during subsequent seasons instead of tilling again.

If you're growing on a fairly large scale, it may be that a low-till approach is ideal for you. This involves combining things like cover cropping, solarization/occultation, mulching, and, occasionally, tilling to manage farm fields. Our good friend and local commercial organic grower Anna Littman utilizes low-till practices, including some tilling, and she has beautiful soil and good productivity to show for it on her multiacre farm.

There are three main machines that we've used for tilling ground: a full-size tractor with a plow attachment, followed by a disc harrow or other cultivator; a walk-behind tractor (BCS is the most common brand); and a garden or walk-behind tiller (Rototiller is the most common brand). Of these, full-size tractors and garden tillers are the most common.

Walk-behind tractor. These machines, like full-size tractors, don't just till; they can be hooked up to a variety of different tools for performing different tasks. They're more effective at eradicating grass and weeds than a garden tiller because they can literally turn the soil upside down (plow). Once the weeds die, you can chop up the clods and fluff and smooth the ground (e.g., till, disc, cultivate, rake). They're too costly for most home gardeners, however, and the majority of large-scale growers opt for full-size tractors. If you happen to have access to a walk-behind tractor, the steps for tilling to prepare planting ground will be the same as those for a full-size tractor.

Garden tiller. This machine pretty much only chops up the soil (tills), mixing in any weeds or grass growing there; most of these plants survive such a chopping and will happily sprout back to life in the newly aerated ground. For this reason it's important to weed thoroughly before using a garden tiller.

TILLING WITH A TRACTOR

If you are preparing a relatively large space for growing—more than 500 square feet—and it's accessible by road (even a rough road), we suggest hiring someone with a tractor and attachments to do the tilling for you. This is much more economical than buying and maintaining your own tractor, unless you are a serious farmer or happen to have other uses for a tractor in your life (they are very handy!).

How to TILL WITH A TRACTOR

1. **MOW THE VEGETATION SHORT.** Leave the debris to be incorporated. Attaching a bush hog (rotary cutter) to a tractor is the best choice for this task when facing a very weedy area; a string trimmer or grass mower may work for smaller or medium areas.

2. **TURN THE SOIL WITH A PLOW.**

3. **WAIT 2 WEEKS FOR THE VEGETATION TO DIE.**

4. **BREAK UP CLUMPS.** Cultivate with a disc harrow, tiller, or other similar attachment.

5. **RAKE OR DRAG THE AREA SMOOTH.** If your tractor person has a log drag or rake to smooth out the soil, great; otherwise, it's time to do some handwork to get things ready for planting.

6. **PLANT!**

The ideal candidate to hire for tractor work is not your local organic farmer but rather hobby farmers, ranchers, retired folks, or landscapers who have the equipment but don't have their own tight planting timeline to stick to. Sometimes folks with tractors will advertise their services in spring through online or in-person bulletin boards, so keep an eye out. You can also post something yourself, or ask at the local watering hole or gas station, wherever older-farmer types tend to hang out in your locale.

Once you establish a relationship with a tractor person, strive to stay in their good graces! The equipment is expensive to buy, heavy and challenging to move, and costly to maintain. Coming over to plow and disc your little (to them) garden is not a money-making endeavor but more of a favor that you pay them for.

If they offer to plow without discing or otherwise tilling, or to till on the surface without plowing, kindly decline. The two processes go together. If they plow without discing or tilling, you are left with huge unorderly waves of soil where weeds will eventually sprout back. If they disk or till without plowing, you will be left with soil that is not actually worked, and the weeds and grass will just come right back. Also, if an area is not mowed short before plowing, subsequent steps will be much less effective and a lot more work.

TILLING WITH A GARDEN TILLER

If your garden is smaller than 500 square feet and doesn't have tractor access, or if you don't have access to a tractor and you want to till with a machine, a garden tiller (Rototiller) will be your best bet.

Larger tillers can be difficult to maneuver, especially for smaller bodies, but they are often more effective than smaller ones at breaking up hard ground.

Although smaller tillers are easier to maneuver, really small ones aren't worth the effort—they barely scrape the surface. As we've mentioned, tilling where grass or weeds are thriving can actually invigorate, rather than eradicate, those robust and unwanted plants. Even though minimizing physical labor may be why you choose tilling in the first place, it's worth the effort of mowing and hoeing, or scraping, the ground before you

TILLER: RENT, HIRE, OR BORROW?

There are many sizes and shapes of tillers, and which one you use depends on your land conditions, body size, and budget. We strongly suggest you rent one (you'll need a truck, van, or trailer to transport it) or pay someone to till for you with their own tiller. If possible, we recommend you avoid borrowing one from a friend. These are heavy, persnickety machines that can easily break, and, for whatever reason, they tend to break more often when they're being borrowed. Renting a tiller for a day or a weekend is not super expensive, and it's definitely worth the value of a peaceful friendship.

TIP: Many tool rental shops offer the same price to rent for one 24-hour period during the week or to pick up on Friday and return on Monday, giving you extra time over the weekend to use the tool at no extra charge.

till to remove as much grass and as many weeds as possible.

Note for tilling on slopes: If your garden is on any significant slope, make sure you till up and down the slope rather than across it, to avoid tipping and potentially hurting the machine and, more importantly, your body.

How to TILL WITH A GARDEN TILLER

1. **MOW THE VEGETATION SHORT.** Then, using a hoe or shovel, scrape away sod and weeds (add it to your compost pile).

2. **TILL ON THE SHALLOW SETTING.** Make a single pass over the area.

3. **TILL ON THE DEEPER SETTING.** Make another pass over the area.

4. **TILL AGAIN ON THE DEEPER SETTING.** If needed, in order to fully loosen the soil, make a third pass.

5. **RAKE THE AREA SMOOTH.**

6. **PLANT!**

Sheet Mulching and Lasagna Gardening

In a forest, the soil is never naked for long. Trees shed leaves, animals poop, plants and mushrooms grow and die. Layers of organic material are constantly being added atop the soil surface and are then broken down by the macro- and microorganisms that call soil home. With sheet mulching and lasagna gardening, we gardeners mimic forest-style soil building and covering to create weed-free and organic matter–rich topsoil in our growing spaces by layering rather than digging.

These two no-till techniques are very similar and involve the same basic principles.

- **Sheet mulching.** This method—the term was coined in the permaculture world—is a loose style of layering carbon- and nitrogen-rich organic materials on top of soil or grass. It's frequently used to mulch around perennials, usually with a layer of cardboard covered in wood chips.

- **Lasagna gardening.** Mother of seven, inn owner, and longtime gardener Patricia Lanza wrote a book by this same title, offering a process and "recipe" for this no-till approach. We don't get into Lanza's recipe here, but if you're curious, check out her book!

The layering method employed in both of these no-till techniques builds soil relatively quickly using materials that are usually considered part of the waste stream. The general principles involve piling all kinds of materials on top of the soil, layer after layer. Over time the layers break down into soil while also smothering most weeds—pretty awesome, right? This is a wonderful way to transform grass into a garden. One thing to keep in

mind: To do it properly requires patience, finesse, and a lot of materials to layer.

The technical differences between the sheet-mulching method and Lanza's lasagna gardening recipe are, more or less, negligible. Lanza's recipe is a little more specific and includes newspaper as the bottom layer with peat moss interspersed with other materials on top.

TIPS FOR SHEET MULCHING

This method of preparing a bed can be presented as almost too good to be true. It can work great, but it can also be a flop if not done properly.

- Have enough materials (you need *a lot*) to make several nice, thick layers.

- Keep everything moist.

- Avoid ingredients that will attract rodents and other critters.

- Make sure your materials are broken down into smallish pieces (big sticks and whole clumps of weeds with their roots attached won't decompose fast enough).

The layered pile needs to be very thick (1.5–3 feet). As the layers break down, the pile will shrink a lot. Without enough materials, you may end up with a bed that has exposed paper or cardboard and only a thin layer of rich,

composted material on top. If this happens quickly, you can simply add more layers on top to keep the process going. Creating a thick enough layered bed requires more material than you probably imagine. We have done sheet mulching only when we have had an influx of weeds, grasses, or cover crops that have been cut; a large amount of vegetable scraps from an event; manure and bedding from cleaning out animal pens; or a mountain of grass clippings or dry leaves from a friendly landscaper.

If you decide to sheet mulch within the walls of a raised bed, begin by layering materials at least twice as high as those walls, otherwise you'll end up with a disappointing, sunken-soil situation. You can keep adding layers as the previous layers break down, but this will prolong the whole process.

Hold off on sowing seeds directly into a sheet-mulched bed until it has broken down significantly, which can take one to six months (depending on temperature and other conditions). Until the layers decompose into soil, plants won't have optimal growth conditions. You can shortcut the process for shallow-rooted plants like onions, lettuce, and chard by adding a 2- to 4-inch layer of finished compost or topsoil and planting in that enriched cap. For deeper-rooted crops like beets or tomatoes, it's worth waiting.

Cardboard more easily contours to the ground and is less likely to blow away if you wet it before laying it down for lasagna gardening.

HOW TO KEEP RODENTS OUT OF YOUR LASAGNA

Incorporating kitchen scraps into your layers is great for adding fertility and managing kitchen waste, but that fragrant food may attract rats, mice, crows, possums, raccoons, and even bears. To keep the critters away, use other greens in conjunction with kitchen scraps and take care to cover any tasty morsels really well with browns. If rats are already a problem in your yard or neighborhood, it's better to omit kitchen scraps altogether.

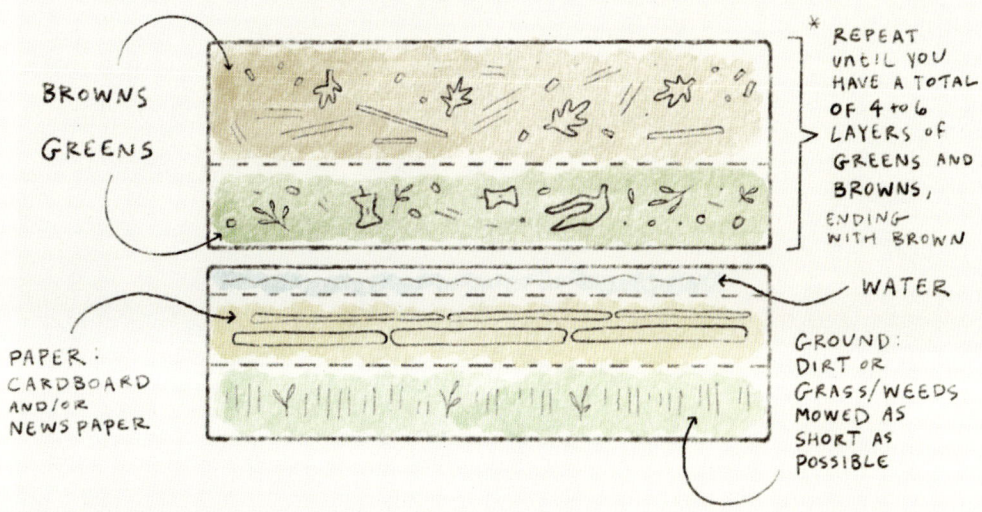

BROWNS

GREENS

* REPEAT UNTIL YOU HAVE A TOTAL OF 4 to 6 LAYERS OF GREENS AND BROWNS, ENDING WITH BROWN

WATER

GROUND: DIRT OR GRASS/WEEDS MOWED AS SHORT AS POSSIBLE

PAPER: CARDBOARD AND/OR NEWSPAPER

How To Make a
SHEET-MULCHED GARDEN BED

Please read Tips for Sheet Mulching on the facing page. If you're new to lasagna gardening or sheet mulching, experiment with a small area first to get a feel for the volume of stuff the process actually requires. You'll likely want to bring in materials from off your property for this trial run, especially the green materials.

Collect Materials

1. **COLLECT "BROWN" AND "GREEN" MATERIALS.** Carbon-rich "brown" materials and nitrogen-rich "green" materials are needed for layering, plus compost and healthy topsoil, if possible. Set them all to one side.

   - **BROWNS:** cardboard, newspaper, straw, dry leaves, dried-out weeds, coconut coir, peat moss, wood chips, and more

   - **GREENS:** grass clippings, food scraps, manure, weeds that are still green, and so on

Prep the Ground for Layering

2. **MOW VEGETATION.** Once you decide where the bed will go, cut the grass or vegetation in that spot as short as possible (save the grass clippings to use for layering).

3. **BUILD RAISED-BED INFRASTRUCTURE (OPTIONAL)** by laying down weed barrier and building walls with rot-resistant wood, salvaged roofing metal, or other materials (see page 66).

Start the Layering Process

4. **PUT SHEET MULCHING INTO ACTION.** Layer wet cardboard and/or newspaper on the bottom of the bed in an overlapping pattern without gaps.

5. **ADD A LAYER OF "GREENS"** 2 to 3 inches thick.

6. **ADD A LAYER OF "BROWNS"** 4 to 6 inches thick.

7. **WATER THE BROWNS** enough that they're evenly moist but not soggy.

8. **CONTINUE LAYERING GREENS AND BROWNS** (the cardboard and/or newspaper is just for the bottom of the bed; subsequent brown layers should be organic materials such as leaves, wood chips, and straw) until you run out of materials or the pile reaches 1.5 to 3 feet in thickness; use a minimum of three layers, though four to six layers are ideal; the bed will shrink in thickness quite a bit as the ingredients decompose into beautiful soil.

Finish the Layering Process

9. **TOP WITH COMPOST, TOPSOIL, OR BROWNS.** To plant right away, top the whole thing with a 2- to 4-inch layer of finished compost or topsoil; then plant shallow-rooted crops like lettuce or onions. To plant later, finish with a layer of browns. Then, keep the bed moist to spur the natural process of decomposition that transforms the layers into soil over a few months.

TIP: *These layers will break down into soil and be ready for plants more quickly when the weather is warm and more slowly when it's cold.*

Basic Solarization and Occultation

This method sounds a little like witchcraft, and it *can* feel magical when you see how it works. Not only is solarization/occultation great for starting a garden from grass, it can also be worked into a no-till or low-till system to prepare planting areas season after season. We both use it regularly, and we *love it!*

Some folks consider this a lazy person's technique. We call it the intelligent way. And it isn't just us. More and more small-scale, no-till, and low-till organic farmers are utilizing this approach to cut down on tillage—without getting overwhelmed with weeds.

Another term for this general practice is *tarping*, which refers specifically to using a large UV-treated silage tarp to occult (block from sunlight) the ground. *Do not* use a standard tarp you would purchase at a hardware store for this purpose, as you will end up with a garden full of shredded plastic fibers!

Tarping was made popular by Jean-Martin Fortier in his great book *The Market Gardener: A Successful Grower's Handbook for Small-Scale Organic Farming*. Just like all of the methods we teach about in this chapter, solarization and occultation can be mixed and matched with other methods. And if you use this method, it doesn't mean you can never till the ground.

DIFFERENCES BETWEEN SOLARIZATION AND OCCULTATION

Both solarization and occultation involve laying an impervious or semi-impervious material, usually plastic, over the ground to kill plants and to warm the earth, which also reduces soilborne pathogens.

Solarization technically refers to the use of a clear material, which creates a greenhouse effect to "cook" the plants beneath. *Occultation* refers to the use of a black or opaque material to omit light (occult) from the area under it while also warming the ground, which smothers and kills plants. In our experience occultation is far more effective. In fact, solarization with a clear material can actually stimulate weed growth. Most people use the term *solarization* whether they're using clear or black material. However, *occultation* is the technical term when using opaque material. We'll continue to use both terms in this section, because very few growers actually use the term *occultation*, though that is what most growers actually do.

HOW LONG DOES IT TAKE TO KILL WEEDS (OR COVER CROPS)?

The time it takes to kill weeds or cover crops with these methods depends on temperature and rainfall and can range from two weeks to six months. Generally speaking, the process takes longer when conditions are cooler and drier, and it goes more quickly with warmer, wetter weather. A good rule of thumb is to leave the ground covered for a minimum of one month when the weather reaches at least 50°F (10°C) on most days. If you plan to garden in spring-time, you can lay material down in fall, and it will feel like a magic trick when you uncover the earth in spring: You'll have an open, weed-free area ready to prepare for planting!

MATERIALS AND SOLARIZATION/ OCCULTATION

Whatever material you use will need to be fairly tough and resistant to the sun's UV (ultraviolet) light; it's going to be lying on the ground, getting rained on, scratched up by rocks and weeds, and exposed to a lot of sun.

For years, Natalie used sheets of roofing metal to occult her garden beds. Since at the time she was also running a building school, there was usually no shortage. Over time, she noticed that this use was pretty hard on the roofing metal, plus that material is large and bulky to store. In general, the best material to use is UV-stabilized plastic. We know it sucks to hear organic gardening teachers espouse the use of something so ecologically malevolent. Please read our short treatise on plastics in agriculture (page 80) to understand more.

Best Materials for Occultation

- Woven polypropylene ground cover, UV treated (DeWitt Sunbelt 3.2 ounce or similar); available from multiple retailers, including Home Depot; rolls from 2 to 12 feet wide (4-foot-wide pieces are excellent for our 3½-foot beds); best for small to medium-size areas

- Low-density polyethylene silage tarps, UV treated; minimum 5 millimeter thickness; available online from Farmers Friend and other retailers; larger pieces from 24 to 50 feet wide and up to 105 feet in length; best for larger areas

Avoid using regular sheet plastic or a tarp from a home improvement store—these will degrade and break apart into a million pieces, polluting your garden soil and causing a huge headache when it comes to cleanup. Trust us, we know . . . it's horrible!

PLASTIC AND WIND

One of the trickier parts of solarization/ occultation is keeping the plastic down in the presence of wind.

In our experience, UV-resistant woven plastic sandbags, filled with sand or rocks or soil that's high in sand and clay, are the most effective. You don't need to fill the bags all the way up, just enough for them to be significantly heavy. If the soil you use to fill the sandbags is moist, add extra to account for it drying out.

Landscaping staples can come in handy if you're using a woven material (not a silage tarp), though they tend to shorten the life of the plastic by piercing holes that end up unraveling the fibers.

Logs and boards can hold down plastic, though they're bulky and cumbersome to store, don't usually conform to the shape of the ground very well, and aren't as heavy per square foot as sandbags and thus not as effective under high winds.

PLASTICS IN AGRICULTURE:
A SHORT TREATISE

I t's easy to make a sweeping statement that plastics of all kinds are inherently bad: They are made of unsustainable hydrocarbons; they're toxic to produce; they inevitably become waste and take tens of thousands of years to break down; they deteriorate into microplastics that pollute waterways, soils, and the bodies of living creatures; their xenoestrogens disrupt the endocrine systems of animals, leading to reproductive harm and other kinds of damage; and plastic products are so cheap that they deincentivize natural crafts and the making and using of handmade objects. The list goes on. Plastic sucks.

At the same time, plastics, like so many ad campaigns in the 1950s claimed, can be miraculous. Have you ever tried to water a garden without a hose? Or without the probably plastic pipes that bring that water to your spigot? Have you walked any distance on a rainy day without "rubber" (probably petroleum-based) soles on your shoes or plastic rain boots on your feet? Yes, plastics are super harmful and have many serious and rippling negative impacts, but they make our lives as we know them possible.

SHORT HISTORY. Plastics became widespread in the 1940s and '50s. Around that time, Dr. Emery M. Emmert, a horticulture professor at the University of Kentucky, was the first to use plastic to warm the earth and extend growing seasons and locations for heat-loving crops; he developed the first plastic-covered high tunnels (like greenhouses). Soon after, in the early 1960s, strawberry growers in New Zealand began using plastic as a ground cover to suppress weeds and preserve soil moisture. In 1965, Israeli innovator Simcha Blass invented the first commercial drip irrigation systems, also made of plastic. With each passing decade, plastic has made its way into every part of the growing process, with agriculture in the United States now utilizing, and disposing of, 816 million pounds of plastic annually.

Biodegradable plastic film (shown here in the closer rows) is a new innovation that suppresses weeds, conserves water, and warms soil without creating long-lasting waste like fossil fuel–derived plastic.

Drip lines deliver water right to plants' roots, conserving this precious resource.

UPSIDES. That's a seriously huge number and an ecological issue that deserves our attention. But there's a lot of nuance here. Drip irrigation, for example, can reduce agricultural water use by 30 to 70 percent. Plastic-glazed high tunnels make vegetable production possible in cooler climates for more of the year, which reduces the amount of fossil fuels and disposable plastic packaging that's needed to bring food to those areas. Using plastic for solarization/occultation minimizes soil disturbance and preserves soil life. In comparison with repetitive tilling, solarization/occultation can make it more doable for small-scale growers (e.g., gardeners like us and our local farmer friends) to produce a significant amount of food without relying on machines or overtaxing our bodies.

The same woven material we like to use for solarization/occultation can be used for weed suppression as crops are growing. Biodegradable eco-plastic films have also been developed for similar applications. These are both more ecologically friendly alternatives to the single-use plastic film you may be familiar with underneath crops on big farms. These more sustainable materials are much more costly than the thinner fossil fuel–based plastic, so funding and support for more sustainable practices on small-to-medium farms are needed to make this a widely accessible option.

DOWNSIDES. While the materials we recommend for solarization/occultation are fairly durable and may last for 10 years or more, that doesn't mean they're impact-free. They are still plastic and will eventually end up in the soil and water, in our bodies, and in the oceans. For us, the difference they make in our ability to grow food for ourselves and our communities feels worth the trade-off.

It's important to know, too, that *synthetic-blend fertilizers and pesticides are the number-one source of agricultural plastic pollution.* These products literally contain plastic—in the form of microplastic beads—to help make them more fluid. These beads go directly into the soil and groundwater.

A PERSONAL DECISION. In reality, we are all participating in "plasticulture" (plastic-dependent agriculture), whether we own and touch the plastic or not. Is it really better to buy plastic clamshells full of mixed greens that were grown with heavy water and plastic inputs in arid Arizona and transported to us via diesel trucks, or is it more ethical to solarize/occult a bed and glaze a high tunnel with plastic so that we can grow our own greens in wintertime? This is a decision for each of us to make on our own.

Part of this reckoning with our relationship with plastics in the garden means recognizing the grief involved. There's great sorrow in the presence of plastics in our bodies, in the ocean, on planet Earth. It makes sense to feel anguish about buying plastic so that we can grow a big garden, especially when we imagine our ancestors accomplishing this task through community interdependence instead. No choice or technique can extinguish this grief, and letting ourselves feel it is part of the process of inner growth that we get to do right alongside our garden.

How to Do
SUPREME SOLARIZATION/OCCULTATION

The basic version of solarization/occultation that we described on page 78 is great for getting a space ready for planting: Kill the plants that are there and wipe the slate clean for whatever you'd like to grow instead. The following "supreme" method takes it a few steps further to build soil fertility and tilth (soil texture). It's a little more time consuming, and it requires more inputs like compost and cover-crop seeds, but the results are worth your time, especially if you're starting out with marginal soil.

1. MOW THE VEGETATION. Shear the area as close to the soil as possible. You can leave the plant material in place to decompose.

2. COVER THE SITE. Use the solarizing/occulting material of your choice (see the options on page 79).

3. PRACTICE PATIENCE. Leave the plastic or other material on the site until the vegetation below it is completely dead (this may take 3 weeks in the heat of summer or up to 6 months or more in a cooler season or place).

4. ADD COMPOST. Spread 1 to 3 inches of compost on top of the dead vegetation.

5. PLANT AND GROW A COVER CROP. (See page 140.)

6. MOW OR CRIMP THE COVER CROP. Do this, ideally, when the crop is flowering. Crimping involves bending and creasing the crop's stalks to kill it. (See Bogwalker's Badass Topsoil Technique on page 84.)

7. SOLARIZE/OCCULT THE COVER CROP.

8. PRACTICE MORE PATIENCE. Wait for the cover crop to die.

9. RAKE AWAY THE DEBRIS. Be sure to save it to use as mulch!

10. PLANT CROPS.

To Create Beds

Depending on your overall plan for the space, you may want to establish beds and pathways rather than managing the area as a field. Natalie used this technique when she created her leaf-shaped garden. By setting up beds, you maximize the amount of topsoil available to your crops. Follow steps 1 through 6 on the facing page.

1. MARK OUT YOUR BEDS. Remember to leave generous paths for comfortable gardening and wheelbarrows. See Chapter 1 for more on layout.

2. MEASURE 6 INCHES IN FROM EACH SIDE OF YOUR MARKED BED. Mark this clearly, then remove the outer markings made in step 1. For example, if your final bed (the original outer marking) is 36 by 96 inches, this new boundary will be 24 by 84 inches.

3. DO A HÜGELKULTUR-INSPIRED METHOD (OPTIONAL). Add 3 inches of wood chips or easily rotting slabs (the rounded parts left over when a sawmill makes round logs into straight boards) to the surface of the inner bed area.

4. DIG DOWN 3 TO 6 INCHES. Move this rich, exquisite soil from the paths and bed edges up to the inner marked boundary you have made. Turn this soil onto the inner bed (leaving room to build the bed walls), with cover-crop bodies down and roots up. Break up clumps as necessary.

5. BUILD RAISED-BED WALLS, if desired, at the original outline of your beds.

6. RAKE. Use a rake to even out the pile to reach the bed walls or achieve the bed shape.

7. PLANT! You can plant a cover crop again or go right into planting a food crop.

Bogwalker's Badass Topsoil Technique

Natalie innovated this technique after creating giant terraces with heavy machines. What was left after the earthmoving were big, beautiful terraces made of clay subsoil with zero topsoil and absolutely nothing growing. She decided to run an experiment based on previous findings and to incorporate hügelkultur, a soil-building technique often used in permaculture. It's based on traditional German and Eastern European practices and was popularized by Sepp Holzer in his book *Sepp Holzer's Permaculture: A Practical Guide to Small-Scale, Integrative Farming and Gardening*.

Lo and behold, the experiment worked—and way better than Natalie could have imagined! Read on to witness the transformation.

THE HÜGELKULTUR-BASED EXPERIMENT

What follows is a tale of something Natalie tried that became a wild success!

Part I: First Cover Crops

In September, directly after the completion of the terrace earthmoving, she and a crew began.

1. They first spread a bed of wood chips on the barren, clayey terraces.

2. They then added a layer of hay by unrolling large round bales over the terraces.

3. They finished with a thin (1- to 3-inch) layer of compost.

4. They planted Austrian winter peas and winter rye into that compost layer. (The winter rye didn't do much, but the winter peas went crazy, growing bigger than Natalie had seen them before.)

5. In spring, when the winter peas started flowering, it was time to terminate, or kill, the cover crop so that all that good, thriving green growth could go down into the soil to feed and build it up.

Natalie developed her "badass topsoil technique" on large terraces that she shaped with a machine. Now the area is a fertile garden space.

When Natalie lifted a shovelful of soil from the terraces in the spring to assess the progress in soil building, she was absolutely floored. She expected to see mostly wood chips and hay, but instead found nearly 6 inches of topsoil! The fact that most of the topsoil formed during winter, when soil organisms are typically less active, was pleasantly shocking. The winter peas had done magical things, turning 8 inches of mostly wood chips and hay into soil.

Natalie was so excited by these result that it was all she could talk about for days. (Chloe can attest to this . . . she heard lots of exclamations like, "Dude!" and "Holy shit!") Natalie's wood chip guy memorably said, "Miss Natalie, that is very impressive." Modest but important praise—it turned out that in addition to this local man being friendly and owning a dump truck and having access to materials, he also holds a degree in horticulture. It boded well that she'd impressed him!

Part II: More Cover Crops

Even though the soil building exceeded Natalie's expectations and veggies could have been planted at that point, she decided against it. (She had plenty of other growing space at that time, so it was easy for her to wait longer

for the terraces.) Instead, to make the soil extra fabulous before planting food crops, she sowed two more rounds of cover crops after terminating the first.

In the spring after the winter peas, she planted sunn hemp, cowpeas, and sorghum–Sudan grass for the summer season. In the fall, she followed that with tillage radish and a small amount of Austrian winter peas for the subsequent winter. Tillage radishes (a.k.a. "driller radishes") help integrate topsoil by carrying it down deep with their long roots.

Conclusion

This whole experiment worked amazingly well in the southern Appalachians, where we are blessed by plentiful rain and many warm spells amid the freezing days of winter. In colder areas of the country (and in some winters here), the timing of the cover-crop planting would not be the same, since winter peas are killed by temperatures below 10°F (−12°C). If you live somewhere colder, it's probably best to start this technique in spring rather than fall.

It's not clear how well this topsoil technique might work in drier conditions, where irrigation would obviously be necessary. If you try it, please let us know how it goes!

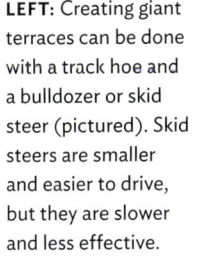

LEFT: Creating giant terraces can be done with a track hoe and a bulldozer or skid steer (pictured). Skid steers are smaller and easier to drive, but they are slower and less effective.

RIGHT: The proof is in the topsoil! Dark, fertile ground enriches the heavy clay that dominated this space just a couple of seasons before.

How to Do
BOGWALKER'S BADASS TOPSOIL TECHNIQUE IN 10 STEPS

1. **START WITH FLAT, BARE SOIL.** Alternatively, mow vegetation very short, occult growth, and rake back debris as in supreme solarization on page 82.

2. **PERFORM A SOIL TEST (OPTIONAL).** A test will identify how much of which minerals (such as phosphorus, boron, zinc, or manganese) the soil needs, and then you can apply these.

   TIP: *Note that many minerals are immobile in soil, so they are better incorporated through tilling rather than simply sprinkling them on top of the soil (see page 113 for more on mineral mobility). If your soil needs significant amounts of immobile minerals, consider tilling them in before the next step.*

3. **SPREAD 2 TO 5 INCHES OF WOOD CHIPS.** They can be fresh or partially deomposed, like these.

4. **ADD 2 TO 5 INCHES OF LIGHTWEIGHT BROWN ORGANIC MATTER.** Hay, straw, and leaves are all good choices. (It's easy to roll out round bales for larger areas.)

5. **ADD COMPOST.** Lay down 1 to 3 inches of finished compost or rich topsoil.

6. PLANT A LEGUMINOUS COVER CROP. Plant with or without another complementary cover crop, and cover very lightly with mulch to keep germinating seeds moist. Water regularly until the seeds germinate. Allow the cover crop to grow to the flowering stage.

7. MOW OR CRIMP THE COVER CROP. Use a T-post to crimp once the leguminous cover is flowering (see page 88 for details).

8. SOLARIZE/OCCULT THE AREA. Place a large UV-treated silage tarp over the cover crop to kill it.

9. RAKE BACK DEBRIS, and prepare the area for planting.

10. REPEAT STEPS 6 THROUGH 8 (OPTIONAL). Repeat twice, if desired, ideally utilizing a variety of cover crops, not necessarily all legumes.

11. PLANT A FOOD CROP!

Crimping Cover Crops

Crimping is the process of bending, creasing, or "squishing" the stems of cover-crop plants to terminate (kill) them. Larger-scale farmers use fancy crimping machines that mount onto and are powered by their tractors. A friend of ours devised a set of crimping shoes he uses to walk over cover crops, accomplishing the same effect. Read on to learn how Natalie likes to crimp cover crops using easy-to-find materials.

Crimping seems to work a little better than mowing to prepare an area for sowing seeds. Crimped and then smothered cover crops will often die back completely, whereas mown cover crops may sprout back readily. Mowing is still a great option, especially if you don't have a buddy to crimp with.

Natalie was inspired to try crimping to terminate a cover crop by the book *The No-Till Organic Vegetable Farm: How to Start and Run a Profitable Market Garden* by Daniel Mays. The idea is that you crimp the stalks before solarization/occultation, which smothers them.

Mays suggests using a 6-foot studded T-post, a green metal fence post with an anchor plate about a foot from the bottom. When purchased at agricultural supply stores, these are relatively inexpensive (about five dollars). Make sure to get the studded T-post and not the flimsy green versions sold at big-box home improvement centers. The latter are the wrong shape and not heavy-duty enough. You'll also need 12 to 16 feet of paracord or other strong, thin rope.

To crimp a cover crop, all you need is a metal T-post, some string, and a friend—no machinery necessary.

How to CRIMP COVER CROPS for Termination

Grab a partner: This method requires two relatively physically capable people who have legs close to the same length and are wearing sturdy work boots.

1. LAY THE T-POST on the ground at one edge of the area to be crimped, with the studs of the T-post up and the rib down.

2. EACH PERSON STANDS ON ONE END of the T-post with their outer foot on the ground and their inner foot on the studs of the T-post.

3. USING ONE END of the paracord, each person attaches their inner foot to the T-post in a way that securely attaches the foot, leaving about a 4-foot "tail" of loose paracord. This tail needs to reach comfortably to the person's hand, so that they can use it to assist in lifting up the T-post that's attached to their foot.

4. THE T-POST PARTNERS WALK in a coordinated way so that their inner feet lift up at the same time. The goal is to raise and lower the T-post in a synchronized rhythm, systematically squishing the cover crops and flattening them in overlapping layers.

NOTE: *Crimping with a T-post is easiest when one person calls out the steps to coordinate the movement.*

Crimping a cover crop this way works incredibly well. We're always pleasantly surprised to look back and see the neat 5-foot rows of cover crop laying down behind us!

Getting Soil Ready for Seeds and Plants

Regardless of what method you use for starting your garden, the last step is always the same. When you've got lovely little seeds full of so much potential and baby transplants that can't wait to sink their roots into real soil, how do you make sure your beds or rows are ready to receive such magic?

Depending on the technique you've used to prepare the ground, you may be ready to plant right away, or extra smoothing and preparation may be in order. A rule of thumb is this: The smaller the seeds or transplants, the smoother the surface of the soil needs to be. Large, healthy transplants adapt to a lumpy-bumpy garden space more easily than delicate starts.

Here's another important principle to remember: The earth does not like to be naked. If you prepare a beautiful seedbed but leave it exposed to the sun for days before planting, you undo some of the work you've done to create a place where life flourishes. Soil life, especially the fungal life that helps deliver water and minerals to plant roots, is killed by direct sunlight, and nitrogen (a crucial plant macronutrient) is volatilized (lost) in the presence of sunlight. For that reason, we try to do this last step of preparing a bed immediately before planting.

If you are direct sowing, of course it will be necessary to leave the soil uncovered while the seeds germinate and begin to grow. The same goes for transplanting in early spring if you live in an area with lots of slugs. Having a naked seedbed is not the end of the world, as you will keep the bed moist throughout the germination process. But once seedlings or transplants are tall enough to poke over mulch and big enough to withstand a little slug pressure, do try to get the ground covered in a timely way. Check out Chapter 4, where we explore mulching strategies to mitigate the damage sun exposure can have on soil life.

ADDING COMPOST AND OTHER AMENDMENTS

Part of preparing a planting space is adding any necessary compost, manure, or other amendments.

If you tilled your soil: Whether you used the double- or single-digging method or tilled with a machine, you hopefully incorporated amendments as you turned the soil, so there will be no need to add them now.

If you decided on a no-till method: You have two choices here. First, you can spread amendments on top of the bare soil and gently mix them in with a hoe or hard rake. Keep in mind that cover crops improve the soil biology and structure in much the same way that compost amends soil, so a no-till bed or field that had been sown with cover crops may or may not need more compost added now. Pick up the soil and feel it and smell it. If it feels moist and a little

LEFT: Use the back of a rake to smooth a seedbed.

MIDDLE: Chloe is sowing seeds by hand (with a tiny helper).

RIGHT: You may sprinkle a powdered amendment onto a bed in preparation for planting.

springy and smells deliciously reminiscent of a forest floor, you're good. If it's crumbly or super sticky and has no smell or a bad smell, there's room for improvement. Also, observe how your cover crops grow to decide whether you'll need to add in more compost later; wimpy cover crops usually indicate wimpy crops to come without some intervention.

Your second choice with no-till beds is to simply layer amendments on top of the soil, either before planting (known as topdressing) or after (sidedressing). It's important to understand that certain mineral amendments (particularly phosphorus, calcium, and boron) are immobile, meaning not readily distributed throughout the soil via biological action and water flow. Those amendments must be mixed in rather than simply sprinkled on top of the earth. (Read more on mobile vs. immobile nutrients, and about topdressing and sidedressing, in Chapters 4 and 5.) Fortunately immobile nutrients don't need to be added frequently because they stick around for a while, due to their inherent properties.

PREPARING SOIL FOR PLANTING SEEDS

Before you plant seeds, the goal is to have a smoothly raked and flat seedbed with little to no debris on the surface. And you definitely don't want any weeds in a seedbed—not even cute baby ones—because they will have a huge head start on your seeds. Depending on the seed germination time, you may not even see your tiny plants come up as the weeds take over.

Tips for Creating an Ideal Seedbed for Planting

- If the soil is clumpy or hard, use a hoe or shovel to break up the clumps. Do this when the soil is moist but not soggy. If it's dry, irrigate and then break up the clumps the following day. If a clump of soil squeezed in your hand oozes or drips, wait for it to dry out.

- If roots, rocks, stalks, or other debris are present, use a rake and/or your hands to remove them.

- If weeds (even tiny baby ones) are present, use a scuffle hoe, other tool, or your hands to remove them completely.

- Run a rake, *tines down*, over the area in a controlled manner that does not go too deep. This will produce a flat, smoothish surface and remove remaining clumps or debris.

- Now run the rake, *tines up*, over the area again without pushing the tool into the soil. Allow it to glide over the top, so you end up with an even and smooth seedbed.

TRANSPLANTING

If you're transplanting small plants, like lettuces, into a bed or row, your planting space must be as smooth and beautifully receptive as if you were sowing seeds.

If you're transplanting bigger plants, like tomatoes or broccoli, there is a bit more flexibility. For example, sometimes when Natalie is transplanting tomatoes, she simply mows the cover crop short, then plants the tomatoes and tops the cover-crop residue with a thick layer of mulch that goes right up to the main stem of each tomato plant. No perfectly smooth bed necessary. Similarly, Chloe will transplant larger plants, like broccoli, directly into a semi-bumpy row that has recently been solarized/occulted, without raking and smoothing. Then, once the danger of slugs has passed, she'll cover the bed with mulch and call it good (she doesn't think the broccoli minds a bumpy atmosphere . . . broccoli is a bit bumpy itself).

Along with these practical considerations, your own aesthetic sense will guide you. Some folks don't mind lumpy beds, others feel calmer with utter smoothness. How you feel about your garden matters, too. Find more about transplanting in Chapter 6: How to Plant a Seed & Get It to Grow.

4
Soil
& Fertility

Soil 101 94

What Makes Soil Good for Growing Vegetables? 96

How to Do a Soil Test and Why 105

Fertility 101 107

Vegetable Fertility Needs 112

Managing Fertility 113

Growing Mediums for Containers 117

Soil 101

Soil is the dark, fertile mystery from which life miraculously sprouts. It is literally the foundation of your garden, and its importance cannot be overstated. The world of soil science is vast, complex, and always evolving. In fact, Western science hasn't yet named, categorized, or begun to understand many of the organisms and functions that occur beneath our feet. Land-based peoples around the world have understood and revered the complex majesty of soil for many thousands of years in mythic, spiritual, relational, and sense-based ways.

Seeds hold the blueprint—the story—of plants, the sunlight provides the energy for growth, and the air shares the biggest building blocks of structure (carbon); but everything else in the body of a plant comes through the soil. It's carried there via water that travels from soil to plant to sky, back to soil in a spiraling journey of life-giving transformation.

This is why soil, soil science, and fertility get two whole chapters in this book. We do our best to explain scientific concepts and principles in plain terms and share simple strategies for interacting with the soil using your body and senses—while also honoring the complexity of soil science.

HOW PLANTS GROW

To begin understanding what qualities the soil needs in order to grow healthy plants, we first look at the bigger picture of how plants accomplish the absolutely magical feat of growing without consuming "food."

Photosynthesis. Animals (including us) eat plants and other animals to get the energy and building blocks needed to live (carbohydrates, proteins, fats, vitamins, and minerals). Plants, in contrast, build and maintain their bodies from a magical reaction called photosynthesis. They transform air and

Up to half or more of the bodies of vegetable plants are underground. Soil is a world unto itself, and one of the most important parts of a garden.

It's time for us to shift our viewpoint and narrative away from the living world as a collection of resources for our benefit, and to understand all as alive.

water (i.e., carbon, oxygen, and hydrogen) from the sky and soil into sugars (carbohydrates), using sunlight as the energy source to break and form chemical bonds needed to do so.

Plants also pull nitrogen, phosphorus, potassium—plant macronutrients (see page 98)—and other mineral and biological elements from the soil to combine with sun-fueled carbohydrates to make cells and tissues.

Plant tissues and their functions.

There are four main types of plant tissues: vascular, epidermal, ground, and meristematic. Within these main groups, there are dozens of specialized cells and systems that perform all manner of processes. They do everything from holding the plant upright to moving water through its body; forming and ripening flowers and fruits; growing roots that exchange nutrients with soil organisms; protecting the plant from heat, cold, diseases, and pests; and much more.

Plants grow most of the mass of their bodies out of sunlight and air. It's quite the

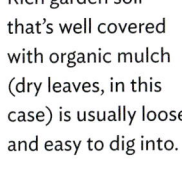

Rich garden soil that's well covered with organic mulch (dry leaves, in this case) is usually loose and easy to dig into.

miracle! But to perform this miracle, they need key ingredients from the soil. Different soil structures, biological actors, and mineral compositions significantly help or hinder plants' ability to grow.

SOIL IS ALIVE

We gardeners sometimes talk about soil as though one kind is "better" or more "alive." It's true that some soils contain more of the elements and creatures needed to support healthy plant growth, and other soils have less. But even in abandoned lots in cities, we find soil nurturing plant growth.

It's time for us to shift our viewpoint and narrative away from the living world as a collection of resources for our benefit and to understand *all* as alive. In many cases, when soil is degraded or less fertile, human abuse is the cause. Similarly, human care can bring vitality and fertility into areas where it may have been compromised.

What Makes Soil Good for Growing Vegetables?

There's a lot going on in the soil! From mineral composition and particle size to biological activity and the movement of air and water, everything has an impact on how well garden vegetables and other plants will grow.

As with so much in life, the ideal garden soil involves *balance* and *quality*: different characteristics and components working together, each with the appropriate qualities to meet the needs of the plants we're tending. This basic principle is important for us to return to when we get overwhelmed with all the specific details.

For crops to thrive, certain soil qualities, traits, and constituents must be in balance within and among themselves.

The well-loved soil in Natalie's garden continues to yield a diversity of beautiful and nourishing crops, year after year, thanks to thoughtful care.

LEFT: See the stripes? The bottom is sand, then silt, then clay suspended in water, which will settle after a few hours. This "shake test" shows you soil composition: Fill one-third of a jar with soil, top with water, shake. Let settle for 48 hours, then measure each layer.

RIGHT: When we engage our senses, we can perceive the vast diversity of soils, even in the same garden. These different colored samples also smell distinct.

Inorganic (Never Alive) Soil Qualities and Traits

- Texture and structure
- Air and water
- Mineral nutrients
- Relative acidity or pH
- Total cation exchange capacity (TCEC)

Organic (Carbon-Based and Once-Living) Soil Constituents

- Decomposing organic matter
- Soil organisms (macro and micro)

INORGANIC SOIL QUALITIES AND TRAITS

Inorganic here doesn't mean agrochemical, but rather non-carbon based. These are the mineral and structural elements of the soil that were never themselves living beings.

Soil Texture and Structure

Soil texture and structure are the physical properties of soil that determine how easily air, water, roots, and critters can move around. They also influence the movement of nutrients within the soil, and from soil to plants (and plants to soil!).

The inorganic part of soil is made up of tiny particles that can be organized into three groups based on size, from largest to smallest: sand, silt, and clay.

Soil texture. While texture also refers to the tactile feel of the soil, the US Department of Agriculture (USDA) groups soils into 12 official classes of texture. The ideal mix for vegetable gardening is around 10 to 20 percent clay, with the rest made up of equal parts silt and sand. You definitely don't need this exact ratio to grow vegetables, but it's a useful reference.

Soil structure. The particles of sand, silt, and clay form aggregates, meaning they clump together. Aggregates, along with organic matter, air, and water, form the basic "architecture" of the soil, or its physical characteristics, such as crumbliness, stickiness, and density. These structural qualities are sometimes referred to as tilth, a word that shares its root with the word *till*.

Soil with good tilth holds together in small clumps, is not very sticky, and has a spongy quality resulting from a balance between particle sizes and ample organic matter. Such soil includes up to 50 percent pore space: Air and water flow through tiny pockets between the particle clumps, and roots can penetrate through them with ease. As you garden, feel the soil with your hands. Imagine that your fingers are plant roots, and ask yourself how inviting this soil would be if they were.

Let's look at the qualities of soil particles that affect tilth.

Clay: Soil nutrients are, chemically speaking, minerals, and some of those minerals—mostly silica, aluminum, magnesium, and iron, mixed with potassium, sodium, and/or calcium—come in the form of clay-size particles.

This unique material (there are actually many kinds of clays, but for our purposes we group them together here) has negatively charged particles with large surface areas that act like little absorptive magnets. If you've ever made pottery and noticed your hands feeling dry and a bit puckered afterward, that's the clay absorbing the oil, water, and other positively charged molecules from your skin, just like it holds on to water and some minerals in the soil.

Clay helps hold and transport nutrients from soil, water, and microorganisms into plant roots, and it carries and holds nutrients that are exuded from roots. It also helps hold on to water and allows plants to suck up water through porous soil, a process known as capillary action.

Silt. Middle-size silt particles, like so many middle children, play an important role in helping big sand and small clay join together to form favorable aggregates (whether visible or microscopic clumps) that aren't too big or too small. Silt also assists with air circulation and drainage.

Sand. Sand is the largest of the three inorganic soil particles, and it increases drainage and air circulation.

Air and Water in Soil

We all know that plant roots drink up water from the soil. Without water, essential nutrients can't be absorbed into the roots to move from the soil into the bodies of plants. But did you know that plant roots also breathe air?

Air and water are crucial for the soil—not only for our cherished plants, but also for the myriad other organisms that make the soil their home and, in turn, help nourish and protect plants.

Air and water belowground need to be able to *move*, just as they do aboveground. Soil that's waterlogged won't have enough air, and plants and other critters will drown. Anaerobic (non-air-breathing) organisms thrive in soggy soil, and many of these, including various fungal rots, are harmful to plants. In contrast, soil that has too much pore space and is full of air can easily lose water and dry out, which is obviously antithetical to healthy plant growth.

WORKING WITH HIGH CLAY SOIL

Clay is super important for proper plant nutrition and for retaining water in the soil. An overabundance of clay, however, causes water and nutrients to get trapped, leaving no room for air or roots. To put it bluntly, overly clayey soil is, functionally, constipated. If your soil is high in clay, it can easily become compacted, especially when wet. Take extra care not to till, dig, transplant, or even intensely weed the soil in this condition. Working wet clay soil can have long-term negative impacts on its structure. Increasing organic matter is the number one remedy for the challenges associated with high clay soil.

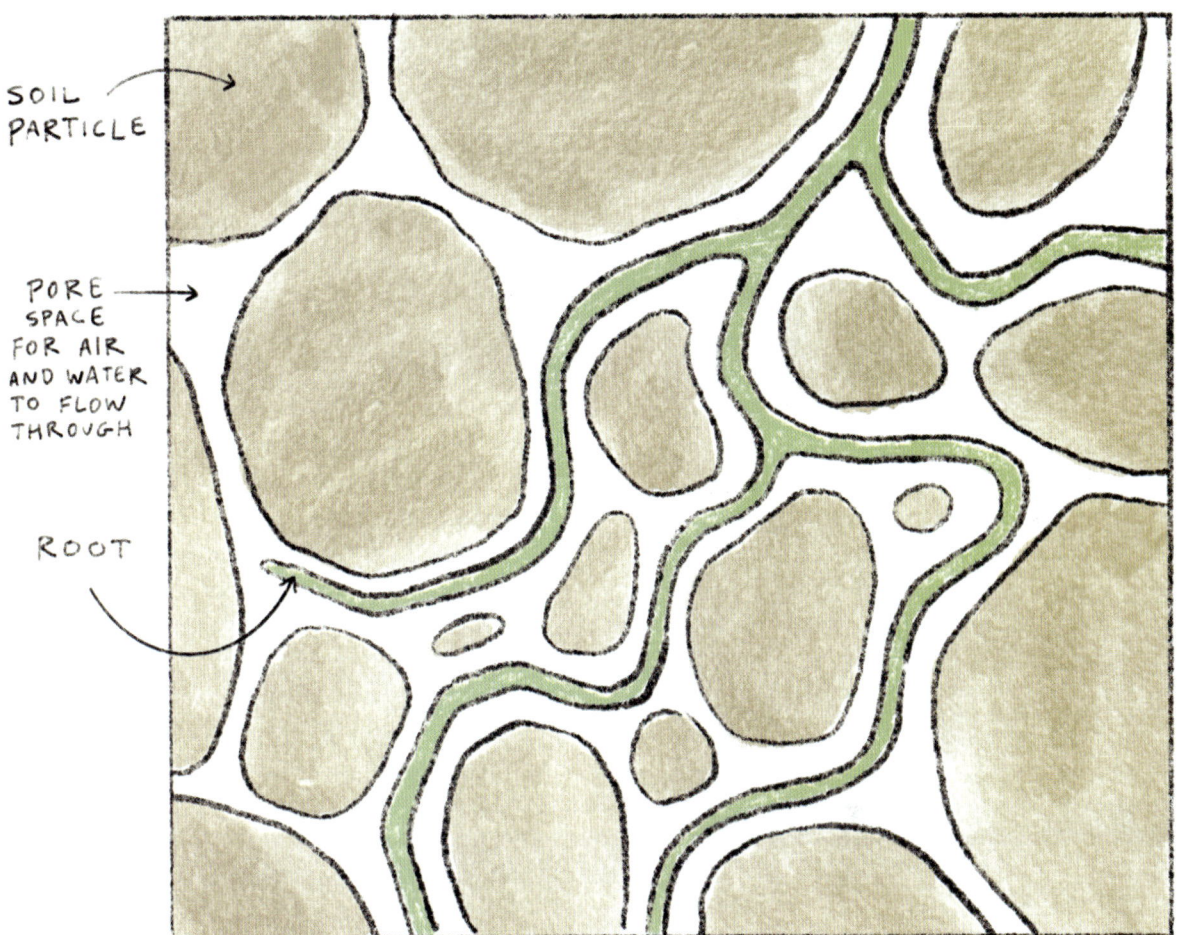

Labels on the illustration:

SOIL PARTICLE

PORE SPACE FOR AIR AND WATER TO FLOW THROUGH

ROOT

It may look uniform, but soil is made up of lots of parts. Here's a simplified image of what's going on up close.

Ideally, garden soil should have a balance of clay, sand, and silt, plus organic matter, so that it stays moist like a wrung-out sponge— not soggy, never bone-dry—capable of retaining some water while also permitting drainage. Soil with an appropriate balance of texture and structure lends itself to a dynamic flow of nutrient-rich water and enlivening, oxygen-rich air.

Mineral Nutrients

Many of the nutrients plants need don't come from sunlight. The minerals and biological compounds in soil provide the "vitamins" that

DON'T LET YOURSELF BE OVERWHELMED BY SOIL SCIENCE

Take a deep breath if you're feeling overwhelmed here. You can always skip this chapter and come back to it later. We find it very interesting and helpful to understand the big picture of soil, its constituent parts, and how they interact with one another, but learning the scientific story of what's going on is in no way necessary to grow healthy plants. Everyone has different learning styles, and we acknowledge that some people just aren't into chemistry and science. In the following sections, How to Do a Soil Test and Why (page 105), Fertility 101 (page 107), and Managing Fertility (page 113), we'll go into more detail about which nutrients plants need for which functions and how to manage them for ideal vegetable goodness. So you can turn to those sections if you want to skip over the *why* and get to the *how* of managing soil fertility.

WHERE DO MINERALS COME FROM?

The presence, or absence, of specific mineral nutrients in soil is dependent on the soil itself and on any amendments we add. The forms these nutrients take are impacted by the activity of soil life and even by the plants that are growing there. But where do the minerals come from in the first place? They come from the rocks that have broken down over time to create soil. They come from air and water moving through the soil. They come from organisms that carried and deposited the minerals in the form of their urine, feces, or whole bodies. Basic mineral elements cannot be created or destroyed; they just move around and transform chemically. Actually, they are created and destroyed in supernovas and other cosmic events, but hopefully those won't happen in your garden!

plants require for every phase of growth and to perform photosynthesis.

Plants need minerals to stay alive. They need them for all their metabolic processes, including growth, reproduction, natural defensive strategies against pests and diseases, and healing wounds or illness. When we eat plants, we consume their minerals, which, in turn, help build our bodies and perform our metabolic processes.

Just like with us (and other animals), the specific needs of different plant species or varieties vary. They all need access to 16 mineral nutrients, some in larger quantities than others. For these minerals to be of use to plants, they must be present in absorbable forms. As the gardener, you want to make choices (such as taking a soil test, adding amendments, using compost, and nourishing soil life) that lead to mineral nutrients being made available for your garden vegetables. The idea is to support their healthy growth and increase their nutrient density for *your* healthy growth when you eat them.

You might think of minerals as being hard like rocks, but mineral nutrients are actually active, changeable substances. It's helpful that we as gardeners understand the changes and movements of mineral nutrients. The main drivers of their chemical changes are soil biology and soil pH, with TCEC impacting how much and where these nutrients move (more on pH and TCEC in subsequent sections). Both living organisms in the soil and chemical compounds from decomposing matter change mineral nutrients into forms that plants can use. The relative acidity (pH) of the soil plays a role in molecularly changing mineral nutrients to make them more or less available to plants. A beautifully complex dance occurs between inorganic mineral elements and the organic constituents of soil, conducted by the mysterious force of acidity, which is, essentially and chemically, the magnetic charge of hydrogen molecules. There's a lot going on here, and every element plays an important role.

Relative Acidity, or pH

A fundamental quality of soil is its relative acidity, or pH, which is a result of the:

- Type of rock that any given soil has been originally derived from
- Volume and frequency of rainfall in the area
- Topography and plants present
- Overall weathering process throughout time
- Soil texture

Some soils are more acidic, some more alkaline, and others neutral. Adding mineral amendments may be futile if soil pH is not addressed, as pH levels set the conditions that affect nutrient movement and availability in the soil. In other words, without the correct soil pH, some minerals will not be available to certain plants.

Most garden vegetables do best with soils that are neutral or just slightly acidic (pH 6.0–7.0), with some variation (muskmelons, for example, prefer slightly alkaline conditions). Other plants and trees have different preferences—like blueberries, which prefer a soil pH of 4.5, which is quite acidic. See page 138 for various ways to adjust soil pH.

Total Cation Exchange Capacity (TCEC)

When you send a soil sample to a lab for analysis, one of the numbers you'll find on the report will be TCEC (total cation exchange capacity) or CEC (cation exchange capacity);

though these have some technical differences, we will use the term TCEC.

TCEC is a measure of the soil's chemical capacity to hold on to and exchange charged particles, which most nutrients in their plant-available forms are. In their book *The Intelligent Gardener: Growing Nutrient-Dense Food* (our current favorite book on soil chemistry and remineralization), Steve Solomon and Erica Reinheimer write, "If the plants are

WHAT EXACTLY IS pH?

The relative acidity (pH) of soil has huge impacts on how that soil interacts with plants. Chemically speaking, pH (potential hydrogen) denotes the number of positively charged hydrogen (H) ions and negatively charged hydroxyl (OH) ions that are present. These charged particles act like magnets, attracting and repelling whatever chemical compounds are also moving through the soil (things like mineral nutrients and water), and thus impacting which nutrients are available to plants and in which forms. It is also a factor in determining which organisms find that soil inviting.

feeding at the dining room table, the nutrients in the soil solution [dissolved in water in the soil] are like the food on their plates. The TCEC is food in the pantry, ready to be brought out and put on the table as needed. The bigger the pantry, the longer the dinner can go on."

The higher the TCEC number, the higher the capacity of the soil to hold on to "extra" nutrients, which are on hand to replace what plants have already taken up through the soil solution. The main contributors to TCEC are clay and humus (a specific kind of organic matter) particles; this means soil that is otherwise well balanced in all the ways we're talking about will also have a good TCEC.

ORGANIC SOIL CONSTITUENTS

Organic matter in soil includes anything that is or was ever alive, but in this discussion we divide it into the dead and the living because living organisms in soil play pretty different roles than decomposing organic matter. Just be aware, however, that they are not truly separate categories, as everything that lives will die and decompose, and decomposition fuels the possibility of more life emerging.

Carbon, a primary component of all organic materials (living and dead, including you and me!), is what links decomposing organic matter with living soil organisms. This powerful element is so central that folks sometimes refer to soil organic matter simply as "soil carbon."

We continue to tip our hats to the plants, who, through photosynthesis, transform carbon dioxide from the air into carbohydrates in their bodies, which are the basis for all solid carbon on this planet.

Decomposing Organic Matter

This is what once was living but now is turning into food and housing for others.

Organic matter is powerful. It positively influences all other properties of soil,

including water retention and drainage, texture, biological activity, and nutrient availability to plants. Up to a certain capacity, for every 1 percent increase in organic matter, crop yields can increase as much as 12 percent.

Increasing soil organic matter can be tricky. Carbon is very volatile: It's constantly moving, being consumed, and returning to the air in the form of carbon dioxide. Up to 90 percent of carbon that's added to agricultural land is lost in the first year. Microorganisms break down the soil's organic matter (things like decomposing mulch, dead plant roots, leaves, and other debris, along with the bodies of other microorganisms) by breaking chemical bonds and eventually *breathing out* (respiring) carbon dioxide, just like we do.

Holding carbon in the soil is beneficial. A goal for many growers is to hold carbon in the soil in the form of stable organic matter, a practice that benefits crops and has extraordinary potential to sequester large amounts of carbon quickly. It also helps curtail some of the harm caused by burning fossil fuels (made of very old plant and animal bodies) and releasing stored carbon into the atmosphere. One simple and effective way to do this is with biochar (which is, essentially, crushed-up charcoal), an extremely stable form of carbon that offers many benefits to garden soil (see page 129 for more on biochar). Adding compost, manure, and cover-crop roots and residues and protecting the living organisms in soil will also add carbon, but this carbon is easier to lose because, as it's broken down, a lot of it is breathed out as carbon dioxide, like we mentioned above.

More organic matter is not always better! Too much organic matter is unlikely to be an issue in your garden, but it can happen—more is not always better! Most productive agricultural soils will have between 2 and 6 percent organic matter (our gardens have between 3.5 percent and 7 percent). Soil with 20 percent or higher organic matter is considered peat or

Some organic matter in soil is clearly recognizable, like the wood chips here, and some is broken down and tiny; it all lends benefits.

muck and won't support the growth of vegetables. Challenges ensue (such as the proliferation of harmful nematodes that destroy plant roots) when soil reaches organic matter levels of only 10 percent.

Not all decomposing organic matter is created equal. Different kinds of soil organic matter play different roles. They can be roughly grouped as "the (recently) dead" and "the very dead."

The (Recently) Dead

- Includes fresh materials like plant debris and insect bodies.

- Adds structure to soil.

- Provides food for decomposers.

- Is a more volatile form of carbon; easier to lose as it gets broken down.

The Very Dead

- Includes more fully decomposed materials.

- Contains important compounds (such as humic and fulvic acids) that dramatically increase nutrient availability and fertility.

- Improves tilth.

- Facilitates the transfer of nutrients and water from soil to roots.

You can aspire to an "ideal" ratio. Though you probably won't be tracking specific percentages, it's good to aim for about 20 percent of the dead (fresher) organic matter and 80 percent of the very dead (more decomposed). What's important here is that you embrace the principle that soil benefits from

a mix of organic matter—including some of the unrecognizable, sweet-smelling, dark-colored, very dead stuff that looks like what you see under the leaves on a forest floor. We provide many techniques for building and maintaining organic matter in soil throughout the book (including adding amendments and reducing loss through no- and low-till practices).

Soil Organisms (Macro and Micro)

The living beings who make their home in the soil are considered part of the overall organic matter content, but because they play somewhat different roles than dead stuff, they deserve to have their very own section. These carbon-based life-forms participate in a continued cycle of consumption and decomposition with recently dead and very dead organic matter (see the preceding section).

There is a whole world happening underground! Just like in the ocean, where great dramas of life, death, and transformation take place among creatures and organisms we never see, the soil is teeming with vitality, pomp, and the near miraculous—much of it entirely invisible to us. If it weren't for the macro- and microorganisms in the soil doing what they alone (and together) can do, none of us air-breathing, plant-eating big guys could live on this planet.

They eat in fascinating ways. Many of them have the ability to digest compounds that other organisms cannot, performing the wizardry that transforms death back into life. They can also alter the chemical structures

There are four types of macroorganisms in soil. These creatures we can see with the naked eye (or a hand lens) are oligochaeta, arthropods, mollusks, and nematodes.

- **OLIGOCHAETA** is a biological name for worms.
- **ARTHROPODS** include mites, ants, spiders, sow bugs, centipedes, beetles, and more.
- **MOLLUSKS,** or soil mollusks, are the terrestrial relatives of the mollusks we know as sea creatures and include snails and slugs.
- **NEMATODES** are roundworms that happen to be the most numerous multicellular animal on Earth, some of which are big enough to see with the naked eye, but many of which require a microscope to be spotted.

The importance of these numerous, diverse, and sometimes mystifying creatures, micro and macro, is both in their direct impacts on plant growth and in their interrelationships with one another. Elaine Ingham, a leading expert on soil life and how it relates to agricultural productivity, coined the term *soil food web* to describe this intricate weaving between and among beings beneath the ground.

On a practical, garden level, we return to the basic concepts of *balance* and *quality*. Some soil organisms are considered beneficial, others are considered harmful, and the relative amounts of each one can determine their impact on our veggies. When we practice basic soil tending by adding and keeping organic matter, reducing soil disturbance, balancing mineral nutrients, and cultivating a diversity of plants, we are also supporting a healthy and teeming community of soil creatures.

Earthworms are the gentle giants of the soil community; many creatures who call dirt their home are too small to see with the naked eye.

of various basic elements, making those elements more available and useful to plants. Additionally, larger soil organisms open up pore space, move nutrients around in the soil, and perform similar chemical transformations as their tinier counterparts. They're small and often unseen, but the beings who live in the soil can do things that we humans cannot, things upon which we daily depend.

These tiny creatures we cannot see with the naked eye fall into one of the following categories: fungi, bacteria, archaea, protozoa, and viruses. Each category includes hundreds, possibly thousands, of species and up to a billion (or more!) individuals in every spoonful of soil.

A MEANINGFUL INFLUENCE

Elaine Ingham, PhD, was a guest lecturer when Natalie studied ecological agriculture at The Evergreen State College, and Natalie recalls how Dr. Elaine's lectures stuck with her more than any others. They still influence Natalie's approach to gardening, especially her commitment to minimizing tillage. If you're into nitty-gritty science and want to learn more, Dr. Elaine's courses are a fantastic resource.

How to Do a Soil Test and Why

One way to get to know your soil—in particular its unseeable aspects like pH, TCEC, and nutrient composition—is to send off a sample to a lab for testing. There are lots of lower-tech ways to understand your soil, too, like observing weeds, smelling the earth, and even tasting. We like to use a combination of techniques, including the laboratory soil test. It's nice to get baseline numbers from these tests and then retest every several years to track changes in your soil. For some micronutrients in particular, it can be very hard to perceive an imbalance through simple observation, and a soil test can point you in the direction of addressing these otherwise imperceptible needs, which can have big impacts.

A friend of ours who grows amazingly beautiful and abundant sweet potatoes, turmeric, and lots of other vegetables found out through a soil test that he could benefit from additional boron. He hadn't thought of this element in his many years of organic farming, compost making, cover cropping, and crop rotation. As a result of the test, he bought some borax and sprinkled a small amount on his fields. The impact was immediate and impressive: healthier, bigger, greener plants all around. Without a soil test, he would have never known.

GETTING A LABORATORY SOIL TEST

Ideal conditions for taking a soil sample are when the soil is fairly dry but not crumbly. If it has recently rained, wait a few days before taking a soil sample. If you live in a very dry area, you may want to irrigate before taking a sample, then wait a day or two after the deep watering to take the sample. Gathering the sample itself is pretty straightforward (see page 106).

What do you do with this sample bag? Most county Cooperative Extension offices will analyze soil samples for free or a small fee. You can search online: "[your county] cooperative extension service." Tests from their labs will give you some baseline data, like soil pH, nitrogen, phosphorus, and potassium levels. Depending on the state, soil tests from Extension offices may be more geared toward chemical agriculture, not organic gardening. For a more ecological approach and a test that will give you information about micronutrients, TCEC, and much more (for a small fee), Logan Labs Soil Testing Services is an excellent choice.

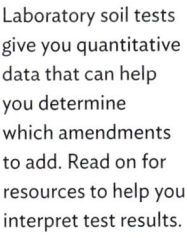

Laboratory soil tests give you quantitative data that can help you determine which amendments to add. Read on for resources to help you interpret test results.

Gathering a SOIL SAMPLE FOR TESTING

1. Remove any mulch or organic material from the soil surface.

2. Use a shovel to make a V-shaped hole about 6 inches deep.

3. Take a narrow slice of one of the sides of the V and put that soil in a clean bucket or other container. If you're testing a large area (more than 10 feet square), take multiple samples and combine them.

4. Perform the same V-hole process in several spots, adding the slices of soil to the bucket.

5. Mix these slices together evenly, then scoop out the required sample size from that blend into a sealable bag. (The lab will tell you how much to send.)

TIP: *If you want to do a lot of soil testing over a very large area, or offer the service to friends or for hire, use a soil-sampling probe or auger in steps 2 through 4. One quick twist and you have a core sample of your soil.*

Managing Fertility

Managing fertility in the garden is an ongoing process. Ideally you care for and enrich the soil in a timely and effective way so that no deficiencies arise. Ideally your plants are healthy, and, ideally, you get good yields. But things don't always go as planned, and all soils are different. In reality, you likely won't become aware of fertility issues until you notice your plants' growth seems stunted, or they are exhibiting signs of deficiency or falling prey to pests or diseases.

When do you add fertility? There are two answers: (1) as you are able, and (2) in response to plant needs at any given time. We'll give a basic overview of what to add and when here, then touch on the types of fertilizers we tend to use. See Chapter 5 for more on fertilizers and amendments.

Tip: When growing in a new area, do a soil test before you plant anything, and add needed nutrients from the beginning.

MOBILE VS. IMMOBILE NUTRIENTS

Some nutrients are very mobile in the soil, moving around easily once dissolved in water. The most notable of these are the macronutrients nitrogen and, to a lesser degree, potassium. These essential nutrients will be washed away by rain or irrigation if the soil contains more than what plants and soil life can utilize at any given moment. Therefore it's important to add only the amount needed and no more. This applies especially to nitrogen—runoff of this growth-inducing nutrient can cause serious problems downstream, as we explained on page 109.

You can mix mobile nutrients into the soil, apply them on top, or provide them through a liquid fertilizer. However you add them, they will find their way to plants' roots (unless you apply them as a foliar spray, in which case they'll be absorbed through the leaves, but this isn't best practice when it comes to adding mobile nutrients).

Other nutrients, notably phosphorus, along with numerous other minerals, are *not* mobile—they don't move through soil easily in water. These are best mixed into the soil before planting, so that they are hanging out where they're needed: in the root zone. Alternatively they can be applied through foliar sprays, which bypass the roots and go straight in through the leaves (but only small amounts of nutrients can be absorbed this way).

Fertility Needs of Various Vegetables

HEAVY FEEDERS	MEDIUM FEEDERS	LIGHTER FEEDERS	NITROGEN FIXERS
Beets	Basil	Arugula	Alfalfa
Broccoli	Carrots	Chard	Beans
Brussels sprouts	Collards and kale	Cilantro	Clover
Cabbage	Leeks	Dill	Peas
Cauliflower	Okra	Mustard greens	Peanuts
Celery	Parsnips	Radishes and daikon	Soybeans
Corn	Peppers and Chiles	Sweet potatoes	Vetch
Cucumbers	Watermelon	Turnips and rutabagas	
Eggplant			
Garlic			
Lettuce			
Muskmelons			
Onions			
Potatoes			
Spinach			
Summer squash/ zucchini			
Tomatoes			
Winter squash/ pumpkin			

Luckily, once immobile nutrients are mixed into the soil, they aren't prone to washing away quickly, so they don't need to be added very often.

See the chart below for a list of plant nutrients and their mobility in the soil.

MIXING IN FERTILITY BEFORE PLANTING

Part of preparing a bed, row, or container for planting can include adding fertility through any number of fertilizers or other amendments. If you're going to be digging or mixing anyway, it's a great time to add compost, manure, worm castings, rock powders, alfalfa meal, and other bulk materials. You may do this once every several years (as in the case of micronutrient rock powders) or each time

Can you spot the bacteria condos? Those bumps on the roots house and feed helpful microbes who transform air into plant food (pretty fancy).

The Mobilities of Plant Nutrients

NUTRIENT	MACRO/MICRO	MOBILITY IN PLANT	MOBILITY IN SOIL
Boron	Micro	Immobile	Very mobile
Calcium	Macro	Immobile	Somewhat mobile
Carbon	Macro	N/A	N/A
Chloride	Micro	Mobile	Mobile
Cobalt	Micro	Immobile	Somewhat mobile
Copper	Micro	Immobile	Immobile
Hydrogen	Macro	N/A	N/A
Iron	Micro	Immobile	Immobile
Magnesium	Macro	Somewhat mobile	Immobile
Manganese	Micro	Immobile	Mobile
Molybdenum	Micro	Immobile	Somewhat mobile
Nickel	Micro	Mobile	Somewhat mobile
Nitrogen	Macro	Mobile	Mobile as NO3-, immobile as NH4+
Oxygen	Macro	N/A	N/A
Phosphorus	Macro	Somewhat mobile	Immobile
Potassium	Macro	Very mobile	Somewhat mobile
Sulfur	Macro	Mobile	Mobile
Zinc	Micro	Immobile	Immobile

you plant (with compost, manure, or nitrogen sources).

If you use a no-till approach, most fertilizers and other amendments can be layered on top, mixed into just the top inch or so of the soil, and/or added in liquid form. Even in no-till systems, we utilize tillage every so often if we identify a deficiency of immobile nutrients that are hard to get down into the root zone without physical mixing. This is a great example of when not to be a purist about any one gardening technique. If you do till to add in immobile nutrients, the soil biology and structure will feel the shock of all that disturbance, but with care and attention it will bounce back.

FEEDING PLANTS AS THEY GROW

The best ways to feed plants as they grow are by adding liquid or solid fertilizers, or by using foliar sprays. Macronutrients can be added with liquids drenched into the soil or with solid fertilizers side-dressed and mixed into the top inch or so of soil, then watered in. Micronutrients are well absorbed through plant leaves and are appropriate for foliar sprays. See more on feeding growing plants in Chapter 6.

What Nutrients Are Needed When?
- Nitrogen is needed throughout periods of green growth, but it hinders flowering and fruiting, so it's best to apply this nutrient before flowering if the part of the plant you want to harvest is a fruit.
- Phosphorus is especially needed during fruiting and flowering, and for root development.
- Calcium is especially needed during fruiting and flowering, but it is also needed throughout the plant's life cycle.
- Potassium is needed throughout the plant's life cycle, and especially to withstand temperature shifts (cold and hot).

- Minerals and micronutrients are particularly important for a plant's defense mechanisms, so they may be indicated if pest or disease problems are present.

FERTILITY, PESTS, AND DISEASES

If you notice a pest infestation, we advise that you address fertility as well as direct pest management. Plants have their own natural defense systems, and when they're healthy and strong, pests and diseases may be present without causing a lot of damage. If plants are weak due to imbalanced fertility, which means

they don't have what they need to defend themselves (much like a human having a compromised immune system), they are more prone to issues with both insect pests and diseases. When plants are already under attack, improving fertility is not going to kill bugs or make them go away, yet it's important to address the underlying reason along with the acute condition (more on pest and disease management in Chapter 8).

When we say that addressing fertility can help prevent pest and disease problems, we mean holistic fertility: a balance of high-quality nutrients in the broad spectrum that plants need. If you overdo the macronutrients, especially nitrogen, this may inhibit natural defense systems, leading to worse pest and disease damage. Nitrogen is a powerful growth stimulant, so in the presence of too much nitrogen, plants grow larger and faster than their other systems are ready for. The unhappy result is a big, green, lush plant that is unable to produce the complex compounds required to ward off pests and diseases or to generate the complex nutrients that our bodies need and that excite our taste buds. Plants grown with an excess of nitrogen are often watery, bland, and wimpy.

HOW TO CHOOSE AMENDMENTS

When it comes to adding amendments to your soil, the options are abundant. Access and convenience are likely at the top of your list in terms of prioritizing what to use when. We have used different amendments over time, depending on what was convenient, easy, and less expensive, or what we were particularly excited about.

For many years Chloe kept farm animals and thus had access to goat, cow, and duck manure, which she happily applied to her garden. Natalie went on a big compost kick in her early 20s and used it enthusiastically on her urban garden. We have both made and applied biochar periodically, along with purchasing and using store-bought amendments.

Since we have regular access to urine (we produce it ourselves multiple times a day), it is a primary nitrogen source for our gardens (see page 131 for more on urine as an amendment), along with a monthly dose of menstrual blood, which contains loads of minerals and bioactive compounds. There is no recipe for perfect soil fertility, and as with the rest of gardening, adding in amendments will depend on the bigger systems your garden is embedded within. See the following chapter for much more detailed information about various fertilizers, including where they come from and how sustainable they are.

OVER-FERTILIZATION IN ACTION

When Natalie's daughter, Hazel, was around three years old, the two of them were tending the garden and side-dressing with feather meal (a concentrated source of nitrogen). Little Hazel loved giving "fairy dust" to the plants, and she decided to give an extra-big dose to a bed of kale. She poured a whole cup of feather meal around the base of each plant—this is a lot! soon as the nitrogen from the feather meal found its way into the soil and up into the kale plants, which didn't take long, those plants became utterly decimated by aphids. Other plants that had received a restrained dusting of feather meal from Natalie's more careful hands didn't succumb to the same sad fate. In the big picture, an enthusiastic gardener learning while doing was totally worth sacrificing those overfed kale plants!

Growing Mediums for Containers

Plants grown in containers have a smaller area for root growth than those grown in the ground, which means the growing medium (soil) you use needs to have a higher concentration of nutrients.

If your garden grows from containers, your relationship with soil will be a bit different than if you're growing in the ground. It's not a good idea to simply fill containers with garden soil; instead, create a medium that addresses the special needs of container-grown plants—hence the term *growing medium* for "soil" in container gardens, because the material may or may not contain actual soil!

Any growing medium still needs to have all of the basic properties and qualities of healthy, fertile garden soil. The conditions in containers, however, are different and more limited than in-ground beds or rows, so there are some special considerations.

FERTILITY

Soil organisms and water obviously can't travel freely from far and wide into a growing medium in a container: It's a relatively small, closed system; spacing is tighter than in the ground; and roots don't have as much room to seek nutrition. For this reason your growing medium should have relatively high fertility and/or you'll need to add fertilizer in the form of liquids and topdressing as your plants grow. All of the fertility sources mentioned in Chapter 5 can be used in container gardening. You can choose to add some to the medium itself and also use liquid amendments, or to side-dress or top-dress as plants grow. If vegetables aren't looking good in a container, the first thing to try is adding more fertility (see Chapter 5 for more on this).

DRAINAGE

Growing mediums in pots need to drain well and not get boggy. Plant roots breathe air, and impervious pots (plastic, metal, glazed ceramic/terra-cotta) don't let air in. So for healthy plants, container gardening mediums must be lighter and fluffier than in-ground garden soil. See page 118 for ingredients that help support good drainage in growing mediums. The cheapest and most accessible one is sand, though perlite and vermiculite are the most effective.

WATER-HOLDING CAPACITY

The smaller amount of growing medium in a container will dry out much faster than soil in the ground. Also, clay particles in garden soil hold on to moisture, and many growing mediums do not contain clay. So you'll need to ensure water-holding capacity in your growing medium. Even with a good blend that retains water well, you'll still need to water container gardens more often than you would plants in the ground. Adding clay to growing mediums is an option, though that can easily result in poor drainage, given such a small system. See the list on page 118 for water-holding ingredients.

WHERE TO FIND, AND HOW TO MAKE, GROWING MEDIUMS

You can purchase premixed container garden growing medium in bags or in bulk, or blend your own. Either way, adding in extra fertility will make or break a container garden.

Buying growing medium. Big-box home and garden stores offer various bagged mixes, many of which contain synthetic fertilizers. Be sure to look for an organic option if you're buying a premade mix. Here in our area, there is a landscaping mulch company that blends a growing medium and sells it by the yard. This is much more affordable than bags but requires a truck to transport each square-yard scoop. If your container gardens are on a rooftop (as is the case with Natalie's greenhouse), bags may be the best option because they are the easiest to transport.

Blending your own growing medium. To blend your own, you might source ingredients from a variety of locations, including home and garden stores, mulch yards, and mail-order gardening supply companies, depending on what's available locally. It's worth the effort to search for local sources, since growing medium is bulky, heavy, and expensive to ship.

INGREDIENT OPTIONS FOR GROWING MEDIUMS

There are a lot of materials you can add to a growing medium, and each one offers different qualities to the final mix.

Biochar. This high-carbon ingredient can improve water-holding capacity and drainage as well as provide structure for biological activity. Make sure to balance the carbon in biochar with additional nitrogen in your mix, otherwise it will "steal" nitrogen from your plants. For more about biochar, see page 129.

Coconut coir. This is basically shredded-up coconut hulls and is considered a more sustainable alternative to sphagnum peat moss, which is removed from sensitive peat bog habitats. Although coco coir offers no nutrition, it provides good structure and has sufficient water-holding capacity. When it's dry, it's hydrophobic (repels water), just like sphagnum peat moss. Once it has absorbed water, it becomes hydrophilic (attracts water) and can hold that water for a long time. Always soak coco coir before using it, and if a medium containing coco coir ever dries out, give it a long, deep watering.

Compost. Whether made from manure or plant-based, compost adds fertility, organic matter, humus, microbial life, and both water-holding capacity and drainage to growing mediums. All container gardening mixes contain compost: It's a must-add ingredient! In fact, you can use 100 percent compost as a growing medium, though that much compost may be hard to come by, and the addition of other materials to improve drainage can be helpful. For more about compost, see page 124.

Fertilizers. See Chapter 5 on fertility and fertilizers to choose which fertility sources to add to your growing medium. Be sure to add something!

Perlite and vermiculite. These naturally occurring minerals are formed under high heat and pressure in Earth's crust. Perlite goes through a process of further heating to puff it like popcorn. They're both mined, but they are abundant. Some people consider them very sustainable, while others question the mining, heating, and distribution systems. Perlite and vermiculite effectively improve both drainage and water-holding capacity of growing mediums and will be present in any premixed medium.

Pine bark fines/pine fines/soil conditioner. This is an affordable product you can find almost anywhere. It's ground-up, partially decomposed bark, a timber industry by-product. Even though most of it comes from pine trees, it's not acidic and has a near-neutral pH. This ingredient adds organic matter and can improve soil texture,

INGREDIENTS FOR GROWING MEDIUMS

COMPOST

SAND

PERLITE

COCO COIR

SYMPHONY FERTILIZER

SOIL

VERMICULITE

PEAT MOSS

WORM CASTINGS

water-holding capacity, and drainage. Like biochar, it's high in carbon (though not as high) and needs to be balanced with additional nitrogen.

Sand. This is the cheapest and easiest-to-get-hold-of option for increasing drainage in a growing medium. Be sure to use coarse or "sharp" builder's sand, not soft-edged play sand.

Soil. Garden soil can make up to 10 percent of your container gardening growing medium, but not all. Garden soil is too dense on its own and won't drain well enough for container gardening, plus you'll need to increase fertility.

Sphagnum peat moss. Peat moss is a common ingredient in premixed growing mediums and in the nursery trade. Although peat moss doesn't provide any nutritional value to plants, it's great at holding moisture and improving texture, behaving similarly to coconut coir. We don't choose to use it much because it's extracted from sensitive peat bog ecosystems in a way that is disruptive and unsustainable for those places. If you do choose to use peat moss, be aware that it's slightly acidic, so you'll want to add a liming agent (see page 138 for a list of options) to balance that. The same hydrophobic/hydrophilic rules apply to peat moss as coco coir.

Worm castings or vermicompost. Earthworm and compost worm (Red Wiggler) droppings are rich in micronutrients, biological activity, and humic acid. They improve texture and overall plant health. If you have access to worm castings/vermicompost, this material will boost your growing medium and make your plants happy. For more about worm castings, see page 124.

Garden soil feels and looks denser than growing medium for a container garden; getting your hands into the soil will help you understand your soil texture.

Recipes for
CONTAINER GARDENING MEDIUMS

A wheelbarrow and hoe are great tools for mixing up your own container garden growing medium.

CHLOE'S SUPER-ACCESSIBLE OPTION

- 1 part premoistened coconut coir
- 1 part pine bark fines (a.k.a. soil conditioner)
- 1 part worm castings/vermicompost (if not available, use more compost instead)
- 2 parts compost
- Appropriate amount of organic fertilizer (based on suggested application of whatever you're adding)

FROM ANNE GIBSON, THE MICRO GARDENER

- 1 part premoistened coconut coir
- 1 part grade 3 vermiculite or coarse sand
- 1 cup to 1 part worm castings/vermicompost (depending on availability; more is generally better)
- 2 parts sieved compost
- Appropriate amount of organic fertilizer (based on suggested application of whatever you're adding)

FROM GAYLA TRAIL, YOU GROW GIRL

- 1 part coarse (builder's) sand, grit, and/or perlite
- 1 part vermiculite (optional, but I like it for water absorption)
- 2 parts rehydrated coconut coir
- 2 parts sieved compost
- Appropriate amount of organic fertilizer (based on suggested application of whatever you're adding)

SOIL-BASED BLEND FROM PLANET NATURAL

- 5 parts peat moss or mature compost
- 5 parts clean builder's sand or perlite
- 1 part garden loam or topsoil
- Appropriate amount of organic fertilizer (based on suggested application of whatever you're adding)

CHALLENGES OF USING MANURE IN THE GARDEN

Excess phosphorus. One challenge with using manure and manure-based fertilizers year after year is that manure has a higher P:N ratio than plants need. Also, phosphorus (P) is less mobile in the soil than nitrogen (N), so you may see a soil buildup of phosphorus over time. Excess phosphorus can inhibit plant growth, so regular soil testing is the best way to keep track of this (we do a soil test every three to five years).

A good way to prevent a buildup of phosphorus in the first place is to alternate between manures and plant-based nitrogen fertilizers, such as alfalfa meal and legume cover crops, nonmanure animal sources like urine (yes, human urine, which we will address below), feather meal and blood meal, or fish emulsion. This diversity tips the scales in the direction of balance, along with providing a broader spectrum of nutrients. Here's an example of how this might look in practice: You apply animal manure for three consecutive years, skip a year or two and use one of the other nitrogen sources just mentioned, then go back to using manure again after the break.

Pathogens. All manure is rich in microorganisms, some that are beneficial and others that are harmful. The harmful guys, called pathogens, can make you sick. Most pathogens break down during the composting process and with exposure to ultraviolet light (sunlight). Methods for aging or composting manure can help with destroying them (see page 125 for more).

Weed seeds. Some manures contain viable weed seeds. The most likely culprit for these unwelcome hitchhikers is horse manure, since these animals only have a single-chambered stomach and they eat lots of plants and their seeds. Even ruminants (cows, goats, sheep, llamas), who have multichambered stomachs, can sometimes pass weed seeds unscathed in their manure. If you're getting manure from a new source, we suggest spreading some in a pot or tray and watering it to take an inventory of the weed-seed bank. It can be a major bummer to bring in nutrient-rich manure full of weed seeds, especially thorny or otherwise noxious weeds, such as Chloe's nemesis, spiny amaranth. If the inventory shows you a lot of nasty weeds, better to pass on that particular manure. If it's weedy, but the weeds are more benign (like clovers

HANDLE THIS MANURE WITH CARE

One exception to the idea that basic composting takes care of pathogens in manure is with swine/pig manure (and, to some degree, human manure). These species can carry pathogens that persist even after composting. It's ideal to let pig and people poop age for at least two years before applying them to a garden. We would only use these types of manure on perennials like trees and shrubs, where they don't make direct contact with the part of the plant that we eat. For more on using "humanure" or "night soil" safely, check out *The Humanure Handbook: A Guide to Composting Human Manure* by Joseph Jenkins.

and grasses) you can apply the manure and plan to wait long enough before planting to make one or two passes over the area with a stirrup hoe to kill most of those baby weed plants. Be sure that you irrigate enough to sprout the seeds, unless it rains sufficiently.

Persistent herbicides. If you can locate manure from organically raised animals, that's ideal! If not, it's worth inquiring what kinds of herbicides were used on anything that the animals have eaten (pasture, hay, other feeds).

One class of herbicides in particular can persist even through the composting process: pyridine carboxylic acids. These include all herbicide products containing active ingredients in the pyridine family, especially aminocyclopyrachlor, aminopyralid, clopyralid, and picloram. If these come into your garden with manure, your vegetable growth can become extremely stunted, or you may even have a barren garden, and this problem can persist for years. At this writing, the following products contain these toxic compounds:

- Curtail
- Forefront
- GrazonNext
- Grazon P&D
- Milestone
- Redeem R&P
- Surmount

A REAL-LIFE EXAMPLE OF TAINTED MANURE

Two of our neighbors got loads of beautiful-looking, nicely composted horse manure from a trusted source that many folks had used in the past. Manure from this stable had always been fine, enriching Natalie's and others' garden soil over the years. These neighbors spread the manure on annual beds—in which they planted peas, kale, carrots, and other seasonal crops—and around raspberry bushes, excited for spring gardening. After a week or two, the raspberries and kale were looking weird, not growing well, and few of the other seeds had germinated; those that had were not thriving or were looking unhealthy.

The neighbors convened and confirmed that the problem was happening for both parties, and it seemed to be connected with the manure. To figure out what was going on, they called the stable and did some detective work. It turned out that the horses had been eating hay from a new source, one that involved a pyridine-based herbicide. A little more research revealed that this compound harms plants in almost all botanical families, heavily limiting what might grow in the beds where the manure had been applied. Several other members of our extended community started mentioning the same problem, and, fortunately, started troubleshooting together on solutions like planting sunflowers and corn that could grow in the toxic situation and would pull the poison into their plant bodies, later to be thrown into the trash.

Up until this point, the idea of getting poisoned manure had been just that, an idea. Having this direct experience and setting eyes on the plants and gardens impacted by it was a wake-up call. If Natalie hadn't phased out of using manure on her garden in favor of cover cropping a few years prior, she would have been in the same boat. The problems caused by life-destroying chemicals are not just "out there" but also can come very close to home.

RIGHT: Pee can really perk up your garden. It's our favorite no-cost organic amendment, and it's really easy to use: Just mix with water and apply.

Then there's the ick factor. This gets in the way for many gardeners who otherwise would love a free and effective fertilizer source. If you're grossed out by using pee as a fertilizer, think about where your other fertilizers come from. Chemical fertilizers are mostly made from fossil fuels, and their manufacture produces climate-warming gases; manure is poop; fish emulsion is basically a dead fish smoothie; alfalfa meal and other vegan fertilizers require lots of energy and machinery to produce. The bottom line: Death and decay and metabolic waste products are what fuel life on this planet. Embracing the beauty of these cycles can turn the "ick factor" into an "awe factor."

HOW TO USE URINE IN THE GARDEN

Adults produce between 100 and 150 gallons of urine per year, containing about 9 pounds of nitrogen and 0.8 pound of phosphorus. As a reference, this amount of fertilizer can grow enough wheat for a loaf of bread every day of the year. The urine our households produce and use in our gardens creates more than enough nitrogen to satisfy the needs of our vegetables. Depending on the size of your garden, you may not need to import any other nitrogen and phosphorus sources. Urine, however, does not replace the important roles of organic matter and mineral-rich amendments, such as kelp or borax, when they're needed (see page 105).

Pee carefully and don't go overboard! As with any nitrogen-containing fertilizer, you don't want to overdo it with urine and end up polluting groundwater. Any amount of water-soluble nitrogen that isn't taken up by green growing plants will wash away. Only use pee on plants that are *already* green and growing (not on germinating seeds, tiny seedlings, or plants that have moved into their fruiting stages).

Pour directly on soil. The easiest way to apply urine is as a soil drench (meaning something poured, or peed, directly onto moist soil). If your soil is dry, dilute the urine with water. Chloe generally favors a 1:1 ratio, while Natalie tends to dilute more, with a 1:3 or 1:5 ratio. Alternatively, you can irrigate immediately after application. If you want to foliar feed with urine, which Natalie likes to do, dilute it to about 10 parts water per 1 part urine.

Note: Never spray undiluted urine directly on the leaves or stems of plants, but rather pour it into the soil about 4 inches from the base of the plant's stem. An appropriate application rate is about 5 gallons per 100 square feet over the course of the growing season. We have never measured this out, as we tend to have fairly large gardens (harder to overdo it) and just apply pee to green growing plants throughout their growth cycle.

Store-Bought Fertilizers and Amendments

There are a whole lot of options when it comes to store-bought fertilizers and amendments. Big-box home and garden centers sell premixed options, whereas more specialized farm and garden stores (online and brick-and-mortar) offer a dizzying array of specific single and mixed amendments. If you happen to live in an area where cannabis cultivation is common, you'll have no trouble finding lots of fancy and specific amendments for your garden veggies (or whatever you want to grow). The cultivation of high-yielding, high-value cannabis usually involves a lot of specialized inputs, so "grow stores" around these operations are usually very well stocked.

For most gardens, using a premixed, general-purpose organic fertilizer will work just fine, in combination with soil-building practices like mulching, making and adding compost, crop rotation, cover crops, and more. If you've had a chance to do a soil test and get your results, you'll have great information on which to base a more personalized amendment plan.

WHERE DO FERTILIZERS COME FROM?

Every product you buy to put into your garden comes from somewhere! Just because it's natural and/or organic doesn't mean that it's a wholly safe and sustainable option. Just because manure, bonemeal, and blood meal are approved for use on organic agriculture doesn't mean that the practices used to produce those materials were organic or humane.

Fertilizers are often animal-based. Many organic fertilizers and amendments come from manures and manure-derived materials, and others are the by-products of the meat and egg industries. On the one hand, industrial animal agriculture can be extremely inhumane and polluting. On the other, purchasing and using agriculture waste products recycles the valuable materials that they are while also being a great help in the garden.

Depending on your personal values and lifestyle, animal-based products may or may not be right for you. Some products explicitly detail what kind of animal operation they come from, while others are more opaque about their specific sources. Harmony and Symphony fertilizers are examples of poultry manure–based products that can be tracked back to a medium-scale, family-run egg operation in New York State.

Plant-based fertilizers aren't always environmentally "green." Plant-derived ingredients in store-bought fertilizers often come from large-scale industrial operations, which have their own not-so-great ecological and social impacts.

Additionally, some plant derivatives have vastly different impacts, depending on whether they were sourced organically or not. Alfalfa meal, for example, is usually genetically modified if it's not organic, resulting in huge herbicide applications and other negative impacts due to its production. Whether organic or GMO, alfalfa production is water intensive and requires fossil fuels and heavy machinery on a large scale. This is just one example.

Rock powders are finite. Some mineral amendments are simply powdered rocks that are high in those minerals. These are often mined and have varying degrees of sustainability. Rock phosphate, for example, is extremely prevalent in organic agriculture, but it's a finite resource from mines with heavy ecological impacts. Plus, rock powders are heavy! Shipping these amendments leaves a huge carbon footprint.

Do your research. When choosing what to add to your garden, we encourage you to

Plants need nitrogen to produce chlorophyll, the pigment that makes them green and plays a key role in photosynthesis.

dig into where the various options come from and make an informed decision about what to buy. You should be able to source many, if not all, of your garden amendments fairly locally and/or make them yourself. If you do purchase things, be sure to use them appropriately and store them carefully so that you can honor the embodied energy and stories they contain.

GENERAL-PURPOSE FERTILIZERS

There is an abundance of general-purpose fertilizers, or fertilizer blends, on the market. If an organic fertilizer of your choice contains between 3 and 5 percent of the macronutrients, it will probably work well. Look for those three numbers on the front of the package or in the description, formatted like this: 4-3-3 (N-P-K, or nitrogen-phosphorus-potassium, in that order).

Other promising and beneficial qualities to look for:

- Slow release
- Presence of calcium, magnesium, and micronutrients
- Presence of biological agents like mycorrhizal spores, beneficial bacteria, and humic and fulvic acids
- OMRI certified, meaning it's approved for use in organic production

NITROGEN FERTILIZERS

Nitrogen is crucial for green growth of all plants. Choose a slow-release option to mix in while preparing beds or containers, or a fast-release option for feeding already growing plants.

For more information on specific nutrient sources, follow the link to our website found on page 364 and check out the Organic Amendment User's Guide from Grow Abundant Gardens.

Alfalfa meal. Good source of all three macronutrients (N, P, and K), plus calcium, micronutrients, and biostimulants (hormone-like growth-inducing compounds); slow release; good stuff, but fairly expensive. Choose organic instead of nonorganic; it's usually genetically modified (GM) if not certified as organic.

Bat guano. Concentrated source of N and P; specific amounts of macronutrients depend on the bats' diet; mined from naturally occurring deposits (beneath bats' sleeping spots); may provide fungicidal and nematicidal properties (can kill fungi and nematodes); fast release; expensive but very effective.

Blood meal. Concentrated source of N; raises soil pH (alkaline); by-product of beef and pork industries; fast release, can burn plants if applied directly to them; mix in right before planting, or side-dress without touching plant stems.

THE DOWNSIDES OF COTTONSEED MEAL IN FERTILIZER

Cottonseed meal, a popular addition to fertilizer, is rarely available from organic cotton production and is likely to contain significant amounts of pesticide and herbicide residues. To get cotton ready for machine harvest, it's standard practice to spray the field heavily with the herbicide glyphosate (Roundup) to kill every plant that isn't cotton. Add to this the labor and water intensiveness of cotton production, plus the prevalence of unfair labor practices in this industry (historically and today), and it may not be a product you want to invite into your gardening life.

Cottonseed meal. Good source of N and P; rarely available organic, most often GMO; tends to have heavy pesticide residues; lowers pH of soil (acid); slow release. See sidebar.

Feather meal. Fairly affordable concentrated source of N; by-product of poultry industry; semi-slow release.

Fish fertilizer (meal or liquid). Good source of N and P in plant-available forms; stimulates biological activity in soils; slow release in meal form, fast release in liquid form; smells fishy; more and more likely to contain microplastics and other toxins that are polluting global oceans.

Prepared poultry manure pellets. Good source of N, P, and K, plus calcium, iron, and some micronutrients; by-product of egg industry; semi-slow release; some products come from organic egg production (Symphony brand), others from nonorganic egg production (Harmony brand), others from broiler operations are less ideal because they contain bedding material.

Soybean meal. High levels of N and K; slow release, takes a while to break down and is best applied pre-planting; choose organic or non-GMO instead of "conventional" GMO.

PHOSPHORUS FERTILIZERS

Phosphorus (P) is especially important for flowering, fruiting, and the development of roots. Most sources are slow release and dependent on soil biology to become available to plants.

Bonemeal (steamed). By-product of commercial red meat industry; very effective, fast-release source of P; also a significant source of calcium and sodium; dust is caustic and harmful to breathe or get on skin. (*Note:* Natalie loves to use this for her onions and garlic.)

Fertoz rock phosphate. Derived from rock phosphate; faster release and more available than regular rock phosphate; lower in heavy metals.

and storing soluble nutrients that would leave the system if the soil were exposed and unplanted. Decomposing bodies of cover crops offer not just more nutrients but more *readily available* nutrients to the next generation of crops that follow them.

Cover crops physically protect your soil. Organisms and nutrients in soil prefer darkness and dampness. When soil is exposed to air and light, it dries out and heats up easily; it then undergoes a fairly rapid loss of nutrients and a dramatic slowing of biological activity. Not to mention that exposed soil (absent of food crops, cover crops, or mulch) is basically a nicely prepared garden bed for existing weed seeds or those that arrive on the wind. Some wild weeds can be used as cover crops (Natalie loves chickweed as a winter cover crop, for example), but most are not suitable for this job. They can easily take over, are harder to kill than cultivated cover crops, may not grow as large, and don't necessarily have the same soil-building properties. See pages 213 and 221 for more on weeds and mulching.

HOW TO WORK WITH COVER CROPS

Cover cropping can be pretty spectacular in terms of soil building and weed management; it can also be a royal pain in the rear if poorly managed.

Keys to Cover-Cropping Success
- Choose the right cover crops for your situation.
- Nail the timing of each step.
- Be ready with the appropriate equipment for termination (and incorporation, if you go that route).

Consider Your Situation
There's an expansive range of choices for cover crops. Their unique and wonderful characteristics can be of real benefit to your soil, your garden overall, and the nutrient

density of what you harvest. So that making a choice doesn't become overwhelming, here are things to think about when deciding what to plant.

Different cover crops have different benefits. The table on pages 142 and 143 should be a good starting point. Definitely take a little time to go deeper to find out more about a particular crop's compatibility with your location and your goals for your garden. Some cover crops are legumes, for example, and collaborate with soilborne bacteria to "fix" nitrogen, which adds fertility to the soil (more about this on page 112). Others have roots that secrete compounds, or exudates, that kill soilborne pathogens and pests and/or suppress the germination of weed seeds. Some cover crops do a great job of scavenging nutrients that would otherwise be washed away or unavailable, and others break up compacted soil with vigorous and extensive root systems. It's empowering to move forward equipped with the clear knowledge of why, when, and where you're planting a particular cover crop.

Austrian winter peas are one of our favorite cover crops: They fix nitrogen, they're delicious to nibble, and they coexist nicely with other cover crops.

Common Cover Crops

Below you'll find a range of common cover crops and their important characteristics. Note that "winter" cover crops are planted in fall; some need time to get established before the frost comes, and others do not.

CROP NAME	WHEN TO PLANT	TIME UNTIL HARVEST	CHALLENGES
Austrian winter peas	Early to midfall	Overwinter (until April or May)	Sometimes very vigorous, sometimes wimpy. Can flop over if grown on its own. Doesn't always survive very cold or highly variable winter temperatures.
Buckwheat	Late spring into midsummer	30–45 days or until frost kill	Will readily self-sow if allowed to mature to seed. Shorter stature and shorter season than other cover crops. Not at all frost tolerant.
Chickweed	Fall or early spring	Not a traditional cover crop; 40–50 days or until it gets too hot	Seeds not available in volume for purchase, so you'll need to cultivate from wild populations. Can transplant from a location where it grows as a "weed," then allow it to go to seed. (We let it seed before removing to make sure it comes back the following fall.)
Cowpeas/ blackeyed peas	Late spring through early summer	65–85 days or until frost kill	Very viny and sprawly—will smother or topple other less-sturdy cover crops. Not at all frost tolerant. Can attract deer, turkeys, and other wild critters.
Crimson clover	Spring, late summer, or early fall	Varies depending on when planted	Not as winter hardy as some other cover crops (down to 0°F/–17°C).
Hairy vetch	Early fall into late fall (can be planted during early frosts)	Overwinter (until April or May)	Not as winter hardy as some other cover crops (down to 5°F/–15°C).
Oats	Early spring or late summer	50–60 days or until frost kill	Freezing will kill oats. Likes cool but not cold conditions (getting the timing right depends on your climate).
Rapeseed and yellow mustard	Early spring or late summer	50–60 days or until frost kill	Not as winter hardy as some other cover crops (down to 5°F/–15°C).
Sorghum-Sudan grass	Late spring into midsummer	60 days or until frost kill	Grows best with very warm/hot temperatures. Very dense and very hard to kill before a frost. Roots exude sorgoleone, a strong allelopathic substance that can inhibit germination of subsequent crops if they're sown right after sorghum Sudan grass. If allowed to set seeds, it can self-sow and become a weed.
Tillage radish and daikon	Fall	Overwinter or until frost kill	Not as winter hardy as some other cover crops (down to 15°F/9°C).
Turnip	Fall	Overwinter or until frost kill	Not as winter hardy as some other cover crops (down to 0°F/–17°C).
White clover	Spring or fall	Long-term cover crop	Not as robust as crimson clover. Does not like to be sown in the heat of summer.
Winter rye/ rye grass	Early fall into late fall (can be planted during early frosts)	Overwinter (until April or May)	Can be challenging to terminate; very important to kill when in flower. Exudes compounds that inhibit germination of other kinds of seeds (allelopathic). Ideally wait at least 1 month after killing rye to plant other crops.

SPECIAL CHARACTERISTICS	COMBINE WITH
Nitrogen fixer (legume). Tasty for humans as pea shoots in early spring. Hardy between 0 and –10°F (–17 to –23°C) but sensitive to temperature fluctuations (won't survive past about 10°F/–12°C if the temp is erratic). Easy to terminate.	Hairy vetch, rape, tillage radish, turnip, winter rye. Easier to harvest and eat when it's the dominant cover crop in a mix.
Attracts and feeds pollinators. Allelopathic action suppresses weed growth. Very fast to grow and cover when temps are warm; accumulates insoluble phosphorus for release to plants later. Wonderful on its own to fill a space for a short time or to add to a mix to give shelter to slower-germinating seeds.	Works well alone or in combination with cowpeas, millet, sorghum–Sudan grass, sunflowers, and sunn hemp. Can be mixed lightly into an early-planted fall cover-crop mixture.
This weed is one of our favorite cover crops! Incredibly nourishing for soil when terminated as it goes to seed (before it becomes long and spindly). Works well with fungal networks to create impressive mycorrhizae in the top 1½ inches of soil. Delicious, nutritious edible. To harvest: Best mowed with scissors, and keep from going to seed. Does not grow in the heat.	When it comes up with other winter cover crops, we leave it instead of weeding.
Nitrogen fixer (legume). Viny and sprawly, so covers a lot of ground and will climb other sturdy cover crops like a trellis. Drought tolerant. Can be attractive to deer and game birds.	Works well alone or with sorghum–Sudan grass, sunflowers, sunn hemp.
Nitrogen fixer (legume). Makes beautiful magenta flower spikes in spring, which attract and feed pollinators.	Austrian winter peas, vetch, winter rye
Very beautiful in growth and in flower! Nitrogen fixer (legume). Viny growth pairs well with taller plants like winter rye. Produces a large amount of biomass in the right conditions.	Austrian winter peas, crimson clover, winter rye
Germinates well in cool, moist soil. An herbal medicine plant for the nervous system: Use immature seeds in the "milky" stage for tincture, and oat straw for tea.	We usually plant oats on their own or alongside a spring planting of Austrian winter peas.
Mustard acts as a biofumigant, helping to reduce soil pathogens like harmful nematodes.	Austrian winter peas, crimson clover, tillage radish, vetch, winter rye
Grows quickly and generates an impressive amount of biomass. Exudes sorgoleone, a strong allelopathic substance that can inhibit weed-seed germination and reduce soilborne pests and pathogens; can provide support for floppy/viny cover crops like cowpeas. Extremely heat tolerant and quite drought tolerant.	Works well alone or with cowpeas, sunflowers, and sunn hemp.
Produces biotoxins that reduce soilborne pests and pathogens; big deep taproot injects biomass, breaks up soil, and scavenges nitrogen.	Austrian winter peas, crimson clover, rapeseed/mustard, vetch, winter rye
Great producer of biomass; breaks up soil by injecting biomass deep into soil. Surprisingly good at growing in marginal places.	Vetch, white clover, winter pea
White clover is a great option if you want a break between growing crops in a given area. It can hold its own against weeds for up to 2 years.	If sowed with light covers (not winter rye), it can persist (if desired).
Very easy to germinate, even in relatively cool temperatures. Very cold hardy (–30°F/–34°C once it's established). Grows fast and thick, creates a lot of biomass. Makes great mulch if harvested before it makes seeds. Exudes compounds that inhibit weed-seed germination. Protects and supports some other cover crops; can inhibit growth of others. Keep the percentage of this seed low in a mix, or it will dominate.	Austrian winter peas, crimson clover, hairy vetch

A diversity of cover crops benefits the soil food web. Each type of cover crop has a unique relationship with the soil microbiome, providing nourishment and structure for billions of organisms within their root systems. While many of these relationships are yet to be fully understood, it's generally agreed that a diversity of species ensures diversity in the soil—and soil loves diversity! Refer to the table on page 142 for help with a diverse approach to cover-crop planting.

Consult your local Cooperative Extension agent. Or talk to your local farmers. Keep in mind that larger-scale growers usually work with tractors, so they can just chop and till in cover crops to terminate them—a process that may or may not be applicable to your garden. Many garden stores and seed companies offer cover-crop mixes for different times of year. These can be great, but they can also include species that may be hard to terminate with your equipment, so

be sure to read the list of what's included before sowing a mix.

Consider starting with the most forgiving cover crops. These cover crops are pretty easy to terminate and aren't a big bother if they end up dropping seeds and becoming "weeds." Other species (see the table on page 142) can be tricky to kill and/or can turn into challenging weeds if accidentally allowed to mature and drop seeds. They all, however, have their advantages and appropriate applications, so don't be afraid to experiment!

The Most Forgiving Cover Crops
- Austrian winter peas (cool season)
- Buckwheat (warm season, short-lived)
- Cowpeas/blackeyed peas (warm season, longer lived)
- Tillage radish/daikon (cool season)

Plant multiple cover crops together. There can be advantages to planting some cover crops alone, but we usually plant them in combination. Leguminous cover crops fix more nitrogen when they are planted in the company of non-leguminous plants that draw nitrogen from the soil. Combinations of cover crops are generally better for the soil and increase biodiversity, but they also require more complex management.

Natalie has approached this in two ways, by planting:

1. Two or more cover crops that have similar life cycles, so they can all be terminated when in flower around the same time.

2. One cover crop that is faster to germinate and grows taller, along with one or more shorter cover crops. The taller crop shelters those beneath it, and then is ideally mowed while it's flowering to give the understory crop(s) time to grow.

The first of these options is relatively straightforward, and we do it a lot. One typical pairing for overwinter or into winter includes Austrian winter peas with a brassica (rape, turnip, or tillage radish), plus wild chickweed, if it happens

Hairy vetch (purple flowers) is viney, while oats (straight stalks) grow upright; they don't get in each other's way and offer complementary benefits.

WHAT CAN I COMPOST?

We get asked this question a lot. The answer, broadly, is all kinds of organic matter, including meat, bones, cardboard, compostable plastics, and more. In reality, your method of composting and the environment where you're composting will rule out some inputs. Every system can readily receive kitchen scraps, leaves, small twigs, weeds, grass clippings, eggshells, and animal bedding. Let's look at potential ingredients more closely.

A balance of "browns" and "greens." An ideal ratio is two-thirds browns to one-third greens.

- *Browns* refers to dry, carbon-rich materials, including dry leaves, straw, small twigs, wood chips, shredded cardboard, and more.
- *Greens* refers to moist, nitrogen-rich materials, including food scraps, fresh grass clippings, weeds that are still green, and other organic matter with similar qualities.

Human food (but be mindful of attracting critters). Adding meat, bones, cooked food scraps, and dairy products to your compost pile may attract critters like rats, raccoons, possums, or even bears. The truth is, these venerable opportunists may come for rotten tomatoes and apple cores, too, but animal products seem to draw them in with more enthusiasm. Depending on your situation, building a critter-proof compost system may behoove you. Also, adding plenty of browns after sumptuous human foods can help balance things out, reduce smells, and, to some degree, deter critters.

Cardboard and compostable foodware. Cardboard and so-called compostable to-go containers and plastics may incorporate easily into your home compost, or they may require the super-high heat of industrial composting to completely break down; their actual compostability varies, with cardboard and paper products breaking down more easily and biodegradable plastics taking longer. There's no harm in adding these to your compost system, as long as you won't be bothered if they happen to be in their original form when the rest of the compost is ready to use. And, like anything in your compost, the more you break down or tear up cardboard and compostable foodware before you add them,

The majority of the "composting" we do happens in the garden beds themselves. When we grow and smother cover crops or add thick layers of organic mulch, we are using a lower-labor way to create compost right where it's needed!

the more easily they'll break down during the composting process.

Garden vegetables and weeds. These are welcome ingredients to any compost system . . . with a few caveats. Many plant pathogens (diseases) aren't killed until temperatures reach over 140°F (60°C), and only the big hot mound method or extra-speedy three-bin system (discussed below) are capable of achieving that. Also, to kill weed seeds, you need that same high heat factor. Taking these facts into consideration:

- If a plant shows signs of disease, burn it, or bag it and toss it in the trash.
- If you put a bunch of mature weeds into a three-bin system or a compost tumbler, or a hot mound that doesn't get turned enough, you may end up sowing those weeds as you spread the resulting compost. When in doubt, add young weeds only!

Hay and animal bedding. These can be great additions, but be sure they don't contain persistent herbicides. If you're getting hay, animal bedding, or composted manure, remember to ask about any sprays that have been used.

See page 128 to read how persistent herbicide in a composted manure supply affected gardens in our community during the writing of this book. The damage will take some effort and ingenuity to remediate. Even though used animal bedding has more of the bedding and less of the poop than a load of manure, it's still worth being cautious here. And return to page 128 for a refresher about which products currently leave persistent chemicals in the soil.

If your hay producer or rancher uses any of those products, or if they have fed their animals hay that was sprayed with them, you don't want their hay, bedding, or manure.

Other compost feedstocks. The following can be added specifically to improve the quality of the finished compost rather than as a way to dispose of the materials themselves.

- Biochar
- Clay (in small amounts)
- Finished compost
- Garden soil
- Granite dust
- Microbial inoculants (intended specifically for compost)
- Micronutrient sources like kelp powder, Azomite, or Sea-90

DOES COMPOST HAVE TO STINK?

One challenge that many gardeners face, especially those in urban or suburban settings, is that compost piles can be pretty stinky! The good news is that they don't have to be. We're not trying to give you the impression that a pile of decomposing organic matter can be odorless or smell like roses—compost will

---

KEEP IT MOIST (BUT NOT TOO MOIST)

A compost pile should be (and stay) about as moist as a squeezed-out sponge. To maintain this moisture level, you may need to water your compost, or you may need to put a roof on it, depending on the climate in which you live. Water is crucial for all of the biological magic that makes compost compost. But more is not better in this situation: Too much moisture can slow composting down and cause anaerobic (without oxygen) decomposition, which creates stinky compost, doesn't produce the same plant-feeding qualities, and is definitely not what we're going for. See the facing page for how to remedy this.

Finished compost (left) doesn't look or smell anything like the rotting veggies and other ingredients that went into it; it's dark, spongy, and sweet-smelling.

have some amount of smell—but it doesn't have to be disgusting. (We even sometimes like it.)

One of the reasons poop smells like poop is because the environment inside the intestines is anaerobic—there's no air in there. Anaerobic decomposition involves different organisms and processes than aerobic (oxygenated) decomposition. When compost doesn't have enough air, usually due to too much moisture, it can definitely smell like poop. The easiest way to remedy this? Balance any moist additions you make with dry, brown materials like dried leaves, straw, or even shredded paper or cardboard. Also, in rainy places like our mountains, covering a compost pile or bin with a tarp or other impervious covering can prevent it from getting waterlogged. Balance is key!

WHEN IS COMPOST READY TO USE?

Finished compost is dark brown, is fairly uniform in size with most particles at ½ inch or less in diameter, and has a sweet or neutral smell. Most importantly, it's not gross. Aside from some remaining large pieces of feedstocks—like bones, eggshells, or sticks—most of the material should be unrecognizably transformed by the original magicians: microbes, air, water, heat, and time.

How quickly compost finishes will also depend on what system you use. We'll go into our recommendations in a moment, but for now, know that two methods—the three-bin system and the tumbler—have a built-in rhythm of doneness. The third system, the big hot mound method, will require you to use your senses to decide when it's ready, though this isn't a tricky thing once you've begun to build a relationship with the qualities of finished compost. If you let your compost cure

How to Use a THREE-BIN COMPOST SYSTEM

In this system, the compost goes from bin to bin to bin. The timing of each move will depend on the condition of the compost in each bin and how quickly each is filled. This method is great for the quantity of kitchen and yard waste produced by one to three households.

1. NEW MATERIAL   2. BREAKING DOWN   3. WELL ROTTED

1. **LAY SOME STICKS OR BRANCHES** down at the bottom of bin 1 (the far left bin). This will allow air to enter into the compost from below as materials get piled on.

2. **LAYER GREEN MATERIALS** on top of the branches. This includes kitchen scraps, grass clippings, crops that are done producing, and more.

3. **ADD A LAYER OF BROWN MATERIALS** on top of the greens. Layer enough straw, small twigs, shredded cardboard, dry leaves, wood chips, and more to cover the green layer.

4. **OPTIONAL: SPRINKLE SOME WATER** atop the brown layer. Do this if your environment is very dry or your greens are not very moist.

5. **REPEAT STEPS 2, 3, AND 4.** Continue this layering process until bin 1 is full. This will likely take 2 to 6 weeks.

6. **ONCE BIN 1 IS FULL,** turn its contents into bin 2. Leave the base layer of sticks in bin 1 behind. Use a pitchfork to do this, adding moisture as you go if the mixture seems dry.

7. **BEGIN THE PROCESS ANEW** in bin 1. Repeat steps 2 through 5.

8. **WHEN BIN 1 IS FULL (AGAIN),** transfer the contents of bin 2 into bin 3. Add water as needed. Then move the contents of bin 1 into bin 2, also moistening if needed.

ONCE ALL THREE BINS ARE FULL, the contents of bin 3 should be ready to use. If not, empty bin 3 into a pile on the ground next to it and move the contents of the other bins one bin to the right. Wait until the pile on the ground seems finished before using the compost (probably another round of filling and emptying).

Quick Compost Alternative

If you're feeling energetic and want to speed up the decomposition process in a three-bin system, you can do this expedited version. It yields finished compost more quickly, but it requires more labor.

1. **FILL BIN 1,** then turn contents into bin 2. Follow the instructions in steps 1 through 6.

2. **DEPOSIT NEW MATERIAL** into bin 1 and turn bin 2 contents into bin 3. Let the contents of bin 3 heat up (this will take approximately 2 to 5 days), then turn it back into bin 2.

3. **LET IT GET HOT AGAIN,** then return it to bin 3. Flip-flop contents back and forth from bin 2 to bin 3 every 3 to 6 days, until compost is finished. Usually this takes about as long as bin 1 needs to completely fill again, depending on your household's compost production.

We don't espouse much plastic stuff, but compost tumblers are pretty useful, especially if you have issues with critters getting into your compost or you have limited space.

from a couple of weeks up to a month or two before using it, you give it the chance to get fully colonized with beneficial microbes. If compost hangs out for too long, these organisms will use up the food that's available to them and die or move on.

THREE SYSTEMS FOR MAKING COMPOST

There are many ways to make compost; here we present three methods. The three-bin system and compost tumblers are great for receiving small amounts of organic waste regularly over time. These methods don't usually generate the heat that the big hot mound style can, so they aren't as effective at killing weed seeds or pathogenic organisms. They also take longer (three to six months minimum) to produce a significant amount of finished, usable compost.

The big hot mound style, in contrast, requires a large volume of organic matter inputs all at once, and it involves physically turning the pile several times throughout the process. This more active approach to composting generates a lot of heat (Chloe has some friends who roasted a turkey—wrapped in foil—in a pile like this!). It can also produce finished compost in as little as a month or two.

As you read over the steps for these three ways to make compost, engage your holistic-thinking mind to help you choose a system that works for you. Brainstorm your goals, clarify your resources, and get honest about your limitations around making compost. *Hint:* Time, space, and materials are significant factors here.

The Three-Bin System

This is one of the simplest composting systems you can easily create yourself.

The bins can be constructed out of recycled pallets. You can use whatever materials you have access to, of course; however, pallet dimensions are perfect, as each bin should

be about 3½ to 4 feet square. You can use metal T-posts and wire or screws to attach the pallets together to form one long rectangular structure that's open on the front side and divided into three bays. Be sure to allow space for a pile of straw, hay, leaves, or other brown covering material (see page 149) next to the three bins. If you aren't using pallets, construct a similar shape (and size, if possible) with what you've got.

Compost Tumblers

Plastic tumblers—self-contained systems that are easy to turn, usually with a crank arm—are a great option for making compost in small spaces and/or to avoid rodent issues. Natalie used this system when she had a temporary rat problem. When she got rid of compost that was accessible to rats—and did some trapping—the rats dissipated. Making compost in a tumbler employs all of the same basic composting principles as the three-bin system: greens and browns, moisture, ideal inputs, and so forth. Just as with other systems, you should always add browns after each addition of kitchen scraps or

whatever other juicy stuff you're composting in tumblers.

Tumblers come in a variety of sizes and qualities, with prices to match. (Natalie likes the Lifetime brand, though there are many good options out there.) These systems aren't cheap and are challenging to construct using scavenged or reused materials, though Natalie has seen some made of repurposed plastic barrels.

Benefits of Compost Tumblers

Tumblers have enough benefits overall to make them worth the expense:

- They prevent rodents and other critters from getting into your compost.
- They take up less space than a three-bin system or big hot mound.
- If you produce a low volume of yard and garden waste, tumblers are ideal.
- Composting in tumblers progresses quite quickly when the weather is warm, keeping up with the pace of inputs.
- A good tumbler is mounted on a sturdy base, spins fairly easily, has a crank arm, and is easy to turn, making it realistic for you to turn it regularly (resulting in a quicker, more oxygenated process of decomposition).

Challenges of Compost Tumblers

There are some potential challenges to think through before deciding if going the tumbler route is right for you:

- They can't fit a large amount of organic material.
- They'll need to be turned at least a couple of times a day.
- It may be tricky to remove finished compost.

Tumblers don't take up a lot of space (a plus!), but they also can't intake a high volume of organic material. So in cold winter climates, these containers can fill up more quickly than the materials break down, creating a backup. Having a tumbler with two compartments or two tumblers will help, because if you are always adding compost to just one tumbler, the compost will never be finished.

Your tumbler will need turning at least a couple of times each day (even when you're not adding materials), so putting it in a well-traveled area will make it much more convenient for you.

When unloading compost from a tumbler, you can't simply pitch finished compost into a wheelbarrow—the tumbler has a mechanical opening from which you'll need to dump or scoop the compost. Moisture and/or bits of compost can get clogged in the opening's mechanisms, so take a close look at that part of a tumbler before you buy to decide if it's the right system for you to work with on a daily basis.

Big Hot Mound Style

One system for making a lot of compost quickly is what we call the "big hot mound style." It's pretty much exactly what it sounds like: You make one big mound *after* accumulating lots of materials rather than adding to a pile or bin as you go.

This method requires more input materials (greens and browns), space, and labor than

A pile of wood chips will naturally become a slow-burning compost pile; adding partially rotted wood chips to garden compost contributes carbon and lots of fungal friends.

the other methods but can result, quickly, in some of the highest-quality compost.

Clearing space for the mound. An ideal size for a big hot compost mound is 5 by 5 by 5 feet. Bigger is fine, too, but it may be hard to turn by hand with just one person. Smaller is also fine; you can go down to about 4 by 4 by 4 feet. Just don't go much smaller, or the pile won't achieve the heat needed to neutralize pathogens and kill weed seeds, and the whole process will take much longer. Since you'll need to turn the mound and pile it up again, look for a flat area without tall weeds growing that's at least 5 by 15 feet (space for two mounds next to each other; one will turn into the other one and be flipped back again over time). A shady spot is fine for a compost mound; you don't need to sacrifice ground that would be good for growing!

Beginning the mound. One important aspect of building a big hot mound is piling it into a straight-sided cylinder and not a conical mountain shape. Stack materials in a ring around the edge, like a doughnut, allowing some to tumble into the middle so that it doesn't become an actual doughnut.

Making the mound. All the foundational concepts for composting are the same here: Alternate layers of different kinds of materials, being sure to sprinkle water on after every dry brown layer so that there is balanced moisture throughout the pile. If you live in a dry place, you may want to water the whole pile with a sprinkler for up to an hour after it's built to ensure the components are nice and juicy and welcoming to all the microorganisms that will do the work of decomposition. But if you're in a rainy place, you might cover the pile with a tarp so that it doesn't get too wet, which slows down the process by cooling the pile and choking out oxygen.

Taking the mound's temperature. After your mound is built, check the temperature every day or two with a compost thermometer or your hand (if you're willing to plunge your arm into the belly of the pile, that is—it's a little messy, but it's also kind of exhilarating). You're checking to see when the temperature peaks rather than looking for a specific temperature. However, 140°F (60°C) will kill most pathogens and weed seeds, so it's good to notice the actual temperature, too, if you're using a thermometer. After the temperature has peaked, it's time to turn the pile.

Turning the mound. *Turning* basically means re-piling all the material again into the same shape right next to the original mound. The role of turning is to introduce oxygen and reinvigorate the microbes so that they can finish the job. Depending on your base materials, moisture content, and outside temperatures, you may need to turn more than once, even more than twice—whatever it takes to get to the finish line of beautiful black gold.

THE COMPOST THERMOMETER

This nifty gizmo looks just like a meat or soil thermometer, but it has a temperature range that's appropriate for compost. It has a round gauge atop a long probe (the longest probe of the bunch is the compost thermometer). It's very gratifying to see the temperature inside your well-built pile soar.

6
How to Plant a Seed

& Get It to Grow

The Magic of Seeds 158

Germination and Seed Viability 160

Ordering Seeds 162

Overview of Planting Methods 170

Setting Up a Seed-Starting System 174

Growing Your Own Transplants 180

Transplanting Baby Plants 184

How to Buy Strong Transplants 190

Direct Sowing 191

When to Plant What 194

The Magic of Seeds

A seed is like a little bundle of memory and possibility, all magically wrapped up tight and sleeping within a protective coat. Seeds breathe and, we believe, dream, until the right conditions arise for their awakening. Planting a seed and watching it grow can be a pinnacle experience of being human and alive on Earth. This simple, natural phenomenon can be spiritual, connective, gratifying, satisfying, hopeful, and awe-inspiring.

Without seeds, there can be no garden and, ultimately, no food for humans or any other animal on the planet. And what's more, all of the seeds that sprout into the vegetables and herbs we enjoy have been carefully coaxed into their current form by many, many generations of our human ancestors. Even if you buy transplants for your garden and don't sow seeds with your own hands, you'll still be conjuring the magic of seeds as you grow with them.

Seeds, like all children, are unique and distinct from their parents in at least a few ways. It's true that a pumpkin seed will always grow another pumpkin-like plant. However, the size, shape, vigor, disease resistance, color, flavor, and many other qualities of the offspring may be surprising and new. In a manner of speaking, seeds listen to the story of their parent plants' lives, then continue telling that story through their own growing.

Choosing and getting to know seeds that are suited for your garden can greatly enhance your experience and your success. Also, recognizing the grandeur of seeds and thanking them for their gifts is a lovely doorway that, when walked through, leads to a deeper connection with the plants you sow and tend. They are like babies, whom we readily love, even though we don't know what their futures hold.

Beet seeds are a funny, bumpy shape and actually contain two to six seeds in one.

Green beans (left) and zucchini (right) are two vegetables that we like to eat when they're immature (the seeds inside aren't yet viable); leave a few to fully mature at the end of the season to save their seeds for future planting.

Germination and Seed Viability

It's time for a quick botany lesson! If you're already familiar with plant sex and the genesis of seeds, this may be a review. We're continually surprised, however, at how many people don't really know the details of how flowers make seeds. This information infuses the gardening experience with extra wonder and useful knowledge.

WHERE SEEDS COME FROM

Seeds are the product of plant copulation. Plants "do it" like this: The female flower part called an ovary is fertilized by male pollen, the plant equivalent of sperm. Instead of being directly deposited, as with animals, plant "sperm" (pollen) flies through the air on the wind; is carried by insects, birds, or other animals; or, in some cases, just falls from the male parts of a flower onto the female parts in the same flower. Different plants have different flower structures and pollination needs. Some

are happy to pollinate themselves, and some will only pollinate with others. Some have "perfect" flowers, with both male and female parts on the same flowers, while others have separate male and female flowers on the same plant, or even male and female flowers on different plants. Whatever shape plants have or journey they undertake, to make a seed, a female ovary needs to be bathed in the right male pollen, at the right time.

Once a female flower is pollinated, a magical process takes place, just like when a baby starts growing in their mother's womb—the flower becomes a seed. Many flowers are actually collections of smaller flowers, and some flowers contain many ovaries. A sunflower, for example, contains hundreds of tiny flowers making up the center of the sunflower head, and the "petals" are actually an adornment of a different kind of flower, called ray flowers. This is why each sunflower makes so many seeds.

Once seeds are fully formed, they "leave home" to find their own place to sprout and grow. Plants have evolved many strategies for seed distribution:

- Some fly on the wind, such as dandelion seeds.

Mature winter squash contains fully mature seeds; carrots are biennial and need a second season of growing before they make flowers and seeds.

- Some grow a fruit around them to be eaten by an animal and then carried far away from the parent plant, later to be dropped in a fertilizer packet called scat.
- Some helicopter down to the soil, in the case of maple samaras.
- Still others find their way into the hands of loving gardeners!

WHAT GERMINATION HAS TO DO WITH IT

Within each seed is the blueprint for an entire plant. Depending on the conditions, seeds can wait for a very long time to sprout, holding that blueprint safely until they perceive the right conditions. Germination, the technical term for sprouting, is the magical process of a seed coming out of hibernation and growing into a plant. If the seed is given certain cues—most vegetable seeds simply need sustained moisture and the right temperature—it germinates.

If a vegetable seed is planted and watered once but dries out before it fully germinates, it won't survive and grow. In the opposite extreme, if a seed is continually submerged in water for days, it's also likely to die from lack of oxygen. For ideal germination and growth, there's a sweet spot for watering seeds: Once or twice a day, let the soil lose saturation between watering, but don't let the soil get so dry that the seed itself dries out.

Along with water, warmth is another key factor that impacts seed germination. Different vegetables have different temperatures at which their seeds will germinate. See the vegetable profiles beginning on page 275 and the appendix for ideal germination temperatures for different kinds of vegetables.

Many seeds, especially those of perennial plants, need all sorts of unique things to happen before they can germinate. For example, seeds of certain types of pine tree must experience fire before they germinate (telling them that nutrients from ash and the clearing force of a wildfire have prepared their seedbed for

them); ginseng seeds need a period of moist, cold conditions, followed by warmth (i.e., winter passing, indicating the beginning of spring); and parsley seeds require abrasion of their seed coat before sprouting (probably because they prefer to be eaten and passed through a digestive tract before sprouting, which guarantees they are far from their parent plant). One way or another, seeds perceive their environment and recognize when conditions are ideal for their growth and thriving.

Fortunately for us gardeners, most vegetables are annuals, and vegetable seeds have such a long relationship with humans that they've learned to trust the simple signals of proper moisture and temperature. To honor this abiding trust, we humans have a responsibility to plant seeds at the right time in conditions where they will thrive. You wouldn't plant a tomato in the shade, or in fall, for instance, as both actions would result in the tomato plant not being able to grow fruits or seeds. For more on timing for specific crops, check out the vegetable profiles beginning on page 275.

Pay attention to the seeds you sow, as your own observations will provide the most accurate and powerful information.

Ordering Seeds

You have a few options when it comes to getting seeds. You can grow and save some of your own, you can barter with other gardeners, or—and it's likely you'll need to do this for at least some of your seeds—you can buy them. This gives you the wonderful opportunity to support small-scale, independent, regionally adapted seed growers and seed companies. In contrast with industrially grown seeds from big-box stores, seeds from these sources will be higher quality, grown in more sustainable conditions, and come in a wider array of varieties adapted to your region and/or to home-garden conditions. We save some of our seeds, order some of our seeds from local growers, and order others from sustainable smallish-scale growers in Maine and Oregon that are not specifically adapted to our local conditions but are adapted to similar small-scale, low-input growing conditions like ours. Whenever possible we avoid purchasing seeds from big-box stores or industrial agribusiness companies.

BEST TIME TO ORDER

Not only is winter usually garden downtime, but it's also when seed companies offer their new stock of seeds. Growers produce most seeds in the green season (spring, summer, fall). Then, after the seeds are mature, they're harvested, dried, cleaned, tested for viability and diseases, packaged, and shipped. Early winter is the time when new seed is ready to go, and it's when seed companies know exactly what they have to offer each year. As interest in gardening and food security continues to grow, seed companies tend to sell out of popular or hard-to-produce varieties very quickly.

PRO TIP: *Order seeds as soon as you're ready, to ensure you get what you're after!*

TAKE INVENTORY

Before you order seeds, take stock of what you've already got. Don't just look at crop or variety names—also look at dates. Seeds are living organisms that are dormant, but they don't stay viable forever. Many types of seeds can last for years, if stored properly; others are shorter lived. Keep in mind that exposure to moisture, heat, and light can decrease a seed's viable life.

LEFT: Natalie enjoys perusing seed catalogs over a cup of tea in the winter.

RIGHT: Chloe flips through her well-organized seed bin to find just what she's looking for.

The first leaves to appear when seeds germinate are cotyledons, or embryonic seed-leaves; unlike the true leaves to come, cotyledons existed within the seed before germination.

How Long Do Seeds Last?

Here's a quick reference that tells you *approximately* how long different types of seeds will be viable under good storage conditions. The following is adapted from a chart made by the folks at Johnny's Selected Seeds, a great source of seeds and growing info.

- **1 year:** carrots, onions, parsley, parsnips, salsify, and spinach
- **2 years:** beets, chives, dandelion, okra
- **3 years:** leeks, most brassicas (e.g., kale, cabbage, broccoli), rutabagas, turnips
- **4 years:** basil, beans, chard, corn, peas, peppers, pumpkins, squash, watermelons
- **5 years:** celery, chicory, cucumbers, eggplant, endive, lettuce, muskmelons, tomatoes

When in Doubt, Do a Germination Test

Since viability is dependent on many dynamic factors (like storage conditions and variety), you can always perform a germination test on a batch of seeds. This will tell you *if* the seeds are still viable and also *how viable* they are. Low germination rates can inform decisions like whether you decide to buy a new batch and compost the old seeds or if you can get away with sowing extra heavily to make up for the lower germination rate. Seed companies do germination tests when they pack seeds, and they generally write the germination rate on their seed packets.

How to Perform a
GERMINATION TEST

1. MOISTEN A PAPER TOWEL (you can also use a large coffee filter) so that it's uniformly damp but not dripping wet.

2. SPRINKLE SEEDS ONTO THE TOWEL OR FILTER. Use at least 10 seeds, making sure they're spread out and not touching each other.

3. FOLD AND ROLL UP THE TOWEL OR FILTER. Do this gently. Roll it up like a burrito, with the seeds inside.

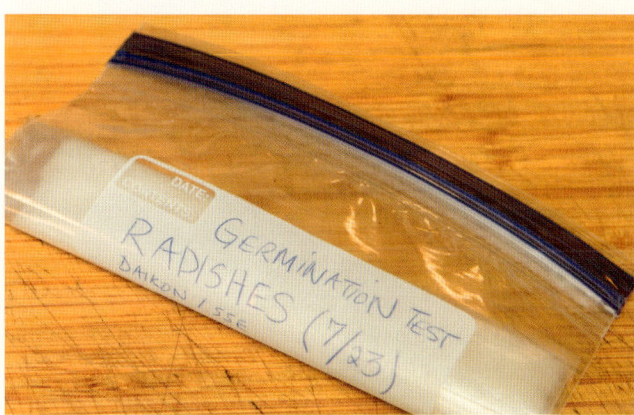

4. PLACE THE GERMINATION TEST (THE "BURRITO") IN A PLASTIC BAG. You can also use a container of some kind. Store the test at the ideal germination temperature for your seeds. Room temperature is fine for most veggies.

5. CHECK ON THE SEEDS EACH DAY AND MOISTEN. Count and record any sprouted seeds; remoisten as needed with a spray bottle to keep things damp but not dripping. Stop the test when 3 days have passed with no new sprouts.

6. CALCULATE THE GERMINATION RATE. Take the total number of sprouts and divide by the total number of seeds. For example: If you start with 20 seeds and 15 of them sprout, your germination rate is 15/20 = 75 percent, which would be low for fresh seeds but fine for a heavier-than-normal sowing in a home garden. This means you would sow extra seeds, since you know only about 75 percent of them will grow.

ORDER ACCORDING TO YOUR GARDEN PLAN

Take a look at your basic garden plan for the coming year before you order seeds. You'll just need a general sense of how much space you'll be planting in and the different kinds of crops and varieties you hope to grow, not a super-detailed complete plan. (See page 39 for guidance on garden planning.)

For most home gardeners, the standard or smallest seed packets available will be sufficient. If you're planning to grow a lot of something—either a large plot or many plantings in succession—you may need two or more standard packets or a larger size packet. Try to order only the amount of seeds you will actually use before they lose viability.

We usually order one or two 4-gram packets of cilantro seed, since we love this tasty herb and sow successions of it every few weeks all season long. Similarly, we order multiple standard packets or a larger packet of beet, carrot, and lettuce seeds, because, like the cilantro, we grow a lot of successions of lettuce, and we grow large plots of beets and carrots. For other crops we generally just order one standard-size packet.

DON'T GO CRAZY!

Trying new things in life can be fun, and your garden is no exception. As you peruse seed catalogs, with their beautiful images and intriguing descriptions, it can be hard to hold back. Even so, we strongly recommend that you limit your explorations to one to five new crops or varieties each year. This way, you can really pay attention to how your new plant friends grow in your garden. When there are just a few of them, you can tend them well and take good notes without neglecting other plants in your garden or other aspects of your life!

LEFT: Immature 'Tennessee Dancing Gourd'

RIGHT (top to bottom): A sampling of midsummer's bounty; garlic is one crop we don't grow from seed, but rather from its own cloves.

A BRIEF HISTORY OF THE
SEED INDUSTRY

For the vast majority of the time humans have been cultivating food crops, seed saving and selection was done by the same people and communities who grew, harvested, and used those plants. This meant that each crop would be engaged with over hundreds of generations to develop adaptations and qualities to suit that climate, those growing conditions, the pests present there, the types of cuisine those folks made and enjoyed, and more. There were—and still are, in some communities—seed-sharing rituals woven into the social and ecological cycles that allowed new seeds to be brought in, lending diversity and novelty to the genetic landscape of food crops in a rhythmic and intentional way. Through these time-tested practices, seeds developed that would thrive in their home ground, outperforming seeds that had developed in other conditions and places.

The first commercial seed companies started up in Europe in the eighteenth century, but since most growers still saved their own seeds at that point (which doesn't cost any money), the industry didn't exactly take off. It wasn't until the early twentieth century, when US commercial seed companies started producing hybrid seeds, that things really shifted from most growers harvesting their own seed to most growers buying seeds.

Hybrids are produced using a time- and labor-intensive process of inbreeding and crossing that's not doable on a small scale. The results are varieties of crops with "hybrid vigor" and superior production and disease resistance than most traditionally bred all-purpose varieties. A downside of hybrids is that gardeners cannot save their own seeds from them and get the same qualities that the parent plants had—they have to keep buying hybrid seeds from their producers. Gradually both the food system in general and the seed-production system specifically shifted toward focusing more and more on profit rather than on community resilience and food sovereignty. Genetically modified seeds (GMOs) came on the scene in the mid-1990s and continue this trend in a much more extreme manner.

Over the past 100 or so years, the seed industry has ballooned in tandem with its equally misguided sibling, the agrochemical industry. The same companies that breed, engineer, and sell over 50 percent of the world's seeds also produce the chemicals those seeds were bred and engineered to rely upon. Their guiding principles are profit and control, not thriving gardens and communities. This is problematic because it traps farmers in dependency on these companies for both seeds and chemicals, and it also strips the seeds of two of their most powerful qualities: diversity and relationship.

SUPPORT LOCAL AND GROWER-FOCUSED COMPANIES

One small way we can resist the perilous trend of seed sacrilege (see A Brief History of the Seed Industry, page 167) is to vote with our dollars and support seed producers who have in mind growers, land, resilience, health, and food sovereignty, as well as the seeds themselves. You'll be able to buy directly from smaller, independent, seed-honoring companies through their websites or catalogs. Exploring catalogs is especially fun—you can leaf through them over cups of tea while your wintertime gardening imagination runs

wild! Do keep in mind that many catalogs are printed before all of the current year's seed is in; some seeds don't make it into the catalog and can only be found online.

Unless you are averse to online shopping, we recommend doing the actual ordering online. It's quicker, and you'll know if anything is already sold out. Plus, you'll receive an email receipt to keep track of what's on the way.

If there are local or regional, independent, high-quality seed producers where you garden, definitely go with their seeds. Plants that are already adapted to your general conditions, especially if they were raised using organic practices, are much more likely to be successful in your own garden. Small producers like this work to carefully select the best version of whatever they are growing, and they truly want growers who use their seeds to have success. You may end up paying a little more for these seeds, but it's worth it on many levels. Even if some seeds were not grown in your region, when they're bred for similar, garden-style, organically managed, lower-input systems, they'll likely thrive in your garden in comparison with seeds that are used to heavy inputs or lots of pampering.

STORE SEEDS FOR OPTIMAL VIABILITY

Once you receive your seeds, store them in a cool, dry, and, if possible, dark environment, like a closet or a shelf in a corner. In humid environments like ours, a plastic tote or other vessel can be really helpful in maintaining a stable microclimate to keep seeds fresh. As an extra layer of protection against moisture, you can add silica desiccant packets to your seed tote (like those you find in jars of vitamins or packages of sushi nori). If a seed packet happens to get wet, don't put it back in the container with the others; instead either dry it completely and/or use it as soon as possible.

Influential and beloved plant-breeder and seed-saver Alan Kapuler created 'Double Red' sweet corn, (high in purple cell-protecting anthocyanins) because he loves colorful, nutritious vegetables.

Two systems for organizing seeds: Chloe categorizes by type, e.g., carrots and tomatoes (left), and Natalie organizes seeds alphabetically by vegetable type (right).

ORGANIZE SEEDS FOR EASE OF USE

One easy way to organize seeds is alphabetically by vegetables (e.g., cucumbers, salad greens, tomatoes). You can also organize them by growing season (placing cool-season crops in one container and warm-season crops in another, with types of crops like brassicas, legumes, or carrot family organized alphabetically), or by seed size (storing larger seeds in their own container, since they take up so much more room). We like to make dividers between categories by cutting rectangles of recycled cardboard and writing on them with a marker; it's simple, easy, and cheap!

GROWING AND TRADING SEEDS

People have been buying and selling seeds for only a short slice of agricultural history. Growing and trading seeds are still wonderful, functional, connective, and generative ways to get seeds for your garden. Seed saving is a fantastic way to get to know the plants you grow more deeply. You'll also connect with the cycles of life in a tangible and magical way.

Our go-to book for basic seed saving is a classic called *Seed to Seed: Seed Saving and Growing Techniques for Vegetable Gardeners* by Suzanne Ashworth, who explores, among other things, seed-saving techniques in a clear, step-by-step way for a wide variety of crops. Rowen White's Seed Seva online program is our favorite digital resource on both the how and the why of seed saving. Once you've saved a few of your own seeds, or if you just find yourself with more purchased seeds than you need, organizing a seed swap is a great way to share the bounty and connect with other gardeners. Together, you'll experience the generosity and abundance of the living world.

Overview of Planting Methods

Over generations of collaboration with our food plants, we humans have developed techniques for growing plants far away from their native territory, elongating the natural growing season where we live, and increasing the chances that our preferred plants will thrive. In the uncultivated wild, plants aren't sown and grown in pots, to be transplanted out to the field . . . but tomatoes also don't naturally grow and produce beautiful fruits in much of the world, either.

Some plants prefer to be planted directly into the soil (called direct sowing or direct seeding). Others perform better in certain climates when they get a head start in pots in a controlled environment and then move to the garden when the weather is warmer and they're big and robust.

We will explore two planting methods: (1) direct sowing and (2) starting your own seeds in pots and then transplanting them to your garden. You can also purchase plant starts to then transplant in the garden.

Whether you decide to direct sow, start your own seeds in pots, or purchase transplants will depend on multiple factors. Some vegetables with sensitive root systems (root crops, such as the carrot, are prime examples) don't survive transplanting well and thus are difficult to start in pots and later move to the garden. Growing your own transplants means you'll have access to a much larger variety of options, since you'll be able to get seed from anywhere. You will also get to cultivate a deeper relationship with those vegetables, having tended to them from seed to table.

Conversely, setting up your own seed-starting situation can be a lot of work and can get pricey. Putting in these resources usually only makes sense if you have a good-size garden (more than a few beds), if you are not able to get the varieties that you want from a nursery or other source, or if you just get really excited about watching baby plants grow (Natalie's dad became one of these people after watching the section on seed starting in our online gardening classes). Otherwise, if you are growing a small garden, it probably makes sense to just purchase your transplants from a nursery, a farmers' market, or another grower.

DIRECT SOWING

Direct sowing is generally less work than growing transplants, but it's only appropriate

Growing these lettuces in a cell tray will make it easy to pop them out and transplant them at the ideal spacing.

LEFT: Direct sowing doesn't require anything but seeds, soil, and water.

RIGHT: Starting seeds in flats or pots can extend the season and make growing heat-loving crops, like these peppers, possible.

for some garden plants, depending on climate. With this method you plant seeds straight into the ground. For direct sowing to work well, you'll need to place seeds at the proper depth and spacing and to keep them moist (not continually saturated) until they germinate (see pages 275 and 358 for more on sowing depths of specific crops).

Watering direct-sown seeds is absolutely crucial. If they dry out, they won't germinate and grow. You need reliable access to outdoor water to successfully direct sow crops. Of course, if you live somewhere with ample rain, the heavens will do some of this work for you. Another consideration with direct sowing is the need to thin the plants at least once (maybe twice) after they come up (see Chapter 7 for more on thinning).

Once the plants emerge, they have some resilience. An advantage of direct sowing is that your new plants are not as sensitive to one missed watering as plants in pots are. The ground outside is able to hold on to water much more easily and abundantly than the soil or growing medium in a little pot.

The plants' roots remain undisturbed. With direct sowing you don't disturb the plant's roots like you do with transplanting. In fact, when you direct sow, you'll never need to do the added work and give the plant the added shock of transplanting, as they'll just

grow where they germinated. If there is a plant that can go either way—can be direct-seeded *or* transplanted—we generally direct sow.

STARTING PLANTS IN POTS

Note: Many of the benefits of starting plants in pots can also be enjoyed when you buy transplants. If you don't have the time or setup to grow your own transplants, this is a great option for you.

Advantages of Starting Plants in Pots

- You'll baby the plants more, which can lead to higher germination rates.

- There's less need to thin plants that you start in pots (unless you plant multiple seeds per pot, which makes sense if you are using old or unreliable seed).

- You can transplant each plant into the soil exactly where you want them to go, at the appropriate final spacing.

- If you are short on seeds, starting them in pots maximizes the chances of each seed growing into a viable adult plant.

- Lastly, and perhaps the most compelling reason to go this route, is that you can extend the growing season.

Many of the garden vegetables we all know and love evolved in places (and climates) that are different from where we grow them now.

Direct Sow or Transplant from Pots?

Every gardener may have slightly different preferences as far as what to sow outdoors directly and what to start indoors. Whether you follow our advice or that of your neighbor who has been gardening forever in your area, it will likely work out just fine. Be sure to keep track of your own garden practices in writing so that you can learn over time what works best for you.

FAMILY NAME	PLANT EXAMPLES	DIRECT SOW	TRANSPLANT FROM POTS	NOTES
Brassicas grown for leaves	Arugula, collards, kale, tatsoi	X	X	These can go either way—they can be sown directly or started in pots. We start the ones that have a longer season, like kale and collards, in pots, and sow the shorter-season ones, like arugula or tatsoi, directly in the ground. Fall kale and collards can also be direct sown.
Brassicas grown for buds	Broccoli, cabbage, cauliflower		X	They tend to require a longer amount of time to mature and require more space than brassicas grown for leaves or roots, so they also require a lot of thinning. We always start these in pots or buy transplants.
Brassicas with an edible root	Daikon, radishes, turnips	X		Like all root crops, these are best sown directly.
Carrot family	Carrots, cilantro, dill, parsnips	X		Even the members of this family that we harvest for their leaves don't like their roots to be disturbed, though dill and cilantro can be successfully transplanted if need be.
Chenopods (Goosefoot family)	Beets, chard, lamb's quarters, spinach	X	See note in next column	These can always be directly sown, but those grown for leaves can also be sown in pots and transplanted.
Cucurbits	Cucumbers, melons, pumpkins and other squashes, zucchini	X	X	These can go either way. If you live in an area with a shorter growing season, starting these in pots, especially cucumbers and melons, gives you a much better chance of success. If cucurbits are sown in pots and transplanted, they must be transplanted *as soon as they're ready* (usually after just 2–3 weeks); they're prone to getting rootbound in pots. We often start a first succession of these in pots, then directly sow a second planting once the soil has warmed. For winter squash, we almost always direct sow.
Daisy family grown for aboveground parts	Chicory, lettuce	X	X	These can go either way; root chicories should be sown directly. We tend to start head lettuce in pots or flats and direct sow cutting lettuce.
Grasses	Corn, millet, oats, wheat	X		To grow a meaningful amount of these crops, you need to sow a lot of seeds; transplanting would be impractical.
Nightshades	Eggplants, peppers, tobacco, tomatoes	See note in last column	X	These generally do better when started in pots, with the exception of potatoes, which are almost always grown from tuber sections and not true seeds.
Pea family	Beans, peas	X		

Some plants are best grown by vegetative propagation (a.k.a. cloning) rather than from seeds.

Sweet potatoes (left) are grown from cuttings (shown growing on tubers), which are then snipped off and planted.

Irish potatoes are grown from sections cut from the potatoes (upper right).

Garlic is grown by planting individual garlic cloves; each clove grows into a whole head.

Tomatoes and peppers, for example, hail from warm regions in South and Central America. These generous immigrants may do fine if they're planted directly in the ground in Los Angeles or Miami, but they won't have time to mature if we direct sow them here in North Carolina (or anywhere else with a winter where temperatures go below freezing for more than a month or two a year). In order to maximize harvests, it's best to give many heat-loving plants a head start in pots in a temperature-controlled environment; this way, they'll already be good-size plants when we put them in the garden, after the danger of frost has passed.

VEGETATIVE PROPAGATION

Some plants aren't typically grown from seeds at all but rather from pieces, cuttings, or sprouts from the parent plant. Garlic, potatoes, and sweet potatoes are examples of common garden vegetables that you won't grow from true seeds. Many herbs are easier to propagate vegetatively than to grow from seed.

Garlic is grown by planting "cloves." The individual pieces of the larger garlic bulb are swollen leaf bases with specialized anatomy that allows a new plant to sprout from them.

Potatoes are cut into pieces and planted directly in the ground. Each tuber, or piece, needs to have at least a couple of eyes, or auxiliary buds, from which new shoots, roots, and leaves will grow.

Sweet potatoes are grown from shoots. These slips, or shoots, grow directly out of the sweet potato itself, a tuber, like other kinds of potatoes. Instead of planting bits of the tuber, you'll break off the slips and plant them in the ground.

Many perennial herbs are propagated vegetatively. Some of them can be challenging to germinate from seed. Examples of these are rosemary, thyme, lavender, and garden sage. In general we buy transplants of these aromatic delights.

Setting Up a Seed-Starting System

There are a lot of ways to set up a seed-starting scene. One important thing to remember is that many of your baby plants will need to be potted up (transplanted into bigger pots) before they go into the garden. Once these plants move to their larger pots, you'll quickly need more seed-starting space. With fast-growing plants like tomatoes or cucumbers, it won't be long before they require a lot more of the limited real estate where you've created ideal seed-starting conditions. When you transplant up peppers and tomatoes, for example, into 4-inch pots, they will take up three to four times the horizontal space that they did when they sprouted in smaller containers. In short: It's best to set up a much larger seed-starting scene than you need just for your original trays or pots.

The basic elements of any system for starting seeds in pots are:

- Warmth
- Water
- Light
- Pots/flats
- Soil
- Seeds

We'll walk through various seed-starting systems that we've used, from least to most complex.

STARTING IN POTS OUTDOORS

Where conditions are appropriate, you can start seeds in pots on a sunny table or bench outdoors. This simple approach works well for sowing in midsummer for fall planting in temperate climates like ours, since the warmth of summer is enough to get seeds going. It does not work, however, for starting tomatoes, peppers, and other summer crops that need to get going before it is warm enough for them to be outside.

It's wise to choose pots based on how large the seeds are and how quickly the plant will grow. Four-inch pots are best for big-seeded, fast-growing plants like squash, while small-seeded plants like kale can be started in a 72-cell tray.

These midsummer-sown Asian cabbage babies do just fine on Natalie's porch railing, where she's screwed on a board for just such a purpose.

If you live in a place that's warm all year, like Florida or Southern California, this may be the only seed-starting system you need. Some considerations here are:

- **Sun.** Shady yards won't cut it.
- **Access to water.** You'll need to water once or twice a day.
- **Wind and rain.** Too much wind is hard on baby plants, and they also don't like heavy rain.
- **Critters.** House cats, chickens, possums, dogs, tiny humans, and other creatures may disturb seeds and pots.
- **Space.** You'll need a surface for your pots, one that can get wet and dirty. An ideal outdoor seed-starting system involves a table or bench that's between waist and chest height, a hose or spigot nearby, and a sunny yard or patio.

THE SUNNY WINDOWSILL

It's possible to start seeds in a sunny, well-heated window. For this to work well, you'll need a fairly large and south-facing window (north-facing if you're in the Southern Hemisphere) with a wide sill or space for a table right next to the window. On warm, sunny days, the baby plants can be brought outside into the sun to get more uniform light exposure, then carried back inside as the day cools off. This method is sweet and simple, but it only works in some houses. One advantage is that the heat indoors is sufficient for germinating most seeds (with the exception of basil, peppers, eggplants, and some others). Refer to the vegetable profiles beginning on page 275 and the appendix for ideal germination temperatures for individual crops.

The windowsill approach also shines as a low-tech approach that's relatively inexpensive. Most of us, however, don't have large, south-facing windows (east-, west-, or north-facing windows will not cut it) that have full sun and enough open space right in front of them for tables covered with plants. Additionally, moving plants in and out each day can become tedious. And it's easy to leave plants outside too long into the cool evening; if you go out with friends after work and the

temperature drops below freezing in that time, you may come home to dead seedlings.

The path of the sun gets higher as the season progresses, so what started as a sunny windowsill in late February or early March may turn into a shady windowsill come late April. This means a lot of trips carrying your baby plants outside to enjoy the sun on nice days and bringing them inside to avoid the cold. It becomes more laborious after you transplant your babies into 4-inch pots and they take up three to four times as much space.

Unless you have great conditions for the windowsill method, we recommend setting up a system with grow lights and heat mats, or using a greenhouse if you've got one. Natalie actually built a wide soapstone windowsill under a large south-facing window above her sink specifically to host flats of baby plants. After a year of using it, moving plants back and forth into the sun, she started using grow lights in a utility room and then finally built a greenhouse.

LIGHTS AND HEAT MATS

With a few grow lights and seedling heat mats, you can easily set up a tiny (or not so tiny) indoor nursery for starting seeds. If you have room in your house, it's great to set up your seed-starting system in a spot you frequent or see often so that you can easily pay attention to it. If you start seeds in an out-of-the-way spot, you'll want to cultivate the discipline to visit them frequently (once or twice a day) to water and to make sure they're in good shape and not drying out. A basement or garage can be an excellent spot, especially if you don't have space in your house or apartment; just be sure that the air temperature wherever you start seeds doesn't go below freezing, even when it gets cold outdoors.

Adjustable Shelves

Use a 4-foot-long, heavy-duty adjustable metal shelf. Grow lights are generally 4 feet long and are easily hung from the shelf above where the plants will grow.

Natalie designed and built her home, making sure to include a sunny, south-facing window with a sill wide enough for a 72-cell tray for baby plants.

Heat Mats

There are a few things to pay attention to when shopping for heat mats:

- **Adjustable thermostat:** When you have a heat mat with one of these, you can dial in the temperature for different seedlings' needs. Very handy.

- **Brands:** Hydrofarm, iPower, and Vivosun are all quality brands that we've used. Other brands may also be good—new ones come on the scene regularly. Just remember, you get what you pay for!

- **Size:** Heat mats come in two sizes to accommodate your seedling trays (see page 181 for more on trays): a 10- by 20-inch mat (to heat one standard "1020" tray) and a 20- by 48-inch mat (to heat four standard 1020 trays). This larger size fits very well on the 4-foot shelf (and is the one we use).

Grow Lights

There are a lot of options out there. Some of this profusion is the result of the booming indoor cannabis industry. If you're a home gardener, you don't need to get too fancy or high tech. Your little plants grow under lights for only a short stint, especially compared to something like indoor cannabis or hydroponic gardens that go through their entire high-yield life cycles in synthetic environments.

The quality of light you use, however, *does* matter. Seedlings grown in low-light settings are prone to legginess (growing too tall and spindly) and tend to lack vigor. We could go deep into the scientific details around light and growing, including the fact that certain plants can utilize different spectrums of light more efficiently than others, but we'll stop here, since for our purposes, it can stay pretty simple.

A lot of plants can fit on one utility shelf seed-starting setup! On the right, Natalie adjusts supplemental lights in her greenhouse so that they're close to the plants.

T5 grow lights. These lights are all you really need to know about. T5 lights are available all over the place, are reasonably affordable, and work well. We have the most experience with fluorescent T5s, though at the time of writing, LED grow lights seem to be advancing (older LED grow lights haven't put out enough light for good growth).

Other grow light options. If you can't find or afford T5 lights, regular fluorescent shop lights can also work—but if you go this route, make sure to hang them low over your pots (just a couple of inches from the top of the green growth) so the seedlings receive sufficient light.

STARTING IN A GREENHOUSE

A greenhouse can host a wonderful nonelectric or low-electricity seed-starting system. Of course to do this, you'll need a greenhouse, which many of us don't have the space or budget for. If you happen to be the fortunate steward of a greenhouse, there are some tricks and tips to starting seeds in that environment.

Heating. You will probably still benefit from bottom heat in a greenhouse in early spring when nighttime temperatures drop down, especially to get the seeds up to ideal germination temperature. *And* if air temperatures get near or below freezing during the time you're starting seeds, you'll likely need another heat source, too (we use a regular electric space heater).

Temperature control and venting. Be sure to install a thermometer in your greenhouse so you can keep track of how warm or cool it's getting. Aside from extreme cold or heat actually killing young plants, huge swings in temperature can stress them and also negatively impact germination. Because greenhouses can easily get too hot on bright, sunny days, even when the air outside is cool, be diligent about checking the temperature and then venting the space as needed. Natalie

has a thermostatically controlled vent and fan in her greenhouse, which has probably saved many plants from being roasted on a day when she was out and forgot to open the door.

Workspace. As with all seed-starting systems, it's nice to have a surface that's between waist and chest height to put your pots or flats on.

Water. Your plants need it, so make sure your access to water from the greenhouse is easy and convenient.

SEEDLING LIGHT NEEDS

Baby vegetable plants need light. They need way more light than houseplants, so you'll want to have your pots or flats in a very sunny windowsill balanced with trips outside, under appropriate grow lights, or in a greenhouse. Household lights, dappled light, or intermittent light won't cut it; your plants will suffer if they don't get what they need.

Germinating seeds just need warmth. Germinating seeds don't *need* any light until the first cotyledons, or seed leaves, emerge. Once you can see those cute and vibrant green faces poke up, light is extremely important. But in that germination "meantime," between your first watering and when seed leaves emerge, you can keep your seedlings in a warm, lower-light environment, if need be. So if you live off the grid and can't use heat mats, can't afford heat mats, or just don't want to buy more plastic stuff, you can keep pots or flats with germinating seeds atop the refrigerator, near a woodstove or heater, in a heated room, or atop a well-built hot compost or manure pile. The tricky part is keeping an eye on them and moving them into a place where they can get their light requirements met as soon as they emerge.

Plastic domes can be useful for germination. You may have seen plastic domes at grow stores or online that can be placed atop seedling trays. These do an excellent job of keeping in warmth and moisture, but they also

Having a greenhouse set up with a hose and watering wand drastically increases ease and efficiency of seed starting. Natalie gardened for over two decades before having this setup.

increase the chances of fungal disease and can trap so much heat that temperatures inside soar. If you'd like to use plastic domes, we recommend doing so *just* during germination and removing them after your seedlings have emerged. Also, keep track of the interior temperature in the dome, and remove it if temps get too hot (over 85°F/29°C for most veggies).

Note: If you have a mixed flat with many kinds of seeds germinating at once, it's unlikely that they'll all sprout at the same time, so this method will pose challenges. It's better to start mixed flats on heat mats and without plastic domes.

WATERING SETUP FOR SEEDLINGS

You'll need easy access to water wherever you start seeds in pots. Use a watering can or hose nozzle that produces a gentle spray of water—not a mist and not a deluge or forceful rush of water.

Some guidelines for watering seedlings:

- **Place a towel or tarp underneath your seedling shelf** or table if you're starting seeds indoors, as watering can be a bit messy.

- **Moisten the soil all the way through.** An easy way to track this is to keep one pot or cell in a tray empty except for the soil itself (no seeds or plants). You can then do the finger test, digging in to check moisture levels without disturbing any of the more delicate neighbors.

- **Keep things evenly moist.** Seed-starting and potting mixes generally contain coconut coir or peat moss, both of which are hydrophobic (repel water) when they're dry but become hydrophilic (hold water well) once they're already wet. If they dry out, you may need to do three or four consecutive waterings with a couple of minutes in between to get them to absorb water again.

Labeling seedlings is important! Larger labels like these white ones have room for info like variety, date, seed source, moonphase; smaller labels like the wooden sticks at left just have space for the basics.

Growing Your Own Transplants

Now that you've got information about getting set up, it's time to dive into the details of caring for baby plants and growing your own transplants.

SOIL OR GROWING MEDIUM

The growing medium, or soil, that you choose for growing transplants is very important. An ideal material will be fine and without large particulates, have a balance of water-holding capacity and drainage, and contain fertility for the plants as they grow and get hungry. Potting soils that are appropriate for container gardening are usually too chunky for seed starting. Similarly, soil dug out of a garden bed isn't ideal because it's likely to be both too chunky and too heavy (dense with clay particles). The following are some considerations.

Choose soil with life. Soil mixes that contain biologically active compounds like worm castings or compost, and that have been inoculated with beneficial bacteria and mycorrhizal fungi, will grow healthier, stronger plants.

Check if you have a fertile mix. Some seed-starting mediums are devoid of plant nutrition. These are great for long-germinating perennial seeds but not for veggies. If your mix doesn't contain compost, worm castings, or another source of fertility, you'll need to transplant your babies very quickly into something richer so they don't starve.

Consider mixing your own. You can mix your own growing medium using coconut coir or peat moss, compost, vermiculite, and perlite, along with amendments. We used to make our own, but no longer. Unless you run a nursery or a large-scale farm, or you happen to make a lot of high-quality compost yourself, the cost savings associated with mixing up your own growing medium is pretty minimal. Plus, premade mediums have been crafted and analyzed for best results and usually contain the ingredients needed to help your transplants grow.

Invest in a high-quality mix, or source high-quality ingredients to make one yourself. The quantity of mix you need for starting seeds is not huge, and the impact that this growing medium will have on your plants' health is big. We've had success with FoxFarm's Ocean Forest and with Vermont Compost Company's Fort Vee and Fort Light.

Melon transplants grow quickly and need spacious, 4-inch pots or the equivalent.

TRAYS AND POTS FOR GROWING TRANSPLANTS

Trays (also called flats) and pots come in a range of shapes and sizes. The size of the seed and the baby plant that you're growing will determine the size of pot you use. For larger gardens and farms, transplants are grown in cells within trays. These trays come in standard sizes that work well with heat mats, lights, and so forth (see page 176 for more on these); if you have been to a plant nursery, you've probably seen them. They are typically 10 by 20 inches and are sometimes called "1020" trays. The more cells (the spaces where soil and seeds will go) per tray, the smaller each individual cell. Individual pots or six-pack or four-pack pots are also available, and some fit neatly into open trays that are 10 by 20 inches. Choose what to use based on the number of transplants you'll be growing, along with your budget and what's available to you.

Pot shapes. We recommend square pots rather than round because they fit more efficiently into trays and/or onto rectangular heat mats.

Pot sizes. The general size recommendations for different garden vegetables apply to pots as well. If you use a pot that's too large,

you'll waste space and may have difficulty transplanting if the root system of your little plant hasn't filled out the entire pot. If you use a pot that's too small, you'll crowd the root system of your emerging transplant, which can have a lifelong impact on growth and vigor. If you notice that a plant is getting big for its pot and you're not ready to transplant it out into the garden yet, move it to a larger pot.

Watering. Do your best to keep your transplants evenly watered. Whatever size pot you use, you'll need to make sure the growing medium stays moist the whole time a seed is germinating and growing (not just moist on the surface).

Tray and Pot Sizes for Different Plants

Here are the trays or pot sizes that we typically use for various plants. Please note that there is some variation in size among different styles of trays and pots.

TRAY OR POT	PLANTS
72-cell trays with each cell being about 1½" × 1½" × 2¼" deep (or equivalent size pots)	Arugula, basil, broccoli, cabbage, eggplants, kale, lettuce, most cut flowers, peppers, spinach, tomatoes (with eggplants, peppers, and tomatoes we'll transplant from 72-cell trays into 4" pots once the plants are large enough)
4" pots or equivalent	Cucumber, muskmelons, watermelons, winter squash, zucchini and other summer squashes (we start eggplants, peppers, and tomatoes in 72-cell trays and transplant them into 4" pots)
Open flats without cells	Celery, leeks, onions

How to SOW SEEDS in Flats or Pots

This whole process is best done outside, as it can get rather messy. It is optimal to be working on a space between waist and chest height, but a plastic folding table, picnic table, or the ground all work great, too! Note that we like to prepare the growing medium the night before we use the soil.

1. **PREMOISTEN YOUR GROWING MEDIUM** (if it's dry at all). Put a hose in the bag and let it flow for a minute or two, then turn off the hose and fluff the medium around to distribute the water evenly. Add enough water so that the medium is evenly moist. It will absorb water over time, so erring on the wetter side at first is better, though don't drown it! Let the growing medium absorb that moisture for several hours (or overnight).

   TIP: *What you're going for is moist but not wet; it should squish like a wrung-out sponge, but not drip when you squeeze a handful of it.*

2. **FILL THE TRAYS.** Find a spot where you can make a mess. Place sheets of cardboard under your trays to catch overflow. Using a scoop (such as an old yogurt container or a 4-inch pot), fill your pots or cell trays loosely to their tops with your growing medium of choice, spreading the medium across the tray (if using) so that it falls into every cell. It's easy to under-fill the cells around the edges of a tray. Be sure to pour growing medium thoroughly around the whole thing, which usually means overflowing onto your cardboard or table.

3. **TAMP DOWN THE MEDIUM.** This will improve water retention and soil-to-seed contact while leaving space on top for the seeds. One option is to use another pot or tray of the same size to press down and level the surface of the growing medium. Another is to lift and drop the pots or trays from about 2 inches up, letting gravity settle the growing medium. Top up any less-full cells or pots.

4. PLACE SEEDS IN THE POTS OR CELLS, RIGHT IN THE CENTER. For large seeds, make small depressions for the seeds with your fingers. For fresh seeds with a high germination rate from a trusted supplier, place one or two seeds per pot/cell. In the case of older seeds that have a dubious germination rate, place three or more seeds per pot or cell.

5. COVER THE SEEDS WITH MEDIUM. Using your scoop, sprinkle ⅛ to ¼ inch of growing medium (more for bigger seeds) over the seeds. Brush off any excess medium around the pots.

NOTE: *Light-dependent germinators (such as lettuce, arugula, dill, basil, and many other herbs) do best without soil on top of them. Simply press these seeds down so that they're nestled in the growing medium.*

6. PRESS DOWN ON THE GROWING MEDIUM WITH YOUR FINGERS. There should be at least a ⅛-inch gap between the top of the growing medium and the top of the pot. This is so that water doesn't overflow and carry away some of your growing medium or, eek, seeds!

7. WATER THE SEEDS GENTLY AND THOROUGHLY. Make sure to use a watering can or hose nozzle that provides a light sprinkle and does not disturb the seeds. A watering can with a "rose" (a diffuser that spreads out the water into droplets) can work nicely. Avoid mister attachments, as these are too gentle and don't deliver enough water to penetrate to the bottom of the growing medium. Ideally, the soil should never dry out completely but will get dryish between waterings.

TIPS: *It's easy to assume you've watered well, when in fact the bottoms of your pots are bone dry. To avoid this problem, we sometimes leave one pot without a seed in it so that we can dig with our finger to assess moisture content. Once- or twice-daily watering usually does the trick, depending on how hot it is.*

Keep an eye on your heat mats and your grow lights to make sure they're not turned up too high, which heats things up too much and causes water to evaporate quickly.

If two seedlings emerge in a single soil cell or pot, gently pinch off whichever you deem less vigorous.

Transplanting Baby Plants

After seeds have germinated and grown into little plants, their root systems will eventually outgrow their pots. The time it takes to do this is quite variable; it only takes cucumbers about 2 weeks, even in a 4-inch pot, before they need more space; but peppers take a month or more before they need to go from smaller cells into 4-inch pots. At this time, when a plant's root system has completely filled out its pot but isn't circling around like a tiger in captivity, you have two choices: Some crops can go straight from their first pots into the ground; for others, you will need to transplant them into bigger pots before they make their final journey into the garden.

Frost- and pest-sensitive crops are usually those that we "pot on," or transplant into larger pots before planting them out. We want them to get as big as they can before contending with the trials and tribulations of the wild world in the garden. In the case of frost-sensitive plants, potting on into larger pots will allow the plants to get a head start, even if outside temperatures aren't quite warm enough for them. For pest-sensitive crops, babying them in pots until they're quite large means that they'll have a fighting chance against pests. In our region, eggplants get decimated by flea beetles unless they're over a foot tall at the time of transplanting or well protected by floating row cover.

Whether you're transplanting into bigger pots or into the ground, the basic steps are the same.

Press down in a circle around transplanted seedlings to make a moat, or a depression where water can settle and percolate down to the roots.

TIPS FOR TRANSPLANTING SUCCESS

Transplanting from small pots into bigger pots, or from any pot into the garden, is a delicate matter. There is a lot of trauma that can be sustained by plants during this process. But if you keep the following tips in mind, your plants will be thrilled to arrive in their new, roomier homes.

Harden Off Your Plants

In preparation for transplanting into the garden, gradually introduce plants to outdoor conditions; this process is called hardening off. It gets them accustomed to sunlight, wind, and temperature variations before transplanting. The result is that they adapt to those conditions before experiencing the shock of serious root disturbance that goes along with transplanting. Hardening off isn't necessary if you're potting up from one size pot to another, because growing conditions will remain the same. It's most important for spring crops that may be especially shocked to leave a warm, protected place.

How to TRANSPLANT YOUR PLANTS

1. **WATER YOUR PLANTS WELL.** Transplanting works best with roots and soil that are moist.

2. **PREPARE THE GROUND** you will be transplanting into (whether a garden bed or growing medium and larger pots).

3. **REMOVE COTYLEDONS** (a.k.a. seed leaves; the plump-looking first leaves that may or may not still be clinging to the stem) and a few true leaves, if there are more than four. Also pinch off and remove extra plants, if there is more than one growing in the pot/cell.

4. **DIG A HOLE** or loosen the soil where you will be transplanting, depending on the size of the plant; for smaller plants, a full-on hole isn't necessary. If you're transplanting into a bigger pot, fill the pot a quarter to a third full and tamp down the growing medium.

5. **REMOVE THE PLANT FROM CONTAINER.** Use a butter knife or other tool to gently lift the plant out of its pot, or turn the pot upside down and gently tap or squeeze it to release the roots.

6. **GENTLY LOOSEN SPIRALING ROOTS** (optional). If the plant is pot bound, loosen roots with your fingers so they aren't tightly bound.

7. **PLACE THE PLANT** in its new home. Lower the plant down into the loosened soil or pot so that the place where the cotyledons used to be is level with the soil/pot. (The one exception to this rule is tomatoes, which we discuss on page 189.)

8. **BACKFILL** around the newly transplanted adventurer. Make sure to completely bury the growing medium and roots with new soil or growing medium; don't let the growing medium from its previous home poke up over the new soil surface.

9. **GENTLY TAMP THE SOIL** or growing medium around the plant. This ensures good soil contact and helps the roots have access to water and nutrients.

   TIP: *When planting out bigger plants like tomatoes and peppers, it can be good to make a little moat a few inches around the plant to encourage water to percolate in a big circle around the plant and encourage outward root growth.*

10. **WATER** your new transplants deeply. This is a good time to share some words of encouragement and gratitude!

Peppers are transplanted twice after sowing: into 4-inch pots to grow bigger, then into the ground. Brassicas are transplanted directly from the tray into the ground.

Start hardening off about a week before you plan to transplant out.

- On the first day, set your plants out for about an hour in direct sunlight, the next day for two hours, and so on, until they are out for five hours.

- Next leave them out for two whole days and a night. If it is particularly windy, hailing, raining super hard, or excessively cold, bring your plants back inside until the extreme weather stops.

- If you have a table or other raised surface to place your pots on, this can help protect them from rodents, meandering cats, or spaced-out humans who might knock them over.

Sometimes we just place the plants outside for a few days before we transplant them into the garden and call it good, especially if outside conditions are not extremely different from what they were used to indoors. Plants are ever so adaptable, thank goodness.

Look for an Overcast Day

Overcast weather is ideal for transplanting. In the absence of cloud cover, you can transplant in the late afternoon or evening. Exposure to bright, prolonged, direct sunlight is stressful for newly transplanted leaf systems when their compromised roots are adapting to so much change. Think of it like this: If you're moving, would you do it on a Sunday, then go to work on Monday without unpacking? Or would you rather move on a Friday and have the weekend to recuperate? Photosynthesis is one of the main jobs plants do, so we can respect them by giving them a solar break after transplanting.

Keep It Clean

It is important to have good hygiene when transplanting, especially with tomatoes, in order to prevent the spread of pathogens. One example of a nasty pathogen is the tobacco mosaic virus. It's highly virulent and can remain in dry soil, leaf debris, or dry

Plants moving from inside to the great outdoors need time to adjust. Starting with a few hours a day helps the transition.

Ouch! Pinching leaves off a baby plant might feel violent, but you're doing it a favor. Fewer leaves mean less water loss and transplant shock.

root matter for up to two years! To prevent the spread of any microscopic ne'er-do-wells (pathogens), take care to wash your hands, tools, and pots between types of plants when transplanting, especially if anything looks fishy.

Use a Tool to Remove Plants

A butter knife, a stiff plant tag, a splint of bamboo, or even a stick works well to help ease your transplants out of their pots. This is much gentler on the plant than pulling it out by its stem or even squeezing the pot to get it out. Indeed, it's ideal to handle transplants by their rootball rather than a stem or leaf. Along with your loosening tool, you can tip the pot on its side, or even all the way upside down, to coax the little plant out with ease. Hold your fingers over the soil, with the stem between your fingers, so you can support the rootball when it slides free of the pot. Natalie likes to use cell trays from Neversink Tools, which are pricey but super durable, and they have a biggish hole at the bottom of the pots that you can poke with a finger to remove the plants. Pretty nifty.

RECOGNIZING MOSAIC VIRUSES

If you have a tomato, pepper, cucumber, eggplant, tobacco, spinach, petunia, or marigold plant with weird discoloration between veins, or mosaic-looking splotches, along with a failure to thrive, you may have a mosaic virus. Tobacco mosaic virus is one of these, but there are several others that behave similarly. This is a really serious situation and requires that you bag up and destroy (not compost, as that can spread the virus) all infected plants, as well as disinfect all tools that have touched them. Two options for destruction are burning (use a paper bag in this case) or throwing in the trash. What a pain in the butt!

Tobacco mosaic virus can come from tobacco. In fact, people who smoke tobacco, especially those who hand-roll cigarettes, need to use special care to disinfect themselves before touching transplants. This pathogen, and others, can also come from seeds, which means even if you are a nonsmoker, you are not necessarily safe. Two effective disinfectants for mosaic viruses are a 10 percent bleach solution and, strangely, a solution of 20 percent nonfat dry milk powder. Tools or hands should be submerged for 1 minute and then thoroughly rinsed. For more on plant diseases, see page 240.

Remove Some Leaves

If your plant has more than four true leaves (not squishy cotyledons, or "seed leaves"), remove a quarter to a third of them before transplanting. Carefully pluck or snip off the leaves at the base of the plant, *not* at the top near the growing tip, which could stop the plant from growing at all. Be careful not to tear the plant tissue. This step can reduce transplant shock by minimizing the amount of water that transpires (evaporates) through the leaves and the amount of aboveground growth that needs to be maintained by the roots.

When transplanting, roots will inevitably be disturbed, and if you don't remove some leaves, this creates an imbalance between the root system and the green growth it can sustain above ground. Removing leaves gives the roots a break and allows green growth and root growth to recover from the stress of transplanting at the same rate. This may seem counterintuitive, but it truly can be helpful!

Dig a Hole and/or Loosen Soil

Depending on the size of your transplant, along with the tilth (texture) of your garden soil, you may simply need to loosen a spot for it or you may have to dig a proper hole. For smaller transplants and softer, looser soil, using a hori hori (garden knife) or your hands to break up the soil is usually just fine. For larger transplants (those in 4-inch pots or bigger), a hand hoe, trowel, or larger shovel tends to work better. If you're working with heavy clay, digging an actual hole and even adding in some sand or compost to lighten it may be your best bet. Whatever your circumstances, the goal is to provide a soft, fluffy home for the transplant so that its roots can spread out in all directions, including downward.

Gently Loosen Roots as Needed

After you've freed the transplant from its pot, take a look at the roots. Ideally they will have filled out the whole amount of growing medium but won't be spiraling around the bottom or

sides. This spiraling is called being "potbound" or "rootbound," and it means the plant has outgrown its tiny home. If you don't see any roots, or if the growing medium quickly crumbles away from the few roots that are present, the plant could use a little more time to fill out its pot and isn't yet ready to transplant.

If a good solid root system is present, or if the plant is potbound, *very* gently loosen the roots by massaging them with your fingertips before transplanting. In the case of a potbound plant, you can be a bit more vigorous with this loosening. It's done to encourage the roots to grow out into the larger pot or garden soil rather than to simply stay within the size and shape of their smaller pot.

Transplant at the Proper Depth

You'll want to transplant most vegetables so that the place on their stem where the cotyledons (seed leaves) were attached is level with the soil or growing medium in their new home. If you didn't see any seed leaves, just transplant ⅛ to ¼ inch deeper than the plant was in its previous home. An exception to this is tomatoes: Bury tomato plants about a third of the way up the stem from the initial growing medium level. You can do this either by digging a deep hole or digging a trench and laying the tomato plants in it at a diagonal. Tomatoes have a wonderful ability to grow adventitious roots from their stems, so this deeper transplanting results in a deeper, bigger root system.

Tamp the Soil

Once the baby plant is settled in its new home (be that a garden bed or a larger pot), take a moment to tamp down the soil all around it. As you do this, be sure to cover up all of the growing medium from the smaller pot it has just evacuated with new soil from its new home. While plants don't do well in dense, highly compacted soil, they do need to have good contact between their roots and the soil particles in order to pull in water and nutrients. The goal here is to snug up the rootball with the soil or medium it's been transplanted into.

Water Your Transplants Right Away!

After transplanting into a bigger pot or into the ground, make sure to water your plants immediately, totally soaking the roots. This reduces transplant shock and gets them off to a good start in their new home. If the garden soil or growing medium that you're transplanting into is dry, moisten it before transplanting. In very dry areas, this can mean running a gentle sprinkler for an hour or two the day before you transplant, then giving it some time to dry out. You don't want to transplant into soaked or soggy soil, which can be easily compacted when worked.

LEFT: You can help transplants adjust to their new freedom by loosening the roots, letting them know they are no longer confined by a pot.

RIGHT: Transplanting seedlings at the right depth, removing lower leaves, and watering well will reduce transplant shock.

How to Buy Strong Transplants

Growing your own transplants is exciting and fun and gives you access to greater variety, but it takes work, equipment, and a fair amount of space. Don't feel like you have to grow transplants to be a good gardener or that you have to grow all of your own transplants to experience the benefits of the process. While we grow many transplants, we also buy some, especially if we just need one or a few of a particular plant.

To be sure you purchase strong, healthy transplants while minimizing the chance of introducing new pests and diseases into your garden, here are tips to keep in mind.

KNOW YOUR GROWER AND ASK QUESTIONS

Put in the time to search for local nurseries or farms in your area that grow their own transplants. Big-box stores may have eye-catching displays out front, but they usually bulk order transplants from huge greenhouses far away. Not only does this send your hard-earned money outside your community, but it also increases the chances of new pests or pathogens hitching a ride on the plants. Plus, the varieties grown for national sales are usually not particularly suited to *your* conditions. These transplants are also more likely to be potbound. If these are the only transplants available to you, don't worry! It's definitely better to use them than to skip growing a garden.

If you find a local grower, ask them questions about where they got the seeds, what growing medium they use, if they've grown these varieties in their own gardens, and so forth. If plants start their life in the presence of chemical fertilizers, it may take them time to adjust to organic growing conditions.

INSPECT THE TRANSPLANTS THOROUGHLY

The greenhouse conditions where most commercial transplants are grown can harbor many pests and pathogens. Use your eyes to carefully inspect any transplants you're thinking of buying to detect problem organisms. Notice general vigor, color, spots, and other irregularities. Look at both the tops and undersides of leaves for pest damage and the presence of actual pests. Pop a plant out of its pot and take a look at the roots. Are the roots spiraling around . . . is it potbound? Some problems are hard to spot visually, but many issues can be detected with the naked eye. If a plant doesn't look healthy or you see pests on it, don't buy it, even if it's on sale!

Root-bound plants will be stressed and less vigorous than seedlings that haven't been left in their pots or cells for too long.

Direct Sowing

Direct sowing is one of the simplest, lowest-input (and lowest-budget) ways to grow vegetables. If it's done correctly, it has lots of advantages over growing or buying transplants for certain crops. Plus, there's something timeless and fulfilling about putting seeds directly into the earth.

If you live in a hot climate with a long growing season, most vegetables can be sown directly. In cooler climates with shorter seasons, some crops need a head start indoors in order to bear fruit. You can find information on sowing vs. transplanting specific crops on page 356 and in the vegetable profiles beginning on page 275.

Advantages of Direct Sowing

- No need to buy seedling mix, flats, pots, heat mats, or lights—or to own a greenhouse.

- Seeds are incredibly cheap in comparison with transplants; one packet of seeds costs about as much as one transplant, sometimes less, and contains lots of potential plants.

- When seeds germinate, they send their first root down toward the center of the earth; direct sowing allows natural root growth to happen unhindered by a wall of plastic or wood in a flat or pot.

One small handful of kale seeds contains the possibility for hundreds of kale plants and thousands more seeds.

- Low-vigor (wimpy) seeds might not make it in a direct-sowing scenario (compared with being babied in a greenhouse), which automatically culls weaker plants.

Even though it's beautifully simple and has lots of advantages, direct sowing is not without its challenges. In making your decision about direct sowing vs. growing/buying transplants, consider your particular growing conditions, along with the specific crop in question. Here are some circumstances when direct sowing is *not* the best option.

Challenges of Direct Sowing

- All seeds have an optimal temperature range for germination; if your soil doesn't warm into that range in the time that you need to start those seeds, your seeds won't germinate (see the table When to Sow, Plant, and Harvest Based on Temperature and Season on page 356 in the appendix).

- Rough or rocky soil can be hard to prepare into a welcoming seedbed; to germinate and thrive, seeds need good soil contact; if rocks or clumps reduce soil contact, seeds can easily dry out before they germinate, especially if they're small seeds.

- Heavy weed pressure can make it difficult for seedlings to thrive; if you know that your garden soil is full of vigorous weed seeds that will grow faster than more tender, slower-growing veggies, direct sowing might not be a great choice.

- Final spacing of your plants is harder to determine with direct sowing; you can't be sure of the germination rate you will get, so your sowing might end up patchy; it's common to sow heavily and then thin plants when direct sowing.

- Thinning, while helpful to ensure a good final spacing, can be challenging for some people; it's hard to kill baby plants, and it's an extra step that needs to happen before the plants grow too large.

How to DIRECT SOW PLANTS

1. **PREPARE YOUR SEEDBED.** Make sure that the top 2 to 4 inches of your soil are loose and fluffy. You can do this by digging, plowing, or, if you've been tending a no-till garden for some time, just removing the mulch to reveal a beautiful, soft, open palette. Run a rake over the bed to smooth out its surface and remove any debris, such as rocks or roots. To do this, first make a pass with the rake tine-side down to grab any big chunks, then flip the rake tine-side up and gently use the flat side to smooth out the bed. (See Chapter 3 for more on no-till gardening and bed prep and Chapter 7 for more on mulch.)

2. **DECIDE ON A PLANTING PATTERN AND MARK IT OUT.** There are three common ways to plant: in rows; in mounds; and broadcast or scattered. We plant most crops in rows, but, depending on the vegetable, we also sometimes plant in mounds (especially with winter and summer squash, cucumbers, and melons). We occasionally broadcast cut-and-come-again greens, cilantro, and dill, but mostly we plant in rows.

   For rows, to create straight furrows at the correct depth and distance apart for the seeds you'll be sowing, use your finger, a furrowing hoe, or a hori hori (see more about tools in Chapter 2). For mounds, push individual seeds down into a mound (about a 12-inch by 12-inch area that has been loosened and amended and is a few inches high). To broadcast seeds, scatter them evenly over a broad area, then rake in gently and cover lightly with mulch or soil.

3. **SOW SEEDS.** Depending on the area you are planting, this can be done by hand or with a device. Rolling walk-behind seeders and jab-style seeders are available for larger gardens and farms. Seeding devices can also be homemade. We mostly sow by hand. Sowing depth depends on the crop you are working with and ultimately on the size of the seed. A rule of thumb is to plant to a depth of two times the width of the seed (see the charts on page 358 for specific planting depths for different crops).

   TIPS: *Some seeds, including lettuce, arugula, dill, basil, and some other herbs, need light to germinate, so check for specific information. You may also want to mark the rows where you plant slow-geminating seeds, like carrots, before covering them so that you can weed around them.*

4. **COVER THE SEEDS.** Good soil contact is crucial for germination and prevents seedlings from getting dried out easily once they germinate. Cover them completely with soil, using your hands or a hoe, then tamp the soil down gently. For light-dependent germinators, press the seeds down into the soil without covering them.

TIP: *For small seeds, sprinkle loose soil on top of them instead of pushing the sides of the furrow in.*

5. **WATER.** Seeds must be kept moist until germination happens. If a seed desiccates before it germinates, it will die. Note, however, that it's possible to kill seeds by overwatering. In most conditions, watering once a day is fine, though in the heat of summer twice a day may be needed. See the Water and Irrigation section in Chapter 7 for more details.

6. **WEED.** All that watering really encourages weed seeds to sprout, too! For veggie seeds that take a long time to germinate, like carrots, weed between rows before your crop germinates. Only do this step if you have clearly marked rows so you are sure to not remove your germinating seeds. Weeding can also happen as the babies are germinating but before thinning.

TIP: *Use a hoe to weed between rows, and then use your fingers to pinch weeds within the row once the seeds have germinated.*

7. **THIN PLANTS TO THE DESIRED SPACING.** Once your baby plants are up, thin out enough of them to achieve the optimal spacing (see Chapter 7 for detailed thinning information; you can also download a video tutorial on thinning from our website; see page 364). Also, keep up with weeding after thinning so that your crops don't have to fend off competition from too many vigorous neighbors.

When to Plant What

Timing is among the most crucial elements of gardening. When should seeds be started in spring? When is it too late for transplanting or sowing hot-weather crops out in the garden? What's the ideal window to start seeds and transplant out for fall and winter gardening? How many times per season can we (and should we) plant each crop to extend the harvest? These are all important questions, and their answers can, to some degree, be moving targets.

We'll do our best to simplify the process and give you a framework for figuring out timing. And we'll share caveats and considerations that help you tune in to the best timing in your specific situation and respond to fluctuating conditions and circumstances.

As the climate gets more and more erratic, nailing the timing with gardening becomes trickier. Plus, broader regions

contain microclimates that each have slightly different garden timing. For example, Natalie's garden is in a frost pocket; temperatures there are typically a few degrees below what they are up the road or even a couple of miles away. Noticing conditions, year after year, provides information to fine-tune planting times in your particular spot.

As with every other aspect of gardening, your own notes and observations are some of the most valuable data you can gather. Be sure to write down sowing and transplanting dates so you can look back and adjust over time.

Factors That Influence When to Plant What

- First frost date (actual and official/predicted)
- Last frost date (actual and official/predicted)
- Days to maturity of the vegetable variety
- Moon phase, sign, and/or other energetics
- Specific soil and weather conditions
- Your availability and other commitments
- Amount of that crop you want to harvest, eat, and preserve, and if you want to do so all at once or over time (succession planting)

OTHER RESOURCES. If the above list feels overwhelming and you just want someone to tell you exactly what to do to get started, here are a couple of other options.

- The Timing Tables starting on page 339 include a key that helps you determine which planting region you're in and when to plant what in your area.
- *The Old Farmer's Almanac* online planting calendar is the best one out there. Simply enter your zip or postal code, and it presents a neat calendar of planting windows for every crop.
- Local seed companies can be another great resource. Many bioregional seed companies include planting calendars in their catalogs

Natalie waters potatoes that were planted in the spring and are looking quite vivacious soaking up the summer sun.

Jack Frost has kissed these Austrian winter peas, which, unlike many garden veggies, contain a natural antifreeze that means they'll bounce back.

and online. These may be more customized to your region.

- Other gardeners in your area are almost always supportive when another gardener is looking for local planting knowledge—seek them out as you tweak the more generalized suggestions we offer in the vegetable profiles section of this book. Now let's delve into the planting factors mentioned above in a bit more detail.

FIRST AND LAST FROST DATES

The last frost date is the last day when temperatures go below freezing (32°F/0°C) in winter or spring, and the first frost date is the day when temperatures fall below freezing for the first time after the summer growing season. If you live somewhere very warm, you may not ever see freezing temperatures. In our North Carolina mountains, and in most of the United States and Canada, the last frost usually happens sometime in spring, and the first frost occurs in fall.

PAY ATTENTION TO TEMPERATURE!

There are lots of things that influence when to plant (see the list, page 194), and it's easy to get psyched out by trying to get everything perfectly right. The only end-all factor is heat and cold. Plants that can't tolerate freezing temperatures will die if they're exposed to that kind of cold. And many plants need a certain number of warm days in order to mature. See the vegetable profiles beginning on page 275 for information on the heat needs and cold tolerance of specific crops.

Each region has an official (predicted) first and last frost date, which are based on averages over time. *The Old Farmer's Almanac* uses these dates to create your planting calendar. These numbers don't claim to be able to predict the weather, but rather they make an informed guess about when the last frost has almost *definitely passed* or the soonest that the first frost is *likely to arrive.*

Trouble is, nobody knows ahead of time when the first or last frost will actually happen each year. And as climate change disrupts global weather patterns, we've seen early warming in spring followed by cold snaps as late as a week after our "official" last frost.

What can you do on your end to prepare for the unexpected and cultivate your garden's resilience?

- Keep your own records so you can form a picture of current weather patterns in your area (rather than rely on historical ones).
- Pay attention to weather forecasts each spring and fall.
- Take precautions to protect seedlings if temperatures dip unexpectedly.

The traditional wisdom in our area is to wait until after Mother's Day in spring to set out frost-sensitive plants. We tend to look at the extended forecast during the first week of May; if we don't see cold in the forecast, we set out these sensitive plants then.

DAYS TO MATURITY

Each variety of each vegetable will have an estimated number of "days to maturity" listed on the seed packet, or online. These numbers can vary greatly from variety to variety of the same crop. For example, 'Scarlet Keeper' carrots take 85 days to mature, while 'Mokum' carrots take just 48 days; that's a difference of more than a month! Considering days to maturity is especially important for early-spring crops that don't like high temperatures (like carrots), midsummer-planted crops for fall and winter harvest (carrots again, among others), and

super-long-season crops like sweet potatoes and some varieties of winter squash.

You want to make sure that spring crops mature before it gets too hot for them, long-season crops get enough frost-free days to mature, and fall crops can mature before it gets too cold and the day length shortens such that growth grinds to a halt. For heat-loving summer crops, knowing the days to maturity will help you determine how late might be too late to put them in the ground, based on when temperatures start to cool off in your area.

MOON PHASE, SIGN, AND OTHER ENERGETICS

For as long as agriculture has been practiced, people around the world have timed planting, tending, and harvesting crops based on the moon phases and signs (what astrological sign the moon is passing through), along with other astronomical, astrological, and ecological phenomena, including wild-plant life phases and animal migrations, also known as the science of phenology. An example of this from around here is to plant corn when the oak leaves are as big as squirrel's ears. This attention to wild nature is a beautiful way to tune in to bigger cycles that we humans are embedded within. There's also some scientific basis for the power of the moon to move water within soil and plant tissues.

If this is your cup of tea, that's wonderful; you might want to explore old-timey gardening with the moon or even biodynamic gardening. If it's not your thing, you'll still be able to grow a garden and harvest delicious food. Natalie has done a lot of moon-phase-oriented gardening; Chloe has done almost none. Both of us have had successes and failures over time with both approaches. You can download a video of Natalie discussing gardening with the moon on our website (see the link on page 364).

Luscious lettuce, which is rather short-lived, can be planted several times per year, in succession, for an extended harvest.

CONDITIONS AND YOUR AVAILABILITY

At this writing, our warm spring soil is sodden from continued heavy rains, and an out-of-the-blue hailstorm just dropped ice chunks as big as golf balls on the garden. Chloe was hoping to transplant peppers today, but the elemental beings at play in the sky had other plans.

As with every other aspect of gardening, your actual moment-to-moment experience is the ultimate decision-maker. If, on paper, a certain day is right for planting but it rains all day, don't plant in the mud just because that's what's on your calendar (that would not only be unpleasant but would cause soil compaction). Similarly, if a particular day is less than ideal weather-wise but that's when you have time to get out and do it, that's when planting needs to happen. We're assuming most of you aren't going to dedicate yourselves to full-time gardening, sacrificing all other obligations and commitments, so give yourself some grace and flexibility.

SUCCESSION PLANTING

Some shorter-lived crops can be sown or transplanted more than once in a season to provide a longer harvest window. This is called succession planting, since two or more rounds of that crop will be planted in succession. Some cool-weather crops can be planted once in spring and once in fall, which is another kind of succession.

Just because something *can* be succession planted doesn't mean it *should* be. Consider how much of that crop you want to eat and/or preserve. Also, in some areas, late-spring plantings of certain crops are often decimated by pests or diseases that tend to strengthen in numbers as warm, wet conditions persist: Planting those crops then can be an exercise in frustration. Refer to the vegetable profiles beginning on page 275 for specific information on succession timing for various crops.

These are the crops we generally plant in succession:

- Cilantro
- Cucumbers
- Dill
- Lettuce
- Snap beans
- Zucchini/summer squash

These are the cool-weather crops we plant once in early spring and once in midsummer for fall and winter harvests:

- Arugula
- Beets
- Broccoli
- Cabbage
- Carrots
- Cauliflower
- Kale
- Radishes
- Turnips

7

Caring for Plants
When They Are Growing

Water and Irrigation 200

Feeding Growing Plants 207

Thinning 210

Weed Management 213

Mulch 221

Trellises and Trellising 229

Water and Irrigation

Water is life! It's as essential to a thriving garden as sunshine, seeds, and soil. Both too much and too little water can be harmful to plants, so striking a balance is key. Watering can take up a lot of time in the heat of summer, so being realistic about what you can do and setting up infrastructure to support ease are critical for holistic garden happiness. No matter where you live and what amount of rainfall you get, there are water-honoring strategies that will help you conserve and utilize water intelligently and efficiently in your garden. Choosing a system that honors both the water itself and *you* will lead to the best results.

HOW AND WHEN TO WATER

Water percolates into soil best when it's applied in a slow, gentle sprinkle. Think of a light spring rain, when you might enjoy a walk outside with an umbrella to protect you. Whatever your watering method, it should ideally deliver a slow, steady amount of water to avoid erosion and runoff. It should deliver enough water—in this slow, gentle manner— so that the soil is moistened at least 5 inches deep and water is not lingering on the surface, as can happen when we apply more water in a shorter period of time.

Assess how much water your plants need. Generally speaking, a vegetable garden needs about 2 inches of water per week. This translates to a little over a half gallon per square foot over the course of a week. The amount of water needed increases when temperatures

Plants drink up sweet water from their roots, so watering at the base of their stem gives them what they need, where they need it.

increase and when plants get bigger and transpire more. Germinating seeds need a little bit of water every day, whereas established plants can go a few to several days without watering.

Crop type, soil type, wind, and other climate conditions can impact water needs as well.

- Crops with shallow roots, like onions and celery, tend to need more frequent watering.
- Deep-rooted crops, like tomatoes and beets, can find their own water underground and don't need as much irrigation.
- When it rains or snows, that counts toward the inches of water your garden needs.
- When it's hot, dry, and windy, more water is lost through transpiration and evaporation, so more watering might be necessary.
- When it's overcast and cool, more water stays in the ground and in plants.

Water slowly and gently. Watering gently, like a soft rain, affects how water penetrates the soil and can have other notable impacts.

- If you water with a nozzle that shoots water in a strong jet or even stand too close with an adjustable nozzle on the "garden" setting, you can totally blast germinating seeds out of the ground.
- Small seeds, like carrots, for example, like to be covered by a tiny bit of soil. Too much soil on top makes a huge obstacle for them to emerge through. Too much water with too much pressure would disturb these small seeds.
- Watering with a strong pressure can also compact soil and hurt baby plants and seedlings.

Track how much water you give your plants. If you're overhead watering using sprinklers, watering cans, or hoses with wands or nozzles, one handy way to judge how much water your garden is getting is to place an empty cylindrical container (like a tin can) in the garden, then water. You can even write lines on the container at ½ inch, 1 inch, and so forth. Be sure the container is a cylinder and

RADIANT RAINDROPS: A PHILOSOPHY TO GARDEN BY

When she was in India, Chloe picked up the book *The Radiant Raindrops of Rajasthan* by Anupam Mishra. It opens with a story of the Hindu deity Krishna getting lost in the Rajasthani desert, a place that only receives about 12 inches of rainfall annually. Krishna comes across a rishi, a Hindu sage, who helps him find his way. In exchange for this kindness, Krishna offers to grant a boon or blessing upon the rishi. This wise person asks that the people of Rajasthan "never suffer from lack of water." Instead of increasing the amount of rainfall in the Rajasthani desert, Krishna gives the blessing in the form of creativity, ingenuity, and care for each drop of rain that falls in this arid region.

The rest of the book is a detailed account of the many ingenious and elegant techniques for rainwater harvesting and storage, methods that have been used throughout history in Rajasthan, supporting thriving communities in the area. The story illustrates how our *relationship* with natural systems can lead to perceived abundance or lack. Our human cleverness is best used to understand, learn from, and adapt to the conditions we find ourselves in rather than try to manipulate or control them.

not wider at the top than the bottom so you get an accurate measure of how much water is hitting the ground.

Consider the time of day you water. The ideal time to overhead water is early in the morning. Less water will evaporate into the cool morning air, and if plant leaves get wet, they won't remain wet long enough to harbor fungal pathogens like powdery mildew. Watering in the evening will also get most of the water into the ground, but if plants remain wet all night, this can cause fungal pathogen problems. Watering in the middle of a sunny day means you'll lose some water to evaporation, and large water droplets on big leaves (like squash and cucumbers) can act like magnifying glasses and concentrate sunlight to the point of burning. We have also noticed more soil compaction in exposed (not mulched) soil that is watered in the heat of the day in direct sun. If it's overcast, you can safely water any old time.

QUALITY WATERING EQUIPMENT

Sometimes in this life, you get what you pay for. We've found this to be true with watering equipment. Indeed, cheap watering wands tend to crap out after one season, if you're lucky, and low-grade watering cans crack or clog easily. Well-made equipment isn't cheap, but if it's taken care of, it will last for many growing seasons and be a worthy investment.

Even if you choose to use a sprinkler or set up a drip system as your main watering method, you'll likely need to do some hand watering. So it's worth investing in the following:

- A well-made watering wand and/or watering can
- High-quality hoses
- Quick-release hose ends (they constrict the flow of water a little, but it makes swapping and moving watering tools so much easier!)

While we haven't done exhaustive trials of watering equipment, here are some brands that we've found to be high quality:

- Craftsman rubber hoses
- Dramm
- DripWorks
- Fiskars
- Fogg-It
- Rain Bird

WATERING METHODS

Irrigation techniques range from low-tech approaches to the completely automated. We'll go over several options here so you can choose whatever combination works best for your garden. Like with everything we share, none of these choices are all or nothing.

When we lived out west, we both used drip irrigation more often because of lack of warm-season rainfall. With this method, veggies get water delivered right to their roots throughout the growing season, without the need to hand water or use sprinklers. Now, living in the southern Appalachians, we've mostly hand watered our kitchen gardens with a hose and a watering wand because we tend to water less frequently. However, in the past few years, we've noticed longer dry spells and are considering incorporating some drip lines in our future gardens. When we're growing field crops, we tend to use sprinklers to cover the larger areas. You can mix and match irrigation techniques, too.

Hand Watering

When you hand water, you go from plant to plant, or bed to bed, with some sort of watering device to deliver water by hand to your garden. Using a hose with a garden nozzle or watering wand or using a watering can or even a bucket are all considered hand watering.

Natalie hand waters with a nice long water wand, walking from bed to bed and checking up on how everyone in the garden is doing.

Pluses of Hand Watering

- It's relatively low cost.
- It requires you to physically visit each of your plants regularly, which can be beneficial for noticing and tending to issues.
- It's super flexible. You can choose where to water and where not to water on any given day.

Challenges with Hand Watering

- It takes time. (When Chloe had an extra-large garden, she'd spend hours watering every few days.)
- If you're using a hose and watering wand, it can be tricky to drag the hose around without plowing over plants or getting the hose tangled around something. *Solution*: Add rounded wooden stakes at the corners of beds as "hose guides" to make movement easier.

Sprinklers

Watering with sprinklers is a popular practice for a reason, but like anything, it has its upsides and downsides.

Pluses of Sprinkler Watering

- If you've got a big garden, the odds are better your garden will get the water it needs (it's common to under-water when hand watering due to the time it requires).
- It's easier to set up than drip irrigation.
- This practice cools the air above and around crops, which can be of benefit in hot places.
- With sprinklers, you can deliver water to large areas in a slow, steady stream with minimal hands-on time.

An oscillating sprinkler isn't just good for summertime waterplay! When mounted atop a ladder, it covers an impressive amount of space.

Challenges of Sprinkler Watering

- Sprinklers are not precise—they cover a large area, but the garden's edges can often get missed.

- Water droplets on plant leaves can cause burning in the presence of strong sunlight, and water that lingers on leaves increases the chances of fungal diseases.

- Water loss due to evaporation can be significant, especially in arid climates (less so in humid places); sprinklers waste more water than other methods.

- You can't use sprinklers to water a single bed (this is where hand watering comes in, even if you use sprinklers as your main system).

There are many kinds of sprinklers to choose from, but the two kinds we use are oscillating sprinklers and impact sprinklers.

Oscillating sprinkler. This sprinkler slowly oscillates back and forth in a wide fan pattern; you may have run through one of these as a child or have one that your own children enjoy running through.

Advantages of Oscillating Sprinklers

- Depending on brand, this sprinkler type can be quite adjustable, which can conserve water, allow crops to get what they need, and avoid wetting paths, roads, and yards.

- Great for small-to-medium rectangular areas (depending on the sprinkler, rounded edges are fine).

- If your garden lies on large, wide, long terraces, or in a relatively rectangular shape like Natalie's, then this kind of sprinkler is superior.

Other Oscillator Considerations

- All-metal versions last longer but may not be as adjustable.

- Natalie likes to tie an oscillating sprinkler to the top of a stepladder to increase the area it covers.

- We strongly suggest getting an oscillating sprinkler that is simple and easy to adjust *in all four directions*.

Impact sprinkler. This sprinkler has a single head with a little wing that pulses against it, making an impact and turning it around in a slow, jerky circle (there is a funky dance move inspired by this kind of sprinkler!).

Advantages of Impact Sprinklers

- It's somewhat simpler to use, and it's a great piece of equipment for watering (but can get pricey for high-quality options).

- They are best for areas that are more rounded or square, rather than long and rectangular.

- This sprinkler covers a larger area than oscillating sprinklers and, perhaps, waters more effectively.

Impact sprinklers like this one can deliver a lot of water over a large circular or semicircular space.

Other Impact Sprinkler Considerations

- Chloe has used Rain Bird brand impact sprinklers on her farm but discovered that they need high pressure to work properly.
- The T-post sprinkler is, basically, the head of an impact sprinkler that you can perch atop a metal T-post for maximum coverage and flexibility (and it's affordable!).

Drip Irrigation

Drip irrigation is a form of "micro irrigation" that slowly releases water over time right in the root zone of plants. It was invented in 1965 by Israeli innovator Simcha Blass and is used on most small- to medium-scale vegetable farms in this and other countries.

Advantages of Drip Irrigation

- In arid climates with little to no summer rain, drip irrigation dramatically reduces weeds between beds since weeds need water to grow.
- It can be set on timers so that the garden is watered whether you're there to turn on the hose or not—a big plus for busy gardeners who want a summer vacation!

Notice the black plastic drip lines at the bases of these pepper plants. They lie right on the soil surface, delivering water to the roots.

- It conserves water; the water slowly drips into the soil and is never airborne, so almost none is lost to evaporation before entering the plants' root zone.

Other Drip Irrigation Considerations

- It requires planning, time, and purchase of materials.
- Since drip lines deliver water only to specific areas, you need to plan your crop spacing accordingly; broadcast seeding isn't so practical with this system. And you need to choose a drip tape that drips at the right distance for the crops you plan to grow.
- Timers are great but can fail at the most inconvenient times (like when they're being relied on to water when the gardener is on vacation!).
- T-tape—the most common type of drip line—isn't super durable. It's easy to damage with a hoe, fork, hori hori, or anything else, for that matter; it can be inconvenient to work around.

Flood Irrigation

Flood irrigation is a low-tech (though not unsophisticated) way to water. It's been used by humans for thousands of years, all over the world, and is still practiced today in certain places and for certain crops. This watering method basically involves shaping garden beds or rows so that they can be flooded

Flood irrigation has been used all over the world for millennia. It requires specific shaping of the land but doesn't require specialized equipment, and it can be done without plastic.

without drowning the plants. Often the plants are planted in elevated rows, and there are valleys that run next to them that are flooded. Such a garden needs to be positioned near a water source to provide flow for the flood. When it's done well, this approach gives deep water to plant roots without ever touching leaves and risking the burning or fungal issues that can come with overhead watering.

This method is used on a larger scale, with pumped water, in corn and rice fields in the southern United States and other places around the globe. It's not so common among small-scale vegetable gardeners here in the land of hoses, sprinklers, and drip tape, but there's no reason not to experiment with it if your garden is close to a creek or stream, or if you collect water in a large tank with access to the garden. You'd still need to use another method for watering germinating seeds and very tiny seedlings, as they might be disturbed by the force of floodwater.

FLOOD IRRIGATION ABROAD

IN SPAIN. When Natalie gardened in Spain, the planting was done on ancient terraces that were all very slightly angled. There was a piscina, a big water tank that doubled as a swimming pool, above all of the terraces. It was fed by tiles that carried water from the buildings' roofs and from a tunnel that went into the mountain a half mile to transport water from a spring. In the past, a network of clay tiles carried the water from the piscina to the terraces, but when Natalie was there, the residents siphoned water from the piscina to irrigate, which worked great, too. Whenever a row was planted, a little ditch was formed next to the crop. Watering was accomplished by flooding each ditch in turn.

IN INDIA. Chloe volunteered at a farm in northern India in a village called Garoh, where a stream flowed through the community. Each family had a set day when they could literally open the floodgates to water their crops. The garden beds were elevated, and the whole garden was on a gentle slope, so that within a few minutes all the pathways would be flooded, with moisture slowly seeping into the mounds where crops were growing. Very cool and totally plastic-free!

Feeding Growing Plants

As plants grow, they continue to require nourishment from the soil. And as they grow bigger, they need more and more of it. If you've prepared and cared for your garden soil well (see Chapter 4), your crops may have what they need without you adding anything extra. If the baseline of your soil is less rich, however, or in the case of "heavy feeders" (crops that require a lot of fertility in order to grow and sufficiently produce), you'll want to feed your plants as they grow.

There are three main ways to do this:

- Foliar feeding
- Fertigating
- Sidedressing/topdressing

You can do any or all of these as forms of basic maintenance or start them as soon as you notice slower growth (and you've ruled out lack of sunlight or water as a cause).

See Chapter 5 for ample information about different types of fertilizers—from feather meal and goat manure to human urine, and about 20 other sources—and to determine which fertilizers make sense for your plants, soil, and climate.

FOLIAR FEEDING

Plant leaves are made up of layers of tissue, like our skin. The outermost layer is called the epidermis and is covered with tiny holes called stomata, which open and close throughout the day based on conditions like heat, humidity, and carbon dioxide saturation of the air. As you may already know, air and moisture exchange happen at the leaf's surface. What's less known is that plants take in nutrition through their stomata and epidermis as well. This is, in some circumstances, a more direct and effective way to feed plants.

When plants are young and their root systems haven't fully developed, or if their roots have been damaged at all, such as during transplanting, they may not be able to take up enough fertility from the soil. Foliar feeding is a great option for bypassing the root system and feeding plants right quick. Similarly, if soil pH is particularly high or low, or a specific nutrient is less available in the soil, giving nutrients to your crops via their leaves is a good option.

Many plant nutrients are water soluble. Plants that are fertigated are given nutrients dissolved in water, which makes them easier for the plants to use.

Keep in mind, however, that foliar feeding is not a substitute for nourishing plants through soil via their roots but rather an avenue to provide easy-to-absorb nutrition quickly in specific circumstances. Foliar feeding with bioactive liquids, such as compost teas, also helps prevent plant diseases from taking hold via the leaves.

Use a pump sprayer. This is the best tool for this kind of application, though a simple spray bottle can work in a pinch. Pump sprayers come in a variety of sizes and usually have a small hand pump that creates pressure within a tank and a hose with a wand that delivers a fine spray.

Filter the foliar food. This is super important so that you don't gunk up the sprayer—something extremely easy to do and annoying to fix. An old T-shirt or a paint strainer bag are good options for filtering.

Dilute the foliar food. For concentrated fertilizers, dilute 1 ounce of fertilizer to 1 gallon water. For liquid amendments, such as compost tea, nettle tea, urine, or menstrual blood, dilute less, between 1:1 and 1:5, with water.

Feed on overcast mornings, every week or two. If the day isn't overcast, try for early morning or late afternoon. Avoid moistening plant leaves in the middle of a sunny day when sunshine can be magnified through the water droplets and burn your plants. Similarly, if you moisten leaves with food too late in the day, they will stay moist all night, which can make them vulnerable to fungal pathogens. Foliar feeding is most effective if you repeat it every one to two weeks for several weeks.

Spray the whole leaf. Be sure to spray all over the leaves, even their undersides, until some liquid drips off.

FERTIGATING

One way to directly feed plants through their roots is to mix liquid fertilizers with water and apply that mixture at the base of your plants. This is known as fertigating. You can fertigate on a small scale by mixing fertilizer with water in a watering can according to the dilution rate for the particular fertilizer. In larger gardens, use a Syphonject, a handy tool that pulls fertilizer from a bucket into the stream of the hose at a measured rate; this makes things a lot quicker and easier. Fertigating is most effective if you repeat it every one to two weeks.

Fertigating

- Much faster in delivering nutrients to a group of plants via their roots compared to spraying each individual leaf surface (foliar feeding).

- Can deliver more nutrition at one time than foliar feeding since plants can take up more nutrients through their roots than their leaves (unless their roots have been damaged or they are very young).

- Can be done any time of day without worrying about burning the leaves if you fertigate at the base of plants.

- Not only feeds plants but also can nourish the living organisms in the root zone.

Foliar Feeding

- Bypasses root systems and soil conditions, so it can deliver certain nutrients (especially immobile minerals that get tied up when pH isn't ideal) right to the plants.

- Can coat leaves with beneficial organisms, protecting them from pathogens.

Whatever nutrients come through the fertigation can be easily utilized at the time of application but will quickly wash away with the water that carries them. Combining good soil care with intentional use of liquid fertilizers is the most effective approach to keeping plants well fed. Neither fertigating nor foliar feeding is a substitute for growing plants in vibrant, living soil.

One disadvantage of both fertigation and foliar feeding, compared with sidedressing/topdressing (see facing page), is that liquid fertilizers tend to be more expensive . . . except for urine, menstrual blood, compost tea, and nettle tea, of course!

SIDEDRESSING/TOPDRESSING

To apply solid fertilizers after plants are in the ground, you can either side-dress or top-dress.

Side-dressing means sprinkling a band of fertilizer alongside a row of crops, mixing it into the soil slightly by gentle cultivation (we often scratch it in with our fingers), and watering it in.

Top-dressing means spreading fertilizer over a larger area, then watering it in. For most garden-scale growing, sidedressing makes more sense than topdressing.

Nitrogen is the most common nutrient applied by side- or topdressing. It's water soluble, and plants need much more of it as they grow larger. Other fertilizers can also be delivered to plants in this way. Clumpy manure or compost can be hard to spread evenly, and caution should be used with extra-dusty amendments so they don't get into your eyes and lungs.

Don't forget to mulch. When you cover your moist fertilizer with mulch (see step 3 in How to Side-Dress), it prevents the nutrients from volatilizing in the heat and light of the sun, thus evaporating away rather than going to the roots. Also, the biological components of fertilizers and amendments that contain living organisms will survive and thrive only in the presence of water, so covering them helps keep them alive and active.

If you have mulched a bed or row that you want to side-dress, make sure to remove the mulch from the area; then side-dress, water, and put the mulch back on.

Depending on what you use to side- or top-dress, you may need to apply it only once during the life of a particular crop. If growth doesn't pick up after one application, follow it up a week or two later with a second one.

How to SIDE-DRESS

1. **DETERMINE FERTILIZER AMOUNT** per plant or row. If you purchase granular fertilizer, check the packaging for application rates. For compost, worm castings, and manure, use one handful per medium to large plant.

2. **SPRINKLE THE FERTILIZER.** Scatter it along the side of a row or around the base of larger individual plants.

3. **MIX IN THE FERTILIZER.** Using your fingers or a small handheld rake or cultivator, scratch the fertilizer into the top 1 to 2 inches of soil.

    TIP: *If you are using a moist substance (e.g., compost, manure), add a layer of mulch once you've mixed in the fertilizer.*

4. **WATER THE AREA.** The water carries the nutrients downward where the plants can take them up through their roots.

Thinning

Thinning (pulling out or cutting some or many seedlings) is a critical step for most plants that are directly sown into the ground rather than transplanted. If you grow a transplanted crop, you can set each plant at the exact spacing you want them to grow. With direct sowing, you'll likely need to thin after the seeds have germinated so that the remaining plants grow with the appropriate space between them.

When we direct sow, we plant seeds much more closely than the desired final spacing because we know a good portion of these baby seeds either won't sprout at all or will die before they become happy little seedlings. It's impossible to have 100 percent germination and survival rates in the real world of nature. A slug might look at your baby plants the wrong way, a neighborhood dog might step on them, or fungal pathogens could infect them, leading to death by the disease known as damping-off.

Because a baby plant can die in any number of ways, each parent plant makes hundreds of seeds. For the same reason, we direct sow at a higher density to ensure we end up with enough plants in a given area. Add to this the fact that seeds can be very tiny and difficult to sow with much spacing accuracy, and you can see that direct-sown beds can become dense with seedlings and can also have gaps here and there. If we leave those plants growing at the original density without thinning, they will suffer due to overcrowding. In short, they need to be thinned to survive and thrive.

You may feel averse to pulling up and killing perfectly healthy-seeming baby plants. We know, it can be hard. But remember that if you don't give them enough space, then all of them are likely to have disappointing growth and be more prone to disease. Without thinning, you might get 30 almost-useless, less-than-pencil-size flavorless carrots, instead of eight beautiful, healthy, tasty, full-size carrots. Yes, it's a bit like playing god, deciding who lives and who dies, but such is the way of gardening. You can download a video tutorial on thinning on our website (see the link on page 364).

It's a tiny but powerful thing: choosing who lives and who dies. Thinning gives remaining seedlings enough room and is essential for sizable harvests.

VEGETABLES THAT MUST BE THINNED

Following is a list of plants that tend to need thinning, as they are often direct-sown close together in rows (see the vegetable profiles beginning on page 275 and the appendix for specific spacing for individual crops).

- Beets
- Carrots
- Chard
- Kale
- Parsnips
- Radishes
- Turnips and rutabagas

LEAF CROPS THAT CAN GO EITHER WAY

The following crops can be grown as large plants with regular spacing in rows, in which case they'll need to be thinned after being direct-seeded, or they can be broadcast or sprinkled and allowed to grow densely for cut-and-come-again harvesting (see Chapter 9). Note that if you want to harvest whole heads of lettuce, the plants will need to be either direct-sown and thinned or planted as transplants.

- Arugula
- Cilantro
- Dill
- Lettuce
- Spinach

VEGETABLES THAT REQUIRE LITTLE OR NO THINNING

The following crops are usually direct sown but have larger seeds. These can be direct-seeded with relative accuracy and require bigger spacing between plants (between 6 inches and 4 feet, depending on the crop; see the vegetable profiles beginning on page 275 and the appendix for specific spacing for individual crops). Thinning is much less of an effort for these crops and is sometimes unnecessary. In the case of squash, melons, and cucumbers, two to five seeds can be planted in clusters at the final desired spacing, then thinned down to one or two plants per cluster after they've germinated.

- Beans
- Corn
- Cucumbers
- Melons (muskmelons and watermelons)
- Okra
- Peas
- Squash (winter and summer)

If you have limited, fresh, high-quality seed (meaning it will likely have a high germination rate), you can sow these vegetables at close to your desired final spacing and only have to deal with a few gaps and a little bit of thinning, rather than needing to thin heavily.

LEFT: These beets would have been bigger and more beautiful if they weren't growing on top of each other.

RIGHT: Bean seeds and seedlings are big and juicy, making sowing and thinning them easy, even for kids.

SPACING BETWEEN PLANTS

The goal with thinning is to achieve ideal spacing, as best you can, while pulling up punier seedlings and leaving the more robust ones. The first step is to get a felt sense of how far away you want the plants to be. (See the vegetable profiles beginning on page 275 and the appendix for final plant spacings.) You should also reference your seed sources, which usually list both how densely to sow and the ideal thinned spacing (your seed sources likely also have more information than we do about the specific variety you're growing).

Additionally, imagine the mature plant in your mind: How big will it be? Add a little extra to that and you'll have the final spacing you should allow between plants.

Pro tip: Cut or break a stick or a piece of cardboard to that final distance and bring it to the garden with you as a measuring tool. You don't need to use it to measure each space, but rather place it near you so that your eyes can gauge which plants to pull up and which to leave.

Ideal spacing vs. healthy plants. Sometimes you have to make a call between ideal spacing and leaving the healthiest plants a little closer together than desired. Use your best judgment here—you'll get a feel for it as you practice. There will be some gaps to begin with, and some spaces that are a little bigger and a little smaller than your ideal when you finish.

Pulling up plants with care. When you pull up or snip off whoever doesn't make the cut, be sure to do so gently. You don't want to accidentally uproot or chop their neighbors, the very ones you hope will stay and grow and eventually feed you.

- If the soil is loose and moderately moist, thinning shouldn't take much physical effort.
- If you pull, brace the soil with your fingers on either side of the plant. With gentle pressure on the soil, use your other hand to wiggle and pull steadily upward.
- Pinch or snip the plants at soil level, or gently pull them up. These methods work equally well, so it's a matter of personal preference.

Note: If the plant doesn't come up easily when pulling, you may want to irrigate deeply, wait a day or two until the soil is semidry, then try thinning again. Or just thin by pinching or snipping.

Eat your thinnings. With many crops, you can eat what you thin: arugula, beets, carrots if they're big enough, chard, cilantro, corn (yes, you can eat the whole corn plant if they're small enough), dill, kale, lettuce, peas, radishes, rutabagas, spinach, and turnips. If you plan to take these treats to the kitchen, keep a basket or bowl with you so that you can collect the thinnings to bring in, wash, and enjoy. Otherwise, thinnings can be composted or fed to chickens or other livestock.

WHEN TO THIN

The key is to thin after all the seeds that are going to germinate have germinated, and ideally after the first wave of casualties have bitten the dust.

Natalie likes to thin in two stages. In stage 1, when the seedlings have grown their first set of "true leaves" (in addition to cotyledons, a.k.a. spongy "seed leaves"), she knows that all the seeds that are going to sprout have sprouted. She then thins to about 1 inch between plants, no matter what kind of crop she's dealing with.

In stage 2, she thins again when the plants are looking big and strong, when they have two or three sets of true leaves, and when it's clear that whoever is going to make it seems to have made it. This is when she thins to the final spacing for that crop.

Chloe does only one round of thinning. It's a time-consuming task, and she's found that once works well enough. Her goal is to thin before the plants look like they're crowding each other—sometime between the first and third set of true leaves, or whenever she finds the time. Larger plants like beans, corn, cucumbers, and squash can usually be thinned earlier in their lives.

Yellow dock is a tenacious taprooted weed with an impressive ability to make abundant seeds. Slicing the flower stalk before those seeds ripen forestalls spreading.

Weed Management

Any plant that's growing somewhere you don't want it to grow is a weed! "Common weeds" are wild or feral plants that are particularly skillful at popping up in garden beds, quickly outgrowing crops, withstanding drought and other stresses, and reproducing themselves. See the table Common Garden Weeds and Their Characteristics, page 216, for the most common weeds we've found in our gardens and how to manage them.

When it comes to dealing with weeds, we don't like using words like *control* or *eradication* but rather prefer the term *management*. Managing weeds, making sure they don't take over your garden, is one of the biggest challenges in growing food. Opportunistic and speedy weeds can compete with vegetables for sunlight, water, and soil nutrients. In fact, US growers spend over $6.6 billion on herbicides each year for weed control. Sure, these plants are unsightly and make your garden seem wild and chaotic, but more to the point, weeds can significantly reduce yields or even choke out your crops entirely if left unchecked.

Not all weeds are created equal, however. Some are somewhat benign and can coexist peacefully with garden plants, with minimal management. It's also true that some weeds are edible and/or medicinal, often with nutritional profiles that outshine the vegetables we favor in their places.

WEED PREVENTION

An ounce of prevention is worth a pound of cure in the world of garden weeds. In other words, you won't have to do much to manage weeds in your garden if you don't have a lot of them growing there in the first place. Plus, the work of preventing weeds is often less backbreaking than the work of giving them the boot once they've established themselves.

Mulch. This is our favorite way of preventing weed seeds from germinating. See page 221 to read about the ins and outs of mulching (which has many benefits beyond weed prevention). Mulching involves covering the soil with an organic or plastic barrier to block newly dropped weed seeds from making contact with the soil and to prevent germination; those already in the soil won't be exposed to enough light to sprout.

Don't let weeds go to seed. You can prevent seeding by hoeing, digging up or pulling entire plants, or simply cutting off the seed heads if seeds are threatening to be released. It helps to understand the life cycle of the particular weed you're dealing with to know when to take action to prevent seed spread if you don't get around to removing the entire plant.

Balance your soil with nutrients. Here again, we can't forget to consider the soil. Balanced nutrients in garden soil can help curtail weed issues. Certain weeds thrive in soils with depleted or excessive nutrients. In fact, weed populations can signal a mineral balance, or imbalance, in your garden's soil. There's a cool spiral-bound book called *When Weeds Talk* by Jay L. McCaman that delves deeply into this subject. Weeds are the triage nurses of the plant world, and they have the incredible ability to survive even in very poor soils. Over time their bodies decay into that same suffering soil, slowly enriching and changing it so that more diversity can flourish. Remember this when you feel compelled to curse the weeds!

Take advantage of cover cropping. In between crops, or sometimes right underneath them, a cover crop can literally cover the soil, preventing weeds from growing in their place. Some cover crops even exude chemical substances that prevent weed seeds from germinating (see more on cover crops in Chapter 5).

HOLISTIC WEEDING

Once again, we return to the holistic principles of balance and quality. We dance with the weeds, employing tools and techniques to prevent them from getting out of hand while at the same time harvesting their bounty and engaging with them as respected members of the web of life.

After pulling or hoeing, for instance, we often leave a lot of weeds on the soil surface to act as mulch and to decompose. During pulling or hoeing, we remove any plant that is likely to sprout back or scatter its seeds. We remove anything actively flowering, as some of these flowers have likely formed seeds or will form them after being pulled. (The only exception for us is chickweed, because it won't sprout during the warm season here in our region.) If we have mulched with straw or other dry matter, we tuck some types of green weeds under the mulch (see the list below). This encourages the nitrogen from the body of the weed to go into the soil instead of into the air. If there isn't mulch, we may lay the pulled weed on the soil surface to desiccate (dry out), decompose, and give its organic matter and some of its nitrogen back to the soil. The exceptions to this are:

- Flowering plants that have made seeds or may make seeds as they dry.

- Anything that has an "R" in the table Common Weeds and Their Characteristics (page 216). This especially applies to "stolon types" and other grasses, which sprout back from nodules on their roots. We pull these out and leave them in pathways or sometimes toss them in a dedicated "noxious weed" compost pile if there are a lot, where they'll desiccate completely and not sprout back.

TOP RIGHT:
Grasses, who co-evolved with grazing animals, are extremely clever at spreading and regrowing after being munched. Rhizomes, shown here, are specialized roots that creep sideways.

BOTTOM RIGHT:
Still-green weeds are great sources of nitrogen. We put those that won't spread (no grasses and no mature seeds) under mulch to feed crops and soil.

An ounce of prevention is worth a pound of cure in the world of garden weeds.

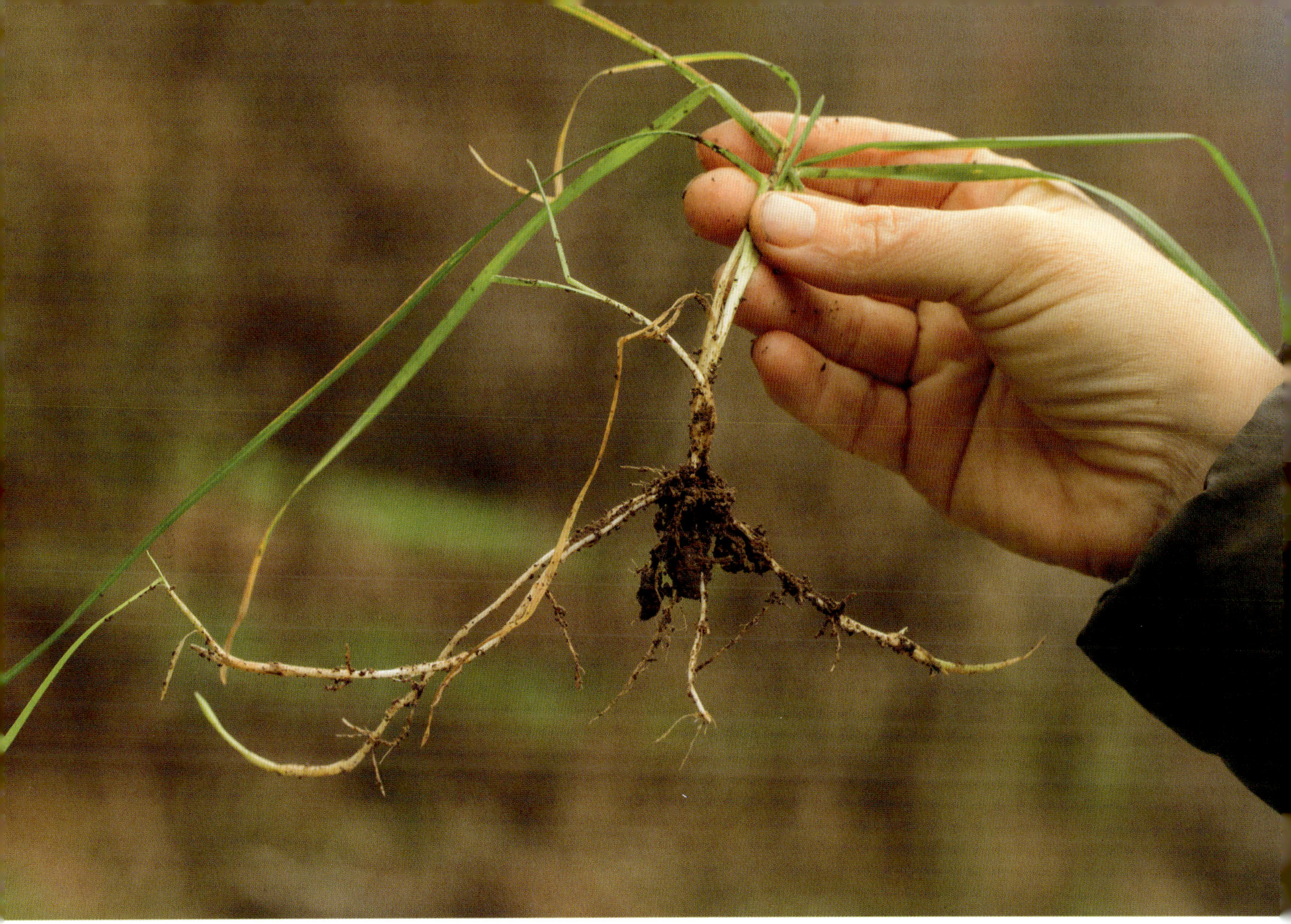

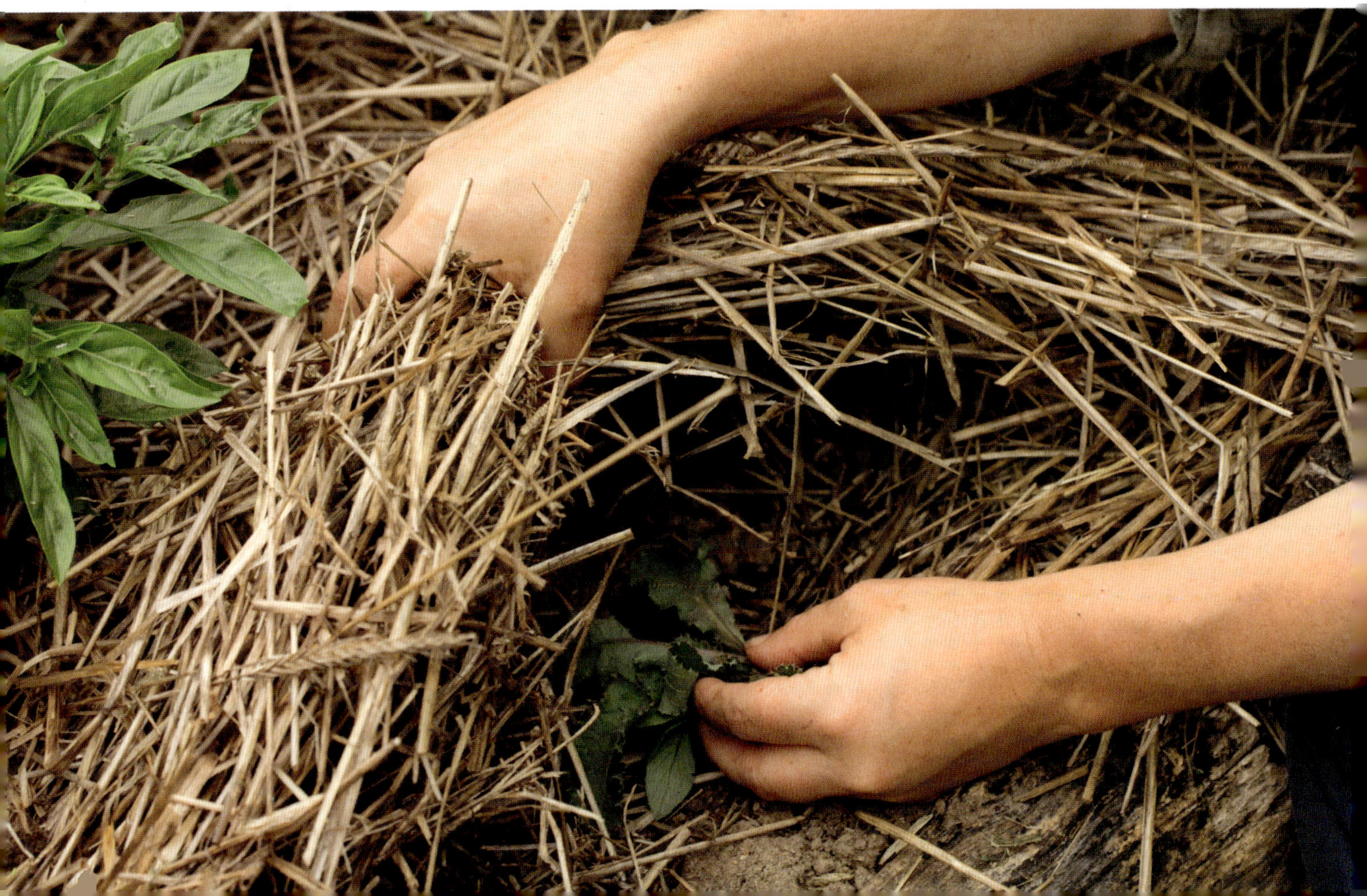

Common Weeds and Their Characteristics

COMMON NAME(S)	BOTANICAL NAME	ANNUAL (A) OR PERENNIAL (P)	BEST WAY TO MANAGE	REMOVE PLANT DEBRIS FROM BED (R) OR LEAVE AS MULCH (L)	NOXIOUS RATING (1 = FRIENDLY, 5 = NEMESIS)	EDIBLE (E) OR MEDICINAL? (M)*	TASTY? Y/N**
Bindweed	Convolvulus spp.	P	Pull, being sure to get runners	R	5		
Chickweed	Stellaria media	A	Hoe, pull, or leave and eat!	L	1	E + M	Y
Creeping Charlie, ground ivy, gill-over-the-ground	Glechoma hederacea	P	Pull, being sure to get runners	R	5	E + M	N
Dandelion	Taraxacum spp.	P	Pull/dig entire plant and root	R	2	E + M	Y
Grasses	Poaceae (grass family)	Some A, some P	Hoe when young; pull when older or if root system is established	R	5		
Lamb's quarters	Chenopodium album	A	Hoe when young, pull when older	L	1	E	Y
Nutsedge	Cyperus rotundus	P	Pull, being sure to get all rhizomes	R	3	E + M	?
Pigweed or amaranth	Amaranthus spp.	A	Hoe when young, pull or harvest to eat when older	L	1 (nonspiny), 5 (spiny)	E	Y (nonspiny)
Plantain	Plantago spp.	P	Pull/dig entire plant and roots	L	2	E + M	N
Purple dead nettle	Lamium purpureum	A	Pull	R	4	E	N
Purslane	Portulaca oleracea	A	Pull	L	1	E + M	Y
Quickweed or gallant soldier	Galinsoga parviflora	A	Pull, ideally before massive seed set; will regrow readily from stems that are left	R	3	E	Y
Slender speedwell	Veronica filiformis	P	Pull, being sure to get runners	R	5	E + M	N
Smartweed or knotweed	Polygonum spp.	Short P or A	Pull, being sure to get runners	R	4	E + M	N
Thistles	Cirsium spp.	A	Pull/dig, ideally before massive seed set	R	4	E + M	N
Yellow dock	Rumex crispus	P	Pull/dig entire plant and root	R	4	E + M	N

*Disclaimer: This book is for educational purposes only. Before you eat wild foods or use wild medicines, be sure you are 100 percent clear on their identification and proper usage, which are beyond the scope of this book. Consult a local expert.

**(according to Natalie and Chloe)

Common Garden Weeds

Those you can eat are marked with *.

AMARANTH*

BINDWEED

CHICKWEED*

CREEPING CHARLIE*

DANDELION*

GRASSES

LAMB'S QUARTERS*

NUTSEDGE

PLANTAIN*

PURPLE DEAD NETTLE*

PURSLANE*

QUICKWEED*

SLENDER SPEEDWELL*

SMARTWEED*

THISTLE*

YELLOW DOCK*

SMART WEEDING

Weeding intelligently requires some understanding of the characteristics of the weeds you're working with. That's why we've included information like whether a weed is an annual or perennial in the table Common Garden Weeds and Their Characteristics (see page 216). This indicates which techniques will be most effective at killing that particular weed and preventing it from regrowing and/or spreading in your garden. If you've got weeds that aren't in this table or you're not sure who you're dealing with, it's worth taking the time to identify them and learn as much as you can about them. Your local Cooperative Extension Service and other local growers (especially older folks) are great resources for identifying weeds in your area.

One of the key factors with smart weeding is timing. Most weeds can easily be eliminated by gently using a stirrup hoe when they're seedlings. After they've gotten established, however, a heavier hoe with more muscle, hand pulling, and/or digging might be required. If you happen to miss the window for evicting weeds as babies, the next key point in time is when they flower and move toward setting seeds. You should either remove or at least cut back weeds before they make seeds, otherwise you could have as

many as several thousand weed seeds landing on your garden soil.

Another consideration for the intelligent weeder is using effective and appropriate tools. As we shared in Chapter 2, using the right tool for the job can make a world of difference. You can download a video demonstration of our favorite weeding tools and how to use them on our website (see link on page 364).

Our favorite weeding tools are the stirrup hoe (a.k.a. scuffle hoe, hula hoe), collinear hoe, wire weeder, field hoe, hori hori, and digging fork. Let's look at why.

Stirrup hoe and collinear hoe. All weeding with hoes is much easier when your veggies have been planted in straight rows. We tend to use the stirrup hoe most of all, while the collinear hoe is especially helpful in tighter spaces. Both these scuffling tools are ideal for slicing and uprooting weeds as seedlings. You simply scrape the tools along the soil, a smidgen below the surface. It's best to do this on a sunny and dry day so that uprooted weeds quickly desiccate (dry out) and die.

Both of these tools have long handles and are used from an upright position, making them easy on your back. We like to start with these tools, as they do the job quickly and elegantly, getting all the weeds that we can without reaching too close to our precious plants.

A challenge with these scuffling tools is that it can be hard to get between or next to vegetable plants without slicing or uprooting them, too. This is where the wire weeder comes in.

Wire weeder. This handheld tool is used in the exact same way as the stirrup and collinear hoes but from a squatting or kneeling position. It's great for cleaning up weeds that are right next to your crops after you've done a pass with either the stirrup or collinear hoe.

Field hoe. This is especially helpful for chopping and even uprooting larger weeds, especially in an in-ground bed or in a field setting. It's more difficult to use a field hoe for weeding in raised beds. To get the most bang for your buck, so to speak, it's worth sharpening a field hoe before using it to weed. (See Chapter 2 for more on sharpening hoes.)

Hori hori and digging fork. Both of these are used to uproot weeds that are beyond slicing, especially those perennial weeds with deep taproots that will resprout if they're simply cut back. The hori hori is smaller and better suited for tight spaces between veggies. But because of its size, using it to uproot a big yellow dock, for example, can require extra elbow grease. In such cases the digging fork puts the power of physics on your side and is ideal for big yellow docks and other plants with deep taproots—as long as you can get the tool in the ground without damaging the nearby veggies you're trying to protect.

EDIBLE AND MEDICINAL WEED MANAGEMENT

A weed can be edible and/or medicinal, but that doesn't mean it should be allowed to run amok in your garden. Some weeds are edible but not particularly yummy (or not yummy to you), while others are medicinal but not the medicine that you need. Also, even amazing and useful weeds can still diminish veggie yields if allowed to grow unchecked.

Two of our favorite edible weeds are chickweed and lamb's quarters, for a lot of reasons!

- Chickweed is purported to have 6 times the amount of vitamin C, 12 times more calcium, and 83 times more iron than spinach.

- Lamb's quarters has 15 times the calcium and nearly 8 times the vitamin C of spinach.

- They grow easily and well during times when lettuce and spinach can be tricky (chickweed in early spring, fall, and throughout winter in some areas, and lamb's quarters in the heat of summer).

We dance with the weeds, employing tools and techniques to prevent them from getting out of hand, while at the same time harvesting their bounty and engaging with them as respected members of the web of life.

- These generous volunteers earn space every year in our garden plan.
- Chickweed and lamb's quarters are relatively easy to kill, so if they start to take over, it's simple to get them back in check.
- They're both genuinely delicious and versatile in many dishes!

Managing chickweed. In our gardens, chickweed is welcomed and allowed to grow underneath fall and winter crops as a ground cover of sorts. It's sometimes even encouraged—Natalie transplanted chickweed into her garden from a friend's when she didn't notice much of her own popping up. When we're ready to plant a new veggie crop in that area, we pull up and lay the chickweed on the soil surface, where it can contribute seeds for later sprouting. Since chickweed is a cool-season crop, those seeds won't sprout until the following fall, when we're happy to welcome them back.

Managing lamb's quarters. We're both partial to an enthusiastic cultivar of lamb's quarters called 'Magenta Spreen' (some people call it "magenta lamb's quarters"). This version of the tasty weed has larger leaves with amazing sparkling magenta accents where the leaves meet the stem. Seeds for this variety are becoming more readily available. If you've got a friend with some, simply transplant or collect its seeds. Both of us have a zone in the garden where we welcome 'Magenta Spreen' to self-sow each year once the weather warms. This means we leave the soil exposed in this area and weed out other plants that may sprout so that we enjoy a self-perpetuating patch of dark, leafy greens all summer.

Clearly we're in strong support of utilizing the nourishing and healing weeds that invite themselves into our gardens. The key is to find a way to allow them to have the space they need without compromising other crops. When this is done well, edible weeds can make up a significant portion of the harvest, and with a very low amount of input from the gardener!

Chickweed is welcome in our gardens. We may gently weed it out in order to direct sow, but mostly we leave it, harvest it, and enjoy it.

Mulch

Soil is never bare and exposed for long in the wild world. In the forest, leaves, branches, and rotting logs contribute to a thick layer of organic duff that covers the ground. In meadows, abundant seeds land and germinate quickly wherever the ground is scratched by critters or otherwise uncovered by wind or water. After disturbance, whatever seeds that were waiting in the soil are keen to take advantage of the open space and sun exposure and jump into growth.

This process of protecting and inhabiting soil is part of the innate intelligence that permeates living systems. Soil that is covered either by decomposing organic matter or living plants remains moist, cool, and dark, making it more hospitable to the myriad organisms who live in that underground world. Plus, when bare soil is exposed to direct sunlight and drying gusts, nutrients and the soil itself can be lost through volatilization and wind erosion.

So if wild ground is always "dressed," why is it so common to see vegetable gardens "naked"? Bare soil can be cultivated with a hoe or other tool to knock down emerging weeds. Since, as we've shared, weeds compete with crops for nutrients, water, sunlight, and space, keeping them at bay is a necessity. Hoeing

is one effective way to do this, but it's labor intensive and results in bare soil, which has its own impacts. In larger-scale mechanized agriculture, tractors with cultivating implements do the job of the hoe to uproot or bury weeds, leaving bare soil behind. As a culture, we've gotten used to the look of this bare soil between crops, but mulching mimics the approach of uncultivated ecosystems and can save labor, water, and weeding time.

Mulching, technically, is the practice of covering the soil around your crops with some kind of organic (i.e., carbon-based) or inorganic (usually plastic) material. It's an ancient way of caring for the ground that has been used by humans since at least 500 BCE in many parts of the world. All manner of materials have been and can be used as mulch, including:

- Animal bedding
- Cover crops that have been cut or crimped
- Paper and cardboard
- Plastic weed fabrics
- Seaweed
- Straw or hay
- Wood chips

We delve into the qualities and considerations for these different mulching materials on page 226.

Here is a stark contrast. Exposed soil (no mulch, left) is dry, cracked, and has weeds emerging in it; covered soil (under mulch, right) is moist, weed-free, and a better home to soil macro- and microorganisms.

Pros of Mulching

- Suppresses weed seed germination and doesn't allow new weed seeds to make contact with soil.

- Builds organic matter (only when using organic mulches, not plastic).

- Protects soil from sun and compaction by rain.

- Prevents erosion and nutrient loss through volatilization (nutrients changing form and being carried away on the wind).

- Holds moisture in the soil.

- Keeps soil cooler or warmer, depending on materials and time of year.

- Creates habitat and provides food for beneficial macro- and microorganisms.

Cons of Mulching

- Organic mulches can harbor pests, insects, and diseases.

- Can be difficult to get enough mulch materials.

- May keep soil too cool or warm, depending on materials and time of year.

- Sheet mulches can be slippery to walk on.

- Can inhibit infiltration of water.

If you read Chapter 4, which explores soil, fertility, and compost in depth, you might be thinking, "Hey, wait a minute, won't adding a bunch of high-carbon material to the garden as mulch tie up nitrogen and inhibit plant growth?" The answer is, wonderfully, no!

Issues with locking up nitrogen happen when lots of high-carbon material is incorporated *into* the soil, but not when it's layered *on top*. The bacteria, fungi, and other organisms that break down that carbon work at a slower pace and in a concentrated area when material is used as mulch rather than mixed in. Nitrogen might be lower in the thin area at the soil surface because it's being tied up dealing with all that carbon, but this doesn't affect the soil farther down where plant roots are hunting for nitrogen.

We mulch as much as possible and strongly recommend that you do it, too. We've noticed, particularly in our humid region, that keeping the soil covered has many benefits, most notably a decrease in the need to weed and water. Natalie also used mulch very successfully in Spain, Washington State, and Arizona, where the climates are dramatically different. There are, of course, challenges to mulching. And as with every aspect of gardening (and life), mulching works best when it's customized to your particular situation and managed mindfully.

WHEN AND HOW TO MULCH

Timing is as important with mulching as it is with weeding and watering. Obviously, if thick mulch can suppress the germination of weed

Exposed soil is a rare sight in our gardens, though we do push the mulch aside when seeds are germinating and during slug season.

seeds, it can also inhibit good sprouting and growth of direct-sown vegetables.

With Direct Sowing

When we direct sow, we wait until the baby plants are about 6 to 8 inches tall before laying down mulch right around them. This not only gives them a chance to germinate in full sun but allows us to weed with a hoe or other tool at least once before adding the mulch.

We've found that the combination of one good weeding and then mulching that day, or after giving hoed weeds a day in the sun to die, is a highly effective strategy for managing weeds. This approach often doesn't require any other steps for the rest of the season. As long as the mulch lasts and stays thick enough, weeds won't grow.

With Transplanting

For transplants from late spring through fall, you can mulch right after you transplant, or mulch can be laid down first and moderately sized veggies (4 inches or taller) can be planted right into it. To do this:

1. Clear a spot in the mulch so you can get to the soil and dig a hole.

2. Plant your transplant in there and smooth out the mulch so that it almost touches the stem of the plant.

One downside of transplanting directly into mulch is that mulch creates an ideal habitat for slugs. When slugs are abundant (usually in early spring here), they will take advantage of the cover and cool moisture and can decimate a bed of plant babies in a single evening. Many other pests also take cover, overwinter, and/ or breed in mulch and plant debris. Some, like striped and spotted cucumber beetles, are deterred by mulch. For more on pests and their particularities, see page 244.

To Retain Moisture

Among the helpful jobs that mulch takes on in the garden is preserving soil moisture. If a rain or watering is light and shallow, however, thick mulch can also prevent moisture from reaching the soil surface. So depending on your climate and conditions, it's a good idea to do a deep watering and *then* lay down mulch to hold in that water. Alternatively, you can mulch right before a heavy rain, as long as it will provide enough moisture to penetrate through the layers to the ground and plant roots. Mulching over drip irrigation is another option; just remember that the drip lines are there and avoid accidentally cutting them later! It won't work well to lay drip lines on top of mulch.

To Moderate Soil Temperature

A final consideration with mulch timing is the impact it has on soil temperature. Mulch acts as insulation and works to keep the ground cool or warm, depending on the season. During the heat of summer, mulch protects soil from sunrays, maintaining a cooler temperature down below. In contrast, during the cooler months, mulch helps hold steady the ground temperature, preventing the upper layers of soil from freezing even as air temperatures drop.

This way, fall and winter crops stay healthy and alive, thanks to the warm blanket of mulch. In early spring, however, we gardeners *want* the soil to warm up, so removing mulch at that time will allow the sun to do its awakening work. In winter it's often beneficial to let the ground freeze to kill overwintering pests and pathogens, but do this only where there are no crops growing.

Amount of Mulch

Whatever material you use for your mulch, and whenever you apply it, make sure to put down a thick enough layer for the mulch to do its job. With organic mulches, you want at least 4 inches of material; even more if you're mulching around larger plants. We like at least 6 inches of mulch for our tomatoes and garlic, for example.

Watering right after mulching stabilizes the material so it doesn't blow away. Aim to pile less mulch right around the stems of your crops, so that the plants receive good airflow and the decomposing organisms that break down the mulch don't also try to devour your growing crops.

Plastic mulches don't need to be layered to increase their thickness, but they do need to be laid down without any gaps between pieces. If you choose paper or cardboard for mulch, make sure to overlap pieces so that no light gets through; wherever it does, weeds will surely grow.

MULCHING CHALLENGES

Mulching has so many upsides, but like anything else, it's not perfect. Here are a few of the challenges we've come across.

Getting Enough Material

If you have a smaller garden, this shouldn't be a big issue, but with larger plots, it can be difficult and sometimes costly. We've had the good fortune of getting to know a landscaper who, in fall, regularly vacuums up dump truck loads of dry leaves from housing development lawns he maintains. Instead of paying to deposit these leaves at a recycler, he's happy to bring them to us so we can use them in our gardens.

If you live in an area with deciduous trees and neighborhoods with lawns, you might be able to strike up a similar kind of relationship. Even if you don't get dump trucks of leaves delivered, you can often collect bags of leaves that folks leave on the curb. In either case here, you may encounter trash, other debris, and even dog poop mixed in with the leaves, so be careful when you spread mulch collected in this opportunistic kind of way.

Weed Seeds, Pests, and Pathogens

The last thing you want to discover is that the mulch you brought in to feed and protect your soil actually introduced a harmful organism. This issue is tricky, since it's hard to know what might be traveling in a load of leaves, straw, or hay.

In the case of hay, you can sometimes visually discern mature weed seeds and choose to purchase "cleaner" hay. Be careful, though, as hay that has few to no weeds may have been treated with a persistent herbicide that you don't want to introduce to your garden, either (see page 128 for more on this). If you can converse with the person who made the hay, that's your best bet; ask about their growing practices to determine if it's hay you want to bring into your garden. If you're getting a large amount of some new mulch

OPPOSITE: We've been lucky to get spray-free, local straw mulch the past few years. It's from a pumpkin patch that uses rye as a cover crop.

LEFT: When we say to apply thick mulch, we mean thick; 5-8 inches! This is crucial for getting all of its weed-suppressing, moisture-retaining goodness.

RIGHT: In moist conditions mulch creates slug habitat, so we push it away from direct contact with plants.

material, you can always apply it in a small area and watch what happens before spreading it all over your garden.

Water Not Infiltrating

Whether rainwater or irrigation water, it will have to soak through that massive mulch layer before finding its way to the soil surface and down to plant roots. With long, slow, deep watering, and in places with consistent and significant rainfall, this isn't a problem. In drier places, however, gardeners will need to put drip lines underneath mulch to direct water right where it's needed, letting the mulch prevent that water from evaporating quickly.

MULCH MATERIALS

What you use for mulch will depend heavily on what you can get your hands on, although taking note of the qualities of the material will influence how you use it. We have utilized the following materials at some point over the years. (We tend to use straw, leaves, hay, and woven weed fabric the most.)

Straw

This excellent and well-known mulch material is a by-product of grain industries. It tends to be low in seeds, since that part of the plant is what has already been harvested out of it, though it isn't totally seed-free.

Almost all commercial straw has pesticide residues in it, though in most cases the levels are somewhat low. If you live in an area that produces organic grains, you may get lucky and find organic straw. Bales of straw aren't super expensive if you're buying only a couple, but the price can add up when you're covering larger areas. Extra-dry straw can blow away in strong winds, so if you live in a windy place, be sure to water it in after you spread it.

Hay

Hay is dried grass, often mixed with other kinds of plants, that's been cut from fields and is most often used as animal fodder.

Depending on the time of year when the hay was cut, and the condition of the field, hay can have a heavy or light to nonexistent weed-seed load.

Hay breaks down faster than straw because it has leaves in it, along with fibrous stalks (straw is almost all stalks). Some hay is sprayed with persistent herbicides; try your best to avoid this (see more on persistent herbicides on page 128). Look for good deals on large round bales of hay that are a bit moldy or otherwise unfit for consumption by animals but are perfect for your garden. If you can get one delivered (they're challenging to transport yourself, even if you have a pickup truck), it will provide mulch for a 1,000-square-foot garden amply for an entire year. It will also be big and bulky and very difficult or impossible to move once it's been opened, so you'll need an area to store it that's accessible to the garden. Smaller square bales are easier to move around and store, though they are much more expensive per unit of actual material.

Dry Leaves

Dry leaves can be an excellent mulch material that you gather for free from people who are keeping their lawns tidy. Dry tree leaves contain high amounts of carbon and minerals

Chloe protects and nourishes a young yacón plant (a species of daisy grown for its sweet, tuberous roots) with dry leaves.

that will benefit the soil as they break down. Even pine and other needles from coniferous trees can be used as mulch and, contrary to popular belief, won't acidify the soil unless you dig them in. To suppress weeds, you'll need thicker layers of pine needles than deciduous leaves, since needles allow more light through.

Like straw, dry leaves can easily blow away. Crushing them a bit before spreading, along with watering them in, helps hold them down.

Fresh Grass Clippings

Some lawnmowers have a bag attachment that catches all the bits you mow. If you mow by hand with a scythe, the clippings are easy to rake up and collect. This fresh material can be a great mulch that adds a nitrogen boost to the soil.

To maximize the amount of nitrogen that goes down into the ground instead of up into the atmosphere, cover grass clippings with a dry mulch of straw, hay, or leaves. And before you use your mowings as mulch, notice what growth stage the grass is in. If the grass has mature seeds (which can be very tiny and hard to see), it might be a better choice to compost that material rather than seed grass in your garden beds as you use it for mulch.

Cover Crops

We use cover crops frequently as mulch. Green cover-crop debris, especially from leguminous plants, can give plants a big boost of nitrogen for growth. Similarly to grass clippings, if you cover the fresh cover crop debris with dry mulch, it increases nitrogen absorption in the soil. If you've got enough cover crop for a thick layer, the top will dry out quickly and become that protective coating.

Weeds

Like grass clippings, green weeds have nitrogen that can boost plant growth while simultaneously covering the soil. With weeds, it can be a little tricky to maximize nitrogen absorption into the soil because you also want them to dry out and die completely. That's why we sometimes like to leave weeds exposed to the sun when we lay them down as mulch, depending on the weed.

Also, be sure to use caution with weeds that sprout from runners or stolons (stems that grow horizontally and can sprout new roots and shoots from their nodes), such as crabgrass, because those weeds spread and keep growing if you lay them in the garden as mulch. Weeds that have matured seeds are equally problematic as mulch and are better off composted. Review the table Common Weeds and Their Characteristics on page 216 to decide what can stay or go.

Crop Debris and Thinnings

Treat these like pulled weeds. One thing to keep in mind is that crop debris can harbor pests and diseases. Make sure to put only healthy crop debris in beds; if something doesn't look healthy or is ridden with pests, it's better to burn it, bag and trash it, or compost it if the issue won't survive composting.

Plastic Mulch

Plastic is the most abundantly utilized mulch material in commercial agriculture (see more about plastics in agriculture on page 80). This can range from very thin single-use plastic film to a biodegradable version of this known as "biofilm" to a more durable woven material like DeWitt Sunbelt. For garden-scale plastic mulching we strongly recommend the latter, as it can be cut to suit your garden beds or rows and used year after year. Also, this woven material lets in water, so it's appropriate for use with overhead irrigation.

If you live in a hot place, white plastic is a great choice, as it reflects sunlight and can keep soil cooler. In cooler climates, consider black plastic, as it absorbs sunlight and warms the soil. Chloe likes to lay down black plastic and cover it with a layer of hay mulch to protect the plastic from damaging sunlight and help hold the plastic in place (though staples and/or sandbags are also needed for larger

WOOD CHIPS AS MULCH

Wood chips are a great mulch for most perennial plants, but they aren't the best choice for most annual vegetables. As wood chips decompose, they tend to harbor more fungal, rather than bacterial, organisms. Soil dominated by fungus is optimal for trees, whereas bacterial dominance is better for annuals. Also, we've found that wood chips don't do a very good job at suppressing weeds unless they are laid very thickly (at least 6 inches thick), which isn't practical in most garden beds.

Additionally, as the wood chips break down, they're hard to remove. Mulch on vegetable beds tends to be put on and taken off throughout the year and from season to season as new crops are planted, seeds are sown, or amendments added. This is one reason wood chips make a better mulch for perennials (where they'll get to stay put). If all you've got to mulch with is wood chips, they're better than nothing, but definitely be aware of these challenges. The one exception to this is using hardwood chips to mulch sweet potatoes. Natalie has done this to good effect. She rotates the sweet potatoes with raspberries, which solves the problem of wood chip removal because the raspberries love this kind of mulch.

pieces). Covered plastic is also more aesthetically pleasing.

To use plastic mulch you can lay strips of it on either side of a row of crops or burn holes in the plastic at whatever spacing you desire. Here are some considerations.

- It's better to burn holes than to cut them because cutting can cause the material to fray, shortening its life and spreading plastic fibers in your garden.

- Once you've burned holes, that piece of plastic mulch will need to be used for crops with that spacing for the rest of its life, so using intact pieces is a bit more flexible.

- To cut pieces to length, we like to use a red-hot machete to burn the edge of the cut and avoid fraying.

Paper Mulch

Using paper for mulching is similar in practice to using plastic, but the paper can be left in place and will break down after one or two growing seasons. Rolls of 100 percent biodegradable brown paper with planting holes are sold at gardening stores and even some big-box home improvement centers. The cost of a roll of paper mulch is much less than a roll of woven plastic mulch, but it will only last for one or two seasons, so the cumulative cost is higher. You'll save time and space, however, because paper mulch doesn't need to be taken up at the end of the season and stored.

Scraps of recycled paper, including newspaper and cardboard boxes, can also be used for mulch. This type of mulching is often called sheet mulching or lasagna gardening and is great around the bases of perennials or when starting a new garden (see page 75 for more on this method). Lay down paper and/or cardboard, then cover it with a thick layer of organic mulch—ideally wood chips for perennial crops like trees and shrubs. Using many smaller bits of paper or cardboard is less practical for annual vegetable gardening, but it's doable if that's what you've got on hand. Be sure to remove plastic tape from cardboard boxes and limit paper that has lots of color ink, which can leach heavy metals into your soil.

Trellises and Trellising

Trellising is a term that refers to any and all kinds of support systems that hold plants up off the ground, from simple stakes to more elaborate arbors. Some plants, like pole beans, require trellising and won't grow well without that kind of support. Other plants will benefit from a lift (but don't necessarily need it), and still others grow fine on their own.

What a delight to harvest beans from a comfortable, standing position, in the shade of a bean trellis tunnel!

BENEFITS OF TRELLISING

In warm, wet areas like our southern Appalachian Mountains, many crops do better when trellised. Even in drier climates, trellising can be an important part of the garden. Here are some advantages of trellising.

- Keeps plants off the moist earth and prevents them from sprawling on the ground (making weeding much easier!).
- Improves airflow around plants, minimizing fungal pathogens.
- Utilizes vertical space, making way for more plants (especially helpful in smaller gardens).
- Eases the physical labor of harvesting; holds veggies up off the ground at a nice height that doesn't require stooping.
- Gives your garden style—looks fun and whimsical and adds beauty.

WHICH PLANTS NEED TRELLIS SUPPORT?

Here's a list of plants that almost always need support, and those that can benefit from it.

Tomatoes

Tomatoes become floppy and disease prone if left to sprawl on the ground. We find that a combination of trellising and pruning leads to the healthiest and easiest-to-harvest plants. Tomatoes do not naturally climb, so they need to be manually attached to whatever trellis you choose. This can be done by tying them with string to a quadripod/tripod, weaving them through a fence panel, twining them around a string trellis, sandwiching them between strings in a weave, or guiding them through the structure of a cage (we'll discuss these trellising techniques in a moment).

Pole Beans

Pole beans are viners that grow upward on the vertical part of any trellis. (Bush-type beans don't need much support, so be sure to check which type you're growing!) These vines can wrap around a pole as thick as 1½ inches in diameter and are happy to climb up something as thin as a string. Many varieties will grow quite tall, but you may or may not be able to reach them up top. If you're growing dry beans, it's worth building a very tall trellis to maximize growth and harvest. In this case, you can bring a stepladder or stool out when you harvest all the beans at once. This isn't practical for harvesting snap (green) beans, because you'll need to gather the beans several times a week for a few weeks.

Peas

Peas have tendrils that climb the horizontal parts of a trellis like a ladder (most varieties of peas are climbing, though some have a bush-type growth habit—be sure you know which kind you've got). Peas are daintier than beans and can only grab onto thin materials like wire or string. They can't climb an actual ladder very effectively.

Cucumbers

Cucumbers climb with tendrils, like peas, though their growth is thicker and more robust, so they can handle bigger spaces between "rungs" on whatever trellis they climb. Unlike peas, cucumbers usually need a bit of encouragement to reach toward a trellis and grab on. Ripe cucumbers are full of water and very heavy, so make sure your trellis is sturdy.

Winter Squash

Winter squash is not frequently grown with a trellis, but some smaller-fruited vining varieties do well with support. This is especially helpful in smaller gardens, since sprawling squash vines take up a lot of space. We have seen winter squash grow up small trees! Ripe winter squash is very heavy; make sure this trellis is extra sturdy. Some folks suggest supporting each fruit inside a pantyhose . . . we've never done this, but it seems like a good use of pantyhose! Bush-type squash doesn't vine, so they won't need or utilize a trellis.

LEFT: This fence panel is supporting beans (dangling fruits), and 'Tennessee Dancing' gourds (spring-shaped tendril and bigger leaves).

RIGHT: The central lead (stalk) of a tomato plant is gently spiraled around the vertical string of a string trellis; this holds the plant upright.

Melons

Melons, like their cousins winter and summer squash, aren't typically grown on trellises, but a trellis is a good idea if you want to save space and get fruits off the ground to reduce the likelihood of rotting. Ripe melons are very heavy, and the stem attachment weakens as they ripen. So, like with trellises for winter squash, be certain your melon trellis is as sturdy as they come. Some folks suggest supporting each fruit inside a pantyhose. Bush-type melons don't vine, so they won't need or utilize a trellis.

Peppers

Peppers don't have tendrils and don't grow vines. However, if they're allowed to grow on their own, they tend to fall over, and their fruits are more likely to rot in contact with the soil. The most important thing when trellising peppers is to make certain that their central stalk is well supported.

Eggplants

Eggplants, like peppers, also don't vine or climb on their own. They're a little more self-supporting than the other summer delight from the Solanaceae family, but they can still benefit from a trellis. When trellising eggplants, their central stalk must be well supported.

Trellises by Crop

PLANT	GROWTH HABIT	TYPES OF TRELLISES	IDEAL HEIGHT
Cucumbers	Tendrils, though fewer than peas; sometimes need encouragement to grab a trellis	Fence panel, string (if it's tough string with good support)	Eye level
Eggplant	Not tendril or vining; needs to be tied on to trellis	Cages, fence panel, stakes, weave	3' (most varieties don't grow taller than this)
Melons	Vining and tendrils; sometimes need encouragement to grab a trellis; very variety-dependent	Fence panel	Eye level
Peas	Horizontal-grabbing tendril (ladder style); will readily grab a trellis	Fence panel, string	Eye level up to as tall as you can reach to harvest (depending on variety; some are shorter)
Peppers	Not tendril or vining; needs to be tied on to trellis	Cages, fence panel, stakes, weave	3' (most varieties don't grow taller than this)
Pole beans	Vertical viners; will readily grab a trellis	Fence panel, quadripod/tripod pole, string	Eye level up to as tall as you can reach to harvest (depending on variety; some will climb as tall as you can build a trellis)
Tomatoes	No tendrils; needs to be tied or twined on to trellis	Cage, fence panel, quadripod/tripod, string, weave	Eye level up to as tall as you can reach to harvest (for indeterminate varieties)
Winter squash	Vining and tendril, sometimes need encouragement to grab a trellis; very variety-dependent	Fence panel or nearby bushes	Eye level (for most varieties) up to as tall as you can reach to harvest for certain enthusiastic climbers

CHOOSING THE RIGHT TRELLIS

The type of trellis you build—its size, style, and materials—will depend on the plant it's going to support and what materials and resources you have available. It also needs to fit into your overall garden plan in a way that works for neighboring plants. When you're deciding whether to trellis something and considering what kind of trellis to build, there are several questions to ask yourself:

- How big and heavy will this plant get? Can the trellis handle the weight?
- Once the plant is occupying the trellis, where will it cast shade? Will that be a problem? Or a boon?
- Will it be easy to harvest this plant from this trellis?
- What materials do you have on hand to build it? What can you easily get?
- What's your aesthetic vision for the trellis? Will it be attractive or whimsical?
- Does the plant climb by twining (attaching itself to the vertical parts of a trellis) or tendrils (attaching itself to the horizontal parts of a trellis, like a ladder), or will it need help attaching to the trellis?

DIFFERENT KINDS OF TRELLISES

Some trellises work for all kinds of veggies; others are specific to one or two crops. Here's a description of several trellising styles and their characteristics.

Metal or Wire Fencing

You can find a number of different types of metal fencing to choose from, including different sizes of welded wire rolled fencing, poultry netting (a.k.a. chicken wire), and hardware cloth. The latter two are not appropriate for trellising. Welded wire cattle panels are our favorite.

Pros of Cattle Panels

- Easy to put up and take down.
- Great for making archway trellises.
- Relatively easy to move around and store for reuse again in another part of the garden or another year.
- Sturdy and need minimal support.

Cons of Cattle Panels

- Come in long, unwieldy 16-foot lengths (we sometimes cut the panels in half with bolt cutters to make them easier to move around and use in shorter beds).
- Pricey.
- Take up space in storage (though they can be stored outside in the elements without any harm done).

Fencing made of thinner wire can work but needs more support and can be prone to bending.

Supports. We use sturdy metal T-posts, which we pound into the ground with a special T-post pounder—basically a pipe with handles that has one end welded shut. You can also pound them with a mallet or even a random scrap of wood, though the official pounder works the best. Be sure to use ear protection, as both post and pounder are

Tomatoes (and many other veggies) get heavy when ripe. Flimsy trellises sometimes fail during fruit set. Here, a strong fence panel does the job well.

metal, and working them into the ground makes *a lot* of noise.

Chloe also has a T-post puller for removing the posts at the end of the season. This tool is well worth the investment if you'll be pounding and pulling lots of posts—it saves your back!

Wooden stakes can also support trellises. Just make sure to use stout, rot-resistant pieces of wood.

Poles and Stakes

Some vining plants, like pole beans, can climb right up straight poles. Other plants that bush out but tend to flop over with the weight of heavy fruits, like peppers, can be supported by simple stakes.

Poles and stakes are usually made of wood or bamboo. In our part of the country, tobacco stalks are traditionally used for staking veggies; other types of straight, fast-growing canes have been used all over the world. More modern materials like PVC pipe or even metal rebar can work, too.

Poles. For pole beans, poles need to be quite tall and either deeply embedded into the earth or anchored with stakes or T-posts so that they're sturdy. Many folks like building conical structures with bamboo poles, reminiscent of the teepees built by Native people of the Great Plains. (More on this on page 235.) Another option is to put vertical poles at either end of a bed or row (with a few in between, if it's a long span) and attach a

bar or string across them. By leaning one end of each pole on the bar and placing the other where the beans grow along the outside of the bed, you effectively make an A-frame tunnel.

Stakes. Shorter than poles, stakes are about 4 feet in length and are pounded 6 to 8 inches deep into the ground next to the central stalk of the plant. Used with crops that don't grab on by themselves, such as peppers and eggplants, stakes will need to be tied to plants with string or another material.

String

Trellising with string is one of the cheapest approaches and doesn't require a ton of space for storing trellising materials between uses. All you need is a fair amount of string and poles to attach the string to.

One style of string trellis involves running a top and bottom wire or pole from the top and bottom of the posts that will be holding it up, creating a rectangle. Then the string is zigzagged up and down from that top and bottom line, creating a row of vertical strands that vining plants like beans can climb up. For plants that climb with tendrils, like cucumbers, the reverse can be done, creating a ladder for plants to climb with the zigzag going from side to side (no top and bottom line are needed in this case).

Pro tip: The key to a good string trellis is to ensure it's strong and secure. If you've got a hoop house or greenhouse, tie the string to the top bar, which should be sturdy.

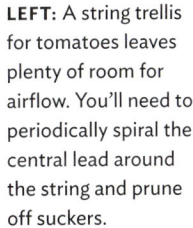

LEFT: A string trellis for tomatoes leaves plenty of room for airflow. You'll need to periodically spiral the central lead around the string and prune off suckers.

RIGHT: Pepper plants are held erect in a weave trellis with wooden stakes between each plant, plus string weaving from stake to plant to stake.

Quadripod trellises can be made out of biodegradable and/or scavenged materials.

Quadripod/Tripod Trellis

Natalie learned this style of trellising while she was gardening in Spain, and it's been her go-to for tomatoes ever since. This can also be a good choice for pole beans and other vining climbers. In Barcelona a giant grass they called caña was used; here in North Carolina, bamboo (also a giant grass!) is a great option.

If someone near you has a bamboo patch, they'd likely be happy for you to thin it out for them. Make sure that the bamboo you harvest is more than a year old, not new sprouts, as older bamboo will last a lot longer and is stronger. There's no need to cure the bamboo before use, since this isn't a permanent structure. Dimensional lumber can also be used for this type of trellis: 2×4s that have been ripped in half to become 2×2s are ideal. Go to page 235 for step-by-step instructions about how to build a quadripod/tripod trellis.

The Weave Trellis

Both Floridian and Californian tomato growers claim this trellising style as their weave, but who invented it doesn't matter for our purposes. The weave is essentially a type of string trellis that works for plants that don't grab onto string on their own. It's good for smaller varieties of tomatoes, as well as for peppers and eggplants.

Commercial growers put sturdy T-posts at the ends of the rows, then put one slender wooden stake in between each plant. We've gotten away with fewer stakes, especially with peppers that don't grow as large as tomatoes. This style of trellising compresses the plants and doesn't allow for great airflow, but it's relatively quick and easy and doesn't require bulky materials. Go to page 236 to see how to create a weave trellis.

Tomato Cages

Tomato cages are those round wire contraptions you see for sale at garden stores. You can make your own out of wire fencing rolled into a cylinder. If you choose this option, make sure that there is room to get your hands through the fencing to prune and pick your tomatoes.

Cages are ideal for smaller gardens (including tomatoes in pots), determinate varieties (those that reach a certain, moderate size and then stop growing), and situations where a bushier growth habit is desirable. This means less airflow and more chance of fungal diseases but potentially more fruits per plant. Tomato cages are bulky and can be a pain to store. Homemade ones can be unrolled for easier storage. Using tomato cages to stake your tomatoes, and tying the plants onto their

How to Build a QUADRIPOD or TRIPOD

Step 1

1. **POUND A STOUT WOODEN STAKE INTO THE GROUND.** The stake should be slightly bigger than the diameter of the taller posts you will use as supports. Pound it 4 to 8 inches deep, then remove it.

2. **PLACE THE BUTT OF A POLE INTO THE RESULTING HOLE.** This could be caña, bamboo, or a 2×2. Then do the same with the other poles (four for a quadripod, three for a tripod).

Step 2

3. **GATHER ALL POLES TOGETHER AT THE TOP.** From their vertical positions, bring them together and tie tightly with string.

An alternative to pounding a stout stake in the ground and removing it is to drive small wooden stakes into the ground to anchor the bases of each pole that makes up the quadripod/tripod. Pound these stakes in at the desired distance for the base of the structure, then attach the longer poles to these anchors with string or wire. Lean the tops in to touch and support one another, then tie tightly with string.

Once the supports are built, tomatoes are planted at the base of each pole. As they grow, they are tied every foot or so to the pole. When tying, make sure to leave room for the tomato "trunk" to grow in diameter as it grows up the pole.

Step 3

How to Create a WEAVE TRELLIS

Once your crops are about a foot tall, you can start weaving.

1. **POUND POSTS OR STAKES.** We like using T-posts at the ends and wooden stakes between every plant, or every few plants.

2. **TIE A LONG STRING** to the post at the end of the bed.

3. **WEAVE THAT STRING** between the plants and posts, from one side of the bed to the other. Move back and forth so the string is on one side of one plant/post, then the other side of the next one. The plants and posts are the warp, and the string is the weft of the weave.

4. **NOW DO IT IN REVERSE.** When you've reached the end of the bed or row, turn around and do step 3 in reverse, sandwiching the plants between two courses of string that crisscross one another.

5. **TIE THE STRING OFF AT THE POST.** Make sure to tie a tight knot that won't come undone.

6. **REPEAT STEPS 2 THROUGH 5 EVERY WEEK OR TWO** as your plants get taller, depending on how fast they grow. Each course of string should be 6 to 8 inches above the last one, supporting the plants as they grow taller.

support, requires the least amount of work throughout the season.

We don't tend to use tomato cages because we grow larger quantities of tomatoes, grow indeterminate varieties that keep growing and growing, and find that other kinds of trellises simply work better for us.

WHEN AND HOW TO TRELLIS VEGETABLES

Aim for getting your trellis installed before the vegetable you're building it for needs the support. This is especially true for pole beans, which live up to their Jack and the Beanstalk fame for fast growth. Resist, however, the urge to build a trellis for direct-seeded crops, like beans and peas, before or right after you sow the seeds. It's much easier to weed with a hoe when there isn't a trellis in the way.

Here's our order of operations for trellising beans and peas.

1. Sow.
2. Once the sprouts reach 2 to 4 inches tall, do a good weeding with a hoe.
3. When they reach 4 to 6 inches tall, mulch heavily.
4. Place/construct your trellis with or right after the mulching.

Since beans and peas are natural climbers, there's no need to affix the plants to the trellis. You can, however, encourage wandering vines and tendrils back toward the trellis as you check on the plants. Sometimes it's even helpful to run extra strings across pea trellises (pressing the plants against the trellis) to help hold them on if they're very heavy with peas.

For transplanted crops like tomatoes, peppers, and eggplant, we put up the trellis either right away after transplanting and mulching or sometime between then and when the plants truly need it. Natalie likes to set up quadripods for her tomatoes before she even plants the tomatoes to reduce the chance of disturbing tomato roots and to get a jump on this task.

For other plants that don't grab on by themselves, you'll need to help them by means of string, wire, strips of fabric, or clips. As you do this, remember that the plant is continually growing, so don't tie anything so tightly that down the line it strangles a stalk.

TOMATOES AND STRING TRELLISES

When grown in greenhouses, tomatoes are most often supported by string trellises. This method of trellising tomatoes can be used outside, too. In essence, it's like staking with wooden or bamboo stakes, but the string becomes the stake.

- Each tomato plant has a string coming down to it from a bar, wire, or rope suspended above.

- As the tomatoes grow, you twine them around the string in a spiral motion. (There's no need to tie the plants to anything with more string, though in commercial operations little plastic clips are often used to attach the tomato stem to the string.)

- You also will need to prune off suckers (side branches) and maintain a single leader or "trunk." You can download a video demonstration of tomato pruning on our website (see the link on page 364).

To create a tomato string trellis outside, you'll need to create a top bar. We've used T-posts with bamboo attached to them to extend their height, then run a UV-resistant rope through holes drilled in the bamboo. Some of our neighbors have figured out another clever approach that involves the same T-post and bamboo posts, but with PVC plumbing Ts on top and lengths of rebar running from post to post.

8

Dealing with Pests
& *Diseases*

Holistic Overview of Pests and Diseases 240

Pest ID and Life Cycles 244

Plant Disease ID and Management 245

No-Spray Ways to Combat Pests and Diseases 250

Organic Pesticides and How to Use Them 254

This elegant caterpillar is the tomato hornworm, larva of the five-spotted hawk moth. Its favorite food? Tomato plants, which it munches to oblivion fairly quickly.

Holistic Overview of Pests and Diseases

Pests, like weeds, are creatures that we perceive as harmful because they compete with us for the food we are trying to grow. Weeds compete with our crops for sunlight, soil nutrients, and water, while insect pests directly consume the plants we'd like to eat or interfere with the growth of those plants. Every single organism on this planet has an important role to play in the beautifully complex web of life, and each has the capacity to do that in a dynamic balance with other organisms. Pests are no exception.

At the same time, insect pests and plant pathogens (diseases, including viruses, fungi, and others) can cause a whole lot of damage when they swing out of balance in our gardens and agricultural fields. All over the world, the majority of pests and diseases that cause serious problems are considered nonnative

invasives. These troublesome creatures hitch rides on cargo; they move around with human-driven commerce. In fact, between 1854 and 2012, 930 nonnative species of insects in the Hemiptera order are known to have invaded the United States with the help of humans. Members of these plant-eating groups include aphids, scales, and whiteflies.

Nonnative insects are problematic because native plants haven't yet evolved defenses against them. Additionally, these pests may not have any natural predators in their new territory, which can lead to population explosions and a serious lack of ecological balance.

We share all this not as a strategy for managing pests in the garden (the problem of invasive species is too big for individual gardeners to manage) but to put pests in context. They are not out to get us. While we can't know for sure, because we've never had a chat with aphids or any others, our bet is that these critters simply want to express their life force like the rest of us do. We've created situations where their ability to do that has some ripples that we don't like, and yes, there are good strategies for managing their impacts and still harvesting healthy veggies.

INTEGRATED PEST MANAGEMENT

Integrated pest management (IPM) is an approach to managing insect pests and diseases that looks at the whole system of a garden and the surrounding area. It's a lot like functional and holistic models of medicine that go beyond merely identifying diseases and trying to destroy them with pharmaceutical drugs. IPM considers many factors, including:

- Habitat manipulation
- Natural predators
- Pest life cycles
- Physical barriers
- Resistant varieties
- Seasonal and climatic rhythms
- Soil fertility
- Targeted use of low-toxicity pesticides

When a pest or disease is taking down your prized tomato plants, the situation can feel scary and urgent, and you may want to rush to the store for a spray. But when your garden is looking good, you may not feel motivated to think about pests and diseases.

IPM works best as a long-term and regular strategy of maintenance, planning, and care; it doesn't serve its true purpose if only applied when there's already an issue at hand. Much like how eating well, calming the mind, exercising, breathing deeply, drinking clean water, laughing, and singing can fortify your body so that it's less prone to picking up sickness, applying IPM to every step of your gardening journey can render your garden more resilient in the face of invasions.

The shiny black dots making lace out of this eggplant leaf are called flea beetles. They're so named because they hop like fleas.

PEST LESSONS
FROM AN OPPORTUNISTIC MOUSE

Natalie learned a lesson about pests and balance from a mouse she once cohabitated with. When she was living at WildRoots, a primitive skills community in western North Carolina, all the meat she ate was roadkill or hunted by friends. Natalie's first house there was a small and ramshackle camper, later to be supplanted with a tent in the national forest, a Catawba-style bark lodge, and then a small straw-clay cabin. In this original camper home also lived a mouse. The wee creature kept Natalie up in the wee hours; it ate her food; it ate the deer hides that she tanned to make her clothes and to sell. This mouse was an unwelcome visitor, to say the least, and yet Natalie, who grew up vegetarian and has a very tender heart, felt horrible about the idea of killing it if she wasn't going to eat it.

She had many conversations about the matter, some with the mouse, and some with other humans. In the meantime the mouse shacked up with another mouse, and there was then a mouse family. Finally Natalie came to the conclusion that all animals defend their home and their food, and if this mouse (now a family of mice) was going to invade her space, she was going to take action. She finally trapped the mice, fed their bodies to the soil, and learned a valuable lesson about balance. Pests in the garden are much like this mouse in the house. When mice and pests live in their natural environments, with their natural limitations, we can live in harmony. When humans start changing the environment, and pests (and mice) no longer exist within natural limitations, it's time to take action.

Natalie and Chloe's Quick Checklist to Keep Pests and Diseases in Check

- ☐ Nourish the soil to keep plants healthy, but don't over-fertilize.

- ☐ Plant vegetables during the seasons they're suited for, in conditions they like.

- ☐ Practice good hygiene with hands and tools to prevent the spread of diseases.

- ☐ Minimize handling wet plants; moisture encourages the spreading of disease.

- ☐ Encourage airflow via sufficient plant spacing, pruning, and trellising.

- ☐ Choose the right varieties for your garden (including disease- and pest-resistant varieties).

- ☐ Employ crop rotation and rest periods to disrupt pest and disease life cycles.

- ☐ Plant a diversity of crops. Some will attract beneficials; if bugs eat a plant or diseases infect something, you'll still have other veggies to harvest.

- ☐ Discern which pests and diseases are a problem in your geographical area and in your garden (before treating them).

- ☐ Use organic sprays, physical barriers, and other natural interventions judiciously.

THE CONNECTIONS BETWEEN SOIL, PESTS, AND DISEASES

The ground is a teeming universe of generative mystery (see Chapter 4 for more on this). It provides mineral nutrients, water, biological relationships, and anchoring that plants need to grow and thrive. What comes from the soil greatly influences a plant's capacity to ward off infections by pathogens and predation by pests.

Even though plants don't have circulatory or central nervous systems like animals do, they still have their own versions of immune systems. To get technical, these are called pathogen-associated molecular pattern (PAMP), PAMP-triggered immunity (PTI), and effector-triggered immunity (ETI). Regardless of what these systems are named or how exactly they work, we, as gardeners, need to understand that healthy plants have an impressive capacity to deter potential pests and to heal from infestations that do happen.

Research shows that organically managed farms and gardens have greater resistance to pest pressure:

- Organic soils contain more biological compounds and relationships.

- Nutrition for plants that comes from them is more balanced.

- They are more inviting to a diversity of insects, including potential predators who like to eat pests.

The Bionutrient Food Association is actively engaged in research connecting the soil practices that lead to healthy, resilient crops in the face of pests with the nutrient density of those crops for human consumption. Evidence suggests that vegetables grown in vital, living soil not only resist pest pressure more effectively than crops grown with industrial, chemical-laden methods, but they are also tastier and more full of nutrients for us humans when we eat them. It's a win-win!

Every single organism on this planet has an important role to play in the beautifully complex web of life, and each has the capacity to do that in a dynamic balance with other organisms. Pests are no exception.

Just like healthy food and exercise prevent sickness in people, nutrient- and beneficial microbe–rich soil gives plants natural resistance to pests and diseases.

So if we haven't already convinced you that tending the fertility and vitality of your soil as a dynamic and diverse community is more than worth the effort, here's another reason! Living soil with lots of organic matter and a blend of available mineral and biological compounds is the basis of effective IPM in any garden.

Another critical piece of the soil-pest-disease connection is a little counterintuitive: Over-fertilizing, especially with nitrogen, can make plants much more susceptible to pests and some diseases. It's more common to over-fertilize when using synthetic products, but this can absolutely be an issue with organic inputs, too. Recall the story in Chapter 4 (see page 110) about Natalie's daughter, Hazel—then around three years old—sprinkling a whole cup of feather meal around the bases of several plants that were shortly decimated by aphids. Other than this, neither of us can remember having serious issues with aphids in our gardening lives. Overdoing the nitrogen causes rapid growth, but it also knocks natural defense systems out of whack, can make plant tissues more appealing to herbivory (getting eaten), and can even disrupt soil biology. Feeding plants to support pest and disease resistance needs to happen in a balanced, holistic way to be effective.

PESTS, DISEASES, AND SEASONS

We regularly hear questions from our gardening students about what to do for their struggling kale plants in midsummer. In most temperate regions this time of year is hot and brimming with insect pests. In our area fungal pathogens abound at this time, too.

Kale is a cool-weather-loving crop that's delectable to many summer insect pests. Although it's possible to grow kale year-round in many areas, we prefer taking a break midsummer because the heat makes it spicier and more bitter, and the pests go to town munching it. Naturally, our answer to students is that

they haven't done anything wrong; growing kale in summertime is a bit of an uphill battle for everyone.

Since we live in a "buy now with one click" culture, it's easy to assume that we can have any veggies we want whenever we want, no matter the season. Certainly this anti-ecological illusion is perpetuated by the selection at most grocery stores. But the truth is, each crop has its ideal season. Weather conditions, like soil conditions, impact how resilient plants are in the midst of an attack. One simple but significant step in applying IPM in your garden is to plant vegetables so they grow in ideal temperatures, and to avoid times when populations of pests are booming. (For specific information on when to plant what, see the vegetable profiles beginning on page 275 and the appendix.)

Pest ID and Life Cycles

Understanding which pest is actually doing damage to your crops is crucial for combating them. See Top 10 Insect Pests: Identification and Management (page 246) to see if any of these common critters happen to be your culprit, and what to do if so. If you're dealing with one that we don't mention, the next step is to lean on your local Extension agent. Almost every county in the United States has a Cooperative Extension office with agents on staff to help growers of all scales. We encourage you to engage these free and low-cost resources, which will be the best suited for your local area.

Another layer of getting to know pests is to understand their life cycles. Sometimes you can nip a pest problem in the bud, so to speak, by removing habitat where they breed or overwinter. And some pests are much easier to kill at certain life stages than others. Here are some questions to explore.

- At what stage are they easiest to eradicate?
- At what stage are they the most detrimental to crops?
- How, where, and when do the pests in your garden complete their life cycles?
- How do they reproduce?
- Where do they overwinter?

You don't need to become an expert on every bug you see (unless that sounds fun, in which case, go for it!). But learning to identify insects and then getting to know how they live, multiply, and feed can tell you whether a particular bug is a friend or foe. Most bugs aren't harmful to crops!

If you know all there is to know about your pests, then you'll know how to approach them. For example, if you know that the mature phase of wireworms (called click beetles) occur in tall, overgrown grassy areas, you may not choose to plant potatoes or another root crop (highly susceptible to wireworm damage) in a place that was recently reclaimed from pasture. Instead you can plant some leafy greens there for a season, which will greatly reduce the wireworm population, then follow that with potatoes.

Here's another example: You discover that flea beetles overwinter in plant debris and emerge in early spring. To reduce damage from these pests, you choose to remove mulch from specific beds, thus limiting their overwintering habitat. You can then avoid planting highly susceptible crops in early spring.

This squash lady beetle larva looks like a tiny Koosh ball, but it's way less fun. They (and the adults) turn leaves into skeletons that are unable to photosynthesize.

Fungal blights are a perennial problem on tomato plants in wet climates like ours.

Plant Disease ID and Management

Diseases, just like pests, are easier to manage if you know what you're dealing with. Proper identification is especially important if you're going to shell out a lot of money on a fancy, specialized pesticide. Since most pathogenic (disease-causing) organisms are microscopic, distinguishing them can be a little trickier than identifying bugs. This is further complicated by the fact that symptoms of nutrient deficiencies can look just like signs of disease. Fortunately many diseases are directly related to certain growing conditions and/or are more likely to show up on certain crops than others. In many cases diseases are carried by pests, and/or pest damage opens entry points

for diseases to infect plant tissues. Holistic care is crucial here!

Check out Seven Common Plant Diseases: Symptoms and Management (page 248) to see if what you're dealing with is listed there and to learn how you might respond. If you don't find clues there as to what's going on, again as with pests, it's time to reach out to your local Extension agent. Many regions have plant pathology laboratories where you can send a sample of your likely diseased plant, and they'll look at it under a microscope. There's usually a fee associated with this service, and we've only done it if something is really weird and we're just so curious, or if an issue is widespread or recurring. Most of the time we just remove diseased tissue or whole plants and practice the management strategies described throughout this chapter. Unless otherwise noted in the table on page 248, 70 percent isopropyl rubbing alcohol and 10 percent bleach solution are both effective disinfectants for most plant pathogens.

BLIGHT-RESISTANT TOMATO

After years of trying all kinds of tomatoes, both of us have come to love the variety 'West Virginia '63'. An all-around good tomato for canning or slicing, it grows vigorously and is significantly resistant to late blight, which can be a serious issue pretty much everywhere. These tomato plants are always the last to succumb to this fungal pathogen. This variety was bred by West Virginia University professor emeritus Mannon Gallegly in 1963 using traditional plant breeding techniques. Growing it in our gardens extends our tomato harvests by weeks or months each year.

Top 10 Insect Pests: Identification and Management

NAME	SUSCEPTIBLE CROPS	TYPE OF DAMAGE
Aphid (Aphididae family)	Many	Failure to thrive; visible presence of aphids sucking sap
Cabbageworm, cabbage looper (*Pieris rapae, Trichoplusia ni, Evergestis rimosalis*)	Many members of the Brassicaceae family (broccoli, Brussels sprouts, cabbage, cauliflower, collards, kale, kohlrabi)	Holes in leaves
Corn earworm (*Helicoverpa zea*)	Corn and tomato are preferred; can attack many kinds of vegetables	Damage to corn silk that can interfere with pollination; direct eating of corn kernels or tomato fruits, creating conditions for fungal pathogens to enter plants where they've been eating
Flea beetle (*Phyllotreta* spp., *Epitrix cucumeris, Disonycha xanthomelas*)	Broccoli, cabbage, eggplant, melons, peppers, potatoes, radishes, spinach, tomatoes, and turnips	Tons of tiny holes (like pinpricks) in leaves
Harlequin bug (*Murgantia histrionica*)	Members of the Brassicaceae family; if they can't find brassicas, they'll eat asparagus, beans, beets, eggplant, potatoes, tomatoes, and a variety of tree fruits	Wilting, browning, and dying due to sucking of plant juices
Mexican bean beetle (*Epilachna varivestis*)	In order of preference: common bean (*Phaseolus vulgaris*, both green and dry varieties), lima beans (*Phaseolus lunatus*), soybeans (*Glycine max*), cowpeas/ blackeyed peas (*Vigna unguiculata*)	"Lacey" leaves, pocks in beans
Squash bug (*Anasa tristis*)	Squash and pumpkins are preferred; can attack all members of the Cucurbitaceae family	Yellow spots that eventually turn brown where bugs suck plant juices and inject a toxic substance, causing Anasa wilt; also causes wilting and death of young or weak plants
Squash vine borer (*Melittia cucurbitae*)	Winter squash, pumpkins, summer squash, melons (less likely)	Holes in squash stems with pithy, mooshy frass (insect excrement) coming out; death or serious suffering of plants
Striped and spotted cucumber beetle (*Acalymma vittatum, Diabrotica undecimpunctata howardi*)	Members of the Cucurbitaceae family, especially cucumbers and melons, but also squash	Holes in leaves and fruit; infection by bacterial wilt that enters those holes and causes wilting of leaves
Wireworm (*Conoderus* spp.)	Beets, grains, onions, potatoes, sweet potatoes; all vegetables are susceptible, but the above are favorites	Tiny tunnels through root and bulb crops

MANAGEMENT TIPS	EFFECTIVE TREATMENTS
Aphid damage tends to be minimal (no treating required); severe aphid damage is often the result of over-fertilizing or plants weakening at the end of their life cycle. Aphids can carry and spread viruses, including cucumber mosaic virus, and aphid "honeydew" (excrement) can cause foliar fungal infections. Spraying infected plants with high-pressure water can remove aphids.	Insecticidal soap and garlic are promising aphid treatments and can be used together. Neem oil kills aphids.
Grow these crops in spring and fall (fewer cabbageworms in cooler weather). Choose red/purple varieties so the "worms" (i.e., caterpillars) are easier to spot. Cover plants with row cover to prevent adult butterflies from laying eggs that hatch into caterpillars. Rotate locations of these crops.	Weekly Bt sprays are quite effective. Regular hand picking and squishing or drowning in soapy water works in smaller gardens. If you use row cover, be sure you don't trap butterflies (adult cabbageworms) inside the cover!
Blacklight and pheromone traps reduce populations of adult moths who lay eggs that pupate into worms (i.e., caterpillars). Handpicking when worms are spotted can help, but they can be hard to see.	Bt sprays can be quite effective, but it's challenging to get the spray onto corn silk or down into developing ears.
Flea beetles are most active in early spring, then populations go down. Larger transplants can withstand some flea beetle damage. The removal of mulch and debris inhibits survival of overwintering larvae, and row cover helps if it's in an area that was absent of flea beetles the previous season. Crop rotation is essential.	Surround WP (kaolin) protects plants from flea beetle damage. Pyrethrins and spinosad kill adults but can kill beneficials, too.
Harlequin bugs are very showy black-and-orange creatures (hence the name) and are therefore easy to spot. They hang out and lay eggs on both sides of leaves, so check there to pick off bugs and squish eggs. Remove debris and hiding places during winter to help reduce populations, and pay special attention to picking and killing bugs in early spring and fall to reduce populations.	Handpick, then squish or drown in soapy water. Surround WP (kaolin) protects plants from harlequin bug damage, and insecticidal soaps and neem oil kill all stages on contact. Be sure to spray on both sides of leaves!
Adults overwinter in debris, like leaves, crop residue, and mulch; reducing these habitats can reduce their populations. Low-growing (nonvining) beans can be covered with row cover. Plant an early patch of beans as a trap crop, then stuff the bean beetle–infested plants into a plastic bag for 1 week before composting. We mostly accept that our bean plants will eventually succumb and give thanks for what we harvest before they do.	Squishing, spinosad, neem oil, and pyrethrins can help, though we haven't had much success with neem oil, possibly because it's so hard to spray every surface of a bean plant, in which case any spray might be hard to use effectively.
Squash bugs like to hang out and lay eggs on the *undersides* of leaves, so check there to pick off bugs and squish eggs. Bugs can be killed in soapy water. For a good trap, lay cardboard or wood near squash plants; the bugs will group underneath it overnight, then you can gather them in the a.m. and drown or squish. Removing debris and hiding places during winter reduces populations.	Sprays are not very effective for adult squash bugs. Physical management practices are the way to go here, along with good soil and plant care.
Squash vine borers are active in June and July, so later plantings can have a better chance. *Cucurbita moschata* (butternut group, including tromboncino summer squash) are much less susceptible. Crop rotation is essential here, as pupae overwinter in the soil. Physically wrapping aluminum foil or pantyhose around the base of squash plants can help protect them.	Once an infestation is happening, inject Bt into the stem/vine with a syringe; insecticidal soap kills eggs on contact. *Note: Once you see damage, meaning borers are already inside the squash stems/vines, it's hard to treat.*
Cucumber beetles can damage plants by eating leaves, stems, roots, and flowers, and they can transmit bacterial wilt. Cucumbers and muskmelons are especially susceptible to bacterial wilt. Lay thick mulch under plants to reduce egg-laying and future populations, then compost far away, or burn debris after crop is done to inhibit survival of overwintering larvae. Crop rotation is essential, as pupae overwinter in the soil.	Neem oil kills adult beetles (be sure to apply on all surfaces, including the undersides of leaves). Pheromone lures and traps help reduce adult populations, and pyrethrins kill adults but can kill beneficials, too.
Wireworms are the larvae of click beetles, which flourish in weeds and tall grasses, including cover crops. Follow a grassy cover crop with a fruiting crop instead of a root crop, and cultivate soil several times before planting to reduce populations. Wireworms love raised beds.	Since wireworms attack underground parts of plants, sprays are an ineffective treatment. *Steinernema carpocapsae* nematodes can be introduced to the soil to consume wireworms, and cultural management practices can be effective over time (see previous column).

Seven Common Plant Diseases: Symptoms and Management

COMMON NAME	SCIENTIFIC NAME	SUSCEPTIBLE CROPS	TYPE OF DAMAGE
Anthracnose	*Colletotrichum* spp.	Beans, chard, cucumber, eggplant, melons, pepper, tomato, spinach, and watermelons	Soft, sunken dark spots appear on fruit but also on leaves and stems. In warm, humid conditions, tiny salmon-colored spores may appear in dark centers of spots.
Blights	Various	Potatoes, tomatoes, and other members of the Solanaceae family; also, to a lesser extent, other vegetables	Signs of early blight: yellow spots with brown edging on leaves when tomatoes set; dark spots on foliage and stem tissue closest to the ground, moving upward. Spots tend to have a slight halo pattern of concentric circles. Late blight shows up as dark, rotten spots on fruits and leaves.
Downy mildew	Various oomycetes from the Peronosporaceae family	Cucumbers, melons, and other members of the Cucurbitaceae family; basil, cabbage, kale, sunflowers	Small, water-soaked splotches are light in color; as damage worsens, they get darker and can distort leaf shape and eventually destroy leaves altogether.
Mosaic viruses	Various	Many	Leaves yellow in a "mosaic" pattern, cup and wilt, become leathery, or turn thin and shoestring-like (filiformity). Plant growth is stunted and plants die.
Powdery mildew	Various	Beans, cucumbers, tomatoes, zucchini and other squash	Very specific and identifiable white powdery spots or coating on upper surface of leaves develops and leads to browning and drying of leaves.
Rusts	Over 8,000 named species of fungi in the Pucciniales order; many are host specific	Asparagus, beans, berries, corn, eggplant, okra, onions, peas, and sweet potatoes	Yellow, orange, or reddish brown blisters (hence the name) show up on either upper surface or underside of leaves or on fruits. Leaves may twist. Advanced infection makes leaves die and fall off.
Wilts	*Fusarium oxysporum* (fusarium wilt), *Verticillium* spp. (verticillium wilt), and others	Basil, cucumbers, eggplants, muskmelons, peppers, potatoes, strawberries, tomatoes, watermelons, and others	Wilting of plants, followed by yellowing, then drying, browning, and death of that tissue. Wilting begins at bottom of plant and moves upward.

MANAGEMENT TIPS	EFFECTIVE TREATMENTS
This fungal disease thrives in warm, wet conditions and can be passed from soil onto plant tissues; layer thick mulch beneath plants to prevent infection and spread. Limit overhead watering and remove and burn or trash infected plants. Practice good hygiene of tools and hands.	Copper-based fungicides, Actinovate AG, Regalia, Serenade ASO
There are thousands of blights; early and late blight are the most common garden blights. Most blights are caused by fungal pathogens, while some are bacterial in nature. Early blight prefers warmer temps, and late blight thrives as the weather cools. Management practices to prevent and reduce blights include using clean hands and tools, pruning and trellising plants for good airflow, mulching to reduce the chance of soil splashing on plants, minimizing overhead watering, growing plants under cover to reduce moisture on leaves, and removing and destroying infected leaves. Crop rotation is especially important with Solanaceae veggies; growing resistant varieties can make a big difference.	For tomatoes, prune affected leaves and do preventive pruning for airflow (very effective). Copper-based fungicides can help prevent and reduce fungal blights (though it's hard to treat a full-blown blight infection). Serenade ASO can also be helpful in the prevention and treatment of late blight.
Downy mildew spores open up in cooler, moist conditions. Limit overhead watering and general leaf wetness. Remove and burn or trash infected plants. Practice good hygiene of tools and hands. DMR (downy-mildew resistant) varieties of basil and cucumbers have been bred for incredibly effective resistance to downy mildew.	Serenade ASO can help treat and prevent downy mildew; hydrogen peroxide products can also help. Regalia is a natural biofungicide that can help prevent downy mildew.
Remove all infected plants from the garden; burn or throw in the trash. Mosaic viruses are often transmitted by insects, so keep up on pest management. Viruses can also be transmitted by tools and hands, so practice good hygiene. Mosaic viruses aren't effectively killed by alcohol, but a 10 percent bleach solution will work, or a 20 percent solution of nonfat dry milk. Infected tools need to be soaked in either of these for 30 minutes. Smokers can transmit tobacco mosaic virus into the garden if they handle dry tobacco or cigarettes and don't wash their hands afterward. If you struggle with these viruses, choose resistant crop varieties when you can.	Management practices are the most effective. Diseased plants cannot be saved by sprays or treatments and can transmit disease; they must be pulled, isolated, and destroyed (not composted). Some mosaic viruses can live for up to 2 years in soil without a plant host.
Powdery mildew thrives in shady or overcast conditions. Avoid overhead watering to minimize spore germination. Prune plants and don't overcrowd to maximize airflow. Remove and burn or trash infected leaves, and do the same with whole plants at the end of the season. Practice good hygiene with tools and hands, and plant resistant varieties. Hydrogen peroxide and neem oil effectively disinfect tools of powdery mildew, along with bleach and rubbing alcohol.	*Bacillus subtilis* products can be used preventively. Sulfur and copper products help treat infections, as does Serenade ASO. Spraying a mixture of 1:1 milk to water also helps.
Rust only lives on living plant tissue, so remove infected plants quickly. Spores open in warmer, moist conditions; limit overhead watering and general leaf wetness. Remove and burn or trash infected plants. Practice good hygiene of tools and hands, and plant resistant varieties, especially if you've noticed the presence of rust in a particular crop.	Copper-based fungicides, sulfur-based fungicides, Regalia
If you know a wilt is present in your soil, plant resistant varieties for the most effective results. Spores live up to 5 years in the soil and require warm, wet, acidic soil to germinate and infect plants, so raise soil pH above 6 to help. Practice good hygiene and long (5- to 7-year) rotations of host plants.	Sprays and other treatments aren't effective for wilts.

LEFT: No bushy plants here! We prune tomato suckers (branching stems) and lower leaves to allow for lots of airflow, reducing rates of fungal blights.

RIGHT: Pests can look, but they can't touch when plants are protected with thin fabric. Be careful to seal the edges so pests don't get trapped inside.

No-Spray Ways to Combat Pests and Diseases

Along with nourishing the ground and planting during the right seasons, there are lots of other tools and techniques (that don't involve pesticides) for preventing pests and diseases from damaging your crops.

NATURAL PREDATORS

Instead of killing bugs yourself, it's always nice to have other bugs or other creatures do the dirty work. Many predatory insects hunt and eat or parasitize garden pests, so make your garden as inviting to these helpful mercenaries as possible. Many of the strategies and approaches that we encourage to promote balance in the garden can also support these beneficial insects. Practices like crop diversity, organic soil fertility management, placing flowering plants within or around your garden, and maintaining wild areas near your garden can attract and feed helpful predators.

Some common flowers that are particularly enticing to natural predators include:

- Achillea (yarrow)
- Chamomile
- Cilantro (coriander)
- Dill
- European goldenrod
- Fennel
- Lavender
- Sedum
- Sweet alyssum
- Veronica

You can also purchase predatory insects to introduce into your garden or greenhouse. This can be highly effective for a period of time, but it can also get pricey. Take the time to research exactly who you're trying to control, who will be most effective at doing them in, and what conditions those predators might need to stick around and establish a population in your garden.

While inviting insect diversity into your garden is a significant step in IPM, it's not the silver bullet that some permaculture perspectives may have you think. A lot of factors influence pest and disease populations and susceptibility. Don't be surprised if you have a beautiful perennial border around your garden and you still see bugs eating your broccoli.

RESISTANT VARIETIES OF GARDEN VEGETABLES

Humans have been in conversation with pests for a long time. As long as we've been selecting and breeding plants, pest and disease resistance have been characteristics we've hoped to coax into stronger expression—by saving seeds from plants that do well in the face of pest pressure; conducting multiyear, multi-stakeholder hybrid breeding projects; and splicing bacterial or other genes into plants to genetically modify them.

Our opinion of genetically modified, or GM, seeds is that they're not respectful of Earth's wisdom or growers' sovereignty, and in the long run they aren't that effective. As for the other methods, they can play vital roles in applying IPM in your garden. One simple step is to try out several different varieties of a crop to see what does well in your conditions. Even if something isn't technically disease resistant, if it thrives in your garden, it will be better equipped to deal with whatever comes. Choosing specifically disease-resistant varieties can be a game changer, especially when it comes to pathogens like fungi and viruses.

HABITAT MANIPULATION

We can create ideal conditions for natural predators by planting flowers to feed them, and we can diminish ideal habitats for pests by raking up plant debris and mowing surrounding areas, and so on. You can practice additional methods of habitat manipulation to encourage prime conditions.

Maximize airflow. To minimize pathogens such as fungal diseases, plant, space, support, and prune your crops for maximum airflow. Fungi don't thrive with drying breezes, so improving airflow can decrease their impact on crops. In humid areas, like where we garden, planting susceptible crops under the cover of a greenhouse or hoop house can make a world of difference in reducing fungal diseases.

Rotate crops and allow for rest periods. This is an essential piece of IPM. Engaging in cycles of crop rotation and fallow (rest) periods can be a longer-term type of habitat manipulation. Both pests and diseases are likely to flourish if you plant the same thing in the same place year after year or season after season. But if you move things around and give sections of your garden a chance to rest, pest and disease life cycles will be disrupted, thus reducing their impacts on your crops over time. Think of this as a rhythmic reset for your garden: Taking away the plants that garden pests and diseases feed on minimizes pest and pathogen populations.

Cull infected plants from affected areas. This is another form of habitat manipulation. When a single plant or a couple of plants seem totally overtaken with a pest or disease, you can either pull out the whole plant or prune off the infected areas and remove that from the garden.

Note: If you aren't sure what's causing the problem, it's best to burn or trash the infected plant parts. This is a precaution we often take with a few individual plants each year.

PHYSICAL BARRIERS

Organic agriculture relies heavily on physical barriers to manage pests. Even with the best IPM practices, some crop-eating bugs are inevitable, especially when you are growing

REST IS IMPORTANT

Many traditional gardening and farming cultures mandate rest every several years and/or incorporate the act of resting land into larger-scale physical rotations. In the Jewish traditions of some of Chloe's ancestors, "shmita years" are part of a sabbatical cycle that rests agricultural fields and forgives debts. We have observed a lowered pest load on plants after giving an area a break from gardening.

Applying diatomaceous earth to an eggplant under attack is a bit like dusting powdered sugar on a cake.

Kaolin. This white clay is another naturally occurring mineral. Composed of tiny mineral particles and crystals—including feldspar, quartz, silica, copper, magnesium, and zinc—kaolin, like DE, is irritating to insects. It doesn't cut and dry insects but rather sticks to plant tissue, thus dissuading insects from penetrating the tissue. While kaolin is sold as a powder, it's meant to be mixed with water and sprayed onto plants; sometimes whole plants are dipped into this solution before transplanting. It's also the main ingredient in an organic pesticide called Surround WP.

Note: Although DE and kaolin are helpful powders, they can irritate your lungs if inhaled. Do not apply them on a breezy day, and please take care when working with them!

in the same area over a long period of time. To protect crops, you can put a physical material between the bugs and the surface of the plants, or you can physically trap and kill bugs. We offer a handful of options for you to choose from:

- Diatomaceous earth or kaolin (white clay)
- Row cover
- Sticky traps
- Your hands (your most valuable tool!)

Diatomaceous Earth and Kaolin Clay

These oft-used powdery substances act as physical barriers between your plants and garden pests. They work best in dry conditions and will need to be reapplied after heavy rain or overhead irrigation.

Diatomaceous earth (DE). Made from the fossilized remains of tiny aquatic organisms called diatoms, DE is primarily silica. If you were to look at it under a microscope, you'd see a bunch of jagged particles. When bugs come in contact with this scratchy stuff, it gets into the cracks of their exoskeletons and their bodies are irritated and cut, which eventually leads to desiccation (drying out) and, finally, death. DE works best when conditions are dry, and it will cut and kill beneficial bugs as readily as harmful ones, so it should be used with caution.

Row Cover

One of the most effective and most commonly used physical barriers is a thin, white fabric called floating row cover (or, simply, row cover). This spun-polyester material comes in various thicknesses and not only protects crops from bugs (and larger critters like crows) but also shelters them from heavy winds and dust, and/or keeps them warm during cool-season growing.

This technique, as far as pest management goes, is only effective against pests that approach plants from the air, such as:

- Bean beetles
- Cabbage loopers
- Cabbage whites
- Cucumber beetles
- Flea beetles

Other pests, like cutworms and wireworms, overwinter in the soil and emerge from there to wreak havoc on crops. Row cover isn't effective for them; all they have to do is crawl up from the soil underneath the row cover. Sneaky creatures!

Securing row cover. The best practice is to drape the fabric over wire or fiberglass supports. This keeps it from resting directly on young plants.

One of the trickier steps to using this effectively as a physical barrier is keeping it secure so that it acts as a true barrier. If it blows away, you're out of luck. And if it isn't held down correctly, pests might enter through gaps between the fabric and the soil, or at the ends of rows. Here are a few methods for securing row cover.

- Use string in a zigzag pattern over the hoops that support the material, tying the string to hooks or eyelets set in the ground or bed edges at or between the base of the hoops.
- Weigh down the edges of the fabric with sandbags or boards.
- Tuck in the edges of the fabric and bury them with a little soil.

None of these techniques is foolproof, especially in windy conditions. If you come up with another clever way of securing row cover, write to us and share the good news!

Regulating temps under row cover.
Row cover does increase temperatures around plants. In spring, fall, and winter, this is a good thing. In summertime, however, it can be problematic. For pest management alone—that is, when you're not also trying to warm things up—choosing a thinner fabric is best.

Sticky Traps
Yes, that's their official name! These physical barriers are more effective for monitoring and identifying pests than reducing populations or protecting plants. They are yellow cards that are coated with a sticky substance and can be placed in different spots throughout your garden or in nearby bushes. The bright color attracts insects, who then get stuck to the card, where you can more easily identify and count them.

You can also wrap double-sided sticky tape (from the drugstore, no special kind) around the stems of plants that seem to be getting munched. Be sure to leave a tail so that you can easily unwrap the tape. Then use a hand lens to identify who tried to crawl up the stem and take a bite.

Your Hands
Using hands, your most valuable tool, to remove bugs can be incredibly effective, especially in small or medium-size gardens: You simply pick off bugs and pinch or cut diseased leaves. Walk through your garden and put your hands on each plant to search for and destroy invaders. It's a wonderful way to tune in more deeply with what's going on in your garden.

Plucked bug bodies can be squashed or dunked in a container with soapy and/ or vinegary water, where they will drown. Infected plant parts should be removed from the garden and composted, burned, or trashed, depending on the pathogen at work. Chloe pays her son Felix 5 to 10 cents per dead pest, which has motivated his interest in entomology.

After trying many methods for killing adult squash lady beetles, we've found "picking and squishing" to be the most effective.

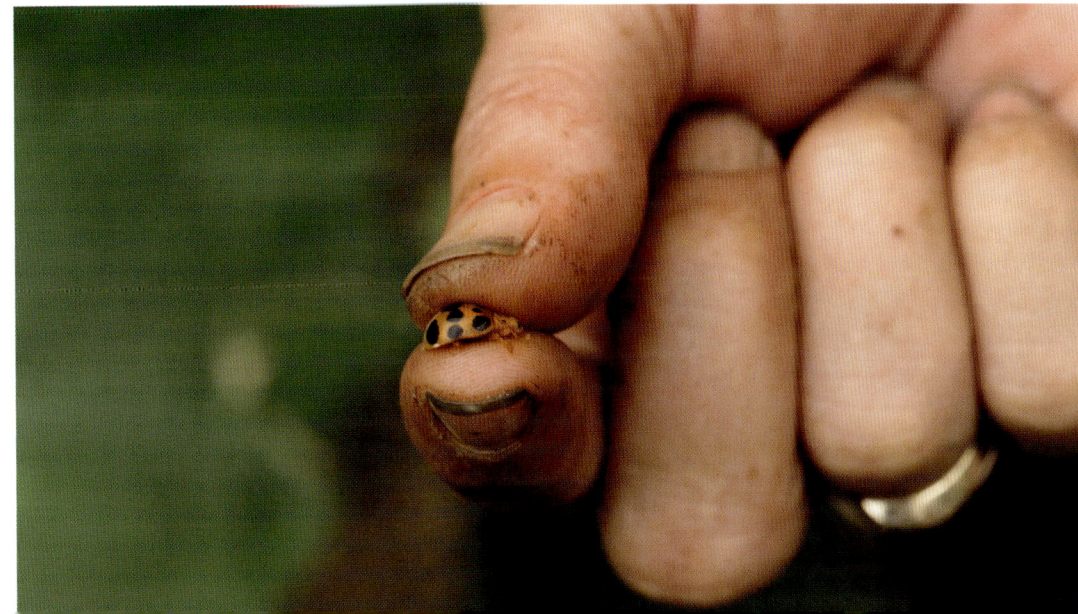

Organic Pesticides and How to Use Them

Humans have made and used pesticides for thousands of years. The vast majority of these products have been derived from plants, minerals, and bacteria, with the birth of the first synthetic pesticide—dichloro-diphenyl-trichloroethane, better known as DDT—coming into use in the 1940s. As you probably know, DDT and other human-made chemical killing agents can be incredibly harmful to humans, birds, beneficial insects, and the life all around us. Consider that naturally derived, organic pesticides can also be quite toxic (though not quite as toxic or persistent in the environment as DDT!) and should be used judiciously.

Thoughtful application of *organic* pesticides can be an essential step of IPM. Even when you reach for such a pesticide or other spray, that doesn't mean it's time to abandon all the holistic considerations we've explored above. You might spray, spray, spray a crop that's not suited to your conditions or that lacks the needed fertility to thrive, yet still not get ahead of the pests or diseases you're fighting. In the process you could hurt beneficial insects and other natural cycles while ending up with a poor-quality harvest despite the spraying.

In our experience even organic pesticides make the most sense when utilized to bridge a gap when pest or disease pressure is heaviest during a crop's life cycle rather than as a crutch throughout an entire season. For example, we spray Bt (*Bacillus thuringiensis*, a bacterial pesticide) on spring brassicas for about a month as they're maturing in late spring and early summer, when cabbage looper and cabbage white populations boom. Similarly, for fall brassicas, we spray starts that were sown in midsummer, when pest populations are high,

POULTRY AS PEST CONTROL

Employing ducks or chickens as part of the garden pest control force is a much lauded practice in the permaculture world. Bill Mollison, one of the fathers of permaculture as we know it, famously said to a fellow gardener who was struggling with slugs eating their veggies, "You don't have a slug problem, you have a duck deficiency." And it's true, ducks like to eat slugs. Chickens do, too. But, like many oversimplified adages, there's a lot of nuance to bringing poultry into a garden system so that they're helpful and not harmful.

Along with slugs and bugs, ducks also like to eat newly emerging vegetable plants, especially in the spring and fall when there isn't a lot of other greenery around. And in pursuit of tasty slugs and other morsels, ducks will indiscriminately stomp on young vegetable plants with their wide feet. Chickens love to eat vegetable plants at any stage, and they have a habit of scratching at the ground with their sharp-clawed feet in a way that disturbs germinating seeds and shallow root systems.

Chloe gardened with free-ranging ducks for many years, learning quickly to protect emerging and newly transplanted veggies until the plants had grown big enough to withstand the ducks' raucous parading. The system worked well for her, in part because the ducks had many acres upon which to roam, including several streams, their favorite places to hang out. Free-ranging ducks in a small or medium-size backyard garden would likely present many challenges.

Chloe has also brought chickens into the garden, but never free-ranging on purpose. Instead, she would run the chickens (contained by moveable fencing) in a garden bed to help prepare it. They would poop and scratch to improve fertility and texture, consume insects, and eat every plant.

TOP: Spray up, down, and all around with a small pump sprayer. Since many pests hang out on the undersides of leaves, upside-down spraying is important.

BOTTOM: When spreading powders like diatomaceous earth, it is important to protect our lungs with a mask. For other pesticides, eye protection is important.

to get them through until temperatures and bug numbers go down. If we have an unusually wet spell in summer and expect fungal issues to skyrocket, we may spray copper or Serenade preventively—though, in all honesty, we mostly select for resistant varieties, plant a diversity of crops, and hope for the best.

Both of us used to be somewhat fundamentalist about not spraying anything on our garden that was purchased in a bottle (we were okay with homemade foliar fertilizers and compost teas). We also both started gardening out West, where it's much easier to grow brassicas than it is in the southern Appalachians . . . and we both love to eat broccoli, cauliflower, and cabbage. Independently, but around the same time, each of us started to spray with Bt during the growth periods mentioned above. We were so pleased with the results (both in terms of delicious brassica harvests and our own humility) that we excitedly shared the news with each other, only to discover, once again, we were walking parallel paths.

STORE-BOUGHT PESTICIDES

According to the USDA, retail sales of organic produce have been increasing about 8 percent per year for the past decade. More farmers are using organic practices, and concurrently, more specialized organic pesticides and sprays are being developed. Some of these products are standardized versions of simple mixtures you can prepare at home (like Safer Brand Insect Killing Soap), while others are expensive biological compounds and formulations that are developed in laboratories and impossible to make at home.

In our experience even organic pesticides make the most sense when utilized to bridge a gap when pest or disease pressure is heaviest during a crop's life cycle rather than as a crutch throughout an entire season.

For a product to be considered organic, it must be approved by the Organic Materials Review Institute (OMRI). This international nonprofit organization determines which input products are allowed for use in organic production and processing, based on standards set by the USDA National Organic Program.

It gets a little complex, but what matters to us home gardeners is that OMRI-listed products can be used in certified organic production, but that *doesn't necessarily mean that they're safe* for pollinators, soil life, or even human life. It basically means that they've passed the same safety standards as any pesticide and that they're more likely to be derived from natural materials, though some synthetics are allowed.

If you're curious to explore the vast world of organic pest and disease management products, we suggest perusing the Arbico Organics website. They sell products, so clearly they have a stake in the game. Yet we've found that they offer pretty clear and balanced information about both products and pests, including helpful tips for ID and organic management that doesn't involve buying stuff from them.

As you look around at what kinds of organic pesticides exist, don't be pulled into the belief that buying one of those products will make all your garden challenges disappear, as the advertising suggests. If you haven't attended to the underlying health of your plants, no spray is going to change that. Also, this is a place where proper pest or disease ID is crucial. There is no use buying and applying a pesticide that doesn't target the exact pest

that is feasting on your crops. So again, not to be a broken record, but we strongly encourage you to approach pests through a holistic lens, applying every aspect of IPM, and to reach for pesticides only when they're called for and are likely to make a difference.

HOMEMADE PESTICIDES

Some household items can be used as pesticides. Like with other organic pest and disease fighters, the fact that something is already in your cupboard or medicine cabinet doesn't mean it's nontoxic to beneficial insects, soil life, wildlife, or even humans! All the same precautions that you would take with any pesticide apply to homemade ones. This includes getting a proper ID on whatever pest or pathogen issue you're addressing so you can match the solution with the problem.

In all honesty we've consistently used only three of the applications in the table on page 259, but the others are commonly referred to in organic gardening lore, so we expect you might be curious about them. We'll go into detail here about the three we use regularly.

Homemade soap spray. This spray is extremely effective against aphids. Occasionally we'll see an infestation of aphids on a crop that is struggling to make it through challenging conditions (like kale seedlings during the heat of summer, on their way to fall planting and a cooler, more appropriate environment). We mix up some soapy water and spray to kill the aphids, knowing that they won't be attracted to the plants once heat stress diminishes.

You might spray, spray, spray a crop that's not suited to your conditions or that lacks the needed fertility to thrive, yet still not get ahead of the pests or diseases you're fighting. In the process you could hurt beneficial insects and other natural cycles while ending up with a poor-quality harvest despite the spraying.

Tobacco tea. This is a broad-spectrum insecticide. In fact, synthetic nicotine-based products (neonicotinoids) are among the most widely used pesticides in the world and are extremely toxic and persistent; many believe that they are partially responsible for colony collapse disorder among honeybees. Homemade tobacco tea is not as persistent in the environment as neonicotinoids are, but it is indiscriminately toxic: It kills any bug with which it comes into contact.

Natalie brews up a bath of this strong stuff when she purchases plant starts from outside sources in order to cleanse them before bringing them into her garden. She's had some bad experiences importing pests through starts, so this is a precautionary step that feels worthwhile to her. It's important here to use organic tobacco, but know that there's always a risk of importing tobacco mosaic virus with the tea. (See page 187 for more on this extremely harmful virus.)

Beer traps for slugs. This simple technique for catching and drowning slugs involves burying tiny cups of beer into garden beds so that their tops are flush with soil level; slugs slither in for the sweet liquid and drown. It works really well in dry conditions. Rain dilutes the beer, rendering it ineffective, so it will need to be replaced frequently during wet periods.

A final note on homemade pesticides: Most of them wash off plants easily during rain or overhead watering. This is also a concern with store-bought pesticides, although many of those have additional ingredients that help them stick to plant parts in light to moderate rain. If you use homemade pesticides, you may need to reapply more frequently to see results.

HOW TO APPLY PESTICIDES

There are a few ways to get pesticides onto your plants, and both when and how you do it will impact their effectiveness. Here are some general guidelines.

- Apply liquid pesticides in the early morning or evening to reduce the risk of sunscald (droplets acting as magnifying glasses and causing sunlight to burn plant leaves).
- Check the weather before applying anything that will wash away with the rain (wait for a dry spell, if you can).
- Trying a pesticide you've never used? Apply the product to a couple of leaves on one plant before spraying a whole patch of plants. This will reveal if it is too strong for the plants you're treating.

Spray bottle or pump sprayer. Either of these work great for applying liquid pesticides. We prefer the pump sprayer because it holds pressure: You pump it up, then spray without continually pumping and tiring your hands. Also, most pump sprayers have nozzles that swivel or are at the end of little tubes, making it easier to reach the undersides of leaves. Remember that many pests hang out where you can't see them; if you spray only upper leaf surfaces, you may miss the mark and waste both your time and whatever pesticide you applied.

Mesh strainer for powdery materials. To apply diatomaceous earth (DE), for instance, place the powder in an ordinary fine-mesh strainer and tap the strainer to dust on the powder, as if you are sprinkling powdered sugar onto a cake. Be sure to wear a dust mask and avoid breathing in DE—and any other powdered products, including fertilizers—and wash the strainer after you use it.

Application schedule. Pesticides or disease treatments are rarely effective in a single dose. Store-bought products will have suggested application intervals on their packaging. Aim for reapplying homemade products at least once a week, or more frequently if the problem persists. There is a risk of over-applying and burning plant tissues, so pay attention as you apply pesticides, and look out for adverse impacts on the crops you're trying to help!

Applications of Common Store-Bought Organic Pesticides

ACTIVE INGREDIENT(S)	BRAND NAME(S)	WHAT IT TREATS	NOTES AND PRECAUTIONS
Biofungicides	Actinovate, Mycostop, Regalia, Serenade, others	Botrytis, damping off, *Fusarium*, powdery mildew, *Pythium*, *Rhizoctonia*, others (depends on the product)	It's very important to know what kind of disease you're fighting and to choose the right product. Many work best preventively and can be expensive but also very effective.
Bt (*Bacillus thuringiensis*)	Various	Caterpillars in the Lepidoptera order, including cabbage loopers, cabbage whites, gypsy moths, tomato hornworms	Toxic to caterpillars of all moths and butterflies; be careful not to spray this on milkweed. The subspecies *kurstaki* is what's used for killing caterpillars.
Copper	Mastercop, others	Various fungal diseases, especially blights and peach leaf curl	This can be irritating to humans topically and toxic internally, and it can damage plant tissues. Try a small area before applying to a whole plant.
Horticultural oils (plant or petroleum-based oils)	Natural Guard, SuffOil-X, TriTek, others	Soft-bodied insects: aphids, leafhoppers, mealybugs, psyllids, scale, whiteflies; powdery mildew	Some are toxic to bees. They can harm plant tissues, especially if applied in high temperatures. They are toxic to fish.
Insecticidal soaps (potassium fatty acids)	Garden Safe, Safer, others	Aphids, soft-bodied insects (but not caterpillars), leafhoppers, mites, scale, thrips, whiteflies	They can harm leaves of certain crops. They are best to use on beans, brassicas, cucurbits, and potatoes. Try a small area before applying to a whole plant.
Iron phosphate	Sluggo	Slugs and snails	It works best when the soil is moist but not soggy. Ideally, apply in early spring and then again a month later to disrupt reproductive cycles.
Kaolin clay	Surround	Colorado potato beetles, cucumber beetles, Japanese beetles, leafhoppers, powdery mildew, scab, thrips	Also mentioned in physical barriers, action is physical but often used as a sprayed slurry. Powder is extremely irritating to the lungs and washes off in heavy rain.
Neem tree derivatives (oil, other extracts)	AzaGuard, Debug products, Ecoworks EC, others	Many kinds of fungal diseases, insects, mites, and nematodes	They can harm some beneficial microbes, though not all. They broadly kill most leaf-eating insects (safe for most beneficials).
Pyrethrins (derivatives of *Chrysanthemum cinerariifolium*)	PyGanic, others	Broad-spectrum killer of over 100 pests	Dangerous to pollinators and other beneficials; it is also toxic to humans if ingested.
Spinosad	Various	Ants, caterpillars, fruit flies, leafminers, mosquitoes, spider mites, thrips, and many others	It is not safe around bees and can be irritating to eyes and skin. Like Bt, it is based on a soilborne bacterium. It is one of the most common pesticides in organic agriculture.
Sulfur	Various	Various fungal diseases, especially rots, rusts, and spots; mites; scab; scale; thrips	Excessive sulfur buildup in the soil isn't good for plants.

Applications of Common Homemade Organic Pesticides

HOMEMADE PESTICIDE	RECIPE	WHAT IT TREATS	NOTES AND PRECAUTIONS
Beer	Pour beer into small cups or dishes buried in the ground so that the rim of the container is flush with the earth	Slugs	Slugs are attracted to the sweet, yeasty aroma, fall into the beer, become intoxicated and disoriented, and drown. It needs to be placed throughout a slug-infested area. Refill beer after evaporation from sun or dilution from rain.
Chili powder	1 tablespoon chili powder with one quart of water and several drops of castile soap	Aphids, armyworms, leaf miners, loopers, spider mites, thrips, and whiteflies	Capsaicin, the active ingredient in chile peppers, can burn your eyes and skin. Similarly to garlic, it works more as a deterrent than an actual killer of bugs. It needs to be reapplied frequently to be effective.
Chrysanthemum flower tea (*Chrysanthemum cinerariifolium*)	½ cup dried flowers in 4 cups of hot water, steep for several hours or overnight	Many insects (broad spectrum insecticide)	It can be toxic to birds and fish— and mammals, too, but only at high concentrations.
Essential oils (citronella, clove, eucalyptus, peppermint, rosemary, tea tree, thyme, others)	Various formulations	Various insects and some fungal diseases	Some actually kill pests, while others deter pests through their strong smell. Volatile oils need to be reapplied frequently. There is very mixed evidence about their effectiveness, and they can get expensive.
Garlic	Concentrate: Purée 2 whole garlic bulbs with a small amount of water; let the mixture sit overnight; strain into a quart jar; add ½ cup vegetable oil, 1 teaspoon castile soap, and enough water to fill the jar. Mix 1 cup of concentrate with 1 quart of water and spray.	Aphids, armyworms, beetles, caterpillars, cutworms, flies, mites, mosquitoes, and larger critters like rabbits and voles	Strong smell deters pests and can kill or seriously disorient some, if applied in high enough concentrations. It needs to be reapplied frequently to be effective.
Soapy water spray	1 tablespoon natural castile soap (not detergent) to 1 quart of water	Soft-bodied insects: aphids, mealybugs and immature leafhoppers, mites, thrips, whiteflies; not very effective on caterpillars	Soft water makes it ineffective. Use distilled water if your water's pH is above 7. Insects must come in contact with moist soap (doesn't work once it's dry) Apply in the morning or evening so it dries more slowly. It can damage plant tissues, so try a small area before applying to a whole plant.
Tobacco tea	1 cup of dry tobacco in 1 gallon of boiling water; steep for a few hours or overnight	Many insects (broad spectrum insecticide)	It can harbor tobacco mosaic virus (see page 187). Nonorganic tobacco can have pesticide residues. It is dangerous to beneficials as well as irritating to our skin and harmful if ingested.
Tomato leaf extract	Concentrate: Pour 1 quart of boiling water over a packed 1-quart jar of fresh, healthy tomato leaves; let steep for 1 hour, then squeeze out liquid through a cloth or paint-strainer bag. Add 1 cup of concentrate to 1 quart water and spray.	Aphids, some caterpillars, spider mites, whiteflies	Do not use on tomato plants or other members of the Solanaceae (nightshade) family.
Vegetable oil spray	Concentrate: 1 cup of oil mixed with 1 tablespoon castile soap. Add 2 tablespoons of concentrate to 1 quart of water and spray.	Soft-bodied insects: aphids, leafhoppers, mealybugs, psyllids, scale, whiteflies; powdery mildew	It can damage plant tissues, so try a small area before applying to a whole plant.

9
Harvesting
& *the End of the Growing Season*

Consider Harvesting When Planning 262

Harvesting Methods 263

Post-harvest Processing 269

The Lifespans of Annual Vegetables 272

Sharing the Harvest 273

Consider Harvesting When Planning

Harvesting the bounty is obviously a joyful and rewarding step in any gardening journey . . . and it also takes some effort and finesse. Proper harvesting methodology, timing, and post-harvest processing of veggies result in bigger yields, healthier plants, and

perkier and tastier vegetables that last longer in the fridge or pantry.

It's important (and motivating) to consider the work of harvesting as you plan and plant your garden. There's a tendency to plan to grow more than you need or have time to harvest; it's paramount that you reflect on this with crops that require regular picking throughout a long harvest window. The best way to learn what it takes to harvest a given crop is to practice: Grow that crop and pay attention to the time and energy required to harvest it properly. Then use that information as you refine your gardening plans in the future.

We strongly encourage you to pay attention to *everything* you're harvesting: Notice children and neighbors watching you in your garden and getting inspired. Let yourself fully feel the satisfaction that comes from picking a basketful of food, and meditate on the notion that you're weaving yourself into a long, braided strand of humans who have done the same. Marvel at the complexity of insect life as you happen upon a tomato hornworm that's been parasitized by wasps. Drink in the healing tonic of tending this tangible connection with the living world.

Not every crop will survive and thrive, but if you're open to the holistic experience of gardening, there will be an abundance of lessons and blessings to harvest along with your vegetables. Each day that you pause in your garden to savor its beauty, to feel the wind and sun on your skin, and to deeply listen to the living world is a harvest day, of sorts. And as you take notes and get to know your garden and yourself as a gardener, you'll harvest the wisdom that will encourage your success and increase your satisfaction over time. Finally, even crops that don't get picked because you planted too much or ran out of time will go on to feed someone. Birds and bugs and microbes are hungry, too, and our harvests can be in the form of nourishing lives beyond our own.

It's best to make clean cuts with sharp harvesting tools (rather than rips or tears) so that plants heal more easily and more quickly and are less likely to be invaded by pests or diseases.

Cutting or snapping leaves at the base of their stems is easier on the plant than if you leave a long stem behind.

Harvesting Methods

Different types of crops are harvested in different ways, at different times of day, using different tools. Each crop is unique, but we can safely make some generalizations when looking at the plant parts we harvest. The following guidelines are all suggestions! We recommend harvesting greens in the early morning, for example, but if it turns out to be high noon or whenever you can actually get out there, that is fine. Both of us have definitely run out to the garden at midday to harvested semi-wilting lettuce for a salad; it's not ideal, but it's still tasty and nourishing.

A basic harvesting principle: *Minimize damage to the parent plant.* This principle applies to any vegetable that gets harvested multiple times over a harvest window. Each time we harvest a leaf or fruit, we leave a wound in its place. The parent plant needs to expend energy to heal this wound, and we want that plant to put its energy into growing more of whatever we just harvested. Furthermore, when we leave stem butts or torn edges after harvesting, these larger wounds invite fungi and other pathogens to infect the plant. So whatever method you use for harvesting, consider its impact on the parent plant and do your best to care for this generous giver of bounty.

LEAVES

We eat the leaves of so many delicious crops: lettuce, arugula, kale, collards, spinach, chard, and more. These plant parts are the photosynthetic surfaces that power plant growth and also transpire both water and air.

Ideal Harvest Time

Early morning is the absolute best time, with late afternoon or early evening coming in second. Transpiration is lower at these times; the plants are wet with dew; and they haven't wilted yet in the blazing sun—leaves will be less prone to post-harvest wilting when they're gathered at these cooler times of day.

In the heat of summer, commercial growers begin their lettuce harvests before dawn, because it makes a huge difference in the shelf life of the lettuce. You don't have to do this, unless harvesting lettuce while watching the sunrise is your thing (it's quite splendid!). But do try to harvest leaves in the first part of the day.

How to Harvest

Larger leaves are usually easy to snap off right where they emerge from the main stem of the plant. This is especially true for kale and collards. Chard and spinach can be snapped but don't break as easily as kale and collards, so for a clean edge, use a sharp knife or pruners to slice them right where they emerge. If you plan to eat the leaves immediately, having a cleanly cut edge won't matter so much. But if you're harvesting chard to store in the fridge or send home with a friend, clean edges will help the leaves last longer.

Leaves removed at the base of their stalks, right where they emerge from the parent plant, make the easiest wounds for plants to heal. Even if you don't plan to eat the stalk, it's better to slice or snap it off and compost it or feed it to the chickens than let a broken stem protrude from the parent plant. Longer stalks mean a harder healing job for the parent plant, plus they create more surface area for fungal and other pathogens to enter.

When lettuce and other tender greens are grown in the cut-and-come-again style—that is, as a full bed or thick row, rather than individual heading plants—a pair of sharp scissors is our tool of choice to give the leaves a haircut. The nice clean cuts heal quickly so the plants can focus on growing bigger for the next cutting. When harvesting lettuce in this way, cut about 4 inches from the ground to stay above the tender young leaves growing at the center of the plant, also known as its basal rosette.

FRUITS

Many of the crops we call vegetables are, botanically speaking, fruits. This includes tomatoes, peas, green beans, peppers and chiles, zucchini, okra, corn, squash, cucumber, and eggplant, among others.

When we harvest fruits, we break them free from the parent plant. Some, like green beans, corn, and tomatoes, come off easily with a simple twist or snap. Others, like okra, cucumbers, zucchini, and peppers, come off more efficiently with pruners or a knife. However you harvest, be sure to make a clean cut that doesn't leave a dangling stem or wide-open wound on the parent plant.

Give your lettuce a haircut every couple of weeks for a long harvest window. Lettuce harvested this way is ready to toss with a dressing!

We find a knife is the best tool to get in and harvest zucchinis, while pruners work well for things like cucumbers and eggplants.

Ideal Harvest Time

Most plants have the highest sugar content in the middle of the day, especially on sunny days. This means that crops such as tomatoes, peppers, and melons will be the sweetest when they're harvested at this time. Another consideration with harvesting fruits, especially those that are ripe when fully mature, is dew. Storage crops like winter squash and dry corn will keep best if they're dry; moisture on their surfaces can lead to mold and rot. For these reasons it's best to harvest most fruits in the middle of the day through early evening rather than in the morning.

Fruits to Harvest at an Immature Stage

Many vegetables that you will harvest as fruits are best to pick and eat when they are immature—the fruits have grown nice and juicy, but the seeds inside are not yet fully mature and viable. These are:

- Cucumbers
- Eggplants
- Green beans
- Okra
- Peas
- Sweet corn
- Zucchini and other summer squash

Knowing a fruit's ideal harvest size is crucial for the tastiest flavor and texture. If you harvest these later, they will likely be tough and not super tasty. If you wait till you have a huge zucchini, for example, the flavor and texture will be inferior compared to one picked when smaller. If you harvest peas when they're mature, they'll be starchy instead of sweet, and harder to digest without cooking. Harvesting underripe fruits will also result in compromised flavor, so knowing what "ripe" means for the specific crop you're harvesting is very important.

Do your best to pick *all* ripe fruits regularly—and by *ripe*, we mean immature in terms of seed production but at the stage we like to eat them. This stimulates the growth of more fruits. The parent plant grows fruit to try to reproduce. When we pick off those fruits, we let the plant know their job isn't done; they should keep flowering and fruiting as long as they can. So whenever you notice overgrown fruits, like blimpy cucumbers or overly fibrous green beans, go ahead and pick those, too. You may not want to eat them, but leaving them on the plant will reduce production of their tender, delicious brethren. You can download a video demonstration of harvesting green beans, along with identifying Mexican bean beetles, on our website (see the link on page 364).

Be aware that the softer fruits mentioned above (tomatoes, peppers, and melons) can become *overmature* if left unharvested for too long; basically, they rot. Even drier fruits and seeds are susceptible to getting munched by critters or molding if left out too long, so be sure to harvest these in a timely manner, too.

ROOTS (AND TUBERS)

Roots and tubers differ from one another botanically, but both grow underground, and both offer us tasty subterranean vegetables, including:

- Beets
- Carrots
- Parsnips
- Potatoes
- Radishes
- Sweet potatoes
- Turnips

It's hard to know by sight when to harvest these vegetables, because you can't always see them swelling with ripeness. The best way to gauge harvesttime is to keep track of the estimated days to maturity. When you reach that number, you can begin digging around to unbury these treasures.

How to Harvest Roots and Tubers

Whether harvesting a root or a tuber, the process is quite similar.

- **In loose soil,** most root crops can be easily pulled out by hand.

- **In denser soil,** do some gentle loosening with a digging fork or hori hori. Start near where the original stem of the plant was, but not right up on it, so you don't skewer your crop.

- **For longer roots** like carrots and parsnips that are growing in dense soil, gently wiggle them after loosening the soil so that their stems don't snap off with the pressure of pulling them up.

- **For deep tubers** like potatoes and sweet potatoes, a digging fork is ideal, but a shovel can work. Dig all around the plant and down at least 12 to 16 inches to loosen the soil without spearing or slicing the tubers themselves.

No tool other than strong hands is needed to harvest garlic from fairly loose soil. Deeper underground crops, like parsnips, almost always require a digging fork.

Fruits to Harvest at a Mature Stage

Some fruits are best harvested when they're mature, when the seeds within are developed and capable of growing new plants. These are:

- Dry beans
- Dry corn and other grains
- Melons
- Peppers
- Tomatoes
- Winter squash

Wait until these fruits have fully matured before harvesting them. That said, toward the end of the season, or in a low-fertility situation, it's a good idea to pick off some *immature* fruits and flowers. When there are fewer fruits on a single plant, each of the remaining fruits has a chance to grow larger. We do this late in the growing season when we know there aren't enough warm days ahead to ripen what's still on the plant. By removing immature fruit, we free the plant to put all its energy into ripening the more mature fruits. This practice, called thinning even though it is different from thinning young plants, is also employed in the pursuit of prizewinning county fair pumpkins!

One or two winter squash plants can yield a lot of food! These beauties get sweeter after several weeks in storage and can keep all winter.

Post-Harvest

To maintain optimal crispness, break the greens off harvested roots right away, whether or not you plan to eat the greens. Even though, for example, carrots look lovely with their greens on, those leaves will continue transpiring (passing water from the root into the air) after the carrot (or daikon or turnip . . .) has been dug up, causing the root itself to go flaccid much more quickly.

Store roots in plastic bags in the fridge, or bury them in straw or sawdust in a cool, dark, humid place like a root cellar. With or without their leaves, roots become floppy and dehydrated if left in direct sunlight. If you can't get them inside right away while you harvest, throw a towel, a piece of cardboard, or, really, anything over them to shield them from the sun.

Breaking off the leaves of carrots and other root crops helps them stay crisp and juicy.

SEEDS

Seeds harvested for eating—namely corn, beans, and grain seeds, plus many spices—are best to pick when fully mature and dry. To test for maturity, pick a small amount and try to break the seed with your fingernail. If you can break it, it's not ready to pick. If it's hard, dry, and cannot be dented or broken with a fingernail, it's ready!

Harvesting Seeds in Humid Places

In wetter areas you'll need to be strategic about harvesting mature seeds so that they don't turn moldy. Once seeds have fully matured, they take a while to dry down. During this drying period they are particularly susceptible to fungal invasions, especially if they're in contact with the ground or in a dense mass with other seeds or vegetation.

Beans. In rainy places like our southern Appalachian Mountains, we occasionally harvest seeds, especially beans, *before* they're completely dry but *after* the pod has started to shrivel a bit. Once picked, we spread out the pods in a protected, sunny, drafty area so they can finish drying without getting rained on, and so that plenty of airflow can minimize mold.

How to CLEAN BEANS QUICKLY

In the case of a big harvest and a desire to get your dry beans cleaned quickly, follow these steps.

1. **SPREAD OUT THE BEANS.** Make sure your beans are bone-dry, then spread them out in their hulls on one half of a tarp or sheet.

2. **FOLD OVER THE TARP.** Fold the other half of the tarp or sheet over them like a taco.

3. **WALK** or, better yet, dance atop them. This breaks the pods and releases the seeds.

4. **WINNOW THE BEANS** from their pods. Do this on a breezy day, or in front of a box fan on a medium setting, by pouring the whole mess from one bucket to another. The force of the air will blow the lighter hulls away, while the weight of the beans will drop them into the bottom bucket.

5. **REPEAT THIS WINNOWING PROCESS** several times, then pick out any remaining bits of hull.

Corn. Sometimes we'll do the same thing with corn that we do with beans if we notice ears getting moldy. Corn, for the most part, is less susceptible to fungus while it dries, because each ear is held up, above the ground, by the sturdy stalk, and the husk also helps shed water. That said, it's key that you check on maturing and drying seeds regularly and take immediate action if you notice the presence of fungi.

Harvesting Dry Beans

To harvest dry beans, either tug or snip each pod off the vine or bush and collect them in a bag, basket, or bucket. We like to harvest into buckets or bins, then either transfer the beans to paper bags or spread them out as described at left to finish the drying process.

Whether the pods (or shells or hulls) are dry when you pick them or take some time to get crispy, the beans are much easier to remove from the pod when completely dry. At this stage, you can shell them out right away or store them in a dry, breezy place for future relaxed shelling.

Harvesting Corn

Harvest mature ears of corn by hand using a quick "pull and twist" action, or you can employ pruners or a knife to remove ears from the stalks. Chloe likes to wear a backpack on her front to easily collect ears of corn instead of hauling a bucket or basket along as she goes. There are specialized harvest sacks made to go frontwise, which are ideal if you plan to harvest a lot of corn or happen to have an orchard to harvest from also.

SHELLING WHILE SHARING

Chloe's elderly mother-in-love enjoys helping on the farm and isn't as mobile as she once was. Each fall she delights in hand-shelling beans with the kids on the front porch while joking and sharing stories. This isn't a super-time-efficient method, but it yields many other valuable gifts beyond the cleaned beans themselves.

Field corn (grain corn) is harvested ear by ear, just like sweet corn. Wearing a backpack front-ways keeps your hands free as you go down the row.

To remove corn seeds from the cobs, be sure they're bone-dry, then either rub two ears together over a bucket or employ any one of many corn-shelling tools available. For large amounts Chloe uses a cast-iron corn sheller that's available from Lehman's.

Harvesting Grain Seeds Other Than Corn

Grains like wheat, rye, and oats require a more elaborate harvesting and hulling process, which we won't get into here. The same general principles of dryness apply. To learn more about growing and harvesting grains, check out *The Organic Grain Grower: Small-Scale, Holistic Grain Production for the Home and Market Producer* by Jack Lazor.

Note: Seed saving is a vast and beautiful topic well worth diving into, yet it is beyond the scope of this work. We direct you to our favorite book dedicated to the subject, *Seed to Seed: Seed Saving and Growing Techniques for Vegetable Gardeners* by Suzanne Ashworth. We also love the work of Rowen White and Sierra Seeds, including her wonderfully comprehensive video course on seed saving.

Post-harvest Processing

What you do with vegetables after their harvest determines how long they will stay fresh and tasty. Some crops barely make it out of the garden before they enter our mouths (like sugar snap peas, in our experience), while others can be stored for months (potatoes, sweet potatoes, field corn, dry beans, garlic, onions, beets, winter squash). If you plan to keep harvested veggies for any length of time, aim to clean, sort, and store them as quickly as possible.

CLEANING

Many veggies that you harvest will have some dirt (or slug poop or grass clippings . . .) on them. These substances can harbor fungi and bacteria that contribute to rotting, so it's critical to clean them off before you store the harvest (except in the case of potatoes). That said, a small amount of dry dirt won't cause harm; in fact, ingesting a little soil can be very beneficial for our own microbiome, especially if that soil is alive with microbes.

Potatoes. They will be plenty dirty when you dig them out, and they should stay that way! Knock off any large dirt clods, but store the spuds unwashed to protect their skin and ensure a longer shelf life.

Leaf crops. Lettuce, kale, chard, spinach, and more shouldn't need to be washed before storing if they've been grown with mulch covering the soil. Without mulch, soil can splash on them during rain or watering. These tender greens keep better if kept dry, so mulching to protect the soil also has the added benefit of simplifying harvesting and post-harvest processing.

All other veggies. Either gently brush or rub dirt off, or wash them. If you wash, be sure to dry everything thoroughly before stowing them in a fridge, root cellar, or other cool-storage situation; excess moisture, like dirt and slug poop, can lead to rotting.

Natalie hangs braided garlic outside under cover to cure, then brings it in before freezing temperatures to protect the harvest and to beautify her space.

SORTING

Since you probably won't be selling what you grow, there's no need to sort out funny or ugly-shaped veggies. But you do want to sort through what you've picked to remove anything showing signs of rot or decay. As the saying goes, "One bad apple can spoil the bunch"; this is also true for vegetables. Unless something is truly rotten, you don't have to toss it out; just put it aside so it's not in direct contact with healthy specimens, and use it first, cutting out the bad spot.

STORING

Most people are used to storing vegetables in the refrigerator, and much of what you harvest will be happy there. However, some crops prefer more moist conditions, while others can handle being out on the counter for a while. Knowing your storage options is important, since you may bring in more veggies than will fit in your fridge, especially during peak harvest season.

Leaf crops. These are first in line for refrigerator real estate. Tender leaves, like lettuce and basil, have the shortest shelf life of the garden bounty, and they're the most sensitive to heat. We tend to harvest leaves as needed, so we don't have to store them at all. If you do harvest a bunch to keep in the fridge, be sure they are dry before you stow them, and put them in a roomy plastic bag with some air space.

Root, tuber, and bulb crops. Turnips, carrots, beets, rutabagas, parsnips, radishes, potatoes, sweet potatoes, onions, and garlic are happier out of the fridge in cool, humid, and dark conditions like a root cellar or pantry. Even so, you can still put most of these root crops in the refrigerator, *except* garlic, onions, potatoes, and sweet potatoes. If you've run out of space in the fridge, root crops should be the first to get evicted to other quarters.

Following are some ideas for storage as well as details about the conditions various vegetables (and fruits) like to hang out in.

Garlic and onions are less sensitive to light and heat than the rest. Natalie loves to braid them and hang them in her cabin, where they're handy to grab as needed and also beautify her space.

Beets, carrots, parsnips, potatoes, radishes, rutabagas, and turnips like to be in cool (45 to 55°F/7 to 13°C), humid, dark, well-ventilated root cellar conditions. These can be approximated in garages, basements, or even pantries. Over time, roots dry out, so burying them in sawdust or shredded straw or even newspaper helps keep them plump because the insulator layer catches and stores moisture rather than letting it evaporate into the air. In the presence of light, potatoes produce chlorophyll (the chemical that makes plants green) and solanine (a toxic glycoalkaloid). The green chlorophyll itself is harmless but warns you of the presence of solanine, which can cause nausea, vomiting, and neurological effects if consumed in high quantities. Be sure to keep potatoes in the dark to keep solanine levels low.

Sweet potatoes like the same conditions as humans do, perhaps a little cooler (50 to 60°F/10 to 16°C ideally, but they can handle as warm as 70°F/21°C). They're happy to hang out in a box, bin, or paper bag on the floor of your kitchen or pantry.

Fruit crops (most of them) don't mind sitting outside the fridge for a couple of days, depending on how ripe they are, or in root cellar–like conditions for a few days to a week. This can be handy if you plan to do any canning or preserving and your fridge is already full. (Sometimes we harvest tomatoes over the course of a week or so in preparation for a big batch of sauce that we'll can. We store each day's harvest in a single layer in a box or bin in a cool space until we're ready to cook them up.) Zucchini, peppers, cucumbers, sweet corn, eggplant, and cabbage (the latter not a fruit, but not exactly a tender leaf) can also do just fine out on the counter or in a cool space for a few days to a week. Winter squash and pumpkins can keep for the whole winter in room-temperature conditions.

Beans, broccoli, cauliflower, okra, and peas seem to be a little less adaptable and store better in the fridge.

Older plants, like humans, tend to have weaker immune systems; they're more susceptible to pathogens. This old cuke gave a lot, and now it is bacterial wilt's time to thrive.

The Lifespans of Annual Vegetables

Annual vegetables (and biennials that we grow as annuals, such as carrots, onions, radishes, and others) traverse the glorious and tragic arc of birth, life, reproduction, and death in a much shorter time than we humans do. Keep this in mind as you tend your garden. Many of our students have shown or described plants to us that are no longer producing well after weeks of harvesting, asking us, "What's going wrong?" The answer, sometimes, is nothing at all. The plant is merely finishing its life and getting ready to die.

We find it fascinating, and a bit disturbing, how deeply the fear of death and worship of youthfulness are embedded into mainstream culture in the United States; these unnatural values even find their way into the garden. Fortunately the garden is also a great place to confront and transform them. As we discuss at length in Chapter 4, death and decay are essential for fertility, growth, and fruiting to occur. Each step in the cycle of life and death is just that: a unique and valuable part of a larger process that cannot exist in a fragmented form.

As we've entered middle age and confronted our own senescence (or the aging process), we've found peace witnessing the beauty of our gardens as they pulse with the natural rhythms of time and change. Here we invite you to do the same: Celebrate growth and harvest while witnessing with reverence the natural endings that make space for new beginnings.

Sharing the Harvest

Canning tomato sauce, and most other food processing projects, are way more fun with friends. And bonus: This kind of party has great party favors.

There is one particularly beautiful trait we get to connect with in our gardens that human society could use more of: generosity. Even if your garden is a 5-gallon bucket on your porch with one big tomato plant growing in it, you'll probably harvest more than you need and have an opportunity to share. The bigger the garden, the more surplus you may have (but remember, don't overdo it and stress yourself out!).

A couple of days before this writing, a friend came over to drop his kids off to play with Chloe's son as she was harvesting 'French Breakfast' radishes, thinking that she had sowed a bit more than she needed. The friend chatted with Chloe as she worked and mentioned that he loved radishes, so she handed him a bunch. This simple act felt so positive and uplifting, as if the tendrils of the generative Earth were reaching out and weaving these two people together with each other, with the radishes, and with the land itself.

For various social, cultural, and economic reasons, it's not easy to make a living as a small-scale commercial vegetable grower (something that needs to change on a policy level!). It is easy, however, to grow enough food to share with friends, your local food pantry, the neighbors who recently experienced a big joy or hardship, or anyone else you think might benefit from a reminder that generosity, abundance, and cooperation are basic qualities of the living world we sprout from.

Ideas for Sharing the Harvest
- Dry flowers that you grow and host a wreath-making party in fall or winter.
- Have a canning party and send everyone home with a jar of homemade salsa or pickles.
- Host a garden-to-table dinner, either for fun or as a fundraiser for something you believe in and want to support.
- Invite a local school or homeschool group to come harvest and taste garden-fresh veggies. (Chloe worked at an educational mini-farm for a time and was amazed at how many things kids were excited to taste, especially if they had picked them themselves.)
- Make a giant pot of soup with veggies from the garden and put it into jars to share with friends or others.
- Place a "free box" in your garden or yard, if it's on a street with foot traffic, and share the bounty there with passersby.
- Plant pollinator crops to feed our insect allies.
- Save and share seeds from your garden.
- Share what you've learned about gardening and invite others to share, too, possibly over garden-grown herbal tea and snacks.
- Talk to your local food pantry and plan to dedicate one row or bed (or more) to growing fresh food for them, making sure you choose something universal that members of your community will like and know how to prepare.

Whatever way you most naturally and joyfully share what your garden shares with you is wonderful and will evolve over time. May your heart and your baskets be full of gratitude as you put your hands in the soil and remember your place in this wild, beautiful, unpredictable, generous, diverse, and delicious family of things.

Vegetable Profiles
& Growing Guides

Arugula 278

Basil 280

Beans 282

Beets and Chard 284

Broccoli and Cauliflower 286

Cabbage 288

Carrots 290

Cilantro 292

Corn 294

Cucumbers 296

Dill 298

Eggplant 300

Garlic 302

Kale and Collards 304

Lettuce 306

Muskmelons 308

Okra 310

Onions 312

Parsnips 314

Peas 316

Peppers and Chiles 318

Potatoes 320

Radishes 322

Spinach 324

Sweet Potatoes 326

Tomatoes 328

Turnips and Rutabagas 330

Watermelons 332

Winter Squash and Pumpkins 334

Zucchini and Summer Squash 337

We're excited to get into the juicy, specific details about growing each vegetable! Here you'll find quick profiles and basic growing guides for 30 common garden veggies; these profiles will help you get started and provide useful reference information as you get to know these tasty, beautiful friends. There's nuance to tending each one, which we share more deeply in our online gardening classes (see the link on page 364). There you can also find step-by-step video lessons on each part of the process for each vegetable (plus some tasty berries that aren't included in this book).

See the appendix for more on these 30 vegetables, including the number of seeds required to plant a 10-foot row of the vegetable, the number of transplants needed per 10 feet of the vegetable, possible yield of the vegetable, and more!

Guide to the Vegetable Profiles

COMMON NAME(S): The name or names you know this vegetable by.

BOTANICAL NAME: Common names can sometimes be confusing, but the botanical (Latin) name of each vegetable is unique. For example: "Beans" could mean common beans, fava beans, chickpeas, soybeans, or any other bean species. Each of these, however, has a unique botanical name to identify it.

PLANT FAMILY: Many pests and diseases like to consume many or all of the plants that share a botanical (plant) family. If you know which veggies are in the same family, you can move them around the garden, ensuring you don't plant them in the same place year after year, to help deter pests.

PLACE OF ORIGIN: Each of our beloved foods has an origin (or origins) and has traveled a long road and gathered stories along the way. We find it fascinating, humbling, and connective to know where our crops come from.

SUN REQUIREMENT: Most garden veggies like a lot of sun; some can handle a little shade; some won't produce well unless they get full sun. Knowing this will help you plan your garden.

NITROGEN NEEDS: Some vegetables need a lot of nitrogen in order to grow well (heavy feeders), others need a moderate amount (medium feeders), while some don't need nearly as much (light feeders). Then there are the incredible nitrogen fixers who partner with soil bacteria to feed themselves. These categories are guides for planning what goes where and which crops follow which. For example: It's best to follow heavy feeders with lighter feeders, nitrogen fixers, cover crops, or a fallow period. Remember, nitrogen is the macronutrient plants need the most in order to grow big and vigorous, but it's by no means the only nutrient they need; see Chapters 4 and 5 for more about nourishing your plants.

GERMINATION TEMPERATURE RANGE (SOIL TEMP): We share the ideal germination temperature, plus the minimum for each crop. This tells you when to direct sow and whether or not to use a heat mat if you're growing your own transplants. Most plants take much longer to germinate at the minimum, rather than ideal, germination temperature.

FROST AND COLD HARDINESS (if the vegetable is frost hardy at all, and to what temperature): Some veggies can handle a little cold, some can handle a lot, and still others will die if temperatures drop below freezing at all. While hardiness temperatures are a good gauge, the level of cold a plant can survive depends on other conditions, too, such as how healthy, strong, and well fed the plant is, and how quickly the temperature drops. Most plants have an easier time handling cold that comes on gradually and can get damaged by a quick drop, even if the low temperature doesn't go below their official tolerance level. Additionally, when it gets and *stays* cold, plants tend to manage that more easily than temperature fluctuations from above to below freezing from day to day or week to week (like we have here in southern Appalachia in winter).

HEAT TOLERANCE: Some veggies can handle very hot weather, while others thrive in cooler temperatures or temperatures that aren't as extreme. Heat that comes on slowly and gradually is easier for plants to manage than huge, quick jumps in temperature.

DIRECT SOW, TRANSPLANT, OR FLEXIBLE: Some crops do best directly sown, others thrive as transplants, and some can go either way.

SEED-SOWING DEPTH: How deeply to plant seeds into the earth or seed-starting medium.

DIRECT-SOWING DISTANCE BETWEEN SEEDS: The distance to plant seeds apart from each other in a row, bed, or container.

FINAL SPACING (thin to or transplant to): The amount of space to leave between plants once they've been thinned (if directly sown) or as you're transplanting.

TRELLIS OR INFRASTRUCTURE NEEDS: Most plants are great at supporting themselves, but certain plants need to climb on a trellis or structure— of the latter plants, some need a stout structure, and others need only a bit of support.

WHEN TO PLANT (in relationship to first and/or last frost): This information will help you time your planting.

SUCCESSION PLANTING: Can this crop be planted more than once per year, and if so, how long between plantings?

ONE-TIME HARVEST VS. HARVEST WINDOW: Crops like cabbage ripen only one head and are done; fruiting crops like green beans, tomatoes, and peppers produce many harvests throughout a window, which means you'll need to keep harvesting to keep them producing. Having an idea of how much time and effort harvesting will require can help you plan.

DAYS TO MATURITY (range): The amount of time it takes for a given crop to be ready to harvest, either from the time the seed is sown or the time the plant is transplanted. Different varieties of the same crops vary in days to maturity, so be sure to check how long the specific variety you are growing will take to mature.

HARVEST SEASON: What time of year will this vegetable find its way to your plate?

COMMON PESTS AND DISEASES: The most common pests and diseases that also like this vegetable.

OUR FAVORITE VARIETY/VARIETIES: We've tried dozens of varieties and have found ones we like; most of them are just generally good garden varieties for organic production, though some are also specifically suited for our region.

REGIONAL VARIATIONS

No gardening book applies perfectly to every region, climate, and ecosystem. Still, the foundations of gardening are basically the same, no matter where you grow.

Where we live and grow now, winters get as cold as –5°F (–20°C), though sometimes lower, and summers get only as hot as 90°F (32°C). If you live somewhere with more extreme conditions than we face, you can adapt our guidance and information, gather a little extra place-based support ("off book," so to speak), and still find a lot of useful goodness in these pages.

If you live in a very different region than we do, here are some things to consider: The planting times in the following vegetable profiles are based on estimated first and last frost dates, so you may need to figure out planting times on your own if you're in the tropics or in an extremely cold place. Also, extreme conditions, like deserts and cold regions, generally require specific techniques for keeping vegetables healthy and happy.

Contrary to popular belief, gardening in the tropics isn't just a matter of throwing some seeds out and watching them grow. Tropical regions host a range of competitive plants (enthusiastic weeds) as well as voracious pests and diseases. Plus, some of the veggies you might be used to eating require a stretch of cooler temperatures to grow well.

The very best way to get specific, place-based gardening advice, no matter where you live, is to talk with other growers in your area. Connect with the Cooperative Extension Service in your county, visit your area farmers' market and chat with local growers, contact local seed companies, knock on doors of houses that have inspiring gardens, get involved with a community garden or gardening club, volunteer at a small-scale organic farm, and read gardening books that are specific to your region or climate.

'Ice-Bred' arugula

Arugula

COMMON NAMES: Arugula, rocket, roquette, rucula

BOTANICAL NAME: *Eruca vesicaria*

PLANT FAMILY: Brassicaceae or cruciferous family

PLACE OF ORIGIN: Mediterranean

Arugula has become a popular salad green in the past several years. You'll find it in plastic clamshells of prewashed mixes, as well as on the tables of fancy restaurants as a "baby green." There are several types of arugula, and they are all native to the Mediterranean region. In ancient Rome and Egypt, consumption of arugula leaves and seeds was said to have an aphrodisiac effect! We haven't found this to be particularly true, but maybe we haven't been eating enough arugula. We like to direct sow our arugula, although it can also be transplanted. Fall- and winter-grown arugula will be sweeter and less spicy than greens that mature in warmer weather. While arugula is quite cold hardy, we tend to cover it with a floating row cover when the weather dips well below freezing.

Sun requirement: Prefers full sun but can tolerate partial shade

Nitrogen needs: Lighter feeder

Trellis or infrastructure needs: No

Temperature

Germination temperature range (soil temp):
Ideal: 40–60°F (4–15°C); min: 40°F (4°C)

Frost and cold hardiness: Yes, to 25°F (–4°C)

Heat tolerance: 80°F (27°C) but prefers cooler than 70°F (21°C)

Spacing

Direct sow, transplant, or flexible: Flexible

Seed-sowing depth: ¼"

Direct-sowing distance between seeds: ¼"–1"

Final spacing (thin to or transplant to): 1½"–4"

Timing

See the Timing Tables on page 339 for specific tips on growing arugula in your region.

When to plant: As early as ground can be worked and up to 1 month before the first frost, skipping the heat of summer

'Astro' arugula

Succession planting: Yes, if you want a lot of arugula, at intervals of 10–30 days until it gets hot, then again after it cools down, up until 1 month before the first frost

One-time harvest vs. harvest window:
Cut-and-come-again

Days to maturity (range): 40–60

Harvest season: Early spring into early summer; fall into winter

Common Pests and Diseases

Flea beetles (most common here), cabbageworms, downy mildew, aphids, bacterial leaf spot

Our Favorite Varieties

We like **'Ice-Bred'** for overwintering because it's tough, delicious, and turns purple when the weather gets cold; and **'Astro'** for spring because it deals with heat well.

STEPS TO GROWING

Planting

- Either direct sow arugula or sow seeds in a 72-cell tray or equivalent to transplant.

- If you're direct sowing, thin to 1½"–4" between plants, depending on how large you'd like them to get (more space for larger plants). Direct-sown arugula will need to be weeded once or twice before it's big enough to mulch.

- If you're going to transplant, do this when plants have gotten a few inches tall, and transplant to the spacing mentioned above.

Growing

- Lay mulch down beside rows of arugula (spacing may not allow for mulch between individual plants) once they've grown to be 4"–6" tall.

Harvesting

- Harvest arugula leaves either by pinching individual leaves on the outside of the basal rosette or giving the whole plant a haircut about 4" above the ground with a pair of scissors.

- If you notice flea beetle damage, you can still harvest and enjoy the less-pristine-looking leaves.

- Repeat harvesting several times after leaves have regrown.

- Eventually arugula will bolt (produce flower stalks); fortunately the flowers are edible and delicious, and they make salads look very pretty.

Basil

COMMON NAMES: Basil; dozens of varieties, including sweet basil, lemon basil, and Thai basil

BOTANICAL NAMES: *Ocimum basilicum* (Genovese basil, Thai basil, others), *O. sanctum* (tulsi or holy basil), *O. minimum* (Greek basil), and others

PLANT FAMILY: Lamiaceae or mint family

PLACE OF ORIGIN: India; Greek basil likely originated in Chile

Basil has been cultivated for at least five thousand years, and its relatives grow in many tropical regions. Domestication likely happened first in India, China, or North Africa. Currently you can find a plethora of basil species and varieties. This herb tastes fabulous with fresh mozzarella and tomato, but basil and its relatives have varying medicinal and other uses as well.

Sun requirement: Prefers full sun but can tolerate partial shade

Nitrogen needs: Medium feeder

Trellis or infrastructure needs: No

Temperature

Germination temperature range (soil temp): Ideal: 80–85°F (27–29°C); min: 70°F (21°C)

Frost and cold hardiness: No

Heat tolerance: 90°F (32°C)

Spacing

Direct sow, transplant, or flexible: Transplant in most places, can direct sow in very warm climates

Seed-sowing depth: ¼"

Direct-sowing distance between seeds: Not usually direct sown, ½"–1¼" if you do

Final spacing (thin to or transplant to): 14"–18" (can be direct sown and harvested as a cut-and-come-again crop with much closer spacing; only in very warm places)

Timing

See the Timing Tables on page 339 for specific tips on growing basil in your region.

When to plant (in relation to first and/or last frost): Sow seeds indoors 45–80 days before the last frost, transplant out after the danger of frost has completely passed. In very warm places, direct sow whenever soil temperature is consistently 70°F (21°C) or warmer.

Succession planting: If you really love basil, you can sow a few rounds 1 month apart. However, this crop has a very long harvest window if properly pinched, so we only do one round.

One-time harvest vs. harvest window: Long harvest window

Thai basil

Days to maturity (range): 85–120 from seeding

Harvest season: Summer

Common Pests

Downy mildew, aphids, slugs, whiteflies, fusarium wilt, bacterial leaf spot, gray mold

Our Favorite Varieties

The **Prospera DMR (downy mildew–resistant) series** from Johnny's Selected Seeds is our go-to here in the warm, wet mountains. We also like to grow **Thai basil** for its unique flavor; it's worth exploring the range of flavors offered by different varieties to find what you enjoy.

STEPS TO GROWING

Planting

- Start basil seeds indoors, ideally on a heat mat and in a heated space, 2½–1½ months before the predicted last frost; they grow slowly! The seeds are very small, so start them in a 72-cell tray or equivalent; transplant into bigger pots if roots have filled out cells before it is warm enough to plant out.

- If you live in a warm or hot climate, basil can also be direct seeded.

- If you started seeds indoors, transplant basil into the garden after the danger of frost has truly passed, and ideally during a spell of warm weather. It can be inter-cropped easily with tomatoes, peppers, or eggplant, or you can plant it on its own.

- Mulch around the plants immediately after transplanting or after they're 4"–6" tall if direct sown.

Growing

- As your basil plants grow, begin pinching off the growing tips from the top of the plant and from side shoots, as well as some side leaves; this will stimulate bushier growth (more branches and leaves) and invite airflow. Visit the basil about once a week to do this early harvest/pruning. Eat whatever you pinch!

Harvesting

- Continue pinching off top and side leaves as desired, up to every few days throughout the season. If you're excited to make a big batch of pesto, you can harvest more heavily and then wait 1–2 weeks to harvest again so the plants have time to recover.

- Before too long, basil plants start flowering. You can pinch off the flowers to extend the harvest for a few weeks, but the power of reproduction will win in the end, and the time of fresh basil will come to a close.

'Provider' bush green beans

Beans

COMMON NAMES: Beans, green beans, string beans, snap beans; dry beans for eating cooked, including pintos and black beans

BOTANICAL NAME: *Phaseolus vulgaris*

PLANT FAMILY: Fabaceae or pea family

PLACE OF ORIGIN: Mesoamerica and the Andes

Different species and types of beans are cooked and enjoyed all over the world both in the green/snap stage and the dry, mature stage. We focus here on the common bean (*Phaseolus vulgaris*) for the sake of brevity and have excluded cowpeas, favas, chickpeas, lentils, and many other fabulous bean species. Cultivating them is similar but different than the common bean, and we encourage you to try as many as you're interested in. All of these plants, also known as legumes or pulses, are rockstars in the garden and the kitchen. Through a cooperative relationship with soil bacteria, they can actually increase plant-available nitrogen in the ground where they grow (this is also called nitrogen "fixing"; you can learn more on page 112). As a result, the pods and seeds that we eat are higher in protein than most other plant-based foods, since nitrogen is a key ingredient in all protein molecules.

Sun requirement: Full sun is ideal, though some varieties (namely "cornfield beans") can tolerate moderate shade.

Nitrogen needs: Nitrogen fixer

Trellis or infrastructure needs: Pole beans can grow very tall and need a trellis with vertical pieces to twine around (conical pole trellis, cattle panel, string coming down from a central tall pole); bush beans support themselves.

Temperature

Germination temperature range (soil temp): Ideal: 75–85°F (24–29°C); min: 60°F (15°C)

Frost and cold hardiness: No

Heat tolerance: 90°F (32°C)

Spacing

Direct sow, transplant, or flexible: Direct sow

Seed-sowing depth: 1"

Direct-sowing distance between seeds: 1"–3"

Final spacing: 3"–10" (closer for pole snap beans, farther for bush dry beans)

Timing

See the Timing Tables on page 339 for specific tips on growing beans in your region.

When to plant: After danger of last frost through 12 weeks before the first frost

Succession Planting: Yes (for snap/green beans only), at intervals of 10–20 days, up until 12 weeks before the first frost

One-time harvest vs. harvest window: Harvest window for green/snap beans; one-time harvest for dry beans

Days to maturity (range): 50–70 for green pole or bush beans; 85–120 for dry pole or bush beans

Harvest season: Summer into fall

Common Pests and Diseases

Mexican bean beetles, bean leaf beetles, vegetable leaf miners, aphids, anthracnose, bacterial brown spot, pythium root rot

Our Favorite Varieties

Bush snap/green beans: **'Provider'** is adaptable, productive, tasty, high-yielding, and germinates well in cooler soil. **'Royal Burgundy'** is resilient and productive and beautifully purple-podded (though they turn green when you cook them).

Pole snap/green beans: **'Kew Blue'** is an English variety of purple-podded pole beans that germinates well in cooler soils and is quite productive and beautiful. **'Northeaster'** is a flat-podded green cultivar that's early to produce and late to get tough.

Bush dry beans: **'Golden Gaucho'** is delicious, resilient, and high yielding given its compact growth habit. It is also quick to dry down.

Pole dry beans: **'King of the Early'** is a mottled red baking bean that is easy to grow, as well as reliable and tasty.

STEPS TO GROWING

Planting

- Direct sow seeds once the soil has warmed and the danger of frost has passed (some varieties, like a couple we mentioned above, will germinate well in cooler soils, while others really need a lot of warmth to get going). Sow with 1"–3" between each seed.

- **OPTIONAL:** Soak beans for about 6 hours or overnight before sowing. Coat them in a *P. vulgaris*–specific legume inoculant before planting to improve growth and yield.

- Keep the seedbed moist but not soggy until seedlings emerge. Beans can rot in the ground if the soil is too wet.

Growing

- Weed around seedlings with a stirrup hoe or wire weeder. Beans may need a couple of weeding sessions before the plants are tall enough to mulch around.

- Mulch thickly around bases of bean plants once they're 6"–8" tall. If you're growing pole (climbing) beans, erect a trellis by the time the beans are 6"–8" tall and start reaching for something to grab with their spiraling vines. If they need early encouragement to wind around the trellis, gently wrap them in the direction they are naturally spiraling.

TIP: *If Mexican bean beetles are a major pest, try mulching with reflective or white plastic mulch to deter them; they don't like bright light.*

Harvesting

- Begin harvesting green/snap beans right when they begin to plump but before the seeds get hard; different varieties of beans are more or less slender, but ripe beans all have a rounded look (even flatter-podded Romano types will have a kind of plumpness); pick and taste some to figure out what size/shape is perfectly ripe for the variety you're growing. They are tastiest if you harvest them before they get too mature, but harvest too early and they won't be as sweet. You can download a video about harvesting snap/green beans, along with identifying Mexican bean beetles on our website (see the link on page 364).

- If you're growing beans to dry for shelling and cooking later, leave all the fruits on the plant to fully mature. If you live in a dry climate, wait for the pods to turn tan or brown and crispy before harvesting. If you live in a moist climate, harvest when the pods begin to wrinkle and the beans inside can't be penetrated with a fingernail. Then bring them to a dry, breezy place like a barn or garage to finish the drying process.

- For green/snap beans, continue harvesting every 2–4 days and pick all mature and any overmature beans; this encourages more flowering and keeps the plants producing more beans.

- Beans are done producing when they don't make any more flowers or, in our region, when the Mexican bean beetles kill the plants.

Beets and Chard

COMMON NAMES: Beet, beetroot; chard, Swiss chard, silverbeet

BOTANICAL NAME: *Beta vulgaris*

PLANT FAMILY: Chenopodiaceae or goosefoot family

PLACE OF ORIGIN: Mediterranean

Believe it or not, beets and chard are the same species! While the two crops are obviously distinct, they are grown similarly. Beets have been bred for big, calorie-rich roots, chard for vigorous and tasty greens. Neither is very susceptible to insect pests in our area, which makes both of them fairly easy to grow. Beets can be stored in a root cellar or similar situation, while chard is heat tolerant and fairly cold tolerant, too, making them generous providers of food nearly all year round.

Sun requirement: Prefers full sun but can tolerate partial shade

Nitrogen needs: Heavy feeders; chard will tolerate lower fertility than beets

Trellis or infrastructure needs: No

Temperature

Germination temperature range (soil temp): Ideal: 65–85°F (18–29°C); min: 40°F (4°C)

Frost and cold hardiness: Yes, to 20°F (–7°C)

Heat tolerance: 80°F (27°C)

Spacing

Direct sow, transplant, or flexible: Flexible; we usually direct sow beets and transplant chard

Seed-sowing depth: ½"

Direct-sowing distance between seeds: ½"–1"

Final spacing (thin to or transplant to): 3"–6" for beets; 6"–10" for chard

Timing

See the Timing Tables on page 339 for specific tips on growing beets and chard in your region.

When to plant: Sow seeds indoors 30–60 days before the last frost (chard); direct sow outdoors when soil has warmed some, and again from 4–8 weeks before first frost date.

Succession planting: We like to grow big beets and, typically, plant just one round in early spring; if you like smaller beets, plant successions up to every 14–30 days. Chard is pretty hardy and has a long harvest window, so we sow it once in early spring and sometimes again in midsummer for fall and winter harvests; if you love it, plant a couple of successions throughout spring and summer up to 4–6 weeks apart.

One-time harvest vs. harvest window: Beets: One-time harvest (but you can pluck beet greens several times before harvesting the root); chard: long harvest window

Days to maturity (range): 50–70

Harvest season: Late spring/early summer and fall/winter

Common pests and diseases

Aphids, black cutworms, scab, cercospora leaf spot

Our Favorite Varieties

‘Lutz Green Leaf’ is the beet for us! It’s big and delicious, with luxuriously large green leaves that are as tasty or tastier than any chard. As far as chard goes, we enjoy ‘**Perpetual Spinach**’, which is sweeter and more tender than most other varieties—and not spinach at all! ‘**Golden Sunset**’ is another tasty and beautiful chard with yellow midribs.

STEPS TO GROWING

TIP: *We recommend direct sowing all root crops in order to avoid disturbing the roots when transplanting. Recently Chloe worked alongside a dear friend and skilled commercial grower, Anna Littman, who transplants beets for weed management purposes with good results. We still direct sow our beets; however, transplanting is an option for those who struggle with weed competition or possibly slugs. If you're going to transplant beets, follow the steps below for chard, using beet spacing.*

Planting

- Directly sow beet or chard seeds at a spacing of ½"–1" between seeds.

- If you're transplanting, sow seeds in a 72-cell tray or equivalent on a heat mat if it's easy; heat mats are not necessary if your seed-starting climate is moderately warm.

- Keep the seedbed watered but not soggy, and cover it with floating row cover if temperatures drop below freezing.

- If you are transplanting, transplant beets or chard into the garden as early as 2 weeks before last frost date, as long as the weather is moderately warm (i.e., may dip down to freezing again but is mostly past frostiness).

Growing

- Weed between rows every week or so as seedlings grow.

- **OPTIONAL:** Thin seedlings to a spacing of 1"–2" between plants once they are 1"–2" tall; this is not the final thinning. Here you will just pinch out seedlings that are right on top of each other.

    TIP: *Beet and chard "seeds" are actually seed clusters, so don't be surprised when multiple babies sprout on top of each other. Thinning is absolutely necessary.*

- When seedlings are 4"–6" tall, do a final thinning to 3"–6" between beet plants. Go with more space if soil fertility is low or if you are planting 'Lutz' beets—they are huge! Or space more tightly if you're growing small beets.

- Final spacing for chard is 6"–10" depending on variety and fertility.

- Mulch thickly between and around plants.

Harvesting

- Harvest chard as needed once it has grown to about 8" tall by snapping or snipping leaves from the outside; you can also lightly harvest beet leaves at this stage and beyond.

- Harvest beets once the roots have gotten plump and round and their "shoulders" have popped above the soil surface.

'Golden Sunset' chard

'Piracicaba' sprouting broccoli

'Snow Crown' cauliflower

Broccoli and Cauliflower

COMMON NAMES AND TYPES: Broccoli and cauliflower

BOTANICAL NAME: *Brassica oleracea* (the same species as cabbage, kale, kohlrabi, and Brussels sprouts)

PLANT FAMILY: Brassicaceae or cruciferous family

PLACE OF ORIGIN: Eastern Mediterranean (broccoli), Turkey (cauliflower)

Broccoli and cauliflower are the youngest relatives of cabbage, kale, and collards. This group is often referred to as the "brassicas" because they are all in the plant family Brassicaceae and have the same genus and species: *Brassica oleracea*. While broccoli and cauliflower are botanically similar to the other brassicas, they are part of the subspecies *botrytis*, meaning "cluster," like a bunch of grapes. You can understand why: The parts that we harvest to eat (actually immature flowers) are indeed clustered and somewhat grapelike in appearance.

Sun requirement: Full sun

Nitrogen needs: Heavy feeder

Trellis or infrastructure needs: No

Temperature

Germination temperature range (soil temp):
Ideal: 55–75°F (13–24°C); min: 40°F (4°C)

Frost hardiness: Yes, to 28°F (–2°C)

Heat tolerance: 75°F (24°C)

Spacing

Direct sow, transplant, or flexible: Transplant

Seed-sowing depth: ½"

Direct-sowing distance between seeds: N/A

Final spacing (thin to or transplant to): 18"–24"

Timing

See the Timing Tables on page 339 for specific tips on growing broccoli and cauliflower in your region.

When to plant: Sow indoors on heat mats up to 2½ months before the last frost; for fall and winter harvest, sow seeds in midsummer and transplant out about 2 months before the first frost.

Succession planting: We plant broccoli and cauliflower once in early spring and again in midsummer for fall and winter harvests. Successions can be planted a couple of times in early spring in climates with cooler summers.

One-time harvest vs. harvest window: One-time harvest for heading varieties; harvest window for sprouting/shooting types

Days to maturity (range): 50–65 (broccoli), 55–80 (cauliflower) from transplanting

Harvest season: Spring/summer and fall

Common Pests and Diseases

Cabbage loopers, flea beetles, aphids, snails and slugs, cabbageworms, cabbage maggots, mites, harlequin bugs, clubroot, black rot, soft rot

Our Favorite Varieties

'Piracicaba' is an open-pollinated, nonheading variety of broccoli from the University of Piracicaba in Brazil. It's delicious and gives tons of good-size mini-heads/shoots instead of one big dense head, plus it's fairly heat and cold tolerant. Natalie enjoys big broccoli heads and likes hybrids 'Monty' and 'Gypsy'.

'Song TJS-65' is a hybrid variety of cauliflower that makes lots of little shoots instead of one big head and is moderately tolerant of heat (cauliflower is generally sensitive to heat).

'Snow Crown' is an adaptable and vigorous heading type of cauliflower.

STEPS TO GROWING

Planting

- In late winter or early spring, sow seeds in a 72-cell tray or equivalent in a protected space that ideally remains warm but not hot (55–73°F/13–23°C).

- If you use a heat mat, put it on a lower setting than other crops; high germination temperatures for broccoli and cauliflower can cause legginess. Ideal germination temperature is 65°F (18°C).

- While your seedlings grow in trays, fertilize them once or twice; these plants are heavy feeders and do well with a nutritious diet.

- Transplant out once they have four to six true leaves and once the weather has warmed up somewhat and won't go below about 30°F (–1°C).

- **FOR FALL/WINTER HARVEST:** Start broccoli and cauliflower outside in midsummer, in a 72-cell tray or equivalent to transplant without any extra heat.

- Transplant out once they have four to six true leaves.

Growing

- While early spring–planted broccoli and cauliflower can handle light frosts, these are the most cold- and heat-sensitive members of the Brassicaceae family, so it can be nice to cover them for the first 3–4 weeks of their lives if it's chilly (though be careful not to cook them under cover if days are warm and sunny).

- **FOR FALL/WINTER HARVEST:** You can cover them with a thin row cover to prevent pests, but take care not to cook the plants under cover on sunny days and not to trap pests inside the row cover.

TIP: *When to spray Bacillus thuringiensis (Bt) for cabbageworms? Most-spring planted crops are in the clear during their early lives, when it's too cold for cabbageworms and cabbage loopers. As plants mature and the weather warms, spraying Bt can be essential for survival. Conversely, midsummer-planted crops are at risk right away, but the pest populations decline as they mature and the weather cools. If you do spray, be sure to do so every 7–14 days during high-pest periods.*

- Fertilize a few times as they grow, unless you've planted them in very rich soil.

- Mulch once plants are 6"–8" tall. In springtime, try waiting to mulch around the plants until they are bigger (8"–10"), as slugs love young brassicas and find refuge in mulch.

Harvesting

- Harvest sprouts or heads once they are big and plump but before they loosen and begin opening. Non-heading varieties will be a little looser at harvest than heads.

- Continue fertilizing, harvesting, and spraying as needed until the end of the harvest. Sprouting varieties will have a long harvest window, while heading varieties are mostly done after you cut off their heads. Some heading varieties do produce side shoots once they're headless.

- **FOR FALL/WINTER HARVEST:** When growing in fall, cover plants with a thick row cover before temperatures go far below freezing; this is essential to keep plants going, and it's worth it if they're still producing.

Cabbage

COMMON NAME: Cabbage

BOTANICAL NAME: *Brassica oleracea* (same species as broccoli, cauliflower, kale, kohlrabi, and Brussels sprouts)

PLANT FAMILY: Brassicaceae or cruciferous family

PLACE OF ORIGIN: Western Europe

Cabbage is the emblematic member of the brassicas—a group of vegetables that includes kale, collards, broccoli, and cauliflower. These plants are all in the family Brassicaceae, and they all have the same genus and species: *Brassica oleracea*. The Latin name Brassicaceae is derived from the Celtic word for cabbage: *bresic*. It was likely hybridized from wild kalelike relatives in the Celtic lands of western Europe. The word *cabbage* itself is an anglicized version of a French word meaning "head," referring to the tight, round ball of leaves that make up this amazing and versatile vegetable.

'Savoy Perfection' cabbage

Sun requirement: Full sun

Nitrogen needs: Heavy feeder

Trellis or infrastructure needs: No

Temperature

Germination temperature range (soil temp): Ideal: 55–75°F (13–24°C); min: 40°F (4°C)

Frost and cold hardiness: Yes, to 24°F (–4°C)

Heat tolerance: 80°F (27°C)

Spacing

Direct sow, transplant, or flexible: Transplant

Seed-sowing depth: ¼"

Direct-sowing distance between seeds: N/A

Final spacing (thin to or transplant to): 18"–24"

Timing

See the Timing Tables on page 339 for specific tips on growing cabbage in your region.

When to plant: Sow indoors 2–3 months before last frost (plan to cover seedlings once they're transplanted if deep freezes happen); for fall and winter harvest, sow seeds in midsummer, about 2½ months before the first frost.

Succession planting: We plant cabbage once in early spring and again in midsummer for fall and winter harvests; in places with cooler summers, a couple of spring successions are possible but not necessary, as this vegetable stores really well.

One-time harvest vs. harvest window: One-time harvest

Days to maturity (range): 60–105 from transplanting

Harvest season: Summer and fall/winter

Common Pests and Diseases

Cabbageworms, cabbage loopers, flea beetles, snails and slugs, root maggots, cutworms, alternaria and bacterial leaf spot, bacterial soft rot, blackleg, black and bottom rot, clubroot, downy mildew, mosaic virus, phytophthora root rot

Our Favorite Varieties

'Early Jersey Wakefield' is a tasty and fast-maturing open-pollinated green cabbage that has been a garden favorite since it was introduced in 1840! This variety is adaptable, compact, and very tasty. For fall-planted Asian Cabbage, we like **'Minuet'** because it's reliable and tasty. **'Savoy Perfection'** is a beautiful, fast-maturing, and reliable savoy (curly-leaved) cabbage.

STEPS TO GROWING

Planting

- In late winter, sow seeds in a 72-cell tray or equivalent in a protected space that remains warm but not hot. If using a heat mat, put it on a lower setting than other crops, as high germination temperatures for young cabbage plants can cause legginess. The ideal germination temperature is 65°F (18°C), so room temperature without bottom heat is usually great.

- **FOR FALL / WINTER HARVEST:** Start cabbage outside in midsummer, without any extra heat. You may need to begin spraying with Bt (*Bacillus thuringiensis*) right away, upon germination, and every 7–14 days, to combat cabbage loopers and worms that are most active in warm weather.

- As seedlings grow, fertilize them once or twice; these plants are heavy feeders and do well with a nutritious diet.

- Transplant out once they have four to six true leaves and, for spring plantings, once the weather is not getting much colder than 28°F (2°C).

Growing

- While spring-planted cabbage can handle some frost, it can be nice to cover them with row cover for the first few weeks of their lives if it's chilly (take care not to cook them under cover if days are warm and sunny).
- After the frosts have ended and the weather has warmed up to perfect pest weather, spray with Bt every 7–14 days to combat cabbage loopers and cabbageworms.

- **FOR FALL / WINTER HARVEST:** Covering with an extra-thin row cover prevents pests, but be careful not to cook the plants under cover on sunny days and not to trap pests inside the row cover. Continuing to spray with Bt is another approach to dealing with pests.

- Fertilize a few times as they grow, unless you've planted them in very rich soil.

- Mulch once plants are 6″–8″ tall. In springtime, try waiting to mulch around the plants until they are bigger (8″–10″), as slugs love to devour young brassicas and find refuge in mulch.

Harvesting

- Harvest cabbage heads once they have formed and are firm and dense when you squeeze them.

- Summer-harvested cabbage should be harvested as soon as the heads firm up, even if you can't eat it all at once (this is a great time to make sauerkraut!).

- **FALL / WINTER-HARVESTED CABBAGE** can be left in the field (covered with thick row cover if/when temperatures go below freezing) and harvested as needed until temperatures drop into the mid-20s °F (around −4°C), or they can be harvested and stored in a root cellar for eating throughout winter. This is also a great time to make sauerkraut, or kimchi if you are growing Asian cabbage.

'Early Jersey Wakefield' cabbage

'Red Cored Chantenay' carrots

Carrots

COMMON NAME: Carrots

BOTANICAL NAME: *Daucus carota*

PLANT FAMILY: Apiaceae or carrot family

PLACE OF ORIGIN: Afghanistan

The wild relatives of carrots have been cultivated and selected for their leaves and seeds since 3000 BCE. (Wild carrots are still used for food and medicine today.) Records show that by 1 CE, people were eating the large, sweet roots of the carrot plant. These roots were originally creamy white in color, but as gardeners selected for larger, sweeter plants, new hues emerged. At first, yellow and purple joined the carrot rainbow, then came the orange that we're so familiar with today. Some folks claim that orange carrots were bred in Holland to honor the country's flag, though others contest this.

Sun requirement: Prefers full sun but can tolerate partial shade

Nitrogen needs: Lighter feeder

Trellis or infrastructure needs: No

Temperature

Germination temperature range (soil temp): Ideal: 75–85°F (24–29°C); min: 40°F (4°C)

Frost and cold hardiness: Yes, to 20°F (–6°C)

Heat tolerance: 80°F (27°C) but prefers cooler temperatures when carrots are forming

Spacing

Direct sow, transplant, or flexible: Direct sow

Seed-sowing depth: ½"

Direct-sowing distance between seeds: ¼"–½"

Final spacing (thin to or transplant to): 1"–1½"

Timing

See the Timing Tables on page 339 for specific tips on growing carrots in your region.

When to plant: Carrots can be sown as early as the ground can be worked, usually 1 month before the last frost, but after the danger of hard freeze has past—if possible, use a soil thermometer to determine if the soil is warm enough for germination. Seeds must be kept very moist for germination, which can take up to 3 weeks at cooler temperatures (this makes spring carrots more difficult to grow than summer-planted fall carrots, because it takes them so long to germinate). Fall carrots are best planted 2–3 months before the last frost. Our main carrot sowing happens in summer for fall and winter harvests, and if we cover the roots with mulch, we often even get harvests into early spring.

Succession planting: Successions of spring carrots can be sown every 20–30 days from about 1 month before last frost through midspring (be sure to use heat-tolerant varieties for spring crops). Fall carrots should be sown just once, 2–3 months before the first frost—the perfect time to sow longer-maturing "storage" varieties.

One-time harvest vs. harvest window: Harvest window for a bed of carrots; single harvest per individual plant

Days to maturity (range): 55–85

Harvest season: Spring, summer, fall, winter

Common Pests and Diseases

Aphids, armyworms, carrot rust flies, cutworms, darkling beetles, garden symphylans, grasshoppers, nematodes, whiteflies, wireworms, black root rot, scab, cercospora leaf spot

Our Favorite Varieties

For spring carrots we go with **'Mokum'**, **'Romance'**, or **'Yaya'** hybrids that can handle maturing in warm weather and have wonderful flavor. These are more "snacking" type carrots, as opposed to the varieties we plant in the summer for fall harvest.

For fall carrots our all-time favorite is a French heirloom called **'Red Cored Chantenay'**. It's sweet, delicious, and very carroty, and each carrot can grow quite large without becoming tough or pithy. We don't know where the name derived from, because they are relatively orange throughout. This carrot's shape is great for us, too: Fat, conical, and not very long, it grows well in our dense and at times rocky soil.

STEPS TO GROWING

Planting

- Direct sow carrot seeds into a smooth and hopefully weed-free (or low-weed) bed or row, with about ¼" between seeds. This amounts to gently sprinkling the tiny seeds, since it's hard to get exact spacing because they're so small.

- **FOR FALL / WINTER HARVEST:** Prepare the bed ahead of time; water it or let it get rained on so that weed seeds germinate, then cultivate with a stirrup hoe to kill those weeds and plant carrots afterward. This doesn't work as well in spring because many seeds won't sprout until temperatures warm. Since carrots take a little while to germinate and their tops are small and slow growing, weed competition can be challenging, so presprouting the weeds in this manner may be worth the extra time and effort.

Growing

- Keep the bed well watered until carrot seedlings emerge. This often means watering more than once a day if it's sunny. Carrot seeds are sensitive to moisture and won't sprout if they dry out even a little.

- As seedlings emerge, weed between rows as needed.

- Once seedlings are about 2" tall, thin carrots either to their final spacing or slightly tighter. If you choose to thin lightly at this stage, you'll have to thin again, but this may make sense because there are various creatures who may like to eat your carrots, and you'll want to have enough left.

- Thin carrots to their final spacing by the time the plants are 4" tall. If you skimp on the thinning, you'll likely have an abundance of thin, small roots not worth harvesting and washing. *Note:* "Baby carrots" that you get at the store are not small carrots but full-size ones that have been cut and ground into uniform sizes.

- Continue weeding, and mulch carrots once they've grown 6"–8" tall.

Harvesting

- Harvest carrots once their rounded shoulders poke up above the soil surface; check the specific days to maturity for the variety you're growing to ensure you're not harvesting too early or late.

- If your soil is loose, simply grab the carrot tops and wiggle-pull them out. If this doesn't work and the tops break off, use a fork or hori hori to loosen the soil around the carrots, then pull them out.

  TIP: *Be careful not to fork or stab the carrots themselves; you want to merely loosen the soil.*

- Harvest all your spring carrots within a window of 1–2 weeks once they are ready.

- **FOR FALL / WINTER HARVEST:** Harvesting can be spaced out over time.

'Leisure' cilantro

Cilantro

COMMON NAMES: Cilantro, coriander, Chinese parsley, Mexican parsley

BOTANICAL NAME: *Coriandrum sativum*

PLANT FAMILY: Apiaceae or carrot family

PLACE OF ORIGIN: Mediterranean

Cilantro is the name for the leafy part of the plant that makes coriander seeds. (In the British Commonwealth, people call the leafy part coriander, too.) It originated around present-day Greece and has been grown for millennia all over Eurasia and North Africa. Coriander seeds and fresh cilantro greens are used in many Eurasian cuisines as well as culinary dishes all over the world. While it isn't a staple veggie crop, it sure is a fabulous and flavorful food plant. We eat a lot of it in salsas, chutneys, and sauces. Yum!

Sun requirement: Prefers full sun but can tolerate partial shade; growing summer cilantro in partial shade can slow bolting

Nitrogen needs: Lighter feeder

Trellis or infrastructure needs: No

Temperature
Germination temperature range (soil temp):
Ideal: 65-70°F (18-21°C); min: 55°F (13°C)

Frost and cold hardiness: Yes, to 15°F (−9°C)

Heat tolerance: 80°F (27°C) but prefers cooler temperatures

Spacing
Direct sow, transplant, or flexible: Flexible; direct sowing is ideal

Seed-sowing depth: ¼"–½"

Direct-sowing distance between seeds: ½"

Final spacing (thin to or transplant to): 2"–6"

Timing
See the Timing Tables on page 339 for specific tips on growing cilantro in your region.

When to plant: First sowing can be about 1 month before the last frost, if the soil has warmed enough for germination to occur well; last sowing can happen about 1 month before the first frost. Cilantro that's gone to seed will often reseed itself in the same patch, in which case you'll notice little cilantro plants coming up in early spring.

Succession planting: If you love cilantro as much as we do, you can sow it every 3 weeks through spring, summer, and into early fall.

One-time harvest vs. harvest window: Harvest window, which can be long if the weather is cool but not freezing. We like to use the cut-and-come-again method, cutting the leaves with scissors about 3″ from the ground.

Days to maturity (range): 45–60

Harvest season: Spring, summer, fall, winter

Common Pests and Diseases

Not many issues; sometimes slugs and snails, aphids, ants, sooty mold, powdery mildew, bacterial leaf spot

Our Favorite Variety

'Leisure' is so named because it's slower to bolt in warm weather than many other varieties, which we like.

STEPS TO GROWING

Planting

- Direct sow cilantro in rows that can be between the rows of other, widely spaced plants, 8″–12″ from each other, with ½″–1″ between seeds. Alternatively, broadcast seed if you feel confident that you're planting in an area with few weed seeds.

- If transplanting, sow seeds in 72-cell trays or equivalent.

- Keep seeds watered well as they germinate and begin to emerge. Cilantro can take up to 3 weeks to germinate at cooler temperatures, and older or lower-quality seed

sometimes does not germinate at all, so don't be discouraged if nothing comes up. Get some new seed and try again.

Growing

- As seedlings emerge, weed between rows as needed.

- When seedlings are 4″–6″ tall, thin to a final spacing of 2″–6″ between plants.

- Mulch around plants if they're growing in a shape that lends itself to being mulched (not if you broadcasted the seeds).

Harvesting

- Harvest a few leaves as soon as they're big enough to warrant harvesting; ideally, pluck a leaf or two from each plant to leave enough foliage to continue photosynthesizing.

- As plants get bigger, use a knife or scissors to give the whole area a haircut to harvest larger amounts, or continue plucking a few leaves from each plant.

- Eventually cilantro plants will bolt (start flowering). You can pinch off the flowers to extend the harvest for a few weeks, but the drive to reproduce always wins, and the time of fresh cilantro comes to a close.

- Fortunately the flowers and seeds of cilantro are also edible and delicious. If you let the seeds mature fully, you'll have coriander seeds, which you can harvest and use as a spice, keep to sow your next round of the crop, or allow to reseed themselves to establish a self-sowing cilantro patch.

- **FOR FALL / WINTER HARVEST:** Fall-planted cilantro can last the longest, as the plant is hardy to 15°F (−9°C). Because of this, if you live in a mild climate, you may be able to harvest cilantro that was planted 1–2 months before the first frost well into winter if it's protected with row cover.

PLANT CILANTRO EARLY AND OFTEN

We like to plant cilantro every few weeks throughout spring to ensure the presence of fresh cilantro for as long as possible into summer. Cilantro has a tendency to bolt (start flowering) as the weather heats up, at which time it becomes less palatable. Gather the seeds that it yields, however, to supply your pantry with coriander.

'Cateto Sulino' flint corn

Corn

COMMON NAMES AND TYPES: Corn, dry corn, field corn, grain corn, popcorn, corn on the cob, maize

BOTANICAL NAME: *Zea mays*

PLANT FAMILY: Poaceae or grass family

PLACE OF ORIGIN: Mesoamerica/Mexico

Corn is a traditional food crop from Mesoamerica that spread first throughout the Western Hemisphere and then around the globe. It's said to have originated in southern Mexico and/or northern Guatemala and is actually the descendant of at least two (some say three) wild relatives. This is somewhat unusual in the world of vegetables; many of them have a distinct, single wild relative. As a result of this unique origin, corn seeds must be removed from the ear to be planted; corn cannot replant itself without the help of humans or some other meddling creature.

Corn has been a staple crop in many cultures throughout the Western Hemisphere for millennia. As a result, a plethora of mythology and folklore surrounds this plant. It's also included in rituals and ceremonies by most corn-growing peoples.

Sun requirement: Full sun

Nitrogen needs: Heavy feeder (though some varieties of grain corn require far less nitrogen than commercial sweet corns)

Trellis or infrastructure needs: Not generally, but sometimes a grid of twine about 3′ in the air helps corn withstand high winds

Temperature
Germination temperature range (soil temp): Ideal: 65–95°F (18–35°C); min: 60°F (15°C)

Frost and cold hardiness: No

Heat tolerance: 95°F (35°C)

Spacing
Direct sow, transplant, or flexible: Direct sow (can be transplanted if absolutely necessary)

Seed-sowing depth: 1″

Seed-sowing distance between seeds: 4″–6″

Final spacing (thin to or transplant to): 6″–12″

Timing
See the Timing Tables on page 339 for specific tips on growing corn in your region.

When to plant: After danger of frost has completely passed

Succession planting: Sweet corn can be sown several times per season, up until about 3 months before the first frost, depending on the days to maturity for the particular variety you plant. In most places, grain corn can be planted only once per year.

One-time harvest vs. harvest window: One-time harvest, though the same variety can be harvested in the "green" (a.k.a. sweet corn) state and the dry state

Days to maturity (range): 60–115

Harvest season: Summer into fall

Common Pests and Diseases
Corn borers, corn earworms, armyworms, black cutworms, corn flea beetles, corn leaf aphids, sap beetles, wireworms, bears, deer, raccoons, rusts, smut (a fungal disease that leads to kernels looking like black mushrooms, known as huitlacoche in Mexico; this fungus is edible and tasty), anthracnose, aspergillus ear rot

Our Favorite Varieties

'Floriani', **'Cateto Sulino'**, and **'Painted Mountain'** are known to be somewhat adaptable as well as tasty. Here in southern Appalachia, Chloe has had great success with **'Cherokee White Eagle'** (a blue-and-white dent corn, great for tortilla and masa for tamales, and for hominy) and **'Cherokee White Flour'** (amazing for cornmeal and baking, also good for hominy; honored as the original Cherokee corn).

'Double Red' is a magenta-colored sweet corn that will stain your fingers and lips when you eat it, which is fun for adults and children alike. It's also tasty and productive.

Different kinds of corn lend themselves to different kinds of cooking and do well in different conditions. For example, corn varieties from desert areas of the Southwest don't like it in Appalachia and vice versa. Try exploring corn varieties well adapted to your region.

STEPS TO GROWING

Planting

- Sow corn seeds in rich soil that has warmed up with 4"–6" between seeds and 30"–38" between rows.

- Plant in a block at least 4' × 4', or as large as is reasonable given your space, rather than in long rows; corn is wind pollinated and won't make kernels unless it's well pollinated, which happens much better in a block.

  TIP: *Protect emerging seedlings from crows, turkeys, and other birds by tying shiny bird-scare tape or plastic shopping bags to stakes throughout the cornfield.*

Growing

- Water at least once every 3-4 days until seedlings emerge.

- Cultivate weeds between corn rows once or twice.

- Thin seedlings as needed to a final spacing of 6"–12" between plants, depending on variety and fertility.

- Mulch around corn plants once they are 6"–8" tall.

- Fertilize once or twice, unless you know the soil where your corn is planted is very rich.

- As ears form and grow plump, inspect the tops of them for corn earworms and remove and squish, or treat with *Bacillus thuringiensis* (Bt) if you notice a lot of them.

Harvesting

- Harvest sweet corn at the "milk stage," when ears are plump with kernels. Squeeze ears to get a sense of ripeness and remove husks to really take a look. Pinch a couple of kernels with your fingernail. If the liquid that seeps out is clear and watery, it is not ready. If it is slightly opaque and milky, it is perfect and ready to harvest as sweet corn. If it is totally white and chalky and you can't see through it, you waited too long.

  TIP: *"Milk stage" is when raccoons and other critters love to come feast on corn. Pay attention and set traps immediately if you notice these marauders.*

- Many varieties of sweet corn are only at ideal ripeness for a few days, so pay attention and harvest quickly when they're ready.

- Harvest grain corn when the kernels have moved through the milk stage into the dry stage. Test for maturity by pressing a fingernail into a kernel. It shouldn't break or even dent the surface.

- If grain corn is almost ready but cold, wet weather is predicted, you can harvest it a little bit early (when you can slightly dent the kernels with a fingernail but not break through) and dry it down in a greenhouse or other warm, dry space.

'Cherokee White Eagle' dent corn

Cucumbers

COMMON NAMES AND TYPES: Cucumbers, cukes; slicing and pickling cucumbers

BOTANICAL NAME: *Cucumis sativus*

PLANT FAMILY: Cucurbitaceae or cucurbit family

PLACE OF ORIGIN: India

Cucumbers hail from what's now known as India, where they have been cultivated for at least three thousand years. The original cukes were probably very bitter and always eaten cooked. The sweet, mild slicing varieties you're more familiar with have been developed only in the past couple of hundred years or so.

Ancient Roman Emperor Tiberius Caesar (42 BCE–37 CE) loved to eat a cucumber relative for its purported enhancement of male virility (guess why?). He ordered horticulturists to provide them for him daily, year-round. In order to achieve this, the plants were grown in proto-greenhouses with glazing made of a mica-like stone over one thousand years before sheet glass was invented.

Sun requirement: Full sun

Nitrogen needs: Heavy feeder

Trellis or infrastructure needs: Yes, strong trellis with horizontal and vertical members. Cucumbers usually don't climb higher than 3'–4'.

Temperature

Germination temperature range (soil temp): Ideal: 75–95°F (24–35°C); min: 65°F (18°C)

Frost and cold hardiness: No

Heat tolerance: 90°F (32°C)

Spacing

Direct sow, transplant, or flexible: Flexible

Seed-sowing depth: ½"

Direct-sowing distance between seeds: Groups of 3 or 4 seeds close to each other, separating groups by 18"–24"

Final spacing (thin to or transplant to): 1 or 2 best plants per group, with 18"–24" between groups.

Timing

See the Timing Tables on page 339 for specific tips on growing cucumbers in your region.

When to plant: Sow indoors as early as 3 weeks before the last frost, or sow outdoors once the danger of frost has completely passed and the soil has warmed. Final sowing should be 2–2½ months before first frost, depending on days to maturity of your specific variety.

Succession planting: Cucumbers can be sown up to every 20–30 days from spring through summer until 2–2½ months before the first frost. We usually just do two or three rounds of them, as each planting has a long harvest window. If you live in a cold climate, you will likely do only one sowing. Pests get worse on each subsequent sowing.

One-time harvest vs. harvest window: Long harvest window for most varieties

Days to maturity (range): 55–65

Harvest season: Summer into early fall in some places, with succession planting

Common Pests and Diseases

Striped and spotted cucumber beetles, squash bugs, aphids, spider mites, leaf miners, pickleworms, black cutworms, squash vine borers, powdery mildew, bacterial wilt, blossom-end rot (actually a calcium deficiency)

THE MANY USES OF CUCUMBERS

Most cucumbers eaten in the United States are pickled. If your goal is to make pickles, be sure to choose a pickling variety or a dual-purpose type. Along with culinary applications, cucumbers have been used to treat scorpion bites, eye irritation, and fevers. These curative practices make a lot of sense, and they affirm the saying "cool as a cucumber." That's because the inside of this vegetable can be up to 20 degrees cooler than the outside air temperature!

- After the danger of frost has passed and the weather has warmed enough that evenings are no longer cool (for us, this happens in early June), and when your transplants are filling out gallon-size pots, transplant eggplants into the garden with 18"–24" between them.

  TIP: *If flea beetle pressure is very heavy, coat the plants with kaolin clay before transplanting. Do so by mixing about 3 cups of clay per gallon of water in a vessel large enough to dunk the whole plants, or by applying the slurry with a sprayer after transplanting, being sure to coat both sides of every leaf.*

Growing

- Some folks prefer to cover eggplants to ward off flea beetles. If you do this, use a very thin row cover, and make sure it's sufficiently weighed down or covered with soil along the edges so that no bugs can sneak in. Remove the row cover once the plants start flowering so that pollinators can do their important work to turn those flowers into fruits.

- Mulch between plants once flea beetle pressure has diminished. Keep them watered, but don't overdo it. Once or twice a week is plenty.

- Stake each plant, put cages around them, or use the weave style of trellis (see page 234) to support eggplants as they become heavy with fruit.

Harvesting

- Harvest eggplants when they are plump and dark in color (depending on the variety; some varieties are lighter when ripe). When ripe and ready to pick, the eggplant will soften slightly. The seeds inside should not be dark, hard, and fully mature. If they are, you waited too long.

- Continue harvesting every few days, removing all mature and overmature fruits, even if they're damaged, because this tells the plants to continue to make flowers and more fruits.

- The eggplant season ends either when the plants run out of steam producing fruits or when frost kills them.

'Diamond' eggplant

Rocambole garlic (harvesting scapes)

Garlic

COMMON NAME: Garlic

BOTANICAL NAME: *Allium sativum*

PLANT FAMILY: Amaryllidaceae or allium family

PLACE OF ORIGIN: Middle Asia

Garlic has been cultivated and used for at least 3,500 years as a culinary and medicinal herb. It can be minced and added near the end of a sauté, dropped into sauces near the beginning of a slow cook, blended into raw sauces (like pestos), or added as whole heads to beans and stews. Garlic is an unusual crop in that it's planted in late fall (in most places), and it grows through the winter. There are lots of different kinds of garlic with varying degrees of pungency and variously sized cloves. This plant is a food, a medicine, and also an ingredient in homemade pesticides (see page 259). It can be used medicinally to kill harmful microbes and fungi, both internally and externally.

Sun requirement: Full sun

Nitrogen needs: Heavy feeder

Trellis or infrastructure needs: No

Temperature

Germination temperature range (soil temp): Ideal: 40–60°F (4–15°C); min: 35°F (2°C)

Frost and cold hardiness: Yes, to –30°F (–34°C)

Heat tolerance: 85°F (29°C)

Spacing

Direct sow, transplant, or flexible: Plant cloves (not true seeds)

Seed-sowing depth: (cloves) 2½"–4"

Direct-sowing distance between seeds: (cloves) 6"–8"

Final spacing (thin to or transplant to): 6"–8"

Timing

See the Timing Tables on page 339 for specific tips on growing garlic in your region.

When to plant: Plant garlic cloves (with their papery peel still on, pointy side up) directly in the ground 2 weeks–2 months *after* the first frost. If you live in a place where the ground freezes solid for much of the winter, make sure to get your garlic in the ground and well mulched before this freeze. Yes, you plant it in fall!

Succession planting: No

One-time harvest vs. harvest window: One-time harvest of bulbs, with a garlic scape harvest about 1 month prior

Days to maturity (range): 220–270

Harvest season: Summer

Common Pests and Diseases
Wireworms, allium leaf miners, white rot, fusarium wilt

Our Favorite Varieties
We like the **rocambole** and **porcelain** types because they produce big, flavorful, potent bulbs with big cloves that are easy to peel. You can't buy these varieties at the grocery store—while the big cloves make for a more pleasurable kitchen experience, they're less profitable to grow because farmers need to use a larger percentage of each plant as "seed" for the following year's crop, and they're more perishable and easily damaged in transport. Yet another reason to grow your own!

STEPS TO GROWING

Planting
- Plant garlic cloves, still inside their papery covering, with the pointy side up, in a furrow or trench that's 2½"–4" deep (deeper for bigger cloves, shallower for smaller cloves). Place cloves 6"–8" apart from one another.

  TIP: *If time and attention allow, and if your soil is not oversaturated with phosphorus (do a soil test to determine this), you can sprinkle a bit of bonemeal into the trench to add phosphorus and encourage root growth and bulb formation.*

- Cover cloves with about 1" of soil, then cover the whole area with a thick layer of mulch right away to tuck them in for successful root development with lack of weed pressure over the winter months.

Growing
- When the ground begins to warm and the garlic starts to grow in springtime, fertilize one to three times to nourish that growth with an all-purpose fertilizer or a phosphorus-heavy fertilizer in combination with urine or other nitrogenous fertilizer.

- Keep garlic watered as it grows.

- Add more mulch if some of the previous layers have broken down over the months. Also weed if you see weeds.

Porcelain garlic

- In early summer each garlic plant sends out a long, curly, cylindrical flower stalk called a scape. Since we want the plants to put energy into producing big, juicy bulbs and not flowers and seeds, it's important to snip or pull these scapes. They are delicious when cooked or pickled!

Harvesting
- Harvest garlic bulbs when about one-third of the leaves have turned brown or yellow. Harvesting too soon or too late reduces the shelf life of your stored garlic, so pay attention during this time.

- Pull up individual plants, using a fork or hori hori to loosen the soil, if necessary.

- Lay harvested garlic in a single layer in a protected, breezy, shady spot to dry for 3–5 days, then clean it by rubbing with a cloth, remove the roots with pruners, and braid or bundle the leaves together. You can download a video about harvesting and braiding garlic on our website (see the link on page 364).

- Hang from a string integrated into the braid or around the leaves in a dry and shady location (a covered porch or barn works well for at least 2 weeks—make sure to bring it in before outdoor temperatures drop below freezing).

- When you take them down from their covered outdoor location, hang the braids inside or cut the bulbs off of the leaves and store them in a root cellar or other cool, dry place.

'Madeley' kale

Kale and Collards

COMMON NAMES: Kale, cole; collards, collard greens

BOTANICAL NAME: *Brassica oleracea* (same species as broccoli, cauliflower, cabbage, kohlrabi, and Brussels sprouts)

PLANT FAMILY: Brassicaceae or cruciferous family

PLACE OF ORIGIN: Eastern Mediterranean and Asia Minor

Kale and collards are the oldest cultivated relatives of cabbage, broccoli, and cauliflower. These leafy brassicas have been grown by humans for at least two thousand years. Their origins are in Eurasia, either in the area now called the Middle East or closer to the Mediterranean. They've also been widely cultivated in the western part of the continent, including on the British Isles, where they form an important part of traditional diets. In fact, the words *kale* and *collards* are Scottish and Anglo-Saxon words (respectively) meaning "cabbagelike." Many old European cultures didn't distinguish between kale and collards, which are, in fact, botanically siblings.

Sun requirement: Prefers full sun but can tolerate partial shade

Nitrogen needs: Medium feeder

Trellis or infrastructure needs: No

Temperature

Germination temperature range (soil temp):
Ideal: 55–85°F (13–29°C); min: 40°F (4°C)

Frost and cold hardiness: Yes, to 20°F (–6°C)

Heat tolerance: 80°F (27°C)

Spacing

Direct sow, transplant, or flexible: Flexible (we usually transplant kale and collards in the spring and sometimes direct sow in the summer for fall and winter harvests)

Seed-sowing depth: ¼"

Direct-sowing distance between seeds: 2"–4"

Final spacing (thin to or transplant to): 12"–18"

Timing

See the Timing Tables on page 339 for specific tips on growing kale and collards in your region.

When to plant: Sow indoors 2 months before the last frost (if you plan to cover seedlings once they're transplanted); for fall and winter harvest, sow seeds in midsummer, about 2½ months before the first frost.

Succession planting: We plant kale and collards once in early spring and again in midsummer for fall and winter harvests. Some gardeners do two successions during each of these times, but our spring plantings usually keep giving until the conditions for kale and collards are less ideal in summer.

One-time harvest vs. harvest window: Long harvest window

Days to maturity (range): 55–75 from sowing

Harvest season: Spring into summer; fall into winter

Common Pests and Diseases

Cabbageworms, cabbage loopers, flea beetles, snails and slugs, root maggots, cutworms, harlequin bugs, alternaria and bacterial leaf spot, bacterial soft rot, blackleg, downy mildew, phytophthora root rot

Our Favorite Varieties

'**Madeley**' kale has won our hearts, palates, and good sense. It's a resilient and tasty variety that makes huge leaves in abundance that look more like collards but stay quite tender. '**Alabama Blue**' collards are a beautiful rainbow of blues, blue-greens, and purples in cooler weather; they stay sweet in some heat and have leaves that remain tender as they get big, even in hot weather.

STEPS TO GROWING

Planting

- Sow seeds in a 72-cell tray or equivalent in a protected space that remains warm but not hot. Keep your heat mat, if using, on a lower setting than you do for other crops; high germination temperatures for young kale and collards can cause legginess. The ideal germination temperature is 65°F (18°C).

- **FOR FALL / WINTER HARVEST:** Start kale and collards outside in midsummer, in pots or directly in the ground, without any extra heat.

Growing

- Fertilize growing seedlings up to a few times with a nitrogen-rich, water-soluble fertilizer, like urine or liquid fish; these plants do well with a nutritious diet.

- **FOR FALL / WINTER HARVEST:** If you see white or grayish-brown butterflies frequenting your garden or notice holes in your baby plants, we recommend you spray with *Bacillus thuringiensis* (Bt) soon after germination to combat cabbage loopers and cabbageworms, which are most active in warm weather. Thin floating row cover is another option for deterring these pests; just make sure you seal the edges and don't trap the pests inside.

- Transplant out once the plants have four to six true leaves and, for spring plantings, once the weather has warmed up some. Space them 12"–18" apart. Water deeply upon transplanting and throughout growing.

- While transplanted seedlings can handle some frost, consider covering them for the first 3–4 weeks of their lives if it's chilly (and if days are warm and sunny, take care not to cook them under cover).

- Fertilize a few times as they grow, unless you've planted them in extra-rich soil.

- Mulch once plants are 6"–8" tall. In springtime wait to mulch around the plants until they are 8"–10" tall, as slugs love to devour young brassicas and find refuge in mulch.

- Spray with Bt as needed, every 7–14 days to combat cabbage loopers and cabbageworms.

Harvesting

- Begin harvesting leaves once there are 8 to 10 true leaves that are of a size worth using in the kitchen.

- Harvest the leaves that are the closest to the base of the plant. If you harvest near the top of the plant, you may inhibit growth.

- Make sure to cut or pluck leaves at the base of the leaf stem; don't leave partial leaf stems attached to the plant.

- Harvest one or two leaves per plant at first, then increase your harvest as the plants get bigger. Kale and collards can handle a heavy harvest, so don't hold back; just be sure to leave four to six decent-size leaves at the top and center of the plant (the part that is growing) to keep photosynthesizing and feeding new growth.

- Summer kale and collards eventually succumb to pests and/or become tougher, spicier, and more bitter in hot weather. Give thanks for what they gave, and don't be too disappointed when the season ends.

- **FOR FALL / WINTER HARVEST:** Continue harvesting greens into winter, covering them with a thick row cover by the time temperatures drop below freezing.

'Rocky Top Lettuce Mix'

Lettuce

COMMON NAMES AND TYPES: Lettuce, salad mix, leaf lettuce, cutting lettuce, head lettuce

BOTANICAL NAME: *Lactuca sativa*

PLANT FAMILY: Asteraceae or daisy family

PLACE OF ORIGIN: Egypt

Lettuce has been cultivated for at least five thousand years and has taken a while to be coaxed into its current tender form—wild lettuces are mostly spiny!

When most people think of lettuce, they think salad. While lettuce certainly shines as a salad green, there are plenty of other fabulous ways to use it: in soup (in Mexican and Italian traditions), as lettuce wraps (use Bibb or romaine), in green smoothies, in tacos or taco bowls, in noodle bowls, and in sauces. Freshness really matters with lettuce, and homegrown lettuce, harvested fresh, outshines anything store-bought many, many times over.

Sun requirement: Prefers full sun but can tolerate partial shade; grow summer lettuce in partial shade to slow bolting

Nitrogen needs: Heavy feeder

Trellis or infrastructure needs: No

Temperature

Germination temperature range (soil temp): Ideal: 70–75°F (21–24°C); min: 40°F (4°C)

Frost and cold hardiness: Yes, to 20°F (–7°C); frost tolerance is variety dependent; winter lettuces are much more cold hardy than spring and summer varieties.

Heat tolerance: 80°F (27°C); heat tolerance is variety dependent; spring and summer lettuces tolerate heat better than winter varieties; most lettuces prefer temperatures at 60–70°F (15–21°C).

Spacing

Direct sow, transplant, or flexible: Flexible

Seed-sowing depth: ⅛"

Direct-sowing distance between seeds: N/A for head lettuce; sow densely for cutting lettuce

Final spacing (thin to or transplant to): 5"–9" for head lettuces; tight spacing for leaf/cutting lettuces

Timing

See the Timing Tables on page 339 for specific tips on growing lettuce in your region.

When to plant: Start indoors 1–1½ months before the last frost, or sow outside starting about 2 weeks before the last frost with cold-tolerant varieties. Plant heat-tolerant varieties through the heat, and then plant cold-tolerant ones again until about 1½ months before the first frost.

Succession planting: Lettuce successions can be sown up to every 3 weeks throughout spring and summer, although we usually take a break from lettuce in the hottest part of the summer; it dislikes high temperatures, and most varieties won't germinate in very warm soil. Resume planting when the cooler season starts to approach.

One-time harvest vs. harvest window: Harvest window for leaf/cutting lettuce; one-time harvest per plant for head lettuces

Days to maturity (range): 45–60

Harvest season: Spring into summer; fall into winter

Common Pests and Diseases

Snails and slugs, armyworms, aphids, crickets, cutworms, darkling beetles, garden symphylans, grasshoppers, leaf miners, nematodes, rabbits, vegetable weevils, whiteflies, groundhogs, downy mildew, bacterial spot, bottom rot, fusarium wilt

Our Favorite Varieties

There are dozens and dozens of varieties of lettuce! Check with local growers to learn what's best in your region. Natalie loves **'Rocky Top Lettuce Mix'** for leaf/cutting lettuce; it's beautiful and tasty and hardy in warmer weather. For head lettuce, we both like **'Optima'** butter lettuce because it's silky and delicious and a bit of a workhorse, tolerating heat and other stressors well. Chloe plants **'Slobolt'** during summer, which, as indicated by the name, takes a long time to bolt (start flowering) even in high temperatures, though it is not as silky as other varieties. For winter lettuce, we like **'Winter Density'** and **'North Pole'**; both are tasty, robust, and reliable.

STEPS TO GROWING

Planting

- Either direct sow lettuce densely in close rows for leaf/cutting lettuce, or sow seeds in a 72-cell tray or equivalent for butter and heading lettuces.

- If you sowed seeds in a flat or pots, transplant head lettuces at a spacing of 5"–9" apart, depending on variety and fertility (larger varieties warrant wider spacing; lower fertility also warrants wider spacing).

Growing

- Weed between rows and between plants as needed.

- Keep plants well watered.

- Fertilize a few times during growth if your soil isn't already rich.

- Mulch between rows or plants once lettuces grow to 5"–7" tall. Wait to mulch, or skip mulching altogether; if you have a robust slug population, lettuce is their favorite.

Harvesting

- Harvest leaf/cutting lettuce by giving the whole lot a haircut with scissors (leaving the bottom 3"–4" of the plants intact) once the plants are 7"–8" tall.

- Harvest head lettuce using a sharp knife once heads have formed and are a good size but haven't started bolting (indicated when a head begins to grow upright with significant space between leaves, ultimately developing a flower stalk).

- Eventually lettuce will bolt; there are, in fact, some varieties called celtuce that have been bred for these edible, crunchy stalks (which are often bitter in regular lettuce varieties).

- **FOR FALL / WINTER HARVEST:** Cover fall and winter lettuces with thick row cover to keep them alive and producing once the temperatures drop below freezing.

PINCH VS. HAIRCUT HARVEST METHOD

When harvesting cutting lettuce, we used to always employ the pinching method (pinching individual leaves) but converted to the haircut method (cutting the whole lot with scissors) because of its ease and effectiveness, and the fact that you typically get a second or third harvest of cutting lettuce with the haircut method.

Muskmelons

COMMON NAMES: Melons, muskmelons

BOTANICAL NAME: *Cucumis melo*

PLANT FAMILY: Cucurbitaceae or cucurbit family

PLACE OF ORIGIN: Iran/Persia

Two distinct groups of melons are commonly grown in the United States: muskmelons (*Cucumis melo*), which include cantaloupes and honeydews, and watermelons (*Citrullus lanatus*). Both are in the Cucurbitaceae family, along with their cousins summer and winter squash, cucumbers, and gourds.

Muskmelons originated in Persia/Iran, whereas watermelons hail from Africa. It is difficult to say when these domestications took place; people have been growing and eating them for a very long time. Both plants took a while to travel the globe but are now known and cultivated wherever there is enough heat for ripening.

Sun requirement: Full sun

Nitrogen needs: Heavy feeders

Trellis or infrastructure needs: Not necessary but can be helpful if you're growing melons in a small space. The trellis will need to be sturdy, and each fruit may need support as it ripens and gets heavy with sweet juice.

Temperature

Germination temperature range (soil temp): Ideal: 75–90°F (24–32°C); min: 65°F (18°C)

Frost and cold hardiness: No

Heat tolerance: 90°F (32°C)

Spacing

Direct sow, transplant, or flexible: Flexible. If transplanting, start in 4" pots.

Seed-sowing depth: ½"

Direct-sowing distance between seeds: 3 seeds in a cluster, with clusters 18" from each other in rows that are 48" from each other

Final spacing (thin to or transplant to): Leave the best-looking plant or two from each cluster with 18" between them in rows.

Timing

See the Timing Tables on page 339 for specific tips on growing muskmelons in your region.

When to plant: Sow indoors right around the time of the last frost; sow outdoors once it's good and hot.

Succession planting: Melons require a long, hot season, so we usually plant one round only. In warmer places, try two or three rounds, with the first being transplants and subsequent rounds being direct sown.

One-time harvest vs. harvest window: Harvest window

Days to maturity (range): 70–90

Harvest season: Summer

Common Pests and Diseases

Cucumber beetles, squash vine borers, black cutworms, squash bugs, fusarium wilt, powdery mildew, mosaic virus

Our Favorite Variety

Muskmelons can be tricky, especially where spring and fall temperatures fluctuate wildly, and where it's hot and wet in the summer (like in the southern Appalachian Mountains). Chloe has had good success with an early-maturing hybrid orange-fleshed melon called **'Hannah's Choice'**. She's also had failures with lots of beautiful and delicious-sounding heirloom melons. If you live in a hotter, drier climate than ours, with a longer growing season, you may find success experimenting with less-forgiving melon varieties.

STEPS TO GROWING

Planting

- If transplanting, sow melon seeds in 4″ pots on heat mats as soon as outside temperatures are consistently above freezing. Transplant melon seedlings out into well-fertilized and potentially alkalized areas about 18″ from each other, with 48″ between rows.

  TIP: *Melons like soil that's neutral to slightly alkaline. If your soil is acidic, consider adding one or two handfuls of wood ash to your planting areas, or use a fast-acting liming agent like hydrated lime (this is caustic, so be sure to use eye, skin, and lung protection and don't overdo it). Other liming agents, like hi-cal or dolomite lime, take longer to impact soil pH; they aren't effective unless applied long before planting. For more on adjusting soil pH, see page 138.*

- If direct sowing, wait until the soil has warmed significantly, and direct sow melon seeds in groups of two to three in well-fertilized and potentially alkalized areas 18″ apart in rows that have 48″ between them.

Growing

- Keep seedlings/transplants well watered but not soggy.

- There will be a lot of space between these tiny plants—be sure to keep it weeded. Once the vines start to run, covering this area, it will be difficult to get in and weed.

'Hannah's Choice' muskmelon

TIP: *We lay down black landscaping fabric and/or an organic mulch all around melons to prevent weeds as the plants begin to vine. Black plastic also helps heat up the soil, which melons like.*

- Feed melons once or twice as they grow.

Harvesting

- Knowing when melons are ready to harvest can be tricky. Muskmelons are so named because they usually have a strong, sweet, melony aroma when they are ready. Sniff your melons when you think they look big enough to eat, and check their skin color, which will change from green to tannish in most varieties.

- Another method for determining ripeness is to press gently on the blossom end (opposite where the stem comes out); a ripe melon will be tender and give a little when you press. Many varieties will also loosen from the vine when they're ready, so give a gentle nudge where the stem meets the plant; if it slips away easily, it's probably ripe.

- Harvest melons as soon as they ripen to encourage immature fruits to also ripen and to avoid rotting; ripe melons will rot quickly!

  TIP: *If you know the temperature will drop in the next 1½–2 months, pick off new flowers or tiny, immature fruits that won't have time to ripen; this encourages the plant to send its energy into the remaining, bigger fruits.*

'Burgundy' okra

Okra

COMMON NAMES: Okra, okro, ladyfingers, okura, bhindi

BOTANICAL NAME: *Abelmoschus esculentus*

PLANT FAMILY: Malvaceae or mallow family

PLACE OF ORIGIN: Ethiopia

Okra originated somewhere in or around Ethiopia, and we know that it was cultivated in Egypt as far back as the thirteenth century BCE. It is in the mallow family (Malvaceae) and has lovely, edible flowers that remind us of its relatives in that family, hibiscus and rose of Sharon, which are close cousins. Okra flowers are so lovely that our students often ask, "What is that flower?" instead of, "What is that vegetable?" when they come upon it in the garden.

Sun requirement: Full sun

Nitrogen needs: Medium feeder

Trellis or infrastructure needs: No

Temperature

Germination temperature range (soil temp):
Ideal: 70–90°F (21–32°C); min: 65°F (18°C)

Frost and cold hardiness: No

Heat tolerance: 95°F (35°C)

Spacing

Direct sow, transplant, or flexible: Flexible, though direct sowing is preferable (transplant only if your season is too short to direct sow)

Seed-sowing depth: ½"

Direct-sowing distance between seeds: 2"–4"

Final spacing (thin to or transplant to): 8"–18"

Timing

See the Timing Tables on page 339 for specific tips on growing okra in your region.

When to plant: Direct sow after the danger of frost has passed and when the soil has warmed, but as early as possible; this is not a quick-growing plant. Germination for this crop doesn't happen under 65°F (18°C), and germination rates are much higher at 70°–85°F (21–29°C). If your season dictates that you sow indoors, do so 4 weeks before you plan to transplant into soil that's good and warm.

Succession planting: In warm and hot places with long growing seasons, plant successions of okra if you love it. Because of its long harvest window and our shorter growing season, we do only one round per year. The plants produce until frost—or when we stop harvesting because we've had our fill.

One-time harvest vs. harvest window: Long harvest window

Days to maturity (range): 50–85

Harvest season: Late summer into fall

Common Pests and Diseases

Not many pest or disease issues, but sometimes leaf-footed bugs, stink bugs, fusarium wilt

Our Favorite Varieties

'Burgundy' is a productive and beautiful variety of okra with red pods and red foliage. **'Cajun Jewel'** is a shorter, squatter okra plant; spine-free; widely adapted to different conditions; and produces abundant grass-green tasty pods.

STEPS TO GROWING

Planting

- Direct sow okra seeds about 3″ apart once temps are good and warm outside, or sow seeds in 4″ pots about 4 weeks before you plan to transplant them into warm soil.

- If you started seeds in pots, transplant to a spacing of about 12″ apart (closer for smaller varieties and wider for larger varieties and lower-fertility situations), being very careful not to disturb the roots.

Growing

- If you direct sow, keep the area watered and weeded as seedlings emerge. Once the plants are about 6″ tall, thin to a spacing of about 12″ apart (same spacing caveats as previously mentioned).

- Mulch between and around plants once they reach 6″–8″ tall.

- Fertilize okra once or twice if your soil is poor.

Harvesting

- Big, beautiful flowers will appear and turn into pods (okra is related to hibiscus). Harvest the pods when they are still tender, usually 4″ or smaller, depending on the variety. Flowers are also edible and tasty, but any flower harvested will mean one less mature pod.

  TIP: *Many okra varieties have scratchy foliage. If you grow one of these, wear long sleeves and possibly gloves as you harvest.*

- Be sure to harvest all ripe and any overripe pods to stimulate further flowering and pod set.

'Burgundy' okra flower

BE CAREFUL NOT TO PLANT TOO MUCH!

Okra is a prolific plant. The pods need harvesting every 2 days once it starts producing; be sure to plan for this, and don't plant more than you can handle! Three to six plants will likely provide ample harvests, unless you have a real thing for okra or love preserving it . . . it does make very tasty pickles.

Onions

COMMON NAME: Onion

BOTANICAL NAME: *Allium cepa*

PLANT FAMILY: Amaryllidaceae or allium family

PLACE OF ORIGIN: Asia

The big, round, bulbing-type of onions that most of us are familiar with are one of the oldest cultivated crops and have been grown throughout Eurasia for at least five thousand years. These pungent, sweet lilies (they're in the same family as the lilies that are grown for their blossoms) are harvested for their flavor as well as their medicinal qualities.

Onions can be grown from seed, sets (tiny bulbs grown the previous year), or transplants. With seeds you'll have a greater variety to choose from, but onion seeds need to be started very early in the season, which may not work with your schedule.

Onions form bulbs based on the number of hours of sunlight, or day length, in their environment. Each onion variety can be identified as a short-, long-, or intermediate-day type. It's important to get the right kind for your latitude. If you grow onions not suited for your region, you'll likely harvest only greens and no nice, juicy bulbs.

Sun requirement: Full sun

Nitrogen needs: Heavy feeders

Trellis or infrastructure needs: No

Temperature

Germination temperature range (soil temp):
Ideal: 60–70°F (15–21°C); min: 45°F (7°C)

Frost and cold hardiness: Yes, to 20°F (–7°C)

Heat tolerance: 85°F (29°C)

Spacing

Direct sow, transplant, or flexible: Transplant onion plants or onion sets or start from seed

Seed-sowing depth: ¼"

Direct-sowing distance between seeds: 1" for seeds, 6"–8" for transplants or sets

Final spacing (thin to or transplant to): 4"–8"

Timing

See the Timing Tables on page 339 for specific tips on growing onions in your region.

When to plant: Sow onion seeds in open flats (not pots or flats of pots) inside, *without* bottom heat, 2–3½ months before the last frost. If buying starts or transplanting your own, set out plants 2 months before last frost or as soon as ground is warm enough to be worked if in a cold climate.

Succession planting: Onions form bulbs in response to changing day length and are not suitable for succession planting. Green onions or scallions can be planted several times throughout the season, since we harvest them for their greens and not their bulbs.

One-time harvest vs. harvest window: One-time harvest

Days to maturity (range): 100–140 from starting seeds; 90–100 from sets

Harvest season: Summer

'Patterson' onions

Common Pests and Diseases

Onion maggots, thrips, botrytis, downy mildew, soft rot, wireworms

Our Favorite Varieties

We've mostly grown onions for cooking and storage rather than fresh eating, and for those purposes we like **'Clear Dawn'** and **'Dakota Tears'** as yellows and **'Rossa di Milano'** as a red. These long-day, open-pollinated varieties are reliable, productive, tasty, and keep well in the right conditions. Natalie tends to order onion starts and usually goes with **'Patterson'** onions (a widely available long-day hybrid variety) for storage onions. Sweet onions like **'Walla Walla'** are delicious but do not store well; be sure to choose a storage variety if you plan to keep them over the winter or another variety if you prefer fresh onions only.

STEPS TO GROWING

Planting

- In our area, for best results and biggest bulbs, we plant onions 1½–2 months before the last frost. The timing may be different where you live. Ask successful onion growers or a local Extension agent for the best timing in your region.

- Start onion seeds in open flats (no cells/pots) without bottom heat 2–3½ months before the last frost. Simply broadcast onion seeds over the soil surface, press them into the soil, and cover with a light sprinkling of more soil.

- If you're going with sets or transplants, order them so that they'll arrive around 2 months before the last frost.

- When onion seedlings are about the thickness of a pencil lead, they are ready to transplant. If they get this big too early, be sure to fertilize and keep them happy in their flat until the ground is workable and it's time to put them out.

- Transplant onion seedlings (or onion sets) 1½"–2" deep and 6"–8" apart.

  TIP: *A sprinkle of bonemeal in the trench where you'll plant onions encourages good root growth and bulb formation. If your soil isn't already overloaded with phosphorus and you can afford bonemeal, it's great to add.*

'Clear Dawn' onions

Growing

- Keep onions well watered, as they have shallow roots.

- Weed around and between onions as needed.

- Mulch onions once they are 6"–8" tall.

- Fertilize a few times during the season, unless you know you have especially rich soil.

Harvesting

- Onions are ready to harvest when the green tops of at least half the plants in the area turn yellow and flop over. At this point, push down the other half and harvest them all within a week.

- Pull onions up by their tops.

- Cure them in the sun on the ground if it is dry, or lay them out on a table in a greenhouse for 2–3 days. If conditions are not dry and you don't have a greenhouse, you can skip this step.

- Braid or bundle onions and hang in a covered space with good airflow and warmth to cure for a minimum of 10 days. This step is crucial if you plan to store the onions.

- Cut off the tops and roots and hang in a mesh sack; store in a crate in a cool, well-ventilated space like a root cellar; or hang braids and bunches in your home (they won't last quite as long as they do in a cooler spot).

Parsnips

COMMON NAMES: Parsnip

BOTANICAL NAME: *Pastinaca sativa*

PLANT FAMILY: Apiaceae or carrot family

PLACE OF ORIGIN: Eurasia

Parsnips originated in Eurasia, where they have been domesticated for millennia. These deep roots have been lauded throughout history for their sweetness, especially those grown in more northern climes. Tribute was once paid from Germany to Rome in the form of parsnips! Parsnips were a primary sweetener in Europe before the import of cane sugar, and they were the main starchy root crop in the colonies of what is now known as the United States and Canada until they were superseded in the nineteenth century by potatoes.

Sun requirement: Prefers full sun but can tolerate partial shade

Nitrogen needs: Medium feeder

Trellis or infrastructure needs: No

Temperature

Germination temperature range (soil temp): Ideal: 55–75°F (13–24°C); min: 45°F (7°C)

Frost and cold hardiness: Yes, to 0°F (–18°C)

Heat tolerance: 75°F (24°C)

Spacing

Direct sow, transplant, or flexible: Direct sow

Seed-sowing depth: ¼"

Direct-sowing distance between seeds: ½"

Final spacing (thin to or transplant to): 2"–4"

Timing

See the Timing Tables on page 339 for specific tips on growing parsnips in your region.

When to plant: Sow parsnip seeds as early as 1 month before the last frost, up until the last frost.

Succession planting: Parsnips take a long time to mature and don't lend themselves to succession planting.

One-time harvest vs. harvest window: Harvest window for a whole patch; they will overwinter in the ground, to be dug as needed. One-time harvest per individual plant.

Days to maturity (range): 105–130

Harvest season: Fall into winter, early spring if overwintered

Common Pests and Diseases

Aphids, leaf miners, carrot rust flies, black cutworms, parsnip canker

Our Favorite Variety

'Harris Model' is a tried-and-true parsnip for the home gardener. It's so reliable and tasty that we haven't found a reason to branch out and try others.

STEPS TO GROWING

Planting

- Direct sow parsnip seeds into a smooth and hopefully weed-free (or low-weed) bed with about ½" between each seed.

- Keep the bed well watered until the parsnip seedlings emerge, which can take up to a couple of weeks. This can mean watering more than once a day if it's sunny. Parsnip seeds are sensitive to drying out and won't sprout unless they're evenly moist.

Growing

- As seedlings emerge, weed between rows as needed.

- When seedlings are about 2" tall, thin parsnips to their final spacing of 2"–4" between plants.

- Continue weeding and mulch parsnips once they've reached 4"–6" tall.

   TIP: *Be careful as you tend your parsnips: Their foliage exudes a milky sap that is irritating to some people's skin.*

'Harris Model' parsnip

Harvesting

- Harvest parsnips once their rounded shoulders poke up from the soil surface; check specific days to maturity for the variety you're growing to avoid harvesting too early.

- Use a fork or hori hori to loosen the soil around the parsnips, then pull them out. Be careful not to fork or stab the parsnips themselves, but simply loosen the soil around them. They grow so deep that just pulling them by hand without loosening usually doesn't work.

- Late January and after, when daylight hours grow longer, harvest any parsnips that are still in the ground, because this change will cause them to turn woody as they prepare to make flowers and seeds.

- If you want to keep eating fresh parsnips into winter, you can harvest all of them and store them in a root cellar or fridge, or you can mulch them heavily and let the ground act as a natural root cellar. If you live in a place where the ground freezes solid, better to dig them up before that happens.

- When leaving parsnips in the ground, there's a risk of them rotting or freezing if freezing temperatures penetrate below a thick layer of mulch, or the parsnips might get munched by critters, but in general we've had good luck with this method.

SWEET REWARDS FOR A DELAYED HARVEST

You can start harvesting as soon as your parsnips are mature, but they get significantly sweeter when left in cold soil to continue to develop after a frost or two.

'Sugar Magnolia' pea

'Sugar Snap' pea

Peas

COMMON NAMES AND TYPES: Peas, snap peas, English peas, snow peas, shelling peas

BOTANICAL NAME: *Pisum sativum*

PLANT FAMILY: Fabaceae or pea family

PLACE OF ORIGIN: Mediterranean or Middle East

Peas are one of the oldest cultivated crops, having been grown since the Neolithic Period or before. They're native to Eurasia, and since they've been in human care for so long, nobody is really sure if their origin point is somewhere in the area now called the Middle East or closer to the Mediterranean. Before and during old-fashioned pea-growing times, wild pea relatives were also collected and eaten. But beware! Many of their wild relatives are poisonous, so it's better to stick to cultivated varieties in your garden.

Sun requirement: Prefers full sun but can tolerate a little shade

Nitrogen needs: Nitrogen fixer

Trellis or infrastructure needs: Yes! Peas climb horizontal members via curly tendrils. Most varieties need a sturdy trellis that's at least 48″ tall; some, like 'Sugar Snap', can grow much taller. We like to use welded wire cattle panels; some folks prefer to make ladders with string or poles. There are short pea varieties that supposedly don't need trellising, but we've found that these still benefit from support, and the yields are so much lower that they're not worth it.

Temperature

Germination temperature range (soil temp): Ideal: 50–75°F (10–24°C); min: 40°F (4°C)

Frost and cold hardiness: Yes, to 28°F (−2°C). This hardiness is for growing plants; for fall peas, freezing temperatures halt flowering and fruit set.

Heat tolerance: 77°F (25°C)

Spacing

Direct sow, transplant, or flexible: Direct sow

Seed-sowing depth: ¾"

Direct-sowing distance between seeds: 1"–1½"

Final spacing (thin to or transplant to): 1"–2"

Timing

See the Timing Tables on page 339 for specific tips on growing peas in your region.

When to plant: Peas are the very first seeds we direct sow in early spring, as early as 3 months before the last frost. Early sowing is crucial here because peas don't like heat. If you have milder springs and summers, your sowing time is more flexible. Natalie used to sow peas with the rest of her early spring crops in April when she lived in the Pacific Northwest. We don't usually grow fall peas, but many folks do, especially in milder climates. Sowing seeds for fall peas happens sometime in July.

Succession planting: They're too sensitive for successions where we live, but in milder climates folks can sow up to every 2–3 weeks through midspring, and again in midsummer for a fall crop.

One-time harvest vs. harvest window: Harvest window

Days to maturity (range): 56–75

Harvest season: Late spring, fall in some areas

Common Pests and Diseases

Aphids, Mexican bean beetles, root-knot nematodes, wireworms, armyworms, cucumber beetles, leaf miners, pea leaf weevils, pea moths, spider mites, thrips, pea enation, fusarium wilt, downy mildew, powdery mildew

Our Favorite Varieties

Since peas are a little hit or miss in the southern Appalachians, we haven't tried lots of varieties, with the exception of the beautiful but a little tough **'Sugar Magnolia Tendril'** pea. Of those we have experimented with, we always go back to good ol' **'Sugar Snap'** for flavor and vigor. If you grow this variety, be sure to erect a tall and sturdy trellis. It's a climber! When Natalie lived in the Pacific Northwest, she loved to grow **'Cascadia'** peas.

STEPS TO GROWING

Planting

- Direct sow seeds as soon as you can work the soil, with 1"–1½" between seeds. Soak peas for about 6 hours, or overnight, before sowing.

   TIP: *We like to coat seeds in legume inoculant (choose one that's specific to peas) before planting if we have it around. This improves growth and yield.*

- Keep the seedbed moist but not soggy until seedlings emerge. Peas can rot in the ground if it's too wet and too cool.

Growing

- Weed around seedlings if weeds emerge (in our region, peas are sown when most weed seeds are still dormant in the cold).

   TIP: *If you experience pressure from birds trying to eat your emerging peas, it will be worthwhile to put up bird-scare tape or plastic bags on stakes. These tactics will deter your feathered friends.*

- Mulch thickly around the bases of pea plants once they're 6"–8" tall.

- Erect a sturdy trellis right after you mulch. Peas climb with curly tendrils on horizontal members, so be sure your trellis has those. Welded wire cattle panels (strong, stiff fence panels) work great, but string or mesh trellises work, too. Check to see how tall the variety you're growing is supposed to get, and build an appropriately sized trellis.

Harvesting

- Peas are ready to harvest when plump but before the seeds get hard (unless you're growing snow peas, which are flat when ripe). Begin harvesting right away, and harvest every 1–3 days.

- Pick all ripe and even overripe peas to encourage further flowering and fruiting.

- Peas produce for a long window if the plants are healthy and temps don't get too hot or cold. Eventually warm weather will reduce vigor and potentially bring in fungal issues; say thanks and goodbye to spring peas at this point.

- If you're growing fall peas, freezing temperatures won't kill the plants but will slow or halt flowering, which in turn means no more pod production.

Peppers and Chiles

COMMON NAMES AND TYPES: Peppers, chiles, pimentos, capsicum, bell peppers, chile peppers, chiltepin

BOTANICAL NAMES: *Capsicum annuum* (all bell peppers and many common spicy chiles, such as jalapeño, New Mexico chiles, pimentos, wax chiles, cayenne peppers, and Thai chiles); *C. frutescens* (tabasco, piri piri); *C. chinense* (habanero, Scotch bonnet); *C. pubescens* (rocoto); *C. baccatum* (most South American aji peppers). Each of these species has been domesticated separately!

PLANT FAMILY: Solanaceae or nightshade family

PLACE OF ORIGIN: South and Central America

Peppers and chiles include both the sweet and the spicy, and most of the ones we're familiar with in the US are the same species. These colorful, flavorful, zesty fruits originated in Peru and the tropical Americas, including Guatemala and Mexico. They have been cultivated and traded throughout the Western Hemisphere since long before European invasion— for at least two thousand years. They continue playing a key role in almost all Native American cooking, from north to south, and have been adopted by cuisines of many parts of the world, especially south and southeast Asia, where you might get hit over the head if you try to tell traditional cooks that chiles are not native to those regions. Peppers have been used medicinally for everything from arthritis to heart health to pain.

Sun requirement: Full sun

Nitrogen needs: Medium feeders

Trellis or infrastructure needs: Not necessary, but we like to support these plants with individual stakes or by using a weave trellis (see page 234) for a row of peppers. This is best done before heavy fruits start to weigh down the plants.

Temperature

Germination temperature range (soil temp): Ideal: 68–95°F (20–35°C); min: 60°F (15°C)

Frost and cold hardiness: No

Heat tolerance: 95°F (35°C)

Spacing

Direct sow, transplant, or flexible: Transplant

Seed-sowing depth: ¼"

Direct-sowing distance between seeds: N/A

Final spacing (thin to or transplant to): 12"–24"

Timing

See the Timing Tables on page 339 for specific tips on growing peppers and chiles in your region.

When to plant: Sow seeds in flats or pots, ideally on a heat mat, and definitely in a warm space, 2½–3 months before the last frost. Peppers grow slowly!

Succession planting: Since peppers require time and significant heat to mature, we plant only one round per year. If you're in a very warm place, you might have luck with two rounds per year.

One-time harvest vs. harvest window: Harvest window

Days to maturity (range): 60–90 from transplant

Harvest season: Later summer into early fall

Common Pests and Diseases

Root-knot nematodes, tomato hornworms, Colorado potato beetles, European corn borers, corn earworms, armyworms, pepper maggots, tobacco hornworms, aphids, cutworms, sap beetles, tarnished plant bugs, flea beetles, blossom-end rot (actually a calcium deficiency), anthracnose, mosaic virus

Our Favorite Varieties

For spicy chiles, we like regular old **jalapeños** because they're productive, reliable, tasty, and only moderately hot. Chloe also loves a yellow Peruvian variety called **'Aji Chinchi Amarillo'** (*C. baccatum*), also known as aji mirasol; it's got an amazing flowery, aromatic, and spicy flavor, and it is extremely resilient and productive.

As far as sweet peppers go, we both like a local open-pollinated variety called **'Ashe County Pimento'** because it reliably produces a lot of small, flat, thick-walled, sweet, flavorful peppers (small peppers are best for cooler climates and places with shorter growing seasons because they mature more quickly). Natalie loves a hybrid sweet pepper called **'Ace'**, a reliable early producer. We also like an open-pollinated "snacker" called **'Lipstick'** because it's—surprise—early producing, sweet, and productive. These are all awesome for packing in school lunches.

STEPS TO GROWING

Planting

- Sow seeds in 72-cell trays or equivalent in a well-heated space, ideally on heat mats, 3 months before last frost. Peppers are slow to grow.

- When seedlings outgrow their original cells or pots, transplant them into larger pots (we go from a 72-cell tray into 4" pots so the plants are nice and big when they finally go out into the garden).

  TIP: *Baby peppers spend a good while in pots, so it's a good idea to fertilize them once or twice.*

- After the danger of frost has completely passed and the weather is warm (likely 2 weeks after the last frost date), and when your transplants are fairly large (about 4"-5" tall), transplant peppers out into the garden with 12"–24" between them, depending on the variety and how big it is likely to get.

- Water transplants well and keep plants regularly watered throughout their growing season—at least once a week. Peppers are fairly drought tolerant.

Growing

- Mulch between plants after risk of slug damage has passed.

- Stake each plant, put cages around them, or use the weave style of string trellis (see page 234) to support your peppers as they become heavy with fruit.

'Lipstick' sweet pepper

WAIT FOR WARMER TEMPS

Peppers are extremely sensitive to cold and can become stunted for life if they get exposed to temperatures below 55°F (13°C) or so, so don't rush to put them out. It's worth waiting until nighttime temperatures are reliably above 55°F (13°C).

Harvesting

- Harvest peppers when they are plump, shiny, and the color that you expect them to be when ripe. All peppers begin green and move through two or three color changes if the growing time is long enough. They can all be harvested as green peppers, but know that while some varieties have been bred to be plump and tasty at the green stage, others have been bred for harvest at a more fully mature stage and a different color.

- Continue harvesting every few days, removing all mature and overmature fruits even if they're damaged, because this tells the plants to continue to make flowers and more fruits.

- The pepper season ends when the plants run out of steam to produce fruits or when frost kills them.

- To extend your harvest in areas where frost comes relatively early, you can pull plants, roots and all, and hang them upside down in a frost-proof location. The peppers will continue to ripen for a couple of weeks!

'Adirondack Red' potatoes

Potatoes

COMMON NAMES AND TYPES: Potatoes, Irish potatoes, spuds, taters, white potatoes

BOTANICAL NAME: *Solanum tuberosum*

PLANT FAMILY: Solanaceae or nightshade family

PLACE OF ORIGIN: South America (Andes mountains)

The Incas may have been the first peoples to cultivate potatoes nearly eight thousand years ago in the Andes Mountains of Peru. Hundreds of varieties are grown in that region today. Many other cultivars are grown around the world; the potato is a well-traveled and much-loved staple food crop. There are currently over five thousand different varieties of cultivated potatoes! People around here refer to potatoes as "Irish taters" to distinguish them from sweet potatoes; in fact, both tasty tubers come from different parts of Peru.

Sun requirement: Prefers full sun but can tolerate partial shade

Nitrogen needs: Heavy feeder

Trellis or infrastructure needs: No, but hilling improves quality of harvest

Temperature

Germination temperature range (soil temp): Ideal: 50–70°F (10–21°C); min: 40°F (4°C)

Frost and cold hardiness: Yes, to 28°F (–2°C)

Heat tolerance: 80°F (27°C)

Spacing

Direct sow, transplant, or flexible: Plant seed potatoes (chunks of potato tubers and not true seeds) directly in the ground.

Seed-sowing depth: (tubers) 3"

Direct-sowing distance between seeds: (tubers) 8"–12"

Final spacing (thin to or transplant to): 8"–12"

Timing

See the Timing Tables on page 339 for specific tips on growing potatoes in your region.

When to plant: As early as 2 months before the last frost for an early crop of "new potatoes"; through mid-spring for later crops of "storage potatoes"

Succession planting: You can plant a few rounds of potatoes or plant varieties that mature in different lengths of time in order to have a staggered potato harvest.

PRESPROUTING

To improve yields, one option is to "chit" or presprout seed potatoes by warming them to 65°F (18°C) in the dark for about 2 weeks, then spreading them out with eyes facing up in a warm (60–70°F/15–21°C) place with some light for another 2 weeks. This stimulates strong, stubby sprouts at the bud end that don't easily break off.

One-time harvest vs. harvest window: One-time harvest. Potatoes can be stored and eaten over a long period of time.

Days to maturity (range): 60–135

Harvest season: Late spring through fall

Common Pests and Diseases

Colorado potato beetles, flea beetles, potato scab, wireworms, tuberworms, white grubs, vegetable weevils, cutworms, Jerusalem crickets, leafhoppers, nematodes, potato psyllid, potato tuberworms, snails and slugs, whiteflies, aphids, early and late blight, fusarium dry rot, black scurf, Rhizoctonia canker, pink rot, powdery scab, charcoal rot

Our Favorite Varieties

'**Yukon Gem**' is a disease-resistant offshoot of the classic '**Yukon Gold**' that we like for the toughness of the plant (not the potato), tastiness, and golden color. '**Adirondack Blue**' and '**Adirondack Red**' are beautiful, antioxidant-rich varieties that don't store as well as others but sure make for a festive platter of roasted potatoes. '**Desiree**' is a late blight–resistant, red-skinned, yellow-fleshed, long-season variety that is highly productive in fertile soil and has a distinctive and delicious taste and texture. *Note:* Potatoes are highly susceptible to a range of viral and fungal diseases, so it's worth purchasing certified disease-free seed potatoes.

STEPS TO GROWING

Planting

- Cut larger seed potatoes into pieces about the size of a hen's egg (approximately 2 ounces), with at least two eyes on each piece. Smaller seed potatoes can be left whole and will be less susceptible to rotting than cut pieces. (For another option, see the aside on presprouting on page 320.)

- Prepare a fertile seedbed with good drainage; dig a trench/furrow that's about 6" deep and 4" wide down the middle.

  TIP: *Don't use fresh manure, compost, or wood ashes on a potato bed; they increase instances of certain diseases and make your potatoes grow a lot of foliage (and not many tubers).*

- Place early-crop or fingerling seed potatoes at a spacing of about 8", and bigger and longer-season potatoes 10"–16" apart. Space rows at least 3' apart (we prefer 4' so that we have plenty of room to gather soil for hilling).

- Cover the potatoes with 3" of soil.

Growing

- Weed as needed when the potatoes are sprouting and growing.

- Water if it's really dry, but don't overdo it, as sprouting seed potatoes can rot in the ground with too much moisture.

- When potato plants are 6" tall, hill them by gently hoeing soil up around the plants so that only about 2" of foliage is still exposed on each plant and the rest is buried. This provides more protected space for tubers to form (between the original seed potato and the soil surface), reduces weeds, and warms the roots. Hill them again when they once again grow 6" above the new (once-hilled) soil level.

  TIP: *Aim to hill twice, once leaving the soil about level with the ground around it, and the second time mounding it up. If you only hill once, do it so that the soil ends up mounded above the surrounding soil level.*

- Mulch after the final hilling to retain moisture and prevent weeds.

- Most varieties of potatoes are drought sensitive, so be sure to water regularly if it doesn't rain.

Harvesting

- When potato plants flower aboveground, they're also forming tubers belowground. Now you can harvest "new potatoes," which will be tasty though more watery and will have fragile skin compared to fully mature potatoes. New potatoes don't store well.

- Potatoes are fully mature when the plants begin to die back. You can hoe them over to encourage maturation once they begin to die. After this, let the potatoes cure in the ground for 2–3 weeks to form thicker skins and improve storage life.

- Dig potatoes with a fork, being careful not to spear the tubers themselves, and eat right away or store in cool, high-humidity, dark conditions, like those found in a root cellar. Don't rinse or clean potatoes before storage; leaving the dirt on and skin unmolested improves storage life.

- In areas where the soil doesn't freeze deeply, potatoes can be kept in the ground several inches deep to overwinter, and you can dig as needed. Be warned that they might rot and/or get nibbled by bugs or critters if you do this, though Chloe has had fairly good success with it.

Radishes

COMMON NAME AND TYPES: Radish, daikon

BOTANICAL NAME: *Raphanus sativus*

PLANT FAMILY: Brassicaceae or cruciferous family

PLACE OF ORIGIN: China

The word *radish* comes from the Latin word *radix*, which means "root." The genus name, *Raphanus*, is a Latinized form of a Greek expression meaning "easily reared." Radishes are, indeed, easily reared. One of the simplest and quickest veggies to grow, they are an encouraging first crop for kids and all beginning gardeners to try.

Radishes have been cultivated in China since as early as the seventh century BCE, and daikons were first cultivated in Japan about 1,300 years ago. We especially like growing daikons because they are so large and lend themselves to a lot of tasty Asian dishes. All kinds of radishes make easy, delicious, crunchy pickles.

Sun requirement: Prefers full sun but can tolerate partial shade

Fertility needs: Lighter feeder

Trellis or infrastructure needs: No

Temperature

Germination temperature range (soil temp): Ideal: 55–85°F (13–29°C); min: 40°F (4°C)

Frost and cold hardiness: Yes, to 20°F (−7°C)

Heat tolerance: 80°F (27°C); spring/summer varieties are more heat tolerant than those best suited for winter, but all radishes prefer cooler temperatures.

Spacing

Direct sow, transplant, or flexible: Direct sow

Seed-sowing depth: ½"

Direct-sowing distance between seeds: ½"

Final spacing (thin to or transplant to): 1"–5" (closer for smaller spring and summer radishes, farther for winter radishes and daikon)

Timing

See the Timing Tables on page 339 for specific tips on growing radishes in your region.

When to plant: Spring/summer radishes can be planted as soon as the ground can be worked in springtime, as early as 1 month before last frost, if the soil has warmed to 40°F (4°C). We sow daikon and winter radishes in late summer, about 1½ months before the first frost. These varieties grow and taste much better when they mature in cooler weather, and they will bolt quickly if it's warm, as they grow large.

Succession planting: Spring/summer radishes are very quick maturing, and you can plant successions of them as close as 1 week apart, though we usually do only one to three rounds of them in spring—warmer weather makes them taste spicier, and our kids don't like that so much.

One-time harvest vs. harvest window: Harvest window for a bed of radishes (especially winter radishes and daikon, which hold well in the soil); single harvest per individual plant

Days to maturity (range): 25–40 (spring/summer), 45–70 (winter and daikon)

Harvest season: Spring into summer for spring/summer radishes, late fall into winter for winter radishes and daikon

WINTER RADISHES: HARVEST OR LEAVE IN THE GROUND?

Smaller, rounder winter radishes (like 'Watermelon' and, to some degree, 'Mini Purple Daikon') can be kept in the ground under mulch and harvested as needed. However, there's a risk that radishes, especially longer daikons, can freeze and rot if temperatures dip below 20°F (−7°C) for more than a few days, if temps fluctuate above and below freezing frequently, or if the radishes are getting munched by critters. The big ones, whose shoulders come inches out of the soil, tend to freeze because it is challenging to pile enough mulch on top of them to properly protect them.

Common Pests and Diseases

Flea beetles (which make the foliage look bad but don't damage the roots), cabbage root maggots, aphids, cutworms, clubroot, powdery mildew

Our Favorite Varieties

For spring/summer radishes, we go with the quick, pretty, and tasty **'French Breakfast'** and **'Easter Egg'** varieties. **'Cherry Belle'** is very fast growing and cute. For winter radishes we love **'Watermelon'** because it's beautiful and sweet and holds incredibly well in the soil. The daikon varieties we love are **'Mini Purple'** (because, well, it's purple and hardy!) and **'Saitaro'**, for its flavor, texture, and hardiness; both are hybrids.

STEPS TO GROWING

Planting

- Sow seeds with about ½" between them.

- Keep the soil moderately moist, and baby radishes will emerge delightfully quickly.

Growing

- As seedlings emerge, weed between rows as needed.

- When seedlings are about 2" tall, thin radishes either to final spacing (1"–5", depending on mature size of variety) or to about twice the final density. If you choose to thin lightly at this stage, you'll have to thin again, but you'll be able to harvest baby radishes you can eat during the process.

- Mulch radishes once they've reached 4"–6" tall.

Harvesting

- Harvest radishes when their rounded shoulders poke up above the soil surface; check the specific days to maturity for the variety you're growing to make sure you're not harvesting too early or too late. Over-mature radishes are spicy, pithy, woody, and disappointing.

- If your soil is loose, you'll be able to simply grab the tops and wiggle-pull them out. If this doesn't work and the tops break off, use a fork or hori hori to loosen the soil around the radishes, then pull them out. Be careful not to fork or stab the radishes themselves; simply loosen the soil around them.

- Harvest all spring radishes once they're ready (within 1–2 weeks).

'Cherry Belle' radish

- **FOR FALL / WINTER HARVEST:** Harvesting can be spaced out over time. You can start harvesting as soon as your radishes are mature. In late January, when daylight hours start getting longer, harvest whatever radishes are still in the ground, because this change will cause them to turn woody as they prepare to make flowers and seeds.

- You can preserve your harvest by making kimchi or pickling. We tend to do this thanks to the influence of a landmate with Korean heritage who has awesome recipes for such things.

- If you want to keep eating fresh radishes into winter, harvest them all and store in a root cellar or fridge, or mulch them heavily and let the ground act as a natural root cellar.

- Daikons tend to poke up way out of the soil when they're ready, so they won't hold well in the ground. Generally radishes are more likely to freeze and turn to mush than other roots like turnips, parsnips, and carrots, so if it's going to get much colder than a light frost, we usually harvest them and store them indoors.

Spinach

COMMON NAME: Spinach

BOTANICAL NAME: *Spinacia oleracea*

PLANT FAMILY: Amaranthaceae or amaranth family

PLACE OF ORIGIN: Iran

First domesticated in Persia (modern Iran) around two thousand years ago, spinach is one of the most common greens in the standard American cooking palate and was the first frozen vegetable to be sold commercially. Spinach was Italian Renaissance icon Catherine de Medici's favorite food. In fact, when she left her home in Florence, Italy, to marry King Henry II of France, she brought along her own cooks who could prepare spinach in the ways she enjoyed. Since this time, dishes prepared on a bed of spinach are referred to as à la Florentine.

In 1929 the American cartoon character Popeye debuted and attributed his incredible strength to eating lots of canned spinach. As a result, spinach became the third most popular children's food in the US, after turkey and ice cream.

Many recipes that come from far stretches of the world simply call for spinach because the writer assumes we are unable to access the greater variety of wild and exotic greens that are used elsewhere.

Sun requirement: Prefers full sun but can tolerate partial shade

Nitrogen needs: Heavy feeder

Trellis or infrastructure needs: No

PRESERVING SPINACH

Blanching and freezing your own garden spinach is a great way to preserve it, and the resulting frozen spinach can be used just like what you would buy at the store. To blanch, submerge the spinach in a pot of boiling water for 2 minutes, then remove and plunge in an ice bath. Squeeze out as much moisture as possible, then pack into freezer bags and freeze.

Temperature

Germination temperature range (soil temp): Ideal: 45–65°F (7–18°C); min: 35°F (2°C)

Frost and cold hardiness: Yes, to 15°F (–9°C)

Heat tolerance: 75°F (24°C)

Spacing

Direct sow, transplant, or flexible: Flexible, but seems to do better direct sown

Seed-sowing depth: ½"

Direct-sowing distance between seeds: ½"–1"

Final spacing (thin to or transplant to): 2"–4"

Timing

See the Timing Tables on page 339 for specific tips on growing spinach in your region.

When to plant: Direct sow spinach around 2 months before the last frost, or start in pots or flats about 2 weeks earlier than that. For fall/winter spinach, sow seeds outdoors as late as 2 weeks before the first frost.

Succession planting: In our erratic mountain climate, we usually plant spinach once in spring and once in fall. If you're in a more mild place, however, plant successions of spinach as frequently as every week for spring and then again in fall. Spinach won't germinate if the soil is above 85°F (29°C), and it doesn't do well in heat, so it's best to take a break in the summer.

One-time harvest vs. harvest window: Harvest window

Days to maturity (range): 45–60 for big leaves, 25–35 for baby spinach

Harvest season: Spring and fall/winter

Common pests and diseases

Leaf miners, aphids, downy mildew, mosaic virus, anthracnose, fusarium wilt

Our Favorite Varieties

'Bloomsdale' is a classic open-pollinated spinach with good productivity, flavor, and cool-soil emergence. **'Space'** is a hybrid variety that's productive in many conditions and resistant to most common spinach diseases.

'Space' spinach

STEPS TO GROWING

Planting

- Either direct sow spinach or sow seeds in 72-cell trays or equivalent to transplant.

- If you're direct sowing, thin to 2"–4" between plants, depending on how fertile your soil is, with more space for less fertile soil.

- If you're transplanting, do so when plants are at least 3" tall; plant at the previously mentioned spacing.

Growing

- Keep the space between and around the plants weeded.

- Water spinach regularly, at least a few times per week. This is not a drought-tolerant plant.

- If there isn't strong slug pressure when you plant spinach, mulch generously with straw or other mulch. If slugs are an issue, wait to mulch until the plants are pretty big.

- Fertilize at least once while the plants are growing, unless you know they're planted in extra-fertile soil.

Harvesting

- Harvest spinach leaves either by pinching or snipping individual leaves on the outside of the basal rosette or giving the whole plants a haircut about 4" above the ground with a pair of scissors.

- Repeat harvesting several times, returning to harvest again after leaves have regrown.

- Eventually spinach will bolt (produce flower stalks), which marks the end of the spinach season.

WILD ALTERNATIVES TO SPINACH

In our cooking we happily substitute nettles, lamb's quarters, and sochan for spinach, though spinach is also tasty and is probably more familiar to most. It's likely that there are wild greens where you live that can act like spinach in many dishes. These alternatives might even be the weeds you've been trying to eradicate in order to plant spinach! See more about edible weeds on page 219. In other climates where spring and fall have a longer reign, spinach thrives!

Sweet Potatoes

COMMON NAMES: Sweet potatoes, sweet taters

BOTANICAL NAME: *Ipomoea batatas*

PLANT FAMILY: Convolvulaceae or morning glory family

PLACE OF ORIGIN: South America (Amazon basin)

Sweet potatoes, like "regular" potatoes, originally come from Peru and have been under cultivation for at least five thousand years. While "regular" potatoes come from the highlands, sweet potatoes come from the jungle. That's why they do most of their growing when temperatures are above 75°F (24°C)—and they don't mind temps above 100°F (38°C). Along with heat, sweet potatoes need a lot of water, so be sure to have an irrigation plan, especially if you're in a drier region. To their credit these plants will produce a whole lot of food even in lower fertility soil. In fact, it's better not to plant them in super rich soil, as high nitrogren will cause them to grow a lot of leaves and fewer, smaller tubers. The leaves are edible and tasty, but what we're really going for is the starchy sweet tuber.

Sweet potatoes are grown from slips, which are vines that grow out of the sweet potato itself, given the right conditions. These vines are snipped from the tuber when they are 4"–8" long and planted directly into soil, where they magically (with plenty of water and the proper soil conditions) take root. You can grow your own slips, or you can purchase them.

Sun requirement: Full sun

Nitrogen needs: Lighter feeder

Trellis or infrastructure needs: No

Temperature
Germination temperature range (soil temp): Ideal: 70–80°F (21–27°C); min: 60°F (15°C)

Frost and cold hardiness: No

Heat tolerance: 105°F (40°C)

Spacing
Direct sow, transplant, or flexible: Slips go directly in the ground (no seeds)

Seed-sowing depth: (slips) 2"-4"

Direct-sowing distance between seeds: N/A

Final spacing (thin to or transplant to): 10"-14" between plants in a row, with 36" between rows

Timing
See the Timing Tables on page 339 for specific tips on growing sweet potatoes in your region.

When to plant: Well after the danger of frost has passed, when nighttime temperatures are consistently above 50°F (10°C) and the soil has warmed above 60°F (15°C)

Succession planting: Not unless you're in the tropics; sweet potatoes need a lot of time and heat to develop tubers.

One-time harvest vs. harvest window: One-time harvest (with option to harvest some greens as they grow)

Days to maturity (range): 90–120 from planting out slips

Harvest season: Fall

Common Pests and Diseases
Flea beetles, Japanese beetles, wireworms, sweet potato weevils, whiteflies, fusarium wilt, sweet potato scurf, white rust

Our Favorite Varieties
It's easy to get slips for '**Covington**', a pretty reliable, productive, and tasty sweet potato with orange flesh and reddish brown skin. '**Murasaki**' is a deliciously dry, white-fleshed, purple-skinned Japanese variety that has a creamy, nutty flavor and is resistant to several common sweet potato diseases.

STEPS TO GROWING
Planting
- Order or grow your own sweet potato slips. These might not be available locally, so figure out where to purchase them and get an order in at least a month or two before you plan to plant them. Be sure to communicate to the provider when you'll be ready to plant them, as it's ideal to get them in the ground right after they arrive.

- Choose a spot to grow sweet potatoes that has loose, fluffy soil and gets plenty of sunlight. Since sweet potatoes aren't

'Murasaki' sweet potato tubers with attached vines and leaves

heavy feeders, you don't need to worry much about fertility; tilth (texture) matters more.

- Using a hori hori or trowel, plant the slips 10"–14" away from each other, 2"–4" deep, so that two nodes (bumps) on their stems are under the soil surface. Leave 36" between rows; these plants will spread out a lot!

- Water slips in deeply, and keep them well watered as they get established.

Growing

- Weed around and between plants a few times as they grow. Sweet potatoes are sprawling vines and will shade out most weeds after they spread out and cover the ground. It's crucial to prevent weeds from growing before the sweet potatoes vine, as it's very difficult to weed once they have. We like to lay down UV-stabilized black weed fabric between rows to prevent weeds as well as heat up the soil.

Harvesting

- Sweet potato leaves are edible and tasty as cooked greens. Harvest a few here and there from the (hopefully) wildly growing vines.

- Harvest sweet potatoes before the ground freezes (even a little), sometime after temperatures start dropping below 70°F (21°C). They need heat in order to grow, and they stop forming tubers when it gets cool. Tubers cluster around where each slip was planted.

- Use a fork to loosen the soil in about an 18" radius around this area, then gently tug on the vine and use your hands to dig up all the tubers.

TIP: *Either wait for a light frost, which will kill back the leaves, then dig, or cut back the foliage with a scythe, string trimmer, or your hands to expose the ground, then dig. It's much easier to dig sweet potatoes once the sprawling vines are out of the way; they can get tangled up in your digging fork if you leave them.*

- After harvesting you must cure sweet potatoes to convert starches into sugars and develop good flavor. To do this you can store them in crates in a warm space (at least 65°F/18°C; 75°F/24°C is best) and wrap the crates in moist paper bags or cotton sheets, remoistening as needed, for 2 weeks or more.

- Another option for curing is to place crates of tubers over a dish of water on top of a heat mat, then cover with blankets to create the ideal curing conditions of 90°F (32°C) and 90 percent humidity for 90 hours (about 4 days). If you have a greenhouse and can put a heater and a humidifier or open crock pot full of water in there, that's an option, too.

- After they're cured, store sweet potatoes at room temperature in a dark space for several months. They don't thrive in cold root-cellar conditions like potatoes; instead, they need some warmth. Room temperature is just fine.

SWEET POTATOES, NOT YAMS

Yams are another crop (*Dioscorea* spp.) and not another name for sweet potatoes. We don't cover yams in this book because they take a very long time to mature and aren't practical to grow outside of tropical and subtropical climates.

Tomatoes

COMMON NAME: Tomatoes

BOTANICAL NAME: *Solanum lycopersicum*

PLANT FAMILY: Solanaceae or nightshade family

PLACE OF ORIGIN: Western South America and Mesoamerica

Tomatoes were domesticated around 700 CE from wild plants in the Andes, which grew in parts of Bolivia, Chile, Colombia, Ecuador, and Peru. There are also wild relatives of tomatoes in Mesoamerica, where the plants were likely domesticated around the same time. Here's a surprising fact: Tomatoes didn't come to Italy until the 1500s and didn't become a central part of Italian cuisine until the 1800s. Tomatillos and husk cherries are tasty tomato relatives that have similar (though distinct) growing habits and are fun to experiment with.

'West Virginia 63' tomato

Sun requirement: Full sun

Nitrogen needs: Heavy feeder

Trellis or infrastructure needs: Determinate varieties need a stake, cage, or weave trellis; indeterminate varieties require a strong and tall trellis. We use welded wire cattle panels, string trellises from a strong top bar (works well inside a greenhouse or hoop house), or sturdy tripod or quadripod trellises.

Temperature

Germination temperature range (soil temp): Ideal: 65–85°F (18–29°C); min: 60°F (15°C)

Frost and cold hardiness: No

Heat tolerance: 90°F (32°C)

Spacing

Direct sow, transplant, or flexible: Transplant

Seed-sowing depth: ¼"

Direct-sowing distance between seeds: N/A

Final spacing (thin to or transplant to): 18"–24"

Timing

See the Timing Tables on page 339 for specific tips on growing tomatoes in your region.

When to plant: Sow seeds indoors, on a heat mat and/or in a heated space, 1½–2 months before the last frost.

Succession planting: Tomatoes require a lot of heat and time to produce fruit and have a long harvest window, so we only grow one round per year.

One-time harvest vs. harvest window: Long harvest window

Days to maturity (range): 60–100

Harvest season: Summer into fall

Common Pests and Diseases

Aphids, flea beetles, tomato hornworms, whiteflies, leaf miners, spider mites, corn earworms, stink bugs, fruitworms, black cutworms, sap beetles, Septoria leaf spot, early and late blights, fusarium wilt, blossom-end rot (actually a calcium deficiency), tobacco mosaic virus

Our Favorite Varieties

There are thousands of tomato varieties, and it's worth trying several to see what you like to eat and what grows well in your conditions. Our standby workhorse tomato has the unpoetic name of **'West Virginia '63'**. It's productive and hardy, creating loads of medium-size, round, tasty, and meaty red tomatoes. It also has the strongest resistance to late blight of any tomato we've tried. It lends itself nicely to canning and sauce making, and it also performs well sliced onto sandwiches.

Chloe also loves the hybrid **'Sungold'** cherry tomato because it's quite productive, beautifully golden, super-sweet, and fruity. Natalie likes the heirloom slicers **'Mortgage Lifter'** and **'Cosmonaut Volkov'** for growing in the southern Appalachians but enjoyed **'Berkeley Tie-Dye'** when she lived in areas with more heat and less blight.

STEPS TO GROWING

Planting

- Sow seeds in 50- or 72-cell trays or equivalent in a well-heated space, ideally on heat mats.

- When seedlings outgrow their original cells or pots, transplant them up into larger pots (we go from a 50- or 72-cell tray into 4" pots so the plants are nice and big when they finally go out into the garden).

  TIP: *Baby tomatoes spend a good while in pots, so it's nice to fertilize them once or twice.*

- After the danger of frost has completely passed, and when your transplants are the size you want (at least 5" tall), transplant tomatoes into the garden with 18"–24" between them, depending on the variety and how fertile your soil is (less fertility will mean wider spacing).

- Tomatoes can grow roots out of their stems, so if your plants are taller than about 8", bury them so that some of the stem is underground and about 8" of the plant is exposed aboveground. Prune off the lower leaves before you transplant them.

Growing

- Water deeply and mulch thickly between plants.

- For smaller, determinate varieties, use a stake for each plant, apply the weave trellis (see page 234), or use a fence panel or piece of fencing as a trellis. You can use tomato cages if you must; we don't like them because it's hard to tend the tomatoes inside and they're bulky to store.

- For larger, indeterminate varieties, use a tall fence panel or piece of fencing securely attached to stakes or T-posts, create a top bar or string for a string trellis, or build quadripod/tripod trellises (see page 234).

- Prune lower leaves off of tomatoes as they grow, about once every 7–10 days. You can download a video demonstration about pruning tomatoes from our website (see page 374).

Harvesting

- Harvest tomatoes when they are plump and the appropriate color when ripe, depending on the variety. They are sweetest when harvested in the middle of the day, afternoon, or evening (not in the morning).

- Continue harvesting every few days, removing all mature and overmature fruits, even if they're damaged; this tells the plants to continue to produce flowers and more fruits.

- The tomato season ends when the plants are killed by late blight or by frost. Give thanks and be sure not to plant tomatoes in the same place again for a few years.

DETERMINATE VS. INDETERMINATE TOMATOES

There are two groups of tomato varieties that have different growth habits: determinate and indeterminate. Determinate plants grow to be a certain size, then stop growing larger as they set fruit. Indeterminate plants are vinier and continue growing even after fruit set; these need lots of support and pruning in order to be productive. Within these groups there are thousands of distinct varieties.

Along with the categories explained above, tomatoes are generally considered to be "saucers," "slicers," and cherries, though there are, of course, some that cross these boundaries. We like tomato sauce and typically grow about four times as many sauce or all-purpose tomatoes as slicers or cherries.

Turnips and Rutabagas

COMMON NAMES AND TYPES: Turnips, salad turnips, neeps, rutabagas, swedes

BOTANICAL NAMES: *Brassica rapa* (turnip); *Brassica napus* (rutabaga)

PLANT FAMILY: Brassicaceae or mustard family

PLACE OF ORIGIN: Eastern Asia (turnip); Russia or Scandinavia (rutabaga)

Turnips and rutabagas are pretty amazing; they are able to grow in cool temperatures when much of the garden has had it. Depending on where you are, and if you have chosen an appropriate time to plant them, they usually don't have to contend with many pests. They are delicious in soups, stews, and roasted vegetable dishes; salad turnips are mild and sweet and delicious eaten raw.

Turnips were bred to have large roots in Eastern Asia. The rutabaga, a hybrid between a turnip and a cabbage, was first cultivated in Russia or Scandinavia, which is why you might hear them referred to as "swedes." These two plants are botanically different, but growing them is pretty much the same. Rutabagas usually require a longer season in order to mature.

Sun requirement: Prefers full sun but can tolerate partial shade

Nitrogen needs: Lighter feeder

Trellis or infrastructure needs: No

Temperature
Germination temperature range (soil temp): Ideal: 60–85°F (15–29°C); min: 40°F (4°C)

Frost and cold hardiness: Yes, to 20°F (−7°C)

Heat tolerance: 75°F (24°C)

Spacing
Direct sow, transplant, or flexible: Direct sow

Seed-sowing depth: ¼"

Direct-sowing distance between seeds: ½"–2"

Final spacing (thin to or transplant to): 2"–4"

Timing
See the Timing Tables on page 339 for specific tips on growing turnips and rutabagas in your region.

When to plant: Sow seeds 1½–2 months before the last frost for a spring crop of those varieties appropriate for growing in spring, and as late as right around the time of the last frost for salad turnips like 'Hakurei' and 'Oasis'. For longer-season turnips and rutabagas, skip the hot summer and sow in late summer or early fall (about 1 month before first frost) for fall and winter harvest and for overwintering turnips and rutabagas.

Succession planting: Salad turnips like 'Hakurei' and 'Oasis' can be planted a few times in spring and fall, 2–3 weeks between plantings. Longer-season turnips and rutabagas are best planted once in spring (we usually skip spring for these because it gets hot quickly here) and once in late summer or early fall for the main fall and winter crop.

One-time harvest vs. harvest window: Harvest window for a bed of turnips or rutabagas; single harvest per individual plant. Turnip greens are edible and tasty, too!

Days to maturity (range): 38–95 (salad turnips are the quickest, and rutabagas take the longest)

Harvest season: Spring and/or fall into winter

Common Pests and Diseases
Flea beetles, aphids, cabbage root maggots, stink bugs, wireworms, black cutworms, powdery mildew, downy mildew, black rot, white rust, clubroot, root knot

Our Favorite Varieties
'**Hakurei**' and '**Oasis**' are our favorite varieties of salad turnips. More like giant, mild radishes than turnips, these hybrids are eaten fresh. For cooking turnips we like '**Gold Ball**' and '**Purple Top White Globe**' because they're beautiful and very tasty. '**Laurentian**' is the only rutabaga we've tried, and we like it. To be honest, we mostly grow turnips, not rutabagas, because they don't take as long to mature.

‘Purple Top White Globe’ and ‘Gold Ball’ turnips

STEPS TO GROWING

Planting

- Direct sow turnip or rutabaga seeds into a smooth and weed-free (or low-weed) bed.

- **FOR FALL / WINTER HARVEST:** Prepare the bed ahead of time. Water it or let it get rained on so that weed seeds germinate, then cultivate with a stirrup hoe to kill those weeds, and plant turnips or rutabagas afterward. This doesn't work as well in spring because many weed seeds won't sprout until temperatures warm.

- Keep the bed well watered until seedlings emerge. Fortunately turnip and rutabaga seeds germinate quickly, even in cooler soil.

Growing

- As seedlings emerge, weed between rows as needed.

- Once the seedlings are about 2″ tall, thin turnips or rutabagas to 2″ apart for salad turnips, or 3″–4″ for larger turnips and rutabagas.

- Continue weeding regularly, and mulch once they've grown to 4″–6″ tall.

Harvesting

- Harvest turnips and rutabagas once their rounded shoulders poke up from the soil surface; check the specific days to maturity for the variety you're growing to make sure you're not harvesting too early or late.

- If your soil is loose, simply grab the turnip or rutabaga tops and wiggle-pull them out. If the tops break off, use a fork or hori hori to loosen the soil around them, then pull them out. Be careful not to fork or stab the turnips or rutabagas themselves; simply loosen the soil. Be sure to harvest and eat the greens if they're in good shape; they're delicious.

- Harvest all of the roots of spring turnips and rutabagas within 2–3 weeks once they are ready.

- **FOR FALL / WINTER HARVEST:** Cover the bed with mulch and harvest as needed, letting the ground act as a natural root cellar. They get sweeter in freezing temperatures, as long as the soil doesn't freeze deep enough to turn them into mush. When leaving them in the ground, there's a risk of the roots rotting if temperatures fluctuate above and below freezing frequently, or the roots might get munched by critters, but we've had good luck with this method.

- Late January, when daylight hours grow longer, harvest any turnips or rutabagas that are still in the ground, because this change will cause them to turn woody as they prepare to make flowers and seeds.

'Early Moonbeam' watermelon

Watermelons

COMMON NAME: Watermelon

BOTANICAL NAME: *Citrullus lanatus*

PLANT FAMILY: Cucurbitaceae or cucurbit family

PLACE OF ORIGIN: Africa

Genetic research has recently revealed that domesticated watermelons probably originated in northeastern Africa, where the sweet fruits have white flesh and bright, striped rinds. These melons were highly prized in the Saharan Desert for their ability to retain water. Cultivation has been ongoing for at least four thousand years—ancient Egyptian art depicts the unmistakable oblong fruits on tables laid for feasting. Over one thousand varieties are now grown throughout the tropical and temperate world. Watermelons can be eaten fresh or pickled, and their rinds can likewise be pickled or cooked. Watermelon juice is extremely refreshing and makes fabulous frozen pops, especially with a squeeze of lime.

Sun requirement: Full sun

Nitrogen needs: Medium feeder

Trellis or infrastructure needs: For growing watermelons in a small space, trellising is a plus. These trellises need to be sturdy, and each fruit needs support as it ripens and gets heavy with sweet juice.

Temperature

Germination temperature range (soil temp):
Ideal: 75–95°F (24–35°C); min: 65°F (18°C)

Frost and cold hardiness: No

Heat tolerance: 95°F (35°C)

Spacing

Direct sow, transplant, or flexible: Flexible.
If transplanting, start in 4" pots.

Seed-sowing depth: ½"

Direct-sowing distance between seeds: 3 seeds in a cluster, with clusters 18" from each other in rows that are 48" from each other

Final spacing (thin to or transplant to): Leave the best-looking plant or two from each cluster with 18" between them in rows.

Timing

See the Timing Tables on page 339 for specific tips on growing watermelons in your region.

When to plant: Sow indoors right around the time of the last frost; sow outdoors once temperatures are good and hot.

Succession planting: Watermelons require a long, hot season, so we plant only one round of them. In warmer places you could do two or three rounds, with the first being transplants and subsequent rounds being direct sown.

One-time harvest vs. harvest window: Harvest window

Days to maturity (range): 70–90

Harvest season: Summer into fall

Common Pests and Diseases

Cucumber beetles, squash vine borers, black cutworms, squash bugs, fusarium wilt, powdery mildew, mosaic virus

Our Favorite Varieties

'Nancy' is a big, juicy, sweet, tender watermelon that we love for neighborhood watermelon feasts; it's too big to be practical for one or two eaters. **'Blacktail Mountain'** is a smaller, delicious, early-maturing and hardy watermelon with crisp, red flesh, bred to ripen in northern Idaho and able to produce mature fruits in most climates. **'Early Moonbean'** is an early-maturing, tasty, yellow-fleshed variety that is very adaptable.

STEPS TO GROWING

Planting

- If transplanting, sow watermelon seeds in 4" pots on heat mats as soon as temperatures are consistently above freezing. Transplant watermelon seedlings out into well-fertilized mounds or strips about 18" from one another in rows that are 48" apart.

- If direct sowing, wait until the soil has warmed (and temperatures have been above freezing for some weeks), and direct sow melon seeds in clusters of three or four, in well-fertilized mounds or strips at the same spacing previously mentioned.

Growing

- Keep seedlings/transplants well watered but not soggy. Once they're established, watermelons have low water needs, as they have deep roots.

- These tiny plants need a lot of space between them because the vines will grow quite large eventually, but at first they will be small, and it's important to keep the space between them weed free.

TIP: *We lay down black landscaping fabric and/or an organic mulch all around watermelons to prevent weeds as the plants begin to vine. Black plastic helps heat up the soil, which watermelons like.*

Harvesting

- Knowing when watermelons are ready to harvest can be tricky. Thump on the melon—if ready, it should produce a low, hollow sound (not a bright, high tone). If you press your fingers against the flesh and it gives a little (doesn't feel totally hard), the fruit is likely ripe.

- Harvest watermelons as they ripen to encourage immature fruits to also ripen.

- If you know the temperature will drop in the next 1½–2 months, you can pick off any new flowers or tiny, immature fruits that won't have time to ripen, which encourages the plant to send its energy into the remaining bigger fruits.

TIPS FOR COLDER-WEATHER GARDENERS

If you live in a climate that is not hot, it's a gamble whether watermelons (and muskmelons, for that matter) will mature and become sweet. Choosing early maturing varieties, mulching with a dark material, and growing in a greenhouse are all ways to increase chances of success. It can also be helpful to extend the season by starting watermelons in 4" pots a couple of weeks before it is warm enough to plant outside.

Another trick is to grow watermelon plants under row cover for the first part of their lives. This will create a warmer microclimate around the plants and will exclude some pests like cucumber beetles and vine borers. Just be sure to remove coverings during flowering so that insects can carry pollen to female flowers and set the stage for fruit formation.

Winter Squash and Pumpkins

COMMON NAMES AND TYPES: Winter squash, squash, pumpkins, calabaza

BOTANICAL NAMES: *Cucurbita maxima* (kabochas, buttercups, Hubbards, 'Red Kuri'); *C. pepo* (delicatas, acorns, pepitas, most pumpkins, zucchinis, and most summer squash); *C. moschata* (butternuts, Seminole pumpkins, cheeses, West Indian calabazas); *C. argyrosperma* (cushaws)

PLANT FAMILY: Cucurbitaceae or cucurbit family

PLACE OF ORIGIN: Mesoamerica and South America

A wide variety of winter squash and pumpkins have been cultivated across the Americas for around ten thousand years. They are a major staple crop of cultural significance to almost all native North and South American tribal peoples. The first cultivated squashes were grown for their big, nutritious, edible seeds, not their flesh. Today's squashes have flesh, seeds, flowers, and leaves that are all edible.

Each species of squash and pumpkin (listed above) has different qualities and characteristics. We find that those in the *C. moschata* (butternut group) are the most resistant to pests and diseases, including the infamous and devastating squash vine borer.

Sun requirement: Full sun

Nitrogen needs: Heavy feeders

Trellis or infrastructure needs: Bush varieties of winter squash have no need of extra support and will not use them, but if you are growing a vining variety—and most winter squash are—in a small space, they can benefit from a trellis. The chassa-howitska, or "hanging pumpkin," mentioned in the favorite varieties section was thus named because it did so well growing up trees. The trellis for these plants needs to be sturdy, and depending on the thickness of the fruit stem and the weight of the variety you are growing, each fruit may need support as it ripens and gets heavy.

Temperature

Germination temperature range (soil temp):
Ideal: 85–95°F (29–35°C); min: 60°F (15°C)

Frost and cold hardiness: No

Heat tolerance: 90°F (32°C)

Spacing

Direct sow, transplant, or flexible: Flexible; we prefer to direct sow. If transplanting, start in 4″ pots.

Seed-sowing depth: 1″

Direct-sowing distance between seeds: Five seeds per mound, 6″–12″ in rows

Final spacing (thin to or transplant to): 24″–36″ between plants in rows, three plants per mound, with 48″–72″ of space between mounds

Timing

See the Timing Tables on page 339 for specific tips on growing winter squash and pumpkins in your region.

When to plant: Sow indoors around the time of the last frost; sow outdoors once temperatures are good and hot.

Succession planting: Winter squash requires a long, hot season, so we plant only one round. In warmer places two or three rounds of quicker-maturing varieties, like spaghetti squash, are possible, with the first being transplants and subsequent rounds direct sown. We get plenty of yield from one planting, and these are a storage crop, so it's not necessary to plant more than one round unless you're planning to sell them.

One-time harvest vs. harvest window: One-time harvest (with optional squash blossom harvest, too)

Days to maturity (range): 85–120

Harvest season: Fall

Common Pests and Diseases

Cucumber beetles, aphids, squash vine borers, pickleworms, black cutworms, squash bugs, squash lady beetle, powdery mildew, blossom-end rot (actually a calcium deficiency), anthracnose

Our Favorite Varieties

In the warm, wet, buggy climate here in the mountains of North Carolina, with a shorter hot season, we have the best success with the *C. moschata* varieties of winter squash. These have relative resistance to squash vine borers and other bugs and issues.

We love the resilience and flavor of **'Seminole Pumpkin'** (chassa-howitska in the Creek language spoken by Seminole people, which means "hanging pumpkin"), originally from the area now called Florida. It produces numerous ribbed, pumpkin-shaped fruits on vines that can sprawl as far as 40'.

STEPS TO GROWING

Planting

- Direct sow winter squash seeds in groups of two or three, in well-fertilized mounds or strips 24"–48" from one another in a row, with 48"–72" between rows. If you have an especially short season, difficulty watering where the squash will grow, or other reasons to transplant, sow winter squash seeds in 4" pots on heat mats as soon as temperatures are consistently above freezing.

- If growing in pots, transplant seedlings after no more than 3 weeks, ideally closer to 2; they grow taproots that want to go directly to the center of the earth and will become easily rootbound and stunted for the rest of their lives if left in pots for too long.

- Keep seedlings/transplants watered, but don't overdo it once they have germinated; winter squash can grow very deep roots and seek out water, and they will do so if they're not overwatered.

Growing

- Once they're established, winter squash has low water needs because of those deep roots.

- These tiny plants need a lot of space between them because the vines will grow quite large eventually, but at first they will be small, and it is important to keep the space between them weed free.

  TIP: *We lay down black landscaping fabric and/or an organic mulch around the squash to prevent weeds as the plants begin to vine. Black plastic can also help heat up the soil, which squashes like.*

Our local landrace derived from 'Seminole Pumpkin' and 'Lofthouse Landrace Moschata'

DEVELOPING A NEW VARIETY

Sometimes many fruits on 'Seminole Pumpkin' won't ripen in our area, so Chloe has been cross-breeding it (in a very unscientific, folk-style-plant-selection kind of way) with faster maturing moschatas, so we have a local landrace developing! Natalie and other community members have picked up Chloe's new landrace and have been continuing to select for the most disease resistant, earliest maturing, and tastiest fruits in our specific conditions.

This has been a wonderfully successful experiment in low-key localized plant breeding. Natalie recently harvested more than one hundred pounds of this variety that was planted in one 3×12 garden bed. Admittedly the vines sprawled to crawl on nearby bushes, but the harvest was still extremely impressive.

Winter Squash and Pumpkins *continued*

- Wrap the stems of your squash plants with aluminum foil or pantyhose when they have four to eight true leaves to prevent attacks from squash vine borers. This is especially important when growing *C. maxima* or *C. pepo*, which are more susceptible to these devastating pests.

TIP: *If you notice withering leaves, investigate the base of the main stem of the plant. Lesions there, with mushy pith erupting from them, suggest that vine borer larvae are feasting within. You can sometimes salvage plants by injecting Bacillus thuringiensis (Bt) directly into the lesions using a syringe.*

Harvesting

- Winter squashes are ripe when their skin is completely hard (can't be broken or deeply dented with a fingernail) and when the stems connecting fruits to vines have become hard, dry, and brown or tan.

- If you know the temperature will drop in the next 1½–2 months, pick off any new flowers or tiny, immature fruits that won't have time to ripen; this encourages the plant to send its energy into the remaining bigger fruits.

TIP: *Many winter squash have tasty, zucchini-like immature fruits that are worth eating; zucchini and summer squash are just varieties of these same species (mostly C. pepo) that have been bred to be tasty at the immature stage. Squash flowers are a delicious ingredient in many Mexican and Guatemalan dishes. It's best to harvest male (pollen-containing) squash flowers earlier in the season rather than female (ovary-containing, fruit-producing) flowers. At the end of the season, all flowers are fair game.*

- Cure winter squash for 7–10 days in warm, dry conditions; this sweetens and improves storage life. Cut fruits from the vines and let them lie in the sun, as long as no rain is predicted. Otherwise, bring them into a house or barn that gets good ventilation and will remain above 70°F (21°C).

Some beautiful specimens of our local landrace of *C. moschata*

Zucchini and Summer Squash

COMMON NAMES AND TYPES: Summer squash, zucchini, crookneck, pattypan, courgette, baby marrow

BOTANICAL NAMES: *Cucurbita pepo* (zucchinis, yellow straightnecks and crooknecks, pattypans, most summer squash); *C. moschata* ('Tromboncino')

PLANT FAMILY: Cucurbitaceae or cucurbit family

PLACE OF ORIGIN: Mesoamerica

Zucchini produces food in a very serious way, so much so that unless you only plant a few plants, you will likely have a surplus that you'll need to find a home for. Zucchini is a type of summer squash, which can be any squash that is harvested before the seeds are mature. All summer squashes have their ancestry in Mexico and Central America, and different varieties have been developed and are cultivated in many parts of the world. The word *zucchini* has Italian origins, and many of the zucchini varieties we know and love were bred in Italy, a country that has given a culinary embrace to many Mesoamerican crops.

Sun requirement: Full sun

Nitrogen needs: Heavy feeders

Trellis or infrastructure needs: Not necessary, unless you're growing 'Tromboncino', which is wild and viny and happily (and elegantly) climbs a trellis. An arched-over welded-wire cattle panel works nicely for this squash; its trombone-shaped fruits hang down in a pleasing and easy-to-harvest way.

Temperature

Germination temperature range (soil temp): Ideal: 85–95°F (29–35°C); min: 60°F (15°C)

Frost and cold hardiness: No

Heat tolerance: 90°F (32°C)

'Costata Romanesca' zucchini

Spacing

Direct sow, transplant, or flexible: Flexible; we prefer to direct sow. If transplanting, start in 4″ pots.

Seed-sowing depth: 1″

Direct-sowing distance between seeds: Three to five seeds per mound, or two to four seeds every 18″–24″ in rows

Final spacing (thin to or transplant to): 18″–24″ between plants in rows, one to three plants per mound with 36″–48″ between mounds

Timing

See the Timing Tables on page 339 for specific tips on growing zucchini and summer squash in your region.

When to plant: Sow indoors around the time of the last frost; sow outdoors once temperatures are good and hot.

Zucchini and Summer Squash *continued*

Succession planting: Successions can be planted as close as 1 month apart throughout the summer season, up until about 2 months before the first frost. We find that one or two rounds is good enough, as these are very generous plants with a long harvest window.

One-time harvest vs. harvest window: Long harvest window

Days to maturity (range): 45–60

Harvest season: Fall

Common Pests and Diseases

Cucumber beetles, aphids, squash vine borers, pickleworms, black cutworms, squash bugs, powdery mildew, blossom-end rot (actually a calcium deficiency), anthracnose

Our Favorite Varieties

For flavor, vigor, beauty, and high yields, we love '**Costata Romanesco**', a deeply ribbed and striped green heirloom summer squash that takes a little longer to start producing than most hybrids but makes tons of fruits with a rich, dense, nutty flavor, even when they've grown fairly large.

'**Tromboncino**' is a great choice if you have trouble with bugs, since it's a *C. moschata* variety and resistant to some of the plagues of *C. pepos*. Be sure to harvest this one when fruits are fairly small and still tender.

For later-season plantings, when pest and disease pressure is highest (at least where we live), we turn toward a hybrid gray-green zucchini called '**Mexicana**', a workhorse that keeps giving even in the boggy conditions of later summer; it's also quite tasty.

STEPS TO GROWING

Planting

- Direct sow summer squash in groups of three to five, in well-fertilized mounds or in groups that are 24"–36" from one another in a row, with 36"–48" between rows. If you have an especially short season, difficulty watering where you'll be growing squash, or other reasons to transplant, sow summer squash seeds in 4" pots on heat mats as soon as temperatures are consistently above freezing.

- If growing in pots, transplant seedlings after no more than 3 weeks, ideally closer to 2; they grow taproots that want to sink into the center of the earth and will become easily rootbound and stunted for the rest of their lives if left in pots for too long.

- Keep seedlings/transplants watered, but don't overdo it once they have germinated; summer squash can grow very deep roots and seek out water and will do so if they're not overwatered.

Growing

- Once established, summer squashes have low water needs because of their deep roots.

- Keep the space between plants weeded and mulch as soon as the plants reach 6"–8" tall.

- Wrap the stems of your squash plants with aluminum foil or pantyhose when they have four to eight true leaves to prevent squash vine borers.

- Monitor for squash beetles, squash bugs, and other pests, and either hand-pick and kill them (squish or drown in soapy water) or treat them with an organic spray.

  TIP: *Covering young plants with row cover can reduce the risk of some pests, but remember to uncover them when they start to flower so that pollinators can work their magic.*

Harvesting

- Be sure to harvest summer squash and zucchini at the right stage, and don't let them get too big. Get an idea of the ideal harvest size for the variety you're growing and harvest every couple of days once they're producing. Generally the smaller the squash, the more tender and delicious, although underripe squash isn't as tasty, so there is a sweet spot.

- Harvest any overmature fruits along with perfectly sized ones to encourage continued flowering and fruiting. Overripe summer squash is usable in things like zucchini bread and crema de calabacín soup.

- Eventually the plants run out of steam and/or get taken down by pests and/or diseases. Wow, summer squash gives so much! Say thank you and then remove the plants, and either compost them if they didn't have a lot of pest issues or burn them if they did.

Timing Tables

These wonderful tools will help you anticipate and plan what to do with each vegetable each month, in your specific region in the United States. Based on frost date information, as well as our knowledge of gardening in different regions, the tables are winnowed down to four climate types, which obviously cannot account for all locations. Elevation also plays a major role in climate and therefore planting times. This information is meant as a jumping-off point, not an exact science.

Timing, temperatures, and soil conditions vary from place to place, so make a point to talk to hyper-local gardeners and farmers for the most accurate information for your area.

Southern Florida, Hawaii, and most of Alaska are not included in these tables. That is because these areas have extreme climates, and gardening there has specificities that are beyond the scope of this book.

These tables apply to outdoor growing only (not greenhouses or high tunnels, but including the use of floating row cover for frost protection). We list multiple opportunities to plant many of these crops. Our intention is to offer you a range of possibilities for when you can plant in your region; this can guide succession planting, but we are not advising that you plant every time it's possible, unless you are growing commercially.

Watering is not included here because irrigation needs vary based on rainfall and other factors that differ by year and bioregion. All plants should be watered after sowing and transplanting, and throughout the season as needed. Please see page 200 for information about watering.

Climate Regions

CLIMATE TYPE	LAST FROST DATE*	FIRST FROST DATE*	APPLICABLE STATES/REGIONS IN THE US
Cold	June 1	Sept 15	Connecticut, Colorado (high-elevation areas), Illinois (northern), Indiana (northern), Iowa, Maine, Massachusetts, Michigan, Minnesota (northern), Montana (most areas), Nevada (parts in the north), New Hampshire, New York (upstate), North Dakota (eastern), Ohio (northern), Rhode Island, South Dakota, Utah (high-elevation areas), Vermont, Wisconsin
Temperate	May 1	Oct 30	Arkansas (northern and central), Arizona (high-elevation areas), California (northern and coastal), Delaware, Georgia (mountainous areas in the north), Kansas (eastern), Kentucky (mountainous areas), Maryland, Nebraska (eastern), New Jersey, New Mexico (high-elevation areas), New York (southern non-mountainous areas), North Carolina (mountainous areas), Oklahoma (northern and eastern), Oregon (western), South Carolina (mountainous areas), Tennessee (eastern and mountainous areas), Utah (northern), Virginia (southern and lowland), Washington (western), West Virginia (mountainous areas)
Warm	April 1	Nov 15	Alabama (non-mountainous areas), Arkansas (central and western), California (lower-elevation northern), Georgia (non-mountainous areas), Kansas (parts of central and southern), Kentucky (central and lowland), Mississippi (non-mountainous areas), Missouri, Nebraska (parts of central and southern), North Carolina (Piedmont region), Oklahoma (southern), South Carolina (Piedmont region), Tennessee (western), Texas (northern)
Hot	Feb 25	Nov 30	Alabama (southern and coastal), Arizona (low elevation areas), California (southern), Georgia (southern and coastal), Florida (most of), Mississippi (southern and coastal), Nevada (southern), New Mexico (low-elevation areas), Texas (southern), Utah (southern)

*Some sources refer to average last frost dates, and some refer to the date when frost danger has completely passed. Here we draw on both and add to them our experience and that of other growers. Keep in mind that climate change adds a lot of variability. See page 194 for more on timing.

WHAT TO DO EACH MONTH IN A Cold Climate* Garden

VEGETABLE	JANUARY	FEBRUARY	MARCH	APRIL	MAY	
Arugula	Rest	Rest	Rest	Direct sowing	Direct sowing, thinning, weeding, mulching	
Basil	Rest	Rest	Rest	Sowing in pots or flats indoors	Caring for plants in pots	
Beans	Rest	Rest	Rest	Rest	Rest	
Beets and Chard	Rest	Rest	Rest	Rest	Bed preparation, direct sowing or sowing in pots or flats indoors, optional first round of thinning and weeding	
Broccoli and Cauliflower	Rest	Rest	Sowing in pots or flats indoors	Sowing in pots or flats indoors, caring for plants in pots	Transplanting, mulching, fertilizing	
Cabbage	Rest	Rest	Sowing in pots or flats indoors	Sowing in pots or flats indoors, caring for plants in pots	Transplanting, mulching, fertilizing	
Carrots	Rest	Rest	Rest	Rest	Bed preparation, direct sowing	
Cilantro	Rest	Rest	Rest	Rest	Bed preparation, direct sowing	
Corn	Rest	Rest	Rest	Rest	Rest	
Cucumbers	Rest	Rest	Rest	Rest	Sowing in pots indoors	
Dill	Rest	Rest	Rest	Rest	Bed preparation and direct sowing later in the month	
Eggplant	Rest	Rest	Sowing in pots or flats indoors	Caring for plants in pots	Caring for plants in pots	
Garlic	Watching and waiting	Watching and waiting	Watching and waiting	Possibly fertilizing and remulching	Possibly fertilizing and remulching	
Kale and Collards	Watching and waiting	Watching and waiting	Sowing in pots or flats indoors, overwintered crop beginning to grow again	Direct sowing or transplanting, mulching, fertilizing, harvest of overwintered crop	Harvesting, pest management for spring crop, end of season for overwintered crop	
Lettuce	Rest	Sowing in pots or flats indoors	Sowing in pots or flats indoors, caring for plants in pots	Bed preparation, transplanting later in the month	Direct sowing, transplanting, weeding, possibly mulching	

JUNE	JULY	AUGUST	SEPTEMBER	OCTOBER	NOVEMBER	DECEMBER
Harvesting	Direct sowing for fall harvests, harvesting spring crop	Direct sowing, thinning, weeding, mulching	Harvesting, frost protection	Harvesting, frost protection	Rest	Rest
Bed preparation, transplanting, weeding, mulching	Pruning, harvesting, fertilizing	Pruning, harvesting	End of season	Rest	Rest	Rest
Bed preparation, direct sowing	Bed preparation, direct sowing, thinning, weeding, mulching, trellising (pole beans)	Pest and disease management, maybe harvesting	Pest and disease management, harvesting	End of season for green beans, harvesting, winnowing, storage of dry beans	Rest	Rest
Thinning, weeding, mulching, sowing successions	Harvesting, thinning, weeding, mulching	Harvesting	Harvesting, end of season	Rest	Rest	Rest
Harvesting, fertilizing, pest management, sowing in pots or flats for fall harvest	Harvesting, pest management, sowing in pots or flats for fall harvest, caring for plants in pots	Harvesting, pest management, transplanting for fall crop	Harvesting, frost protection	Harvesting, end of season	Rest	Rest
Harvesting, fertilizing, pest management, sowing in pots or flats for fall harvest	Harvesting, pest management, sowing in pots or flats for fall harvest, caring for plants in pots	Harvesting, pest management, transplanting for fall crop	Harvesting, frost protection	Harvesting, end of season	Rest	Rest
Thinning, weeding, mulching	Harvesting spring crop, direct sowing for fall	Harvesting, thinning, weeding, mulching	Harvesting	Harvesting	Harvesting	Harvesting, end of season
Bed preparation, direct sowing	Harvesting, sowing successions, thinning, weeding, mulching	Harvesting, sowing successions, thinning, weeding, mulching	Harvesting, frost protection	Harvesting, frost protection	End of season	Rest
Bed preparation, direct sowing	Sowing successions, thinning, mulching, fertilizing	Harvesting sweet corn	Harvesting dry corn	Rest	Rest	Rest
Direct sowing, transplanting	Trellising, thinning, weeding, mulching, pest management	Harvesting, weeding, mulching, pest management	Harvesting, end of season	Rest	Rest	Rest
Direct sowing, thinning, weeding	Thinning, weeding, mulching, harvesting, sowing successions	Thinning, mulching, harvesting, sowing successions	Harvesting, end of season	Rest	Rest	Rest
Transplanting, mulching, trellising, pest management	Pest management, fertilizing	Harvesting, pest management, fertilizing, maybe end of season	End of season	Rest	Rest	Rest
Harvesting scapes	Harvesting and curing, optional braiding of bulbs	Rest	Rest	Planting and mulching	Watching and waiting	Watching and waiting
Harvesting, pest management	End of season for spring crop, sowing in pots or flats for fall and overwintering	Transplanting for fall and overwintering	Transplanting, mulching, fertilizing, pest management	Harvesting and frost protection	Harvesting, frost protection	Harvesting, frost protection
Transplanting and direct sowing, thinning, mulching, fertilizing	Harvesting, sowing successions, thinning, mulching, fertilizing	Harvesting, sowing cold-tolerant varieties for fall	Harvesting, frost protection	Harvesting, frost protection	Rest	Rest

VEGETABLE	JANUARY	FEBRUARY	MARCH	APRIL	MAY	
Muskmelons	Rest	Rest	Rest	Sowing in pots indoors	Caring for plants in pots	
Okra	Rest	Rest	Rest	Sowing in pots or flats indoors	Caring for plants in pots	
Onions	Rest	Sowing in open flats indoors	Caring for plants in flats	Caring for plants in flats, ordering plants if you didn't start your own, maybe transplanting outdoors	Bed preparation, transplanting, fertilizing	
Parsnips	Sweetening under mulch	Sweetening under mulch	Sweetening under mulch, harvesting when first leaves emerge	Rest	Bed preparation, direct sowing	
Peas	Rest	Rest	Bed preparation and direct sowing if the ground thaws	Bed preparation and direct sowing	Thinning, trellising, weeding, mulching, direct sowing	
Peppers and Chiles	Rest	Rest	Sowing in pots or flats indoors	Caring for plants in pots	Caring for plants in pots, transplanting into 4-inch pots, fertilizing	
Potatoes	Rest	Rest	Rest	Rest	Bed preparation, planting for summer use and storage	
Radishes	Rest	Rest	Rest	Bed preparation, direct sowing, thinning, weeding	Thinning, weeding, mulching, harvesting, sowing successions	
Spinach	Watching and waiting	Watching and waiting	Watching and waiting	Bed preparation, direct sowing, harvesting overwintered crop	Direct sowing, thinning, mulching, weeding, fertilizing	
Sweet Potatoes	Rest	Rest	Rest	Rest	Bed preparation, growing slips	
Tomatoes	Rest	Rest	Rest	Sowing in pots or flats indoors	Caring for plants in pots	
Turnips and Rutabagas	Rest	Rest	Rest	Rest	Bed preparation, direct sowing salad turnips	
Watermelons	Rest	Rest	Rest	Sowing in pots indoors	Caring for plants in pots	
Winter Squash and Pumpkins	Rest	Rest	Rest	Rest	Sowing in pots or flats indoors	
Zucchini and Summer Squash	Rest	Rest	Rest	Rest	Sowing in pots or flats indoors	

JUNE	JULY	AUGUST	SEPTEMBER	OCTOBER	NOVEMBER	DECEMBER
Transplanting early in the month, mulching, weeding, fertilizing	Weeding, mulching, fertilizing	Harvesting	Harvesting, end of season	Rest	Rest	Rest
Transplanting, weeding, mulching	Harvesting at the end of the month	Harvesting	End of season	Rest	Rest	Rest
Weeding, mulching, fertilizing	Fertilizing	Harvesting, curing	Harvesting, curing	Rest	Rest	Rest
Weeding, thinning, mulching	Weeding, thinning, mulching, fertilizing	Growing	Harvesting or allowing to overwinter and get sweeter	Harvesting or allowing to overwinter and get sweeter	Harvesting or allowing to overwinter and get sweeter	Sweetening under mulch
Harvesting	Harvesting, end of season for spring planting, direct sowing for fall harvest	Thinning, weeding, trellising	Harvesting	Harvesting, end of season	Rest	Rest
Bed preparation, transplanting, mulching	Fertilizing, trellising, pest and disease management	Harvesting, pest and disease management	End of season	Rest	Rest	Rest
Hilling	Weeding, pest management	Harvesting	Harvesting later plantings and later varieties	Rest	Rest	Rest
Harvesting	Direct sowing for fall crop	Direct sowing for fall crop, thinning, weeding, mulching, pest management	Thinning, weeding, mulching, harvesting	Harvesting, end of season	Rest	Rest
Thinning, mulching, harvesting	Harvesting, end of spring season	Direct sowing for overwintering and early spring harvest	Direct sowing for overwintering and early spring harvest, thinning, mulching, fertilizing	Mulching and frost protection for overwintering	Watching and waiting	Watching and waiting
Planting slips, mulching, weeding	Weeding, mulching	Harvesting some greens	Harvesting greens and roots, curing	Harvesting, curing, end of season	Rest	Rest
Transplanting, pruning, mulching, fertilizing, trellising	Pruning, trellising, pest and disease management	Pruning, trellising, pest and disease management, possibly harvesting toward end of month	Pruning, pest and disease management, harvesting	Harvesting, end of season	Rest	Rest
Direct sowing for fall	Thinning, weeding, mulching, sowing successions of turnips	Thinning, weeding, mulching, harvesting, sowing successions of turnips	Thinning, weeding, mulching, harvesting	Harvesting, mulching, frost protection	Harvesting, frost protection, end of season	Rest
Fertilizing, weeding, mulching	Fertilizing, weeding, mulching, harvesting early varieties	Harvesting	Harvesting, end of season	Rest	Rest	Rest
Direct sowing, mulching	Mulching, weeding, fertilizing, pest and disease management	Fertilizing, pest and disease management	Harvesting, curing	Harvesting, curing, end of season	Rest	Rest
Bed preparation, direct sowing, sowing successions in pots or flats, transplanting	Pest and disease management, weeding, mulching, transplanting successions, maybe first harvest	Weeding, mulching, pest and disease management, harvesting	End of season	Rest	Rest	Rest

WHAT TO DO EACH MONTH IN A Temperate Climate* Garden

VEGETABLE	JANUARY	FEBRUARY	MARCH	APRIL	MAY	
Arugula	Harvesting	Harvesting	Harvesting, direct sowing	Direct sowing, thinning, weeding	Harvesting	
Basil	Rest	Rest	Sowing in pots or flats indoors	Caring for plants in pots	Bed preparation, transplanting, weeding, mulching	
Beans	Rest	Rest	Rest	Bed preparation, direct sowing, frost protection as needed	Bed preparation, direct sowing successions, thinning, weeding, mulching	
Beets and Chard	Rest	Rest	Rest	Bed preparation, direct sowing or sowing in pots or flats, first round of thinning and weeding	Direct sowing or sowing in pots or flats, thinning, mulching	
Broccoli and Cauliflower	Rest	Sowing in pots or flats indoors	Sowing in pots or flats indoors, transplanting, frost protection as needed	Transplanting, mulching, fertilizing, frost protection as needed	Growth, harvesting, pest management	
Cabbage	Harvesting in some places	Sowing in pots or flats indoors	Sowing in pots or flats indoors, transplanting, frost protection as needed	Transplanting, mulching, fertilizing, frost protection as needed	Growth, harvesting, pest management	
Carrots	Harvesting	Harvesting, end of season for fall crop	Bed preparation, direct sowing if soil has consistently warmed enough	Bed preparation, direct sowing, thinning	Thinning, weeding, mulching	
Cilantro	Frost protection and harvesting	Frost protection and harvesting	Harvesting, sowing in pots or flats indoors	End of season of fall crop, bed preparation and direct sowing or transplanting of spring crop	Thinning, weeding, harvesting, bed preparation, and sowing successions	
Corn	Rest	Rest	Rest	Rest	Bed preparation, direct sowing	
Cucumbers	Rest	Rest	Rest	Direct sowing, or sowing in pots and transplanting	Sowing successions, pest management, and trellising	
Dill	Rest	Rest	Rest	Rest	Bed preparation, direct sowing	
Eggplant	Rest	Rest	Sowing in pots or flats indoors	Tending to plants in pots, transplanting into 4" pots	Bed preparation, transplanting into quart or gallon pots, transplanting out, pest management	
Garlic	Watching and waiting	Watching and waiting	Watching and waiting	Fertilizing and remulching	Fertilizing and remulching	
Kale and Collards	Harvesting, frost protection	Harvesting over-wintered crop, sowing spring crop in pots or flats indoors	Sowing in pots or flats indoors, end of season for overwintered crop	Direct sowing or transplanting, mulching, fertilizing, frost protection as needed	Growth, harvesting, pest management	
Lettuce	Rest	Sowing in pots or flats indoors	Sowing in pots or flats indoors	Direct sowing, transplanting	Direct sowing or transplanting successions, thinning, mulching	

JUNE	JULY	AUGUST	SEPTEMBER	OCTOBER	NOVEMBER	DECEMBER
End of season	Rest	Direct sowing for fall and winter harvests	Direct sowing, thinning, weeding	Harvesting, frost protection	Harvesting, frost protection	Harvesting, frost protection
Pruning, harvesting,	Pruning, harvesting, fertilizing	Pruning, harvesting, fertilizing	End of season	Rest	Rest	Rest
Trellising (pole beans)	Pest management, harvesting	Harvesting, pest management, possibly end of season	End of season for green beans, harvesting, winnowing, storage of dry beans	Rest	Rest	Rest
Harvesting, thinning, mulching	Harvesting, direct sowing for fall and winter harvests	Harvesting, end of season for spring planting, direct sowing for fall and winter harvests	Thinning, mulching	Harvesting, thinning, mulching	Harvesting, end of season	Rest
Harvesting, pest management, end of season for spring crop	Sowing for fall/winter harvest in pots or flats	Caring for plants in pots, pest management, transplanting	Transplanting, mulching, fertilizing, pest management	Harvesting, frost protection	Harvesting, frost protection	End of season
Growth, harvesting, pest management, end of season for spring crop	Sowing for fall/winter harvest in pots or flats	Caring for plants in pots, pest management, transplanting	Transplanting, mulching, fertilizing, pest management	Harvesting, frost protection	Harvesting, frost protection	Harvesting, frost protection
Harvesting	Harvesting, end of spring crop, direct sowing fall crop	Thinning, mulching	Growth	Harvesting, frost protection	Harvesting, frost protection	Harvesting, frost protection
Harvesting, sowing successions	Harvesting, sowing successions	Harvesting, sowing successions	Sowing for winter	Harvesting, sowing for winter at beginning of month	Harvesting, frost protection	Harvesting, frost protection
Sowing successions (sweet corn only), thinning, mulching, fertilizing	Thinning, fertilizing, maybe harvesting sweet corn	Harvesting sweet corn	Harvesting dry corn	Harvesting dry corn and end of season	Rest	Rest
Weeding, mulching, trellising, pest management	Harvesting, pest management	Harvesting, end of season	Rest	Rest	Rest	Rest
Thinning, mulching, harvesting, sowing successions	Thinning, mulching, harvesting, sowing successions	Sowing for fall and winter harvests in some places with milder winters	Harvesting	Harvesting and possibly end of season	Harvesting and end of season	Rest
Planting, pest management	Pest management, fertilizing	Harvesting, pest management, fertilizing	Harvesting, pest management, maybe end of season	End of season	Rest	Rest
Harvesting scapes, possibly harvesting bulbs	Harvesting and optional braiding bulbs, curing	Rest	Rest	Planting and mulching	Planting and mulching	Planting and mulching
Harvesting, pest management, possibly end of spring crop	Direct sowing or sowing in pots or flats for fall/winter harvest, end of spring crop	Direct sowing or sowing in pots or flats, transplanting, pest management	Weeding, mulching, fertilizing, pest management	Harvesting, frost protection	Harvesting, frost protection	Harvesting, frost protection
Harvesting, sowing successions, thinning, mulching	Harvesting, sowing successions, fertilizing, thinning, mulching	Harvesting, sowing successions, sowing winter varieties for transplant, fertilizing, thinning, mulching	Direct sowing or transplanting winter varieties	Harvesting, frost protection	Harvesting, frost protection	Harvesting, frost protection

VEGETABLE	JANUARY	FEBRUARY	MARCH	APRIL	MAY	
Muskmelons	Rest	Rest	Rest	Sowing in pots indoors	Sowing in pots indoors, bed/mound prep and transplanting	
Okra	Rest	Rest	Rest	Sowing in pots or flats indoors if you plan to transplant	Bed preparation, direct sowing, transplanting	
Onions	Sowing in flats indoors to grow your own starts	Sowing in flats indoors, tending plants in flats, or ordering plants or sets	Bed preparation, transplanting, mulching if ground is dry enough	Bed preparation, transplanting, mulching	Weeding, mulching, fertilizing	
Parsnips	Harvesting	Harvesting, end of season for fall/winter crop	Rest	Bed preparation, direct sowing	Bed preparation, direct sowing, weeding, thinning	
Peas	Rest	Bed preparation and direct sowing	Thinning, weeding, direct sowing	Thinning, trellising, sowing successions in areas with cooler summers	Harvesting, end of season in places with warmer summers. In places with cooler summers: harvesting, trellising, sowing successions, thinning	
Peppers and Chiles	Rest	Sowing in pots or flats indoors	Sowing in pots or flats indoors, caring for transplants	Transplanting into 4" pots	Bed preparation, transplanting, mulching	
Potatoes	Rest	Rest	Bed preparation, planting for earlier harvest	Bed preparation, planting for earlier harvest, hilling, weeding, mulching	Bed preparation, planting for later harvest, hilling, weeding, mulching	
Radishes	Harvesting, end of season	Rest	Bed preparation, direct sowing	Direct sowing, thinning, weeding, mulching, pest management, harvesting of fast varieties	Harvesting, end of season	
Spinach	Rest	Rest	Bed preparation, direct sowing	Direct sowing, thinning, mulching	Thinning, mulching, harvesting	
Sweet Potatoes	Rest	Rest	Rest, ordering slips if you don't plan to grow them	Growing slips	Growing and planting out slips	
Tomatoes	Rest	Rest	Sowing in pots or flats indoors	Transplanting into 4" pots	Bed preparation, transplanting, pruning, trellising	
Turnips and Rutabagas	Harvesting, frost protection	Harvesting, frost protection	Harvesting, end of season, sowing salad turnips for spring harvest	Weeding, thinning, mulching, harvesting salad turnips	Harvesting salad turnips	
Watermelons	Rest	Rest	Rest	Sowing in pots indoors	Bed/mound preparation, transplanting	
Winter Squash and Pumpkins	Rest	Rest	Rest	Sowing in pots indoors if you plan to transplant	Bed/mound preparation, transplanting or direct sowing, pest management	
Zucchini and Summer Squash	Rest	Rest	Rest	Sowing in pots indoors if you plan to transplant	Bed preparation, direct sowing, sowing in pots, transplanting, pest management	

JUNE	JULY	AUGUST	SEPTEMBER	OCTOBER	NOVEMBER	DECEMBER
Fertilizing, weeding, mulching	Fertilizing, weeding, harvesting some varieties	Harvesting	Harvesting, end of season	Rest	Rest	Rest
Thinning, mulching, fertilizing	Harvesting, pest management	Harvesting	Harvesting	End of season	Rest	Rest
Fertilizing	Harvesting, curing	Rest	Rest	Rest	Rest	Rest
Weeding, thinning, mulching, fertilizing	Growing	Growing	Growing	Harvesting	Harvesting	Harvesting
Rest in places with warmer summers. In places with cooler summers: harvesting, sowing successions, thinning, trellising	Sowing successions in places with cooler summers	Thinning, weeding, trellising in places with cooler summers	Harvesting in places with cooler summers	Harvesting in places with cooler summers, end of season	Rest	Rest
Bed preparation, transplanting, fertilizing	Harvesting, trellising, fertilizing	Harvesting, trellising, pest and disease management	Harvesting, pest and disease management	Harvesting, end of season	Rest	Rest
Hilling, weeding, mulching, harvesting early crop	Hilling, weeding, mulching, harvesting early crop	Harvesting, storing, end of season	Harvesting, storing, end of season	Rest	Rest	Rest
End of season	Rest	Bed preparation, direct sowing	Thinning, weeding, mulching, pest management	Thinning, weeding, mulching, harvesting	Harvesting, mulching, frost protection	Harvesting, frost protection, end of season
Harvesting, end of season	Rest	Direct sowing for fall and winter harvests	Direct sowing, thinning, mulching, fertilizing	Direct sowing, thinning, mulching, fertilizing, harvesting	Harvesting, frost protection	Harvesting, frost protection, end of season
Planting out slips, weeding, mulching	Weeding, tending	Harvesting greens	Harvesting early varieties in some areas, curing	Harvesting, curing, end of season	Rest	Rest
Pruning, transplanting successions, trellising, pest and disease management	Pruning, trellising, pest and disease management, early harvesting	Pruning, trellising, pest and disease management, harvesting	Harvesting, possibly end of season	End of season	Rest	Rest
Rest	Bed preparation, direct sowing for rutabagas	Direct sowing for turnips and rutabagas	Thinning, weeding, mulching, fertilizing	Thinning, weeding, mulching, harvesting some varieties	Harvesting, frost protection	Harvesting, frost protection
Weeding, mulching, fertilizing	Weeding, mulching, fertilizing, harvesting some varieties	Harvesting	Harvesting, end of season	Rest	Rest	Rest
Weeding, mulching, pest management	Weeding, mulching, pest management	Pest management	Harvesting, curing, end of season	Rest	Rest	Rest
Sowing successions, pest and disease management, thinning, fertilizing, harvesting	Pest and disease management, harvesting	Pest and disease management, harvesting, possibly end of season	Harvesting, end of season	Rest	Rest	Rest

WHAT TO DO EACH MONTH IN A **Warm Climate* Garden**

VEGETABLE	JANUARY	FEBRUARY	MARCH	APRIL	MAY		
Arugula	Harvesting	Harvesting, sowing in pots or flats indoors	Direct sowing or transplanting, thinning, weeding	Harvesting, weeding, thinning, mulching	Harvesting, end of season		
Basil	Rest	Sowing in pots or flats indoors	Sowing in pots or flats indoors, caring for transplants	Bed preparation, transplanting, weeding, mulching, sowing successions	Pruning, harvesting, fertilizing, transplanting successions		
Beans	Rest	Rest	Rest	Bed preparation, direct sowing	Bed preparation, direct sowing, thinning, weeding, mulching, trellising (pole beans), pest management		
Beets and Chard	Rest	Rest	Bed preparation, direct sowing or sowing in pots or flats indoors	Direct sowing or sowing in pots or flats indoors, thinning, weeding, mulching	Harvesting, thinning, weeding, mulching		
Broccoli and Cauliflower	End of season for fall/winter harvest, sowing in pots or flats indoors for spring planting	Sowing in pots or flats indoors for spring planting	Transplanting, mulching, fertilizing	Harvesting, pest management	Harvesting, pest management, possibly end of season		
Cabbage	End of season for fall/winter harvest, sowing in pots or flats indoors for spring planting	Sowing in pots or flats indoors for spring planting	Transplanting, mulching, fertilizing	Harvesting, pest management	Harvesting, pest management		
Carrots	Harvesting	Harvesting	Bed preparation, direct sowing	Bed preparation, direct sowing, thinning, weeding	Thinning, weeding, mulching, harvesting		
Cilantro	Harvesting	Harvesting	Bed preparation, direct sowing or sowing in pots or flats and transplanting	Bed preparation, direct sowing, sowing successions	Harvesting, sowing successions		
Corn	Rest	Rest	Rest	Bed preparation, direct sowing	Sowing successions, thinning, fertilizing		
Cucumbers	Rest	Rest	Sowing in pots indoors	Direct sowing, transplanting those already started in pots	Sowing successions, trellising, weeding, mulching, fertilizing		
Dill	Rest	Rest	Rest	Bed preparation, direct sowing	Thinning, mulching, weeding, harvesting, sowing successions		
Eggplant	Rest	Sowing in pots or flats indoors	Sowing in pots or flats indoors, transplanting into 4" pots	Caring for plants in pots, transplanting into 4" pots or quart or gallon pots	Transplanting, pest management		
Garlic	Watching and waiting	Watching and waiting	Watching and waiting	Possibly weeding, fertilizing, remulching	Possibly weeding, fertilizing, remulching, harvesting scapes		
Kale and Collards	Harvesting, frost protection, sowing in pots or flats indoors	Transplanting out, direct sowing, end of season for overwintered crop	Harvesting, pest management	Harvesting, pest management	Harvesting, possibly end of season for spring crop		
Lettuce	Harvesting, frost protection, sowing in pots or flats indoors	Sowing in pots or flats indoors	Direct sowing, transplanting, sowing successions, harvesting	Sowing successions, weeding, thinning, mulching, fertilizing	Harvesting, sowing successions, thinning, mulching, fertilizing		

JUNE	JULY	AUGUST	SEPTEMBER	OCTOBER	NOVEMBER	DECEMBER
Rest	Rest	Direct sowing or sowing in pots or flats	Sowing successions	Harvesting, frost protection	Harvesting, frost protection	Harvesting, frost protection
Pruning, harvesting, fertilizing, direct sowing successions	Thinning, weeding, mulching, fertilizing	Pruning, harvesting, fertilizing	Pruning, harvesting, fertilizing	Harvesting, end of season	Rest	Rest
Pest and disease management, harvesting	Sowing successions, pest and disease management, harvesting	Thinning, weeding, mulching, trellising (pole beans), pest and disease management, end of spring harvest	Trellising (pole beans), pest and disease management	End of season for green beans, harvesting, winnowing, storage of dry beans	Rest	Rest
Rest	Rest	Bed preparation and direct sowing late in month	Thinning, mulching	Harvesting, thinning, mulching	Harvesting, end of season	Rest
End of spring crop	Rest	Sowing in pots or flats for fall crop	Bed preparation, transplanting, pest management	Transplanting, mulching, weeding, fertilizing, pest management	Harvesting, frost protection	Harvesting, frost protection
End of spring crop	Rest	Sowing in pots or flats for fall crop	Bed preparation, transplanting, pest management	Transplanting, mulching, weeding, fertilizing, pest management	Harvesting, frost protection	Harvesting, frost protection
Harvesting, end of season for spring crop	Rest	Direct sowing fall crop	Thinning, mulching	Harvesting some varieties	Harvesting, frost protection	Harvesting, frost protection
Harvesting, end of season	Rest	Direct sowing or sowing in pots or flats for transplant at end of month	Thinning, weeding, mulching, sowing successions, transplanting	Harvesting, sowing successions for winter	Harvesting, frost protection	Harvesting, frost protection
Sowing successions, thinning, fertilizing, maybe harvesting sweet corn	Thinning, fertilizing, maybe harvesting sweet corn, pest management	Harvesting sweet corn and/or dry corn	Harvesting dry corn	Harvesting dry corn	Rest	Rest
Sowing successions, trellising, harvesting, pest management	Sowing or transplanting successions, trellising, harvesting, pest management	Harvesting, pest management	Harvesting, pest management	Harvesting, end of season	Rest	Rest
Thinning, mulching, harvesting, sowing successions	Thinning, mulching, harvesting, sowing successions	Thinning, mulching, harvesting, sowing successions	Sowing for fall/winter harvest in places with warmer winters	Harvesting	Harvesting, maybe end of season	Maybe harvesting, end of season
Pest management, fertilizing	Harvesting, pest management, fertilizing	Harvesting, pest management, fertilizing	Harvesting, pest management, fertilizing	Harvesting, maybe end of season	End of season	Rest
Care, harvesting scapes	Harvesting, optional braiding bulbs, curing	Rest	Rest	Bed preparation, planting, mulching	Bed preparation, planting, mulching	Bed preparation, planting, mulching
Rest	Sowing in pots or flats	Direct sowing or transplanting for fall crop, pest management	Transplanting, mulching, fertilizing, pest management	Harvesting	Harvesting, frost protection	Harvesting, frost protection
Harvesting, sowing successions, thinning, weeding, mulching, fertilizing	Harvesting, thinning, mulching, fertilizing	Harvesting, sowing successions	Rest	Direct sowing winter varieties or sowing them in pots or flats	Harvesting, frost protection	Harvesting, frost protection

VEGETABLE	JANUARY	FEBRUARY	MARCH	APRIL	MAY	
Muskmelons	Rest	Rest	Sowing in pots indoors	Bed/mound preparation, direct sowing or transplanting	Fertilizing, weeding, mulching	
Okra	Rest	Rest	Rest	Bed preparation, direct sowing or sowing in pots or flats	Bed preparation, direct sowing, transplanting, thinning, mulching	
Onions	Starting seeds indoors or tending plants in open flats	Tending plants, ordering plants if you didn't start your own, transplanting	Bed preparation and transplanting, mulching	Weeding, mulching, fertilizing	Fertilizing	
Parsnips	Harvesting	Harvesting	End of season for overwintered crop, bed preparation, direct sowing for spring	Bed preparation, direct sowing, weeding, thinning, maybe mulching	Weeding, thinning, mulching	
Peas	Bed preparation and direct sowing	Thinning, mulching, weeding, direct sowing	Thinning, mulching, trellising, direct sowing in areas with cooler summers	Harvesting, end of season	Rest	
Peppers and Chiles	Sowing in pots or flats indoors	Sowing in pots or flats indoors, caring for plants in pots	Transplanting into 4" pots, fertilizing	Bed preparation, transplanting, mulching	Fertilizing, trellising	
Potatoes	Rest	Preparing for planting, planting for early harvest	Preparing for planting, planting for early harvest	Planting for winter storage, hilling, weeding, mulching	Hilling, weeding, mulching	
Radishes	Rest	Bed preparation, direct sowing	Thinning, weeding, mulching	Harvesting	Harvesting, end of season	
Spinach	Harvesting, frost protection	Harvesting, frost protection, bed preparation, direct sowing	Direct sowing, thinning, mulching	Thinning, mulching, fertilizing, harvesting	Harvesting, end of season	
Sweet Potatoes	Rest	Rest	Rest	Growing or ordering slips	Bed preparation, growing and planting out slips	
Tomatoes	Rest	Sowing in pots or flats indoors	Caring for plants in pots, transplanting into 4" pots	Transplanting, pruning, trellising	Pruning, pest and disease management, sowing successions, trellising	
Turnips and Rutabagas	Harvesting	Harvesting, end of season	Rest	Rest	Rest	
Watermelons	Rest	Rest	Sowing in pots indoors	Bed/mound preparation, direct sowing or transplanting	Fertilizing, weeding, mulching	
Winter Squash and Pumpkins	Rest	Rest	Rest	Bed/mound preparation, direct sowing or starting in pots or flats indoors	Direct sowing, transplanting, pest management, mulching	
Zucchini and Summer Squash	Rest	Rest	Rest	Bed preparation, direct sowing, planting in pots or flats indoors, transplanting	Sowing successions, transplanting, pest management, thinning, mulching	

JUNE	JULY	AUGUST	SEPTEMBER	OCTOBER	NOVEMBER	DECEMBER
Fertilizing, weeding, mulching, harvesting some varieties	Fertilizing, weeding, harvesting some varieties	Harvesting	Harvesting, end of season	Rest	Rest	Rest
Harvesting, thinning, mulching	Harvesting	Harvesting	Harvesting	Harvesting	End of season	Rest
Harvesting, curing	Rest	Rest	Rest	Rest	Rest	Maybe sowing in open flats indoors
Growing	Growing, direct sowing for fall/winter harvest	Growing, direct sowing for fall/winter harvest	Disease management, growing, direct sowing	Harvesting	Harvesting	Harvesting
Rest	Rest	Rest	Direct sowing for fall harvest	Thinning, mulching, weeding, trellising, harvesting	Harvesting, end of season	Rest
Harvesting, pest and disease management, trellising	Harvesting, pest and disease management, fertilizing	Harvesting, pest and disease management, fertilizing	Harvesting, pest and disease management, fertilizing	Harvesting, pest and disease management, fertilizing	Harvesting, end of season	Rest
Weeding, harvesting early crop	Harvesting, end of season	Rest	Rest	Rest	Rest	Rest
Rest	Rest	Direct sowing	Direct sowing, weeding, mulching, pest management	Thinning, weeding, harvesting	Harvesting, frost protection	Harvesting, end of season
Rest	Rest	Rest	Direct sowing or sowing in pots or flats for fall/winter harvests	Direct sowing, transplanting, thinning, mulching	Transplanting, thinning, mulching, harvesting, frost protection	Harvesting, frost protection
Planting out slips, weeding, mulching	Fertilizing, pest management	Harvesting greens	Harvesting greens	Harvesting tubers, some varieties and in some areas	Harvesting, curing, end of season	Rest
Pruning, trellising, pest and disease management, maybe harvesting	Succession planting, pest and disease management, pruning, harvesting, trellising	For summer harvest: end of season. For fall harvest: pruning, trellising, pest and disease management, maybe harvesting	Pruning, trellising, harvesting	Pruning, trellising, harvesting	End of season	Rest
Rest	Rest	Bed preparation, direct sowing for rutabagas	Direct sowing for turnips and rutabagas	Thinning, weeding, mulching	Thinning, weeding, mulching, harvesting some varieties	Harvesting, growing
Fertilizing, weeding, mulching	Fertilizing, weeding, harvesting some varieties	Harvesting	Harvesting, end of season	Rest	Rest	Rest
Direct sowing, weeding, mulching, pest management	Pest management	Pest management	Pest management, harvesting, curing	Harvesting, curing, end of season	Rest	Rest
Sowing successions, pest management, weeding, thinning, harvesting	Pest management, harvesting	Pest management, harvesting	Pest management, harvesting, maybe end of season	Maybe harvest, end of season	Rest	Rest

WHAT TO DO EACH MONTH IN A Hot Climate* Garden

VEGETABLE	JANUARY	FEBRUARY	MARCH	APRIL	MAY
Arugula	Harvesting	Direct sowing, thinning, weeding, harvesting	Direct sowing, thinning, weeding, harvesting	Harvesting or end of season	End of season
Basil	Rest	Rest	Sowing in pots or flats indoors, direct sowing if it's warm enough	Thinning, weeding, mulching, fertilizing, maybe sowing successions	Pruning, harvesting, thinning, weeding, mulching, fertilizing, sowing successions
Beans	Rest	Bed preparation, direct sowing	Bed preparation, direct sowing, thinning, weeding, mulching, trellising (pole beans)	Pest and disease management, trellising, thinning, weeding, mulching	Pest and disease management, harvesting
Beets and Chard	Harvesting, bed preparation, direct sowing or sowing in pots or flats, thinning, weeding	Harvesting, direct sowing or sowing in pots or flats, thinning, weeding, mulching	Harvesting, thinning, weeding, mulching	Harvesting	Harvesting
Broccoli and Cauliflower	Sowing in pots or flats, transplanting, mulching, fertilizing	Transplanting, mulching, pest management, fertilizing	Harvesting, pest management	Harvesting, pest management	Harvesting, pest management, end of season
Cabbage	Sowing in pots or flats, transplanting, mulching, fertilizing	Transplanting, mulching, pest management, fertilizing	Pest management	Harvesting, pest management	Harvesting, pest management, end of season
Carrots	Harvesting, bed preparation, direct sowing, thinning, weeding, mulching	Harvesting, bed preparation, direct sowing, thinning, weeding, mulching	Harvesting, bed preparation, direct sowing, thinning, weeding, mulching	Harvesting, bed preparation, direct sowing, thinning, weeding, mulching	Harvesting, thinning, weeding, mulching
Cilantro	Direct sowing	Direct sowing	Direct sowing, thinning, weeding, mulching, harvesting	Direct sowing, thinning, weeding, mulching, harvesting	End of season
Corn	Rest	Bed preparation, direct sowing	Sowing successions, thinning, mulching, fertilizing	Sowing successions, thinning, mulching, fertilizing, harvesting sweet corn	Thinning, fertilizing, maybe harvesting sweet corn
Cucumbers	Rest	Rest	Bed preparation, direct sowing or sowing in pots or flats for transplanting	Thinning, mulching, transplanting, fertilizing, trellising, pest management	Harvesting, pest management
Dill	Direct sowing, thinning, mulching, harvesting	Direct sowing, thinning, mulching, harvesting	Direct sowing, thinning, mulching, harvesting	Thinning, mulching, harvesting	End of season
Eggplant	Sowing in pots or flats indoors	Tending to plants in pots, transplanting into 4" pots	Transplanting into quart or gallon pots, pest management	Transplanting, pest management	Harvesting, mulching, trellising, pest management, fertilizing
Garlic	Watching and waiting	Possibly fertilizing and remulching	Harvesting scapes	Harvesting, optional braiding bulbs or harvesting scapes, curing	Harvesting, optional braiding bulbs, curing, end of season
Kale and Collards	Direct sowing or sowing in pots or flats, transplanting, mulching, fertilizing, pest management	Transplanting, thinning, weeding, mulching, pest management	Harvesting, pest management	Harvesting, pest management, end of season	Rest

JUNE	JULY	AUGUST	SEPTEMBER	OCTOBER	NOVEMBER	DECEMBER
Rest	Rest	Rest	Bed preparation, direct sowing	Direct sowing, transplanting, mulching	Direct sowing, thinning, weeding	Harvesting, frost protection
Pruning, harvesting, thinning, weeding, possibly end of season	End of season	Rest	Direct seeding	Thinning, weeding, mulching	Pruning, harvesting, fertilizing, maybe end of season	End of season
Harvesting	Harvesting	Bed preparation, direct sowing	Direct sowing, thinning, weeding, mulching, trellising (pole beans), maybe harvesting	Trellising (pole beans), pest and disease management	Pest and disease management, harvesting	End of season for green beans, harvesting, winnowing, storage of dry beans
Rest	Rest	Bed preparation, direct sowing or sowing in pots or flats, thinning, weeding	Bed preparation, direct sowing, thinning, mulching, weeding	Harvesting, direct sowing, thinning, weeding, mulching	Harvesting, direct sowing, thinning, weeding, mulching	Harvesting, thinning, weeding, mulching
Rest	Rest	Sowing in pots or flats	Sowing in pots or flats, transplanting, mulching, fertilizing, pest management	Sowing in pots or flats, transplanting, mulching, fertilizing, pest management, possibly harvesting	Sowing in pots or flats, transplanting, mulching, fertilizing, pest management, harvesting	Transplanting, mulching, fertilizing, harvesting
Rest	Rest	Sowing in pots or flats	Sowing in pots or flats, transplanting, mulching, fertilizing, pest management	Sowing in pots or flats, transplanting, mulching, fertilizing, pest management	Sowing in pots or flats, transplanting, mulching, fertilizing, pest management, harvesting	Transplanting, mulching, fertilizing, harvesting
Harvesting	Rest	Rest	Bed preparation, direct sowing	Bed preparation, direct sowing, thinning, weeding, mulching	Harvesting, bed preparation, direct sowing, thinning, weeding, mulching	Harvesting, thinning, weeding, mulching
Rest	Rest	Rest	Bed preparation, direct sowing or sowing in pots or flats for transplanting	Bed preparation, direct sowing or sowing in pots and flats and transplanting	Harvesting, thinning, weeding, mulching	Harvesting
Harvesting sweet corn and/or dry corn	Harvesting dry corn	Harvesting dry corn	Rest	Rest	Rest	Rest
Harvesting, end of season	Rest	Rest	Bed preparation, direct sowing or sowing in pots or flats and transplanting	Thinning, mulching, trellising, pest management	Harvesting, pest management	Harvesting, end of season
Rest	Rest	Rest	Direct sowing	Direct sowing, weeding, thinning, mulching	Direct sowing, thinning, weeding, mulching, harvesting	Direct sowing, thinning, weeding, mulching, harvesting
Rest	Rest	Sowing in pots or flats	Transplanting, pest management	Pest management, trellising, fertilizing	Harvesting, pest management, fertilizing, end of season	Rest
Rest	Rest	Rest	Rest	Rest	Planting and mulching	Planting and mulching
Rest	Rest	Rest	Direct sowing or sowing in pots or flats and transplanting	Direct sowing or sowing in pots or flats and transplanting, mulching, fertilizing, pest management	Sowing in pots or flats, direct sowing, transplanting, mulching, fertilizing, pest management, harvesting	Sowing in pots or flats, direct sowing, transplanting, mulching, fertilizing

VEGETABLE	JANUARY	FEBRUARY	MARCH	APRIL	MAY	
Lettuce	Sowing in pots or flats indoors	Direct sowing, transplanting, fertilizing	Transplanting, thinning, mulching, fertilizing, harvesting	Harvesting	End of season	
Muskmelons	Rest	Sowing in pots indoors	Bed/mound preparation, direct sowing, transplanting	Fertilizing, weeding, mulching	Fertilizing, weeding, harvesting some varieties	
Okra	Rest	Bed preparation, direct sowing	Bed preparation, direct sowing, thinning, mulching	Bed preparation, direct sowing, thinning, mulching	Harvesting	
Onions	Fertilizing, mulching	Fertilizing, mulching	Fertilizing, mulching	Harvesting, curing	Harvesting, curing, end of season	
Parsnips	Growing	Maybe harvesting	Harvesting	Rest	Rest	
Peas	Thinning, weeding, direct sowing	Harvesting, thinning, weeding, mulching, direct sowing in areas with cooler summers	Harvesting, thinning, trellising, maybe end of season	Harvesting, end of season	Rest	
Peppers and Chiles	Sowing in pots or flats indoors	Bed preparation, transplanting, mulching	Fertilizing, trellising	Harvesting, trellising	Harvesting, trellising	
Potatoes	Bed preparation and planting	Bed preparation and planting, hilling	Hilling, weeding, mulching	Harvesting, hilling, weeding, mulching	Harvesting, end of season	
Radishes	Bed preparation, direct sowing	Bed preparation, direct sowing, thinning, weeding	Thinning, weeding, mulching	Harvesting	Harvesting, end of season	
Spinach	Direct sowing, thinning, mulching, harvesting	Direct sowing, thinning, mulching, harvesting	Thinning, mulching, harvesting	Harvesting, end of season	Rest	
Sweet Potatoes	Rest	Rest	Bed preparation, growing slips or ordering them	Growing and planting slips	Weeding, mulching, planting, fertilizing	
Tomatoes	Rest	Sowing in pots or flats indoors	Transplanting, pruning, trellising	Pruning, sowing successions, trellising	Pruning, transplanting successions, trellising, harvesting	
Turnips and Rutabagas	Direct sowing, thinning, weeding, mulching, harvesting	Thinning, weeding, mulching, harvesting	Harvesting	Harvesting, end of season	Rest	
Watermelons	Rest	Sowing in pots indoors	Bed/mound preparation, direct sowing, transplanting	Fertilizing, weeding, mulching	Fertilizing, weeding, harvesting some varieties	
Winter Squash and Pumpkins	Rest	Bed preparation, direct sowing	Direct sowing, thinning, weeding, mulching, pest management	Direct sowing, thinning, weeding, mulching, pest management	Direct sowing, thinning, weeding, mulching, pest management	
Zucchini and Summer Squash	Rest	Bed preparation, direct sowing, sowing in pots or flats, transplanting	Sowing successions, pest management, thinning	Thinning, weeding, mulching, pest management, fertilizing, harvesting	Pest management, harvesting, end of season	

JUNE	JULY	AUGUST	SEPTEMBER	OCTOBER	NOVEMBER	DECEMBER
Rest	Rest	Rest	Direct sowing or sowing in pots or flats and transplanting	Direct sowing or sowing in pots or flats and transplanting, weeding, mulching, fertilizing	Direct sowing or sowing in pots or flats and transplanting, weeding, mulching, fertilizing, harvesting	Direct sowing or sowing in pots or flats and transplanting, weeding, mulching, fertilizing, harvesting
Harvesting	Harvesting, direct sowing or transplanting	Fertilizing, weeding, mulching	Fertilizing, weeding, harvesting some varieties	Harvesting	Harvesting, end of season	Rest
Harvesting	Harvesting	Direct sowing, harvesting	Thinning, mulching, harvesting	Harvesting	Harvesting	End of season
Rest	Rest	Rest	Rest	Sowing in flats	Sowing in flats, transplanting, weeding, mulching	Transplanting, weeding, mulching, fertilizing
Rest	Rest	Rest	Bed preparation, direct sowing	Bed preparation, direct sowing, weeding, thinning, mulching	Weeding, thinning, mulching, fertilizing	Growing
Rest	Rest	Rest	Rest	Rest	Rest	Bed preparation and direct sowing
Sowing in pots or flats, harvesting	Sowing in pots or flats, caring for plants in pots, harvesting	Bed preparation, transplanting, mulching	Bed preparation, transplanting, mulching, fertilizing	Fertilizing, trellising	Harvesting, trellising	End of season
Rest	Rest	Rest	Rest	Rest	Rest	Rest
Rest	Rest	Rest	Direct sowing	Direct sowing, thinning, weeding, mulching, pest management	Weeding, thinning, pest management, harvesting	Harvesting
Rest	Rest	Rest	Rest	Bed preparation, direct sowing	Direct sowing, thinning, mulching, fertilizing	Direct sowing, thinning, mulching, fertilizing, harvesting
Weeding, mulching, planting	Harvesting greens, weeding, mulching	Harvesting greens and possibly roots	Harvesting greens and possibly roots	Harvesting, curing	Harvesting, curing, end of season	Rest
Harvesting, end of season	Sowing in pots or flats or taking cuttings	Transplanting, pruning, trellising	Pruning, trellising, pest and disease management, maybe harvesting	Pruning, pest and disease management, harvesting	Harvesting, end of season	Sowing seeds in pots or flats
Rest	Rest	Rest	Bed preparation, direct sowing for rutabagas	Direct sowing turnips and rutabagas	Thinning, weeding, mulching	Thinning, weeding, mulching
Harvesting	Harvesting, direct sowing, sowing in pots or flats and transplanting	Fertilizing, transplanting, weeding, mulching	Fertilizing, weeding, harvesting some varieties	Harvesting	Harvesting, end of season	Rest
Direct sowing, mulching, pest management	Pest management, harvesting, storage	Bed preparation, direct sowing	Pest management, mulching, weeding, thinning	Pest management, fertilizing	Pest management	Harvesting, curing, end of season
Rest	Rest	Bed preparation, direct sowing or sowing in pots or flats and transplanting	Sowing successions, pest management, weeding, mulching, thinning	Pest management, thinning, weeding, mulching, harvesting	Harvesting, end of season	Rest

Appendix

When to Sow, Plant, and Harvest BASED ON TEMPERATURE AND SEASON

PLANT	MIN. SOIL TEMP °F (°C)	IDEAL SOIL TEMP °F (°C)	DIRECT SOW (DS), TRANSPLANT (T), OR FLEXIBLE (F)	
Arugula	40 (4)	40–60 (4–15)	F	
Basil	70 (21)	80–85 (27–29)	F	
Beans, dry, pole and bush	60 (15)	75–85 (24–29)	DS	
Beans, green, pole and bush	60 (15)	75–85 (24–29)	DS	
Beets	40 (4)	65–85 (18–29)	F	
Broccoli	40 (4)	55–75 (13–24)	T	
Cabbage	40 (4)	55–75 (13–24)	T	
Carrots	40 (4)	75–85 (24–29)	DS	
Cauliflower	40 (4)	55–75 (13–24)	T	
Chard	40 (4)	65–85 (18–29)	F	
Cilantro	55 (13)	65–70 (18–21)	E	
Collards	40 (4)	55–85 (13–29)	F	
Corn, dry	60 (15)	65–95 (18–35)	DS	
Corn, sweet	60 (15)	65–95 (18–35)	DS	
Cucumbers	65 (18)	75–95 (24–35)	F	
Dill	40 (4)	60–70 (15–21)	DS	
Eggplant	60 (15)	75–85 (24–29)	T	
Garlic	35 (2)	40–60 (4–15)	DS	
Kale	40 (4)	55–85 (13–29)	F	
Lettuce, head	40 (4)	70–75 (21–24)	T	
Lettuce, leaf	40 (4)	70–75 (21–24)	DS	
Muskmelons	65 (18)	75–90 (24–32)	F	
Okra	65 (18)	70–90 (21–32)	F	
Onions	45 (7)	60–70 (15–21)	DS	
Parsnips	45 (7)	55–75 (13–24)	DS	
Peas	40 (4)	50–75 (10–24)	DS	
Peppers and chiles	60 (15)	68–95 (20–35)	T	
Potatoes	40 (4)	50–70 (10–21)	DS	
Radishes and daikon	40 (4)	55–85 (13–29)	DS	
Spinach	35 (2)	45–65 (7–18)	F	
Sweet potatoes	60 (15)	70–80 (21–27)	DS	
Tomatoes	60 (15)	65–85 (18–29)	T	
Turnips and rutabagas	40 (4)	60–85 (15–29)	DS	
Watermelons	65 (18)	75–95 (24–35)	F	
Winter squash and pumpkins	60 (15)	85–95 (29–35)	F	
Zucchini and summer squash	60 (15)	85–95 (29–35)	F	

Chart source: Gardener's Supply Company

COOL WEATHER CROP/ WARM WEATHER CROP	FROST HARDINESS °F (°C)	HEAT TOLERANCE °F (°C)	AVERAGE DAYS TO MATURITY
cool	25 (–4)	80 (27)	40–60
warm	No	90 (32)	85–120
warm	No	90 (32)	85–120
warm	No	90 (32)	50–70
cool	20 (–7)	80 (27)	50–70
cool	28 (–2)	75 (24)	50–65 from transplant
cool	24(–4)	80 (27)	60–105 from transplant
cool	20 (–6)	80 (27)	55–85
cool	28 (–2)	75 (24)	55–80 from transplant
cool	20 (–7)	80 (27)	50–70
cool	15 (–9)	80 (27)	45–60
cool	20 (–6)	80 (27)	55–75
warm	No	95 (35)	60–115
warm	No	95 (35)	60–115
warm	No	90 (32)	55–65
cool	25 (–4)	85 (29)	55–80
warm	No	95 (35)	100–120 from seed; 55–88 from transplant
cool	–30 (–34)	85 (29)	220–270
cool	20 (–6)	80 (27)	55–75
cool	20 (–7)	80 (27)	45–60
cool	20 (–7)	80 (27)	45–60
warm	No	90 (32)	70–90
warm	No	95 (35)	50–85
cool	20 (–7)	85 (29)	100–140 from seed; 90–100 from sets
cool	0 (–18)	75 (24)	105–130
cool	28 (–2)	77 (25)	56–75
warm	No	95 (35)	60–90 from transplant
cool	28 (–2)	80 (27)	60–135
cool	20 (–7)	80 (27)	25–40 in spring/summer; 45–70 in winter
cool	15 (–9)	75 (24)	45–60 (big leaves), 25–35 (baby spinach)
warm	No	105 (40)	90–120 from transplant
warm	No	90 (32)	60–100
cool	20 (–7)	75 (24)	38–95
warm	No	95 (35)	70–90
warm	No	90 (32)	85–120
warm	No	90 (32)	45–60

Seed Spacing, Depth, and Amounts OF SEEDS NEEDED

Planting depths are not subject to change based on conditions. Seeds should be planted at a depth of about twice their width/diameter. Thus, bigger seeds get planted deeper than small seeds. If you're planting seeds that are light-dependent germinators (e.g., lettuce, some herbs), you can press them into the soil surface without covering them with soil. Or if you are direct sowing a lot of seeds, spread the seeds in an extremely shallow furrow, sprinkle soil lightly on top of them, and then pat them in. Some unique varieties of indigenous crops adapted to desert conditions can be planted much deeper; use this table as a reference, and always learn as much as you can about the specific varieties you'll be growing.

PLANT	SEED-SOWING DEPTH (IN INCHES)	DIRECT-SOWING DISTANCE BETWEEN SEEDS (IN INCHES)	FINAL SPACING BETWEEN PLANTS IN ROW AFTER THINNING (IN INCHES)	NUMBER OF SEEDS PER 10 FEET	WEIGHT OF SEEDS/ 10 FEET OF ROW
Arugula	¼	¼–1	1½–4	120–240	0.5 g
Basil	¼	½–1¼	14–18	n/a	n/a
Beans, dry, pole and bush	1	1–3	3–10	30–40	14–28 g
Beans, green, pole and bush	1	1–3	3–10	60–120	28–56 g
Beets	½	½–1	3–6	120–240	2–3.5 g
Broccoli	½	n/a	18–24	n/a	n/a
Cabbage	¼	n/a	18–24	n/a	n/a
Carrots	½	¼–½	1–1½	240–480	1 g
Cauliflower	½	n/a	18–24	n/a	n/a
Chard	½	½–1	6–10	120	2–5 g
Cilantro	¼–½	½	2–6	240	4 g
Collards	¼	2–4	12–18	30–60	0.25 g
Corn, dry	1	4–6	6–12	20–30	7–14 g
Corn, sweet	1	4–6	6–12	20–30	7–14 g
Cucumbers	½	3–4 seeds per hill, 18"–24" apart	18"–24" between hills of 1–2 plants	15–40	1–2 g
Dill	⅛–¼	½–2 (or broadcast)	4	30–60	0.125 g
Eggplant	½	n/a	18–24	n/a	n/a
Garlic	2½–4	6–8	6–8	15–20	227–454 g
Kale	¼	2–4	12–18	30–60	0.25 g
Lettuce, head	⅛	n/a	5–9	n/a	n/a
Lettuce, leaf	⅛	n/a, sow densely	n/a, do not thin	1,200–2,000	3–6 g
Muskmelons	½	3 seeds per cluster, 18" apart; rows 48" apart	18	20	1 g
Okra	½	2–4	8–18	30–60	2–4 g
Onions	¼	1 for seeds, 6–8 for transplants or sets	4–8	120	0.5 g

PLANT	SEED-SOWING DEPTH (IN INCHES)	DIRECT-SOWING DISTANCE BETWEEN SEEDS (IN INCHES)	FINAL SPACING BETWEEN PLANTS IN ROW AFTER THINNING (IN INCHES)	NUMBER OF SEEDS PER 10 FEET	WEIGHT OF SEEDS/ 10 FEET OF ROW
Parsnips	¼	½	2–4	240	1.5 g
Peas	¾	1–1½	1–2	80–120	28–56 g
Peppers and chiles	¼	n/a	12–24	n/a	n/a
Potatoes	3	8–12	8–12	10	0.9–2.3 kg
Radishes and daikon	½	½	1–5	120	1–2 g
Spinach	½	½–1	2–4	120–240	1–2.5 g
Sweet potatoes	2–4	n/a	10–14; rows 36" apart	n/a	n/a
Tomatoes	¼	n/a	18–24	n/a	n/a
Turnips and rutabagas	¼	½–2	2–4	120–200	0.25–1 g
Watermelons	½	3 seeds per cluster, 18" apart; rows 48" apart	18	20	1 g
Winter squash and pumpkins	1	5 seeds per mound, mounds 48"–72" apart; rows: 6–12	48–72 between mounds of 3 plants; rows: 24–36	10–20	1–6 g
Zucchini and summer squash	1	3–5 seeds per mound, or 2–4 seeds every 18"–25" in rows	36"–48" between mounds of 1–3 plants; 18"–24" between plants in rows	8–10	2 g

Plant Spacing for Garden Beds

PLANT	FINAL SPACING BETWEEN PLANTS IN ROW AFTER THINNING (IN INCHES)	NUMBER OF ROWS THAT CAN FIT IN A 36"–42" BED	DISTANCE BETWEEN ROWS (INCHES)
Arugula	1½–4	3–4+*	4–8
Basil	14–18	2+ or 3	18–24
Beans, dry, pole and bush	3–10	2–3	24–30
Beans, green, pole and bush	3–10	2–3	24–30
Beets	3–6	2+ or 3	18–24
Broccoli	18–24	2+	18–24
Cabbage	18–24	2+	18–24
Carrots	1–1½	3+	18–24
Cauliflower	18–24	2+	18–24
Chard	6–10	2+ or 3	18–24
Cilantro	2–6	3+	8–12
Collards	12–18	2	24–30
Corn, dry	6–12	3	30–38
Corn, sweet	6–12	3	30–38
Cucumbers	18–24 between hills of 1–2 plants	1	48–56
Dill	4	2+ or 3	18–24
Eggplant	18–24	2+	18–24
Garlic	6–8	3–4	10–12
Kale	12–18	2+ or 3	18–24
Lettuce, head	5–9	3+	6–10
Lettuce, leaf	n/a; do not thin	3+	6–10
Muskmelons	18	1	48–56
Okra	8–18	2	24–30
Onions	4–8	3+ or 4	10–12
Parsnips	2–4	2+ or 3	18–24
Peas	1–2	2+	18–24
Peppers and chiles	12–24	2+	18–24
Potatoes	8–12	1	48–56
Radishes and daikon	1–5	3+ or 6; 2+ or 3 for daikon	6–12
Spinach	2–4	2+ or 3	18–24
Sweet potatoes	10–14	1	36
Tomatoes	18–24	2	24–36
Turnips and rutabagas	2–4	2+	18–24
Watermelons	18	1	48
Winter squash and pumpkins	48–72 between mounds of 3 plants; rows: 24–36	1	48–56
Zucchini and summer squash	18–24 between plants in rows; 1–3 plants per mound, with 36–48 between mounds	1+	48

*"+" means this spacing works with intercropping a small complementary crop

DETERMINING THE RIGHT PLANT SPACING

It's very important to give your plants enough room to grow, seek out nutrition in the soil, and receive sufficient airflow. This care will, in turn, maximize your harvest. Here are some guidelines for determining the right spacing for your garden crops.

- Different varieties of the same crops may have different needs for space (for example, slender spring carrots vs. fat fall storage carrots). When possible, look up the spacing recommendations for your specific variety.

- Most seed packets have specific information about spacing for that crop and variety; if you don't see this on the packet, look on the seed company website. Often seed companies print the same information on packets for all varieties of a given species, but they may provide more variety-specific info online.

- You can sometimes get away with tighter spacing if you've got richer soil and plenty of water.

- If you have poor soil or a shortage of water, you'll generally have better yields with wider spacing (though this isn't a stand-in for irrigating, improving the soil, and/or feeding your crops).

- The more tightly spaced your plants, the more competition there is for water, light, and soil nutrients.

- Your garden conditions are unique; take notes to fine-tune future spacing choices.

- If you live in a warm, moist place (like we do), try wider spacing to ensure airflow and reduce the prevalence of fungal diseases on susceptible plants.

Possible Yields of Common Vegetables

PLANT	POSSIBLE YIELD PER 10-FOOT ROW (IN POUNDS)	POSSIBLE YIELD IN POUNDS PER PLANT
Arugula	2–4	0.125–1.5
Basil	n/a	0.5–1.5
Beans, dry, pole and bush	1	0.25
Beans, green, pole and bush	4–6	0.5–1
Beets	10	0.2–0.3
Broccoli	4–6	1–3
Cabbage	10	2–4
Carrots	12	0.2–0.3
Cauliflower	4–6	0.75–2.5
Chard	8–10	1–2
Cilantro	n/a	0.5 –1
Collards	8–10	1–2
Corn, dry	10–15 ears	1–3 ears
Corn, sweet	10–15 ears	1–1.5
Cucumbers	20	3–5
Dill	n/a	0.25–0.5
Eggplant	11	5–8
Garlic	2–4	0.25–0.75
Kale	10	1–5
Lettuce, head	5	0.25–.75
Lettuce, leaf	5–8	0.5–1
Muskmelons	8–12	4–8
Okra	6–8	1–5
Onions	8–12	0.25–0.5
Parsnips	5–8	0.2–0.3
Peas	4–6	3–5
Peppers and chiles	5–18	1–5
Potatoes	15–65	1.5–5
Radishes and daikon	1–5	0.1–0.5
Spinach	4–8	0.25–1
Sweet potatoes	20–50	2–5
Tomatoes	12–18	5–15
Turnips and rutabagas	8–12	0.25–0.5
Watermelons	10–15	5–10
Winter squash and pumpkins	20–50	10–35
Zucchini and summer squash	12–20	5–18

NOTE: These numbers come from a combination of agricultural research station data from Michigan State University and Louisiana State University plus our own experience. The amount you ultimately harvest from your garden may differ significantly from these numbers. Factors that impact yields include plant variety; soil fertility; sun exposure; water; pressure from pests, diseases, and weeds; and how and when you harvest. Use the numbers above as a quick reference to plan your garden. As you start bringing in the bounty, keep track of actual yields for each specific variety. Your place-based data will be the most useful for future planning.

Acknowledgments

Thank you to the hands and hearts of uncountable ancestors,
who whispered to soil with quiet devotion,
who have nurtured, selected, protected, and passed on
seeds and understandings, meanings and medicines,
stories stirred into stews.

Thank you to the garden, that place of mundane joy and loving labor,
a place where the wild and the tended embrace,
where we remember we are part of it all—
not masters, but kin.

Thank you to the mountains that cradle the watersheds,
and for the rains that wander down
to kiss roots awake;
for the miracle of water finding its way
just as we do.

Thank you to the magic that makes things grow—
the unseen stirring inside seeds,
the curl of vine toward sunlight,
the holy hunger of bees.

Thank you to the light dancing in dewdrops on dill,
luscious lettuces on summer plates
the pleasure of parsnips melting in your mouth
the first bite of a homegrown tomato—
a taste that stops time.

A reminder:
even in chaos,
we are invited to tend, to transform, to begin again.

Thank you to the mystery, the Earth,
and the small and holy parts we humans are invited to play.

It turns out that creating a book is a lot like growing a garden: It's a collaboration between many beings who share their magic to make something that's greater than the sum of their parts. We did not write this book alone, and here we express gratitude to some of the folks who supported us along the way.

Without the engagement, inspiration, curiosity, and faith of the thousands of students and followers who have studied gardening with us, none of this would have happened. Thank you! Deep appreciation for the chrysalis magic in which our gardening work together has metamorphosed from a Wild Abundance class into the Growing Wise Gardening School.

Thank you to the team, especially: Sarah Tew for incredible photography and patience; Kaylee Walters for doing what needs to be done willingly and well; Meghan Gemma for excellent research and writing skills; Amy DeCamp for being instrumental in making the Online Gardening School happen; Alivia Ruiz, who became a videographer because we needed one; Eve, who turned our disparate documents into something coherent. Thanks to professional videographer and photographer Mason McDonald, who made our videos the best they could be, and to video editor Connor Reveley.

To our already published beloved friends and colleagues Juliet Blankespoor, Asia Suler, and Rebecca Beyer, who paved the way and nourished us with inspiration. Rebecca Beyer also contributed significantly to the sections on soils, compost, and garden planning.

A bow and a twirl to Cindy Spitzer, our book midwife and the fairy godmother of this project. She magically appeared and unveiled the mystery of the publishing process, turning this book into something real, and helping us believe in ourselves. Cheers to Elizabeth at Aloha Redland, who welcomed us at her little piece of paradise; that book retreat led to a productive process and a deeper commitment. Daniel Foor, friend and author of *Ancestral Medicine*, told us about the need for a book proposal, and Lindsey Warf made ours too beautiful to turn down; thank you. Thanks to George, Sunshine, Nadi, and Carleen for reviewing the timing tables for their climates.

Everyone at Storey Publishing has been incredible, particularly Sarah Slattery, Carleen Madigan, and Carolyn Eckert.

Natalie thanks her parents for introducing her to gardening, and her mom for paying her to weed, which got her into the habit of loving being in the garden. Also, her gardening mentors: Elaine Ingham, Pat Labine, and Russ Fox. She thanks Frank Salzano, father of Hazel, and master of the poetry of the planets, and Matty Semkowich for patiently loving her through the conclusion of creation.

Chloe thanks her farm-partner for 10 years and coparent for life, Cailen Campbell, for loving the land and being crazy enough to try actually living by his values, for teaching her a lot about gardening, and for bringing her and Natalie together. Also, her gardening mentors: Steve Gliessman and Robbie Jaffe, Doug Gosling, Michelle Vesser, Humberto Zuñiga, Martín Prechtel, and many others.

Thanks to our kids, Natalie's daughter Hazel and Chloe's son Felix, for sharing us with this project and tolerating our sometimes-divided attention, weekend working, and missed opportunities to go out and play. Also for posing with vegetables, picking slugs for a dime apiece, and adorning the gardens with laughter.

We live in a miraculous corner of the earth that's covered in greenery and crisscrossed with clear mountain streams. This ecological haven also hosts humans who think botany is sexy and that bringing homegrown and wildcrafted delicacies to potlucks is the way to party. We're so grateful for the incredible community of Earth-loving people we get to share our lives with, many of whom are avid gardeners we continue to learn with and from. In particular we'd like to thank Yanna Fishman and Doug Elliott, Mary Morgaine and Hart Squire, Peter Belt, Chama Woydak, Leon Birstein, Anna Littman and the late Patricia Allison, Chuck Marsh, and Frank Cook.

Finally, we thank each other. Our collaborations bring out the best in us and create beauty that we couldn't conjure alone.

Resources to Download from the Growing Wise Gardening School

As a companion to this book, we're offering a bundle of free online resources to enhance your learning. You can access them from our website: **GrowingWise.net/book-bonuses**

In 2020, at the onset of the global COVID-19 pandemic, dozens of followers reached out to us seeking advice about how to become independent of global food supply chains. As a result we created a collection of in-depth online gardening classes to share what we've learned in our decades of experience. Since then thousands of students from all over the country and around the world have learned from us, with amazing gardens to show for it. The fulfillment we felt watching people feel more capable and confident to grow their own food inspired us to write this book!

Growing Wise, our online school, hosts the most comprehensive online gardening classes in the world (as far as we can tell). They have been utilized and enjoyed by both total newbies and people who have been gardening for years. The classes cover gardening foundations and advanced techniques, and they include step-by-step growing guides for over 25 veggies, herbs, and berries. Students also have unlimited access to Chloe through the online classroom and live Q&As to ask questions and get personalized advice in their gardens. We've received incredibly positive feedback from totally new gardeners and from folks who have gardened for years.

The bonus goodies we're offering here enhance this book and are just a tiny taste of our Growing Wise programs, which we hope you also check out!

VIDEO LECTURES

10 Veggies That Will Really Feed You

When Can You Start a Garden?

Deciding Which Veggies to Plant

Gardening with the Moon

Crop Rotation

VIDEO DEMOS

Guide to Thinning

How to Prune Tomatoes

Harvesting and Braiding Garlic

How to Start a Garden from Grass: Double-Digging and Single-Digging Options

Essential Weeding Tools and How to Use Them

Harvesting Green Beans and the Mexican Bean Beetle

PRINTABLES

These printable worksheets are referenced in Chapter 1 and are super useful for planning your garden.

What Veggies to Plant? Worksheet

Holistic Inquiry Exercise Worksheet

CURATED RESOURCE LISTS

On our website you'll find links to the places where we order all of the goodies that help us garden, specifically:

Our Favorite Sources for Tools

Places to Source Fertilizers and Amendments

Where to Find Seed-Starting Supplies

Best Quality Weed Fabric, Organic Pesticides, and Irrigation Equipment

Seed Companies We Love

BELOVED BIBLIOGRAPHY

Our website has an extensive list of other great gardening books. Many of them dive deeper into specific topics, and we share what we love about each one. There you will find books on:

Soil and Fertility

Urban and Suburban Gardening

Container Gardening

Permaculture

Gardening in the Desert, Tropics, and Cold Places

Market Gardening and Small-Scale Farming

Season Extension and Fall/Winter Gardening

Seed Saving and Plant Breeding

Food Preservation

Cookbooks That Center Garden Produce

Index

Page numbers in **bold** indicate tables or charts. Page numbers in *italics* refer to photographs or their captions.

A

access, 23, 37
achillea, 250
acidifiers, 139
acorns (*Cucurbita pepo*), 334–336
aesthetics/beauty, 22–23, 37
aging manure, 125–126
airflow, maximizing, 251
aji peppers (*Capsicum baccatum*), 318–319
alfalfa, **113**
alfalfa meal, 136
alkalizers, 138–139
allelopathic plants, 23–24, **25**
amaranth (*Amaranthus* spp.), **216**, *217*
amendments
    biochar, 129–130
    biological, 139
    choosing, 116
    cover crops, 140–147
    manure, 125–128
    preparing soil and, 90–91
    raised beds and, 68
    store-bought, 134–139
    urine, 131–133
    wood ash, 131
    worm castings, 124
angles, right, 24
animal bedding, composting, 150
anthracnose, **248–249**
aphids, **246–247**, *246*
aragonite, 138
Arbico Organics, 256
arthropods, 104

arugula (*Eruca vesicaria*), **40**, **41**, **42**, **113**, **172**, **181**, 194, 211, 278–279, *278*, *279*, **340–341**, **344–345**, **348–349**, **352–353**
Ashworth, Suzanne, 269
attention, 21
aubergine (*Solanum melongena*), 300–301
audiobooks, 51
Austrian winter peas, *141*, **142–143**, 144, *195*
availability, timing of planting and, 194, 197
azomite, 138

B

bacteria, nitrogen fixers and, 112, *114*
bacterial inoculants, 139
barriers, physical, 251–253
basalt, 138
basil (*Ocimum basilicum*), **40**, **41**, **42**, **113**, **181**, 280–281, *280*, *281*, **340–341**, **344–345**, **348–349**, **352–353**
baskets, 55
bat guano, 136
bean beetles, 252
beans (*Phaseolus vulgaris*), **41**, **12**, **113**, **172**, 211, *211*, 229–230, *229*, *230–231*, **231**, 265, 266, 267–268, 271, 280–281, 282, **340–341**, **344–345**, **348–349**, **352–353**

beds
    raised, 18, 29–30, *63*, **64**, 65–68
    rows vs., 18, 26–27
    solarization/occultation and, 83
    styles of, 18, 28–30
beer traps, 257, **259**
beetroot (*Beta vulgaris*), 284–285
beets (*Beta vulgaris*), *10*, *35*, **40**, **41**, **42**, *112*, **113**, **172**, 194, 211, *211*, 266, 271, 284–285, *284*, **340–341**, **344–345**, **348–349**, **352–353**
bell peppers (*Capsicum annuum*), 318–319
berms, 22
bhindi (*Abelmoschus esculentus*), 310–311
bindweed (*Convolvulus* spp.), **216**, *217*
biochar, 118, 129–130, *129*, 150
biofungicides, **258**
biological amendments, 139
Bionutrient Food Association, 242
black beans (*Phaseolus vulgaris*), 282–283
blackeyed peas, **142–143**, 144
black walnut, **25**
blight-resistant tomatoes, 245
blights, 245, **248–249**, *250*
blood meal, 136
body dimensions, as guide, 23
Bogwalker's Badass Topsoil Technique, *63*, **64**, 84–87, *84*, *86–87*
bonemeal, 136

boron (B), 108, 111, **114**

brinjal (*Solanum melongena*), 300–301

BrixBlend basalt, 138

broad forks, 58, 59

broccoli (*Brassica oleracea*), 37, **40**, **41**, **42**, **113**, **172**, **181**, 194, 271, 286–287, 286, **340–341**, **344–345**, **348–349**, **352–353**

Brussels sprouts, **113**

Bt (*Bacillus thuringiensis*), 254, **258**

buckets, 54–55

buckwheat, **142–143**, 144, *147*

bug spray, 51

bulldozers, *85*

bush beans, **41**, **42**, *282*

buttercups (*Cucurbita maxima*), 334–336

butternuts (*Cucurbita moschata*), 334–336

C

cabbage (*Brassica oleracea*), **40**, **41**, **42**, **113**, **172**, *175*, **181**, 194, 271, 288–289, 288, 289, **340–341**, **344–345**, **348–349**, **352–353**

cabbage loopers, **246–247**, *246*, *252*

cabbage whites, *252*

cabbageworms, **246–247**, *246*

calcium (C), 108, 111, **114**

capsicum (*Capsicum baccatum*), 318–319

carbon, **114**

cardboard, composting, 149–150

carrots (*Daucus carota*), **40**, **41**, **42**, **113**, *161*, **172**, 194, 211, 266–267, *267*, 271, *272*, 290–291, *290*, **340–341**, **344–345**, **348–349**, **352–353**

carts, garden, 54, *54*

cattle panels, 232–233

cauliflower (*Brassica oleracea*), **40**, **113**, **172**, 194, 271, 286–287, *286*, **340–341**, **344–345**, **348–349**, **352–353**

cayenne peppers (*Capsicum annuum*), 318–319

celery, **113**, **181**

chamomile, 250

change, using and responding to, 10–11

charcoal, *130*. *See also* biochar

chard (*Beta vulgaris*), *34*, **40**, **41**, **113**, **172**, 211, 269, 284–285, *285*, **340–341**, **344–345**, **348–349**, **352–353**

cheeses (*Cucurbita moschata*), 334–336

chickweed (*Stellaria media*), **142–143**, **216**, *217*, 219–220, *220*

chicory, **172**

chiles (*Capsicum annuum*), **40**, **113**, 318–319, **342–343**, **346–347**, **350–351**, **354–355**

chile peppers (*Capsicum baccatum*), **259**, 318–319

chiltepin (*Capsicum baccatum*), 318–319

Chinese parsley (*Coriandrum sativum*), 292–293

Chloe's Super-Accessible Option, 121

chloride (Cl), 108, 111

chlorine, **114**

chlorophyll, *135*, 271

chrysanthemum flower tea (*Chrysanthemum cinerariifolium*), **259**

cilantro (*Coriandrum sativum*), **40**, **41**, **42**, **113**, *115*, **172**, 194, 211, 250, 292–293, *292*, **340–341**, **344–345**, **348–349**, **352–353**

clay, 97, 98, 150

clothing, 50

clover, **113**, **142–143**

cobalt, **114**

coconut coir, 118, *119*

cole (*Brassica oleracea*), 304–305

collards/collard greens (*Brassica oleracea*), **40**, **113**, **172**, 304–305, **340–341**, **344–345**, **348–349**, **352–353**

collinear hoes, 218–219

commercial fertilizers, macronutrients in, 110

companion planting, 28

compost and composting, 68, 90–91, 118, *119*, 124, 130, 148–155, *148*, *149*, *151*

composting manure, 125–126

compost teas, 139

compost tumblers, 153–154, *153*

conditions, timing of planting and, 194, 197

container gardening
 amendments and, 130
 fertility and, 117
 fertilizers and, 118
 garden design and, 18
 growing mediums for, 117–121, *117*
 images of, *32*, *34*
 overview of, 32–34
 See also pots

Cooperative Extension offices, 105, 144

copper (Cu), 108, 111, **114**, **258**

coriander (*Coriandrum sativum*), 250, 292–293

corn (*Zea mays*), **40**, **113**, *168*, **172**, 211, 265, 266, 268–269, *269*, 271, 294–295, *294*, *295*, **340–341**, **344–345**, **348–349**, **352–353**

corn earworms, **246–247**, *246*

cottonseed meal, 136

cotyledons, *163*

cover crops, 84–85, 87, 88–89, *88–89*, 140–147, *140*, *141*, *144*, *147*, 214, 227

cowpeas, **142–143**, 144

creeping Charlie (*Glechoma hederacea*), **216**, *217*

crimping cover crops, 87, 88–89, *88–89*

crimson clover, **142–143**

crooknecks (*Cucurbita pepo*), 337–338

crop debris, as mulch, 227

crop groupings, 37

crop rotation, 36, 37, 251

cucumber beetles, 252

cucumbers/cukes (*Cucumis sativus*), 36, 38, **40**, **41**, **42**, **113**, **172**, **181**, 187, 194, 211, 230, **231**, 265, *265*, 271, *272*, 296–297, *297*, **340–341**, **344–345**, **348–349**, **352–353**

cushaws (*Cucurbita argyrosperma*), 334–336

cutting lettuce (*Lactuca sativa*), 306–307

D

daikon (*Raphanus sativus*), **40**, **41**, **42**, **113**, **142–143**, 144, **172**, 322–323
dandelion (*Taraxacum* spp.), **216**, *217*
decomposing organic matter, 102–103
delicatas (*Cucurbita pepo*), 334–336
Deppe, Carol, 51
design
    different approaches to, 24
    elements of, 18
    from patterns to details, 8
    planning versus, 16–17
    sample, 26
diatomaceous earth (DE), 252, *252*, *255*, *257*
digging forks, 55, 58, *58*, *59*, 219
digging shovels, 58, 59, *59*
digging spades, 59
dill/dill weed (*Anethum graveolens*), **40**, **41**, **42**, **113**, **172**, 194, 211, 250, 298–299, *298*, *299*, **340–341**, **344–345**, **348–349**, **352–353**
direct sowing
    advantages and challenges involving, 191
    mulch and, 223
    overview of, 170–171, **172**
    process of, *171*, 192–193, *192–193*
    thinning and, 210
    See also seeds
diseases
    fertility and, 115–116
    holistic overview of, 240–243
    identifying, 245
    management of, 245
    mulch and, 224
    no-spray ways to combat, 250–253
    resistance to, *243*
    symptoms and management of, **248–249**
diversity, 9
dolomite lime, 138
double-digging, *63*, **64**, 69–71, *69*
downy mildew, **248–249**
drainage, 117
drip irrigation, *81*, 205, *205*
dry corn (*Zea mays*), 294–295
dry leaves, as mulch, 226–227

E

edges, using, 9
edible weeds, 219–220
effector-triggered immunity (ETI), 242
eggplants (*Solanum melongena*), **40**, **41**, **42**, **113**, **172**, **181**, 187, 231, *231*, *241*, 252, 265, *265*, 271, 300–301, *301*, **340–341**, **344–345**, **348–349**, **352–353**
endomycorrhizal inoculants, 139
energy, catching and storing, 7
English peas (*Pisum sativum*), 316–317
essential oils, **259**
eucalyptus, **25**
European goldenrod, 250

F

feather meal, *115*, 136
feedback, applying, 9–10
feeding plants, 207–209
fencing, as trellis, 232–233
fennel, 250
fertigating, *207*, 208
fertility
    components needed for, 107–111
    container gardening and, 117
    managing, 113–116
    pests and diseases and, 115–116
    requirements for, 112
    of various vegetables, **113**
fertilizers
    container gardening and, 118
    general-purpose, 135
    macronutrients in, 110
    nitrogen, 135–136
    phosphorus, 136–137
    potassium, 137–138
    sidedressing and, 209
    store-bought, 134–139
    synthetic, 109
fertoz rock phosphate, 136
field corn (*Zea mays*), 294–295
field hoes, 56, 219
fish bonemeal, 137
fish fertilizer, 136
flat beds, 18, 28–29

flats, sowing seeds in, 182–183
flat shovels, 58, 59
flea beetles, *241*, **246–247**, *246*, 252
flood irrigation, 205–206, *206*
foliar feeding, 207–209
foodware, composting, 149–150
frost/frost dates, 194, 195–196, *195*
fruits
    harvesting, 264–266
    phosphorus (P) and, *110*
    storing, 271
    See also individual plants
fungal blights, *245*, 250
furrowing hoes, *46*, 56, 57–58, *57*

G

gallant soldier (*Galinsoga parviflora*), **216**, *217*
garden carts, 54, *54*
garden plan
    cover crops and, 146
    garden design and, 16–17
    making, 39–43
    sample, *16–17*
    seeds and, 165
garden tillers, 74–75
garlic (*Allium sativum*), 15, **40**, **41**, **42**, **113**, *166*, 173, *173*, **259**, 266, *270*, 271, 302–303, *302*, *303*, **340–341**, **344–345**, **348–349**, **352–353**
genetically modified seeds (GMOs), 167
Genovese basil (*Ocimum basilicum*), 280–281
germination, 160–161, 163–165, *163*, *164–165*
Gibson, Anne, 121
gill-over-the-ground (*Glechoma hederacea*), **216**, *217*
gloves, *48*, *50*, 51
goldenrod, **25**, 250
grain corn (*Zea mays*), 294–295
granite dust, 137, 150
grape hoes, 56, 57

grasses
  as mulch, 227
  as weeds, *214–215*, **216**, *217*
Greek basil (*Ocimum minium*),
  280–281
green beans (*Phaseolus vulgaris*), *160*,
  265, *282–283*
greenhouses, *177, 178, 179*
green manure. *See* cover crops
greensand, 138
ground ivy (*Glechoma hederacea*), **216**,
  217
grower-focused companies, 168
growing mediums
  for container gardening, 117–121,
  117
  for growing transplants, 180
  recipes for, 121
  sowing seeds in, 182–183
  See also soil
grow lights, 176–178, *177*
guano, 136, 137

H

habaneros (*Capsicum chinense*),
  318–319
habitat manipulation, 251
hairy vetch, **142–143**, *144*
hands
  caring for, 49
  pest removal and, 252, *253*, *253*
  as tools, 48
hand watering, 202–203
hardening off, 185–186, *186*
harlequin bug, *115*, **246–247**, *246*
harvesting
  methods for, *262*, 263–268, *263*,
    264, *265*, *266*, *269*
  planning for, 262
  processing after, *268*, 269–271, *270*,
    273
  sharing after, *11*, 273
hats, 50
hay
  composting, 150
  as mulch, 226

hayforks, 55
hazel hoes, 57
head lettuce (*Lactuca sativa*), 306–307
heat mats, 176–177
herbicides, in manure, 128
herbs, perennial, 173
high-calcium (hi-cal) lime, 138
high-phosphorus liquid fish hydroly-
  sate, 137
hoes
  hand, 52–53, *52*
  mixing growing medium with, *121*
  types of, *46*, 56–58, *56, 57*
  weeding and, 218–219
holistic thinking, 3–11, *25*
holistic weeding, 214
Holmgren, David, 5
holy basil (*Ocimum sanctum*),
  280–281
Holzer, Sepp, 84
hori hori, *49, 49*, *52*, 219
horticultural oils, **258**
Hubbards (*Cucurbita maxima*),
  334–336
hügelkultur, 66, 84–85
human food, composting, 149
Humanure Handbook, The (Jenkins),
  127
humic acid products, 139
humidity, harvesting seeds and, 267
humus products, 139
hybrids, seeds for, 167
hydrogen, **114**

I

immobile nutrients, 113–115, **114**
impact sprinklers, 204–205, *205*
India, irrigation in, 206
Ingham, Elaine, 104, 107
insecticidal soaps, **258**
integrated pest management (IPM),
  241–242, 243, 251, 254, 256
Intelligent Gardener, The (Solomon and
  Reinheimer), 101, 107
interactions, 7
intercropping, 28
inventory of seeds, 162–163

Irish potatoes (*Solanum tuberosum*),
  173, 320–321
iron (Fe), 108, 111, **114**
iron phosphate, **258**
irrigation, *81*, 200–206, *205, 206*

J

jalapeño peppers (*Capsicum annuum*),
  318–319
Jenkins, Joseph, 127

K

kabochas (*Cucurbita maxima*),
  334–336
kale (*Brassica oleracea*), **40**, **41**, **42**,
  113, *115*, **172**, **181**, 194, 211, 243,
  269, 304–305, *304*, **340–341**,
  344–345, **348–349**, **352–353**
kama, *52, 53, 53*
kaolin, 252, **258**
Kapuler, Alan, *168, 219*
kelp, 138
King, Franklin Hiram, 5
knives, *48, 49*, *52*, *52*, 265
knotweed (*Polygonum* spp.), **216**, *217*

L

laboratory soil tests, 105–106
ladyfingers (*Abelmoschus esculentus*),
  310–311
lamb's quarters (*Chenopodium album*),
  172, **216**, *217*, 219–220, *219*
lasagna gardening, *63*, **64**, 75–77, *76*
lavender, 250
layout, 18, 22, 26–27
Lazor, Jack, 269
leaf lettuce (*Lactuca sativa*), 306–307
leaves
  harvesting, 263–264
  as mulch, 226–227, *226*
  post-harvest processing of, 269
  removing, *187*, 188
  storing, 271
  See also individual plants

leeks, **113**, **181**

lettuce (*Lactuca sativa*), **40**, **41**, **42**, **113**, **172**, **181**, 194, *197*, 211, *264*, 269, 306–307, *306*, **340–341**, **344–345**, **348–349**, **354–355**

light requirements
    for seedlings, 178–179
    See also sunlight

lights, for starting seeds, 176–178

liming agents, 138–139

location, 9, 18, 22

M

macronutrients, 108–109, 138. *See also individual nutrients*

macro-organisms in soil, 104

magnesium (Mg), 108, 111, **114**

maintenance, 23

maize (*Zea mays*), 294–295

manganese (Mn), 108, 111, **114**

manure, 125–128, *125*, **126**

marginal, valuing, 9

marigolds, 187

materials, using right, 11

maturity, days to, 194, 196

Mays, Daniel, 88

medicinal weeds, 219–220

melons (*Cucumis melo*), **172**, *181*, 211, 231, *231*, 266, 308–309

mesh strainers, 257

metal fencing, as trellis, 232

methods, trying different, 62

Mexican bean beetle, **246–247**, *246*

Mexican parsley (*Coriandrum sativum*), 292–293

microbial inoculants, 150

micronutrients, 111, 138, 150. *See also individual nutrients*

millet, **172**

mineral nutrients, 99–100, 107

Mishra, Anupam, 201

mobile nutrients, 113–115, **114**

moisture retention, mulch and, 223

Mollison, Bill, 5

mollusks, 104

molybdenum (Mo), 108, 111, **114**

moon phases and signs, 194, 196

mosaic viruses, 187, **248–249**

mound culture, 66

mound style compost system, 154–155, *154*

mulch
    amount of, 223–224, *224*
    challenges involving, 224, 226
    importance of, *221*
    materials for, 221, 226–228
    overview of, 221
    process for, 222–224
    pros and cons for, 222
    sidedressing/topdressing and, 209
    timing of, 222–223
    weeds and, 214

multiple functions, ensuring, 7

music, 51

muskmelons (*Cucumis melo*), **40**, **113**, **181**, 211, 308–309, *308*, *309*, **342–343**, **346–347**, **350–351**, **354–355**

mustard greens, **113**

N

natural patterns and cycles, 8

neem tree derivatives, **258**

neighborly relations, 11

nematodes, 104

New Mexico chiles (*Capsicum annuum*), 318–319

nickel, **114**

nitrogen, *214–215*

nitrogen (N), 108–110, **114**

nitrogen fertilizers, 135–136

nitrogen fixers, 112, 113

No-Till Organic Vegetable Farm, The (Mays), 88

nutrients
    macronutrients, 108–109, 138
    in manure, 125, **126**
    micronutrients, 111, 138, 150
    mobile vs. immobile, 113–115, **114**
    See also individual nutrients

nutsedge (*Cyperus rotundus*), **216**, 217

O

oats, **142–143**, *144*, **172**

observation, 7, 8

occultation, *63*, *64*, 78–79, 78, 79, 82–83, *82–83*, 87

okra (*Abelmoschus esculentus*), **40**, **113**, 211, 265, 271, 310–311, *310*, *311*, **342–343**, **346–347**, **350–351**, **354–355**

okro (*Abelmoschus esculentus*), 310–311

okura (*Abelmoschus esculentus*), 310–311

Old Farmer's Almanac, The, 194, 196

oligochaeta, 104

onions (*Allium cepa*), 10, **40**, **41**, **42**, *112*, **113**, 181, 271, 272, 312–313, *312*, *313*, **342–343**, **346–347**, **350–351**, **354–355**

ordering seeds, 162–163, *162*, 166

organic constituents in soil, 97, 102–104

Organic Grain Grower, The (Lazor), 269

Organic Materials Review Institute (OMRI), 256

organic matter, decomposing, 102–103

oscillating sprinklers, 204, *204*

outdoors, starting in pots, 174–175

over-fertilization, 116

oxygen, **114**

P

Palmer, Nigel, 139

PAMP-triggered immunity (PTI), 242

paper mulch, 228

parsnips (*Pastinaca sativa*), **40**, **41**, **42**, **113**, **172**, 211, 266, *266*, 271, 314–315, *315*, **342–343**, **346–347**, **350–351**, **354–355**

pathogen-associated molecular pattern (PAMP), 242

pathogens, in manure, 127. *See also* diseases

patience, 62

pattypans (*Cucurbita pepo*), 337–338

pawpaw, 5

peanuts, **113**

peas (*Pisum sativum*), **40**, **41**, **42**, **113**, **172**, 211, 230, **231**, 265, 271, 316–317, *316*, **342–343**, **346–347**, **350–351**, **354–355**

peat moss, *119*, 120, 139

pepitas (*Cucurbita pepo*), 334–336

peppers (*Capsicum annuum*), **40**, **41**, **113**, **172**, 181, *186*, 187, *205*, 231, **231**, *233*, 266, 271, 318–319, *319*, **342–343**, **346–347**, **350–351**, **354–355**

perennial crops, 5

perlite, 118, *119*

permaculture, 5–11, *5*, *6*

pesticides
    homemade, 256
    how to apply, 257–259
    organic, 254–256, *255*
    store-bought, 255

pests
    fertility and, 115–116
    holistic overview of, 240–243
    identifying, 244, **246–247**, *246*
    life cycles of, 244
    mulch and, 224
    no-spray ways to combat, 250–253
    organic pesticides and, 254–256
    removing, *253*
    resistance to, *243*

petunias, 187

pH adjusters, 138–139

pharmaceuticals, in urine, 132–133

phenology, 196

pH levels, 100–101, 108

phosphorus (P), 108, 110–111, *110*, **114**, 127, *137*

phosphorus fertilizers, 136–137

photosynthesis, 94–95, *135*

physical barriers, 251–253

pickling cucumbers (*Cucumis sativus*), 296–297

pigweed (*Amaranthus* spp.), **216**, *217*

pimentos (*Capsicum annuum*), 318–319

pine, **25**

pine bark fines/pine fines, 118, 120

pinto beans (*Phaseolus vulgaris*), 282–283

piri piri (*Capsicum frutescens*), 318–319

pitchforks, 55, *55*

Planet Natural, 121

plantain (*Plantago* spp.), **216**, *217*

planting
    direct sowing, 170–172
    overview of, 170–173
    starting in pots, 171–173
    in straight rows, 24
    timing of, 194–197
    transplanting, 180–181, 184–190
    See also seeds

planting depth, 189

plants
    allelopathic, 23–24, **25**
    crop placement for, 37
    feeding and growing, 115, 207–209
    growth process of, 94–95
    height of, 37
    number of, 38
    preparing soil for, 90–91
    selecting, 35–36
    separating by season, 40, **40**
    space requirements for, 40–41, **41–42**
    spacing between, 212
    thinning, 193, 210–212
    tissues of, 95
    See also transplanting

plastic
    biodegradable, *80*
    as mulch, 227–228
    pots made from, 33
    short treatise on, 80–81
    solarization/occultation and, *78*, *79*, 79
    wind and, 79

pole beans, **41**, **42**, 229–230, **231**

poles, 233

pollution, *109*

polyculture, 28

popcorn (*Zea mays*), 294–295

potassium (K), 108, 111, **114**, *137*

potassium fertilizers, 137–138

potassium sulfate, 138

potatoes (*Solanum tuberosum*), 27, **40**, **41**, **42**, **113**, 173, *173*, *194*, 266, 269, 271, 320–321, *320*, **342–343**, **346–347**, **350–351**, **354–355**

pots
    fabric, 34
    glazed ceramic, 33–34
    for growing transplants, 181
    metal, 34
    miscellaneous, 34
    plastic, 33
    sizes for, 181, **181**
    sowing seeds in, 182–183
    starting plants in, 171–173, 174–179
    wooden, 34
    See also container gardening

poultry, as pest control, 254

poultry manure pellets, 136

powdery mildew, **248–249**

predators, natural, 250

propagation, 173

pruners, 48, 49, *49*, 52, *52*, 265

pruning, *21*, 250

pumpkins (*Cucurbita pepo*), **113**, **172**, 334–336, **342–343**, **346–347**, **350–351**, **354–355**

pump sprayers, 255, *257*

purple dead nettle (*Lamium purpureum*), **216**, *217*

purslane (*Portulaca oleracea*), **216**, *217*

pyrethrins, **258**

Q

quadripod trellises, 234, *234*, 235, *235*

quickweed (*Galinsoga parviflora*), **216**, *217*

R

Radiant Raindrops of Rajasthan, The (Mishra), 201

radishes (*Raphanus sativus*), **40**, **113**, **172**, 194, 211, 266, 271, 272, 322–323, *323*, **342–343**, **346–347**, **350–351**, **354–355**

raised beds
    comparison of methods and, 63, **64**
    design and, *18*
    filling, 67–68
    flat and sunken vs., *18*
    materials for, *65*, 67, **67**, *68*
    paths and, *29*
    pros and cons for, 29–30
    setting up, 65–68
rakes, hard, 49, *49*
rapeseed, **142–143**
reasons for gardening, 14–15
'Red Kuri' (*Cucurbita maxima*),
    334–336
redundancy, 7
redwood, **25**
reflection, questions for, 15
Regenerative Grower's Guide to Garden
    Amendments, The (Palmer), 139
Reinheimer, Erica, 101, 107
renewable resources, 8
requirements for garden, 19–21
Resilient Gardener, The (Deppe), 51
rest, 51
rhizomes, *214–215*
rhizosphere, 20
rhododendron, **25**
rocket (*Eruca vesicaria*), 278–279
rock phosphate, 137
rock powders, 134
rocoto (*Capsicum pubescens*), 318–319
rodents, 76
roots
    harvesting, 266–267
    storing, 271
    transplanting and, 188–189, *188–*
        189, *190*
    See also individual plants
roquette (*Eruca vesicaria*), 278–279
round shovels, 59
row covers, *250*, 252–253
rows
    vs. beds, *18*, 26–27
    planting straight, 24
rucula (*Eruca vesicaria*), 278–279
runoff, agricultural, 109
rust, removing from tools, 48
rusts, **248–249**

rutabaga (*Brassica napus*), **40**, **113**, 211,
    271, 330–331, **342–343**, **346–**
    347, **350–351**, **354–355**
rye grass, 140, **142–143**

S

salad mix (*Lactuca sativa*), 306–307
sand, 97, 98, *119*, 120
Scotch bonnets (*Capsicum chinense*),
    318–319
Sea-90, 138
seabird guano, 137
seasons
    pests and diseases and, 243
    separating plants by, 40, **40**
sectors, 9
sedum, 250
seeds
    direct sowing, 90, 191–193, *192–193*
    germination and, 160–161, *163–*
        165, *163*, *164–165*
    growing, 169
    harvesting, 267–269
    images of, *158*, *159*, *166*, *191*
    industry surrounding, 167
    labeling after sowing, *180*
    local and grower-focused compa-
        nies for, 168
    ordering, 162–163, *162*, 166
    organizing, *162*, 169, *169*
    overview of, *158*
    preparing soil for, 90–91
    setting up system for starting,
        174–179
    sowing in flats or pots, *174*, *175*,
        176, *177*, 182–183, *182–183*
    storing, 168
    timing of planting and, 194–195
    trading, 169
    viability of, 160–161, *163*, 168
    weeds and, 214
Seed to Seed (Ashworth), 269
Seminole pumpkins (*Cucurbita*
    moschata), 334–336
Sepp Holzer's Permaculture (Holzer),
    84
shake test, 97

sheet mulching, 63, **64**, 75–77
shelling peas (*Pisum sativum*), 316–317
shelves, adjustable, 176–177
shovels, 48–49, *49*, *58*, 59, *59*
sidedressing, *115*, 209
silt, 97, 98
silverbeet (*Beta vulgaris*), 284–285
single-digging, 64, 71
skid steers, 85
slender speedwell (*Veronica filiformis*),
    216, *217*
slicing cucumbers (*Cucumis sativus*),
    296–297
slugs
    beer traps for, 257
    mulch and, *222*, 224
smartweed (*Polygonum* spp.), **216**, *217*
Smith, Joseph Russell, 5
snacks, 51
snap beans (*Phaseolus vulgaris*), 194,
    282–283
snap peas (*Pisum sativum*), 316–317
snow peas (*Pisum sativum*), 316–317
soap spray, homemade, 256–257, **259**
soft rock phosphate, 137
soil
    air and water in, 98–99
    basics of, 94–95
    composition of, *99*
    ease of digging and, *95*
    fertility and, *107*, *112*
    growing mediums and, *119*, 120, 121
    for growing transplants, 180
    importance of, *94*
    inorganic qualities and traits of,
        97–102
    mineral nutrients in, 99–100, 107
    mulch and, 223
    organic constituents in, 97,
        102–104
    pests and diseases and, 242–243,
        243
    preparing, 90–91
    quality and balance in, 96–104
    for raised beds, 67–68
    relative acidity of, 100–101, 108
    requirements for, 19–20
    testing, 105–106, *105*, *106*

soil, *continued*
    texture and structure of, 97–98, *97, 120*
    transplanting in, 188, *189*
    weeds and, 214
    See also amendments; growing mediums
soil compaction, 72
soil conditioner, 118, 120
soil damage, reducing, 72
soil organisms, 103–104
solarization, 63, **64**, 78–79, *78, 79, 82–83, 82–83,* 87
Solomon, Steve, 101, 107
solutions, small and slow, 10
sorghum–Sudan grass, **142–143**
sorting after harvesting, 271
soybean meal, 136
soybeans, **113**
space requirements, 40–41, **41–42**
spades, *58, 59*
Spain, irrigation in, 206
spearhead spades, *58, 59*
sphagnum peat moss, *119,* 120
spinach (*Spinacia oleracea*), **40, 113, 172, 181,** 187, 211, 269, 324–325, *325,* **342–343, 346–347, 350–351, 354–355**
spinosad, **258**
spotted cucumber beetles, **246–247,** *246*
spray bottles, 257
sprinklers, 203–205, *204, 205*
spuds (*Solanum tuberosum*), 320–321
squash (*Cucurbita* spp.), **40, 41, 42, 113,** *161,* **172, 181,** 211, 230, **231,** 265, 266, 267, 334–336, *335, 336,* **342–343, 346–347, 350–351, 354–355**
squash bugs/beetles, *244,* **246–247,** *246, 253*
squash vine borers, **246–247,** *246*
stack and pack, 10
stakes, 233
starting a garden
    overview of methods for, *63,* **64**
    patience and, 62

    See also design; garden plan; planting
sticky traps, 252, 253
stirrup hoes, *25, 48,* 56–57, *56,* 218–219, *218*
storing harvest, 271
straw, 226
string, trellising with, *231, 232, 233,* 237
string beans (*Phaseolus vulgaris*), 282–283
striped cucumber beetles, **246–247,** *246*
succession planting, 36, 194
Sudan grass, sorghum–, **142–143**
sulfur (S), 108, 111, **114,** 139, **258**
summer squash (*Cucurbita pepo*), **40, 113, 181,** 194, 211, 265, 334–336, 337–338, **342–343, 346–347, 350–351, 354–355**
sunflower hull ash, 138
sunken beds, 18, 30, *30*
sunlight, 19, 22, 37
sunscreen, 50–51
swales, 22
sweet alyssum, 250
sweet potatoes (*Ipomoea batatas*), **40, 113,** 173, *173,* 266, 271, 326–327, *327,* **342–343, 346–347, 350–351, 354–355**
sweet taters (*Ipomoea batatas*), 326–327
Swiss chard (*Beta vulgaris*), 284–285

T

T₅ grow lights, 178
tabasco (*Capsicum frutescens*), 318–319
taters (*Solanum tuberosum*), 320–321
tatsoi, **172**
technology, 10
temperature
    planting and, 195
    under row covers, 253
Tennessee Brown rock phosphate, 137
termination of cover crops, 145–147
terraces/terracing, 18, 31, *31, 84, 85*

Thai basil (*Ocimum basilicum*), 280–281, *281*
Thai chiles (*Capsicum annuum*), 34, 318–319
thermometers, compost, 155
thinning(s), 193, 210–212, *210,* 227
thistles (*Cirsium* spp.), **216,** *217*
three-bin compost system, *148,* 152, 153
three-tine hoes, 56, 57
tillage radish, **142–143,** 144
tilling with a machine, *63,* **64,** 72–75
timing tables, 194, **339–355**
tobacco, **172,** 187
tobacco tea, 257, **259**
tomato cages, 234, 237
tomatoes (*Solanum lycopersicum*), 21, **40, 41, 42, 113,** 137, **172, 181,** 187, 229, **231,** *231, 232,* 237, 245, *245,* 250, 266, 328–329, *328,* **342–343, 346–347, 350–351, 354–355**
tomato hornworms, *240*
tomato leaf extract, **259**
tools
    bare-bones, 48–49
    for care of gardener, 50–51
    caring for, 47–48
    cleaning, 47
    for digging, 58–59
    hoes, 56–58
    for moving things, 54–55
    purchasing, 47
    quality of, 46
    sharpening, 48
    small hand, 52–53
    storing, *47*
topdressing, 209
topsoil
    native, 67–68
    purchased, 68
    See also growing mediums; soil
total cation exchange capacity (TCEC), 100, 101–102, *101,* 105, 108
tractors, tilling with, 73–74
trading seeds, 169

Trail, Gayla, 121
transplanting
    buying strong plants for, 190
    growing plants for, 180–181
    mulch and, 223
    preparing soil for, 91
    process of, *170, 171,* 184–189, *184, 185, 186, 189*
trays for growing transplants, 181, **181**
trellises and trellising, *9, 21,* 229–237, *229, 230–231, 232, 233, 234, 235, 236*
tripod trellises, 234, 235
'Tromboncino' (*Cucurbita muschata*), 337–338
trowels, 49, *52,* 53
tubers
    harvesting, 266–267
    storing, 271
    See also individual plants
tulsi basil (*Ocimum sanctum*), 280–281
turnips (*Brassica rapa*), **40, 113, 142–143, 172,** 194, 211, 266, 271, 330–331, *331,* **342–343, 346–347, 350–351, 354–355**

U

urine, 131–133, *133*
USDA, 255, 256

V

vegetable oil spray, **259**
vegetables
    composting, 150
    lifespans of annual, 272
    post-harvest processing of, 269
    resistant varieties of, 250
    See also individual vegetables
vegetative propagation, 173, *173*
vermicompost, 120
vermiculite, 118, *119*
veronica, 250
vertical space, 10
vetch, **113**
viability of seeds, 160–161, 163, 168
videos, gardening, 51

W

Walker, Rohini, 5
waste, absence of, 8
water and watering
    container gardening and, 117
    equipment for, 202
    flow and, 22
    methods for, *200,* 202–206, *203*
    mulch and, 226
    overview of, 200–206
    rainwater, 8
    requirements for, 20
    for seedlings, 179, 181, **181**
    in soil, 98–99
    timing of, 200–202
    transplanting and, 189
    when direct sowing, 193
water bottles, 50
watermelons (*Citrullus lanatus*), **40, 113, 181,** 211, 332–333, *332,* **342–343, 346–347, 350–351, 354–355**
wax chiles (*Capsicum annuum*), 318–319
weave trellises, *233, 234, 236, 236*
weeds
    common, **216,** *217*
    composting, 150
    direct sowing and, 193
    edible and medicinal, 219–220
    managing, *25, 27,* 213–214, *213, 218*
    in manure, 127–128
    in mulch, 224
    as mulch, 227
    prevention of, 213–214
    smart weeding and, 218–219
    solarization/occultation and, 79
West Indian calabazas (*Cucurbita moschata*), 334–336
wheat, **172**
wheelbarrows, 54, *121*
white clover, **142–143**
white potatoes (*Solanum tuberosum*), 320–321
wilts, **248–249**
wind, solarization/occultation and, 79
windowsills, starting plants on, 175–176

winter rye, **142–143**
winter squash (*Cucurbita* spp.), **41, 42, 113,** *161,* **181,** 211, 230, **231,** 266, 334–336, **342–343, 346–347, 350–351, 354–355**
wire fencing, as trellis, 232–233
wire weeders, 52, *52,* 219
wireworms, **246–247,** *246*
wood ash, 131, *131,* 138–139
wood chips, *154,* 228
wooden handles, oiling, 47
worms and worm castings, 104, *104, 119,* 120, 124, *124,* 139

Y

yarrow, 250
yellow dock (*Rumex crispus*), 213, **216,** *217, 218*
yellow mustard, **142–143**
yellow straight (*Cucurbita pepo*), 337–338
Yeomans, P. A., 5
yield, obtaining, 7

Z

zinc (Zn), 108, 111, **114**
zones, 9
zucchinis (*Cucurbita pepo*), **40, 41, 42,** *48,* **113,** *160,* **172, 181,** 194, 265, *265,* 271, 334–336, 337–338, *337,* **342–343, 346–347, 350–351, 354–355**